Export Promotion Strategies

Theory and Evidence from Developing Countries

Edited by
Chris Milner
Loughborough University

HARVESTER WHEATSHEAF

New York · London · Toronto · Sydney · Tokyo · Singapore

First published 1990 by
Harvester Wheatsheaf
66 Wood Lane End, Hemel Hempstead
Hertfordshire HP2 4RG
A division of
Simon & Schuster International Group

Typeset in 10/12pt Times by
Keyset Composition, Colchester, Essex

Printed and bound in Great Britain by
BPCC Wheatons Ltd, Exeter

British Library Cataloguing in Publication Data

Export promotion strategies: theory and evidence from
    developing countries.
    1. Developing countries. Exporting. Promotion
    I. Milner, Chris, 1950–
    382.63091724

ISBN 0-7450-0517-9

1 2 3 4 5   94 93 92 91 90

Contents

Contributors

V. N. Balasubramanyam is Professor of Development Economics at the University of Lancaster.

Dipak R. Basu is Lecturer in Economics at the University of Lancaster.

Karl Bennett is Associate Professor of Economics at the University of Waterloo, Ontario, and Research Associate at the Institute of Social and Economic Research at the University of the West Indies.

Jagdish N. Bhagwati is Arthur Lehman Professor of Economics and Professor of Political Science at Columbia University.

Tim Congdon is Economic Adviser at Gerrard and National, London.

H. David Evans is a Senior Research Fellow at the Institute of Development Studies, University of Sussex.

Rodney E. Falvey is Reader in Economics at the Australian National University.

Norman Gemmell is Lecturer in Economics at the University of Durham.

David Greenaway is Professor of Economics and Director of the Centre for Research in Economic Development and International Trade (CREDIT) at the University of Nottingham.

Hal Hill is Head of the Indonesia Project and Senior Research Fellow in Economics at the Research School of Pacific Studies, Australian National University.

Chris Milner is Reader in Economics at Loughborough University and Research Fellow of the Centre for Research in Economic Development and International Trade (CREDIT) at the University of Nottingham.

Peter Montiel is an Economist in the Research Department of the International Monetary Fund.

Chong-Hyun Nam is Professor of Economics at Korea University.

Richard Pomfret is Professor of Economics at Johns Hopkins School of Advanced International Studies, Washington.

Geoffrey Reed is Lecturer in Economics and Research Fellow of the Centre for Research in Economic Development and International Trade (CREDIT) at the University of Nottingham.

Peter Warr is Senior Fellow at the Research School of Pacific Studies, Australian National University.

Figures

Tables

Preface

My interest in trade policy reform issues in developing countries was first aroused by my involvement during 1983 in a UNIDO-funded study of trade policy in Mauritius. I was required for the first time to apply principles of trade theory and the theory of commercial policy to the analysis and evaluation of actual conditions and policies. I claim no responsibility for Mauritius' success in the last decade in expanding and diversifying its non-traditional exports, though many of the trade policy changes implemented by the government of Mauritius are in line with what I advocated at the time of the study! Involvement subsequently with other studies of import and export policies in Madagascar, Burundi, Syria, Cameroon, Kenya and Barbados has widened my understanding of the constraints, political, economic and administrative, on trade policy reform, though it has not dented my conviction that sustainable export promotion requires, among other things, the lowering or dismantling of trade restrictions that encourage the inward orientation of domestic producers. Of course a developing country, such as Mauritius, with its very small domestic market has appreciated longer than most that exports were necessary for growth and industrialisation. But need and ability are different considerations. Despite limited natural resources and capital, and despite its remoteness from the industrialised markets, Mauritius has been able to expand its manufactured exports substantially. This must be a source of encouragement to other developing countries.

The circumstances of developing countries may vary considerably, however, from those of Mauritius. The aim of this book is to provide perspectives on export promotion from a wide range of developing countries and from a wide range of specialists in the field. I am delighted that so many well-known economists with a specialism in this area have been willing to contribute to this book. They are all very busy and active economists and I am grateful for their considerable efforts. I hope that their contributions will be appreciated by scholars and policy-makers alike.

My thanks must go to a number of people and organisations. David Greenaway (Nottingham) has given me much encouragement with this project and much convivial company during the fieldwork on several of the studies referred to above. Maxwell Stamp PLC London is the firm of economic consultants who first took me to Mauritius in 1983 and thereby stimulated my interest in policy reform issues in developing countries. I have continued to give advice to them since 1983 on the trade policy studies referred to above. Su Spencer has, as ever, provided excellent secretarial support in the preparation of the final manuscript.

The acquisition of operational experience in developing countries inevitably involves periods away from work and home. I am grateful to my university and department for supporting my work in this area. I am even more grateful to my wife, Ruth, and children, James and Elizabeth, for coping so admirably during my absences.

Chris Milner
Loughborough University

Abbreviations

CARICOM	Caribbean Community and Common Market
CARIFTA	Caribbean Free Trade Area Association
CGE	computable general equilibrium
CMCF	CARICOM Multilateral Clearance Facility
CVD	countervailing duty
DFI	direct foreign investment
DLC	domestic letters of credit
DUP	'directly unproductive profit-seeking activities'
EER	effective exchange rate
EOI	export-oriented industrialisation
EP	export promotion
EPZ	export processing zone
GATT	General Agreement on Tariffs and Trade
IDB	Inter-American Development Bank
IRR	internal rate of return
IS	import substitution
ISI	import-substituting industrialisation
LDC	less developed country
MTN	Multinational Trade Negotiations
NBER	National Bureau of Economic Research
NIC	newly industrialising country
NPV	net present value
NTB	non-tariff barrier
PPP-EER	purchasing-power parity exchange rates
QR	quantitative restriction
RCA	revealed comparative advantage

SAL	Structural Adjustment Loan
SAP	Structural Adjustment Programme
SSA	sub-Saharan Africa
VER	voluntary export restraints

1

The issues and outline of the book

Chris Milner

1.1   Introduction

The choice of trade strategy or orientation by a developing country may
be viewed as problematic for a number of closely related reasons. First,
there are different perspectives on the relationship between trade and
growth in developing countries. Second, there are alternative views on
the way in which trade strategy or orientation influences trade performance. Third, there are conflicting attitudes towards the appropriate role
for government policy and market forces.

Orthodox neo-classical theory assumes that trade is important, because exposure to world prices encourages the efficient allocation of
resources. By contrast, there is a strong strand of thinking in development theory which assumes that domestic rigidities mean that relative
prices are of negligible importance in influencing the level and composition of economic activity. It is, according to this school of thought, the
level of external demand that influences the trade or export performance
of developing countries. In the context of this book, however, it should be
noted that both perspectives or schools of thought view trade as being
important or desirable; the former because it encourages efficient use of
resources (with alternative potential uses), and the latter because it
permits the use of potentially idle resources. The focus of this book is not
therefore on the importance or otherwise of trade, and by implication
exports. It focuses, by contrast, on the means of achieving trade or export
expansion, i.e. with the issues surrounding the second and third areas of
controversy identified above.

Of course, the trade–growth link is not a sterile debate for our present
purpose, since the judgement is likely to fashion one's views on the form

1

and content of trade policy. The orthodox neo-classical perspective is, for instance, more likely to be associated with advocacy of neutrality or outward orientation, resulting from restricted government intervention. It is important, however, to view the issues of trade orientation and of the degree of government intervention as analytically separate issues. Outward orientation can be market-led or intervention-led. Inward orientation can be removed by dismantling protectionist instruments and operating under a free-trade regime. Alternatively exports can be promoted by interventions that explicitly or implicitly subsidise exports or exportables production. It is, in fact, the relative merit of seeking to achieve export promotion by means of these alternative approaches that is one of the two key issues investigated in this book. The other is the theoretical and empirical 'case' for export promotion or outward orientation.

1.2   The issues

The choice of trade strategy or 'case' for export promotion is fashioned by both theoretical arguments and/or by empirical evidence. The book is concerned with both; it seeks to challenge policy-makers in developing countries to consider a range of questions. Are static gains likely to result from resource reallocation and X-efficiency improvements, if outward orientation is increased? Are dynamic productivity gains likely to result from exposure to greater competition and access to larger markets in world markets than in protected domestic markets? Are outward-orientation strategies easier and less costly to manage or administer? These are a series of questions raised by theory. The robustness of the assumptions underpinning alternative theoretical perspectives needs to be reviewed. But answers to the above questions can also be elicited from the empirical evidence; cross-country and case-study. Is there systematic cross-sectional evidence of higher growth performance being associated with greater outward orientation? Is the evidence susceptible to alternative explanations?

Given the diversity of conditions and factors that might account for cross-country variations in growth performance, reliance on cross-sectional evidence may be dangerous. Country-specific or region-specific case-study material is likely therefore to add much new richness to the empirical debate. By devoting half of the volume to such case-studies from around the world, the intention is to reduce the dependence on crude cross-country comparisons. The costs and benefits of alternative trade strategies may be more clearly identifiable and more easily related to alternative theoretical perspectives.

The case-studies are also designed to offer detailed insights into whether there are alternative means of promoting exports and whether it is possible to rank alternative approaches. At the strategic level, the volume is concerned with the consequences or relative effectiveness of pro-exportables bias, free trade or neutrality of incentives and of mixed strategies of selective import substitution and export promotion. In terms of specific policy instruments the need is to investigate the degree of complementarity and substitutability between alternative instruments such as the exchange rate, border taxation and fiscal measures in formulating effective export-promoting trade regimes. Similarly we need to consider what are the advantages and disadvantages of generalised export promotion for all activities as opposed to discriminatory or selective export promotion for enclave activities only in export processing zones (EPZs). Again the intention will be to investigate such issues from first principles and from case-study evidence.

1.3   Outline of the book

The contributions are organised into three major parts. Part I provides a critical evaluation of the general 'case' for export promotion (EP). In Chapter 2 Jagdish Bhagwati outlines the case for outward orientation. He reviews a wide range of the issues identified above, but places a considerable amount of weight on political economy arguments in favour of trade liberalisation and the elimination of rents associated with protectionist regimes. A counterbalance to Bhagwati's advocacy of EP policies is provided in Chapter 3 by David Evans. It is not intended to provide the case against export promotion, but rather a critical assessment of the theoretical and empirical support offered by liberal trade economists. Finally in this part, David Greenaway and Geof Reed review the existing cross-country evidence on trade orientation and economic performance. These authors recognise that the empirical evidence of a causal link between outward orientation and export performance and in turn between export performance and growth is not conclusive, but are more confident about the limitations of strongly inward-oriented strategies.

Part II of the book contains four essays, which seek to provide a theoretical analysis of alternative, possible and specific instruments of export promotion. In Chapter 5 I investigate the relative incentive implications of import-substitution and export-promotion policies within a general equilibrium framework. The essay considers the problem of strategic conflict, and the symmetrical nature of the relative or true protection/promotion effects of import liberalisation and export subsidisation when reducing the anti-export bias associated with import-substitution policies. Trade regime bias is also influenced by other policy instruments. Thus in Chapter 6 Peter Montiel examines the role of the exchange rate and domestic financial policies in export promotion and the trade liberalisation process. This essay identifies the role of short-run exchange rate and stabilisation policies in avoiding economic conditions that would threaten the sustainability of outward-oriented trade reforms designed to change relative prices. It also examines the role of fiscal and financial policies in the longer-term management of the real exchange rate.

Where trade and other policy instruments continue to generate an anti-export bias (for whatever reason), export promotion or at least reduced anti-export bias can be achieved by means of compensatory financial/fiscal measures to exports. In Chapter 7 Rodney Falvey and Norman Gemmell provide an analysis of measures available for such purposes. The authors also set up a formal framework to identify the potential advantages and disadvantages of alternative compensatory export measures aimed at lowering distortions induced by protection of the importables sector. The appropriate form and level of export subsidisation are shown to be sensitive to factors such as patterns of substitutability and factor mobility between sectors. Not surprisingly under second-best conditions, complete compensation for an initial distortion may *not* be desirable! Finally in this section, Peter Warr (Chapter 8) studies in detail one form of 'second-best' intervention to promote exports, namely export processing zones. This essay studies the benefits and costs of EPZs in Indonesia, South Korea, Malaysia and the Philippines and reviews the relationship between the welfare effects of EPZs and the host country's economic policies. Consistent with the conclusions of the previous essay, Warr argues that if the home economy is distorted, limited welfare gains *may* be achieved from EPZs. However, the experience of EPZs has not been what some countries had hoped for. There are no simple, single means of achieving export promotion!

Case-study material for developing countries is often not extensive or not easily accessible outside the countries themselves or international agencies such as the World Bank. The seven case studies in Part III are therefore valuable in themselves as self-contained studies. But they are intended to constitute an integral element in the overall structure of the volume. The country or country-group studies provide a vehicle for evaluating both the arguments for and alternative means of export promotion set out in the first two parts. The cases have been chosen to give geographical spread, variety of policy experience and strategy, and a range of trade and growth performance and of opinion.

The section starts with the case of Korea, a (now) strongly outward-oriented newly industrialising country (NIC) with an exceptional export performance in the last two decades. In Chapter 9 Chong -Hyun Nam examines the role of exports in Korea's recent economic development, and examines the extent to which export promotion has been intervention as opposed to market-led. The author argues that, until very recently, outward orientation was implemented through the 'export-subsidy' rather than 'free-trade' route. Indeed government intervention has tended in the Korean case to achieve greater overall neutrality than most other developing countries, but not without costs which should be considered by countries seeking to imitate the Korean 'success'. Imitation of trade policies alone is in any case likely to be inadequate, since Korea's export performance is not explained by its trade policies alone: infrastructure investment and macroeconomic stability are also important. Two alternative Asian experiences are provided in Chapters 10 and 11. In Chapter 10 Hal Hill examines the Indonesian experience in the post-oil boom period. He argues that Indonesia's trade policy reforms were both necessary and creditable. However, he also takes up the earlier theme that export promotion involves much more than simply placing exporting firms only on a free-trade footing. The author identifies many remaining constraints to international competitiveness (inefficiencies in the large state enterprise sector, remaining regulation and protection in many sectors, inadequate physical and social infrastructure). He also examines the threats to the political sustainability of Indonesia's export strategy.

Feasibility, rather than sustainability, is the theme of Balusubraman-yam and Basu's essay (Chapter 11) on India's export performance and policies since the early 1950s. The neglect of exports in the 1950s and early 1960s is explained by the desire for self-sufficiency, on grounds of economic nationalism rather than as a result of economic arguments associated with structuralist thinking. By the time 'export pessimism' views were less fashionable in the 1960s, the prospects for efficient export promotion within the context of India's planning system were limited. The essay argues that in the absence of an economic rationale about the appropriate form and scale of promotion and given the highly bureaucratic system for administering export incentives, the outcome has been a tendency towards excessive and indiscriminate subsidisation of exports. Indeed the authors doubt whether piecemeal liberalisation of the foreign trade regime is wise if the complex system of industrial licensing and investment controls is to remain.

An alternative aspect of the sustainability issue is examined in detail in the Latin American context by Tim Congdon in Chapter 12. The author repeats the argument that the disparity between the successful and unsuccessful exporters in Latin America reflects differences in the overall orientation of policies: the more successful exporters adopted more outward-looking policies through import liberalisation. However, the essay focuses also on the difficulty of reconciling trade liberalisation with inflation control, with particular emphasis on the comparative experiences of liberalisation in Chile (in the 1970s) and in Mexico (in the 1980s). Congdon argues that continuous reliance on devaluation (as advocated often by economists at the World Bank) to maintain competitiveness may threaten the sustainability of reform by undermining domestic financial confidence. Exchange rate overvaluation is an important constraint on export competitiveness, but inflation control (which may conflict in the short term to some degree with export promotion) is required for sustainable policy reform.

The final three case studies offer different regional perspectives on trade policy reform. In Chapter 13 Karl Bennett examines the Caribbean experience with export promotion. In particular he contrasts the experience of the 1960s and 1970s, when the emphasis was on a regional approach to export promotion, with the 1980s which have seen a greater emphasis on extra-regional exporting. Intra-regional export promotion proved in the case of CARICOM to be predominantly (regional) import substitution. Given policy deficiencies and inconsistencies in the customs union arrangements, and the smallness of the regional market, this offered limited scope for industrial expansion. The experience in general of developing countries forming preferential regional trading arrangements has not been very encouraging. They have not been a source of significant growth of exports and of reduced dependence on external/industrial markets. As I have argued elsewhere (Greenaway and Milner, 1990a) regional arrangements are better not viewed as an alternative to extra-regional export promotion.

The Caribbean is in general a high per capita income region in terms of developing countries, and one with the large US economy nearby. The immediate prospects for export promotion in sub-Saharan Africa (SSA) might seem by contrast to be relatively low. In Chapter 14 David Greenaway examines the relatively modest steps taken away from generally highly protectionist policies in this large number of low-income countries. He focuses on the role of externally sponsored trade policy reform, in particular on the role of the World Bank's Structural Adjustment Lending (SAL) programme in reducing anti-export bias. Although it is too early to generalise about the success of the SAL programme or about the sustainability of policy reform in this region, the author identifies some 'successes' for the SAL programme and some significant demonstration effects. The sustained export performance of Mauritius and recent reforms in Tanzania, for example, may help to create internal pressures across sub-Saharan Africa for further liberalisation. The internal resistance to change is not to be underestimated, however!

In the final case study Richard Pomfret (Chapter 15) examines economic performance and export-promotion policy in the countries of the Mediterranean region. It offers an overview of policies across the region, and some greater detail about the liberalisation experiences of Israel, Turkey and Malta. This region is not subject to the same locational disadvantages as sub-Saharan Africa or resource limitations as the Caribbean or many sub-Saharan African countries, and Pomfret places particularly strong emphasis on national policies in explaining export and economic performance. He concludes (p. 297) that 'The crucial element in the successful national policies has been not to favour production for the domestic market over production for export.'

The simple message in the above quote is a recurring theme of the essays in this volume. The nature of the internal constraint on export growth in many developing countries is relatively easy to identify and describe. The means of reducing that constraint and sustaining an efficient export-promoting trade strategy are less easy to specify in operational terms. The ensuing chapters do seek to offer, however, valuable insights (theoretical and practical) into the formulation of an export-promotion trade strategy and into the use of appropriate policies for sustainable export promotion in developing countries. The structure and content of the book were designed to satisfy this aim!

PART 1

The 'case' for export promotion
Theory and evidence

2

Export-promoting trade strategy: Issues and evidence

Jagdish N. Bhagwati

2.1 Introduction

The question of the wisdom of adopting an export-promoting (EP) trade strategy has a habit of recurring in the developing countries. Develop-ment economics was born in an atmosphere of export pessimism at the end of the Second World War. However, the remarkable success of the few economies that pursued export-promoting policies, in defiance of prescriptions for import-substituting (IS) policies that the pessimism inspired, swung the weight of academic opinion behind the EP strategy by the late 1960s. Aiding this process were numerous academic findings from research projects around the world which probed these EP successes, and equally the failures of the IS countries.[1]

However, the debt crisis of the 1980s, the sluggish world economy and the continuing depression of primary product prices have revived export pessimism afresh. It is time again therefore to examine the old and new arguments which question the wisdom of the EP strategy.

After the Introduction, section 2.2 briefly reviews the early post-war arguments in support of the misguided export pessimism. Section 2.3

This is an extended version of an article published in edited form in *The World Bank Research Observer* (Bhagwati, 1988). Thanks are due to Armeane Choksi, Martin Wolf, Constantine Michalopoulos, Sarath Rajapatirana, Swaminathan Aiyar, Mohsin Khan, Vittorio Corbo, Adrian Wood and Bela Balassa for helpful comments and to Sunil Gulati, Susan Hume, Douglas Irwin and David Laster for research assistance. Thanks are due to the World Bank for allowing the material to be reproduced in this volume. The World Bank does not accept responsibility for the views expressed herein which are those of the author and should not be attributed to the World Bank or to its affiliated organisations.

states the precise content of an EP strategy, sorting out some of the confusion that bedevils much of the current debate. Section 2.4 considers a few salient lessons that have emerged in the studies on the advantages of the EP strategy, focusing on those that are particularly pertinent today. Section 2.5 then examines several new sources of scepticism concerning export-promoting trade policies. The contrasts between the old (post-war) pessimism and the new pessimism prevalent today are then exploited briefly in section 2.6 to draw a central policy lesson for the developing countries, especially in regard to the present multilateral trade negotiations (MTNs).[2]

2.2 The first export pessimism

It is well known that export pessimism characterised the thinking of most influential development economists and policy-makers in the developing countries after the Second World War. The most articulate proponents of the pessimist school of thought were the two great pioneers of development economics: Raul Prebisch (see Prebisch, 1952, 1984) and Ragnar Nurkse (see Nurkse, 1959). Interestingly, however, their diagnoses had significant differences.

Prebisch considered the terms of trade of primary products, then the chief exports of developing countries, to be secularly declining exogenously to the policies of the developing countries. Left to themselves, producers in the developing countries would themselves have then responded to this exogenous secular price shift by industrialising. Government intervention in the shape of either (trade tariff) protection or (domestic subsidy) promotion would be then unnecessary and unjustified in this instance.[3] By contrast, Nurkse's export pessimism related to the notion that the absorptive capacity of foreign markets was low and that they simply could not accommodate imports from developing countries on a sufficient scale as developing countries accelerated their development. Therefore, export pessimism explicitly meant 'elasticity' pessimism; and, as all students of international economics will immediately recognise, the case for government intervention then follows.[4] Nurkse, therefore, advocated what he called a policy of 'balanced growth'.

Paradoxically, however, Nurkse (1953) was mindful of the costs of indiscriminate protectionism, having also written about the collapse of the world trading system during the 1930s. That 'balanced growth' could only mean government incentives to assist industrialisation appears therefore to have been a prescription that combined uneasily with the caveats that Nurkse expressed about protection. By contrast, Prebisch's brand of pessimism did not justify protectionism but was nevertheless widely used by his followers to do so in Latin America.

The export pessimism of these influential economists, in any event, was cast in the mould of 'natural' forces and phenomena that the developing countries faced. Nurkse, for instance, wrote about increasing economy in the use of raw materials and a shift further from natural to synthetic materials, both dampening the demand for developing countries' exports over time.

Developing countries could do nothing to change these conditions at the source, just as one cannot do anything about bad weather. But their policies had to adjust to these conditions, just as one can buy an umbrella against the rain. (By contrast, as I note below, the second export pessimism of the 1980s is rooted in protectionist threats, which can indeed be addressed at the source and hence has critically different implications for developing countries' policies.)

The export pessimism following the Second World War was to prove unjustified by the unfolding reality.

1. World trade did not merely grow rapidly during the 1950s and 1960s, it grew even faster than world income. In fact, the growth rates in both output and trade were unprecedented for such sustained periods (see Table 2.1).
2. Within the aggregate performance, the economies that shifted quickly to an EP strategy (as defined more formally below) experienced substantial improvements in their export performance. This is particularly the case for the four Far Eastern economies: Hong Kong, Singapore, South Korea and Taiwan, but by no means confined to them. In fact, the dramatic rise in these economies' share of trade in GDP over this period made them 'jump off' the Chenery-type regression lines for trade-to-GDP ratios and per capita incomes in a dramatic fashion. If anything, these regressions show a falling trade-to-GDP ratio as per capita income rises, whereas these successful exporters showed a spectacular rise in their trade shares as their per capita incomes grew rapidly.[5]

Clearly, history has sided with economists such as Cairncross (1962) and Krueger (1961), who had been among the foremost critics in raising doubts about export pessimism.

While the evidence of successful trade expansion buried export pessimism decisively, the economic analysis underlying the reasons that Nurkse and others had advanced in support of such pessimism was also to prove enlightening. It also has a bearing on the dissection of the resurgent, second export pessimism prevalent today. Thus, Nurkse had

Table 2.1   Post-war growth rates of world output and trade.

	World output (annual growth rate)	World trade (annual growth rate)
1953–63	4.3	6.1
1963–73	5.1	8.9
1973–83	2.5	2.8

Source: Hufbauer and Schott (1985), Table A-1, p. 97.

embraced Robertson's classic phrase: trade as 'an engine of growth'. This established a rather strong and direct link in the export pessimists' minds between external conditions and internal expansion. In a classic throwback to this form of argumentation, Arthur Lewis (1980) argued more recently in a much-quoted passage:[6]

> The growth rate of world trade in primary products over the period of 1873 to 1913 was 0.87 times the growth rate of industrial production in the developed countries; and just about the same relationship, about 0.87, also ruled in the two decades to 1973 . . . . We need no elaborate statistical proof that trade depends on prosperity in the industrial countries. (p. 556)

But, it is evident from several analyses,[7] the latest being by Riedel (1984), that such stable relationships (which suggest the exclusive dominance of 'demand' in determining trade performance) simply cannot be extracted from the export experience of developing countries in the post-war period. Indeed, the export performance of these (and indeed other) countries must be explained by domestic incentives (or 'supply') more than by external (or 'demand') conditions. It is worth restating the main arguments supporting this conclusion:

1. While Lewis addresses the linkage between developed countries' incomes and developing countries' exports of primary products, Riedel (1984, Table 4) shows that even this aggregate developing-country relationship is not stable. The stability, in turn, obviously cannot be maintained for individual developing countries.

2. Again, it is important to note that the post-war period has seen a dramatic shift in the export composition of developing countries towards manufactures. Developing countries' exports of manufactures grew threefold over the 1955–78 period, representing one-fourth of overall exports. Manufactures are now close in magnitude to the other non-fuel exports such as food, minerals and agricultural raw materials. Of course, the successful exporters of the post-war period dominate this shift. But their experience, based on domestic policies, precisely proves the point that one goes seriously wrong if one assesses trade potential by mechanical linkages to developed-country income expansion.

The most compelling aggregate statistics in fact are that during the prosperous 1960s developing countries' exports of manufactures grew nearly twice as fast as the developed countries' incomes. The expansion of developing countries' trade over the 1950s and 1960s occurred in the context of an environment where protection in the developed countries was diminishing sharply as a consequence of first the elimination of quotas, and then the reduction in tariffs. Even during the troubled 1970s, developing countries' exports of manufactures grew more than four times as rapidly as the developed countries' income.[8]

The only key question that has remained at issue, therefore, is what has been called the 'fallacy of composition' – can all, or most, developing countries become successful exporters simultaneously? Or, focusing on the successful Asian exporters, the question may be put wittily: can the Asian export model be successfully exported to all? The suspicion still lingers that the success of a few was built on the failure of the many, and that if all had shifted to the EP strategy, none would have fared well.

There are two distinct sources of this worry. The first presumes that markets would not be able to absorb all of the exports that would materialise if developing countries shifted to an EP strategy. The second argues that while the markets could be found, they would be closed by protectionist measures, provoked by the import penetration and outcries of market disruption. The second source is the major cause of export pessimism today, while the first source was the one that afflicted the earlier wave of export pessimism. I now examine the former argument, and defer discussion of the latter.

First, as I shall argue more fully below, the fear that world trade would have to grow by leaps and bounds if most developing countries pursued an EP strategy is unwarranted. For this fear follows from trying to put all countries on the curve as estimated in Cline (1982), however adjusted, for the Asian exporters with very high ratios of trade to national income. The pursuit of an EP strategy, as discussed in section 2.3, simply amounts to the adoption of a structure of incentives which does not discriminate against exports in favour of the home market. This does not imply that the resulting increases in trade-to-income ratios will be necessarily as dramatic as in the Far Eastern case. To infer otherwise is simply a *non sequitur*.

Second, the share of developing countries in the markets for manufactures in most developed countries has been, and continues to be, relatively small. While there are obviously variations in individual industries, in the aggregate the share of manufactured exports from developing countries in the consumption of manufactures in the developed countries runs even today at a little over 2 per cent. 'Absorptive capacity' purely in the market sense, therefore, is not *prima facie* a plausible source of worry.

Third, a chief lesson of the post-war experience is that policy-makers who seek to forecast exports typically tend to understate export potential by understating the absorptive capacity of import markets. This comes largely from having to focus on 'known' exports and partly from downward estimation biases when price elasticities for such exports are econometrically measured. Experience underlines the enormous capacity of wholly unforeseen markets to develop when incentives exist to make profits; and 'miscellaneous exports' often represent the source of spectacular gains when the bias against exports, typical of IS regimes, is removed on a sustained basis.

Fourth, trade economists have increasingly appreciated the potential for intra-industry specialisation as trade opportunities are provided and seized. The experience of the European Community (EC), where the progressive dismantling of trade barriers within the EC led to increased mutual trade in similar products rather than to massive reductions in scale of output in industry groups within industrial member states, has only underlined this lesson.[9] There is no reason therefore to doubt that such intra-industry trade in manufactures among developing countries and between them and the developed countries can also develop significantly, difficult as it is to forecast with plausible numbers.

Finally, if we reckon also with the potential for intra-developing country trade (where again policies can change to permit its increase), and the possibility of opening (again by policy) new sectors such as agriculture and services to freer trade, then the export possibilities are even more abundant than the preceding arguments indicate.[10]

Export pessimism, if traced to market forces as in the post-war period, is then unwarranted. If, however, it is traced to policies (that is, to protectionism) as is the case today, this is a different matter which I turn to later.

Therefore, while the post-war export pessimism was unjustified, it did provide a key rationale for the widespread adoption of inward-looking or IS trade policies in many developing countries. The export-promoting strategy was shortchanged, in consequence.

There were other contributory factors in this outcome. Thus, trade restrictions were adopted to protect the industries that had grown up in Latin America during the Second World War, which had provided artificial inducement to set up domestic capacities to produce interrupted supplies from traditional, competitive suppliers abroad.[11] Then there was a reluctance to devalue which, combined with high rates of inflation, implied that these developing countries had continuously overvalued exchange rates which amounted to a *de facto* IS trade policy.[12]

2.3   Export-promoting trade strategy: What is it?

What exactly is meant by an export-promoting trade strategy? Unless we are clear on that critical question, we cannot properly debate the merits of the strategy and its alternatives. Clarification of the question is therefore important, especially as the everyday usage of this phrase evokes many different notions that are wholly unrelated.

The definitions of EP and IS that are most widely accepted, and indeed the ones proposed and used by the sophisticated international economists who have long studied these matters theoretically and empirically, relate to incentives. The incentive-related definition states that a country is following the IS strategy if the effective exchange rate for the country's exports (EER_x) is less than for its imports (EER_m). These effective exchange rates measure the incentives to export and import-substitute respectively. Thus, EER_x would include, for a peso-currency country, not just the pesos earned at parity from a unit dollar's worth of export, but also any export subsidy, tax credits, special credits, etc. (It would also include, say for tractor export, the subsidy on input of steel that is used in the exported tractor; so that there is no distinction between EER comparisons defined on value added or gross value, for the purpose at hand.) Similarly, EER_m would add to the parity any import duty, import premia resulting from quantitative restrictions (QRs) and other charges. If then a dollar's worth of exports fetches altogether 100 pesos, whereas a dollar's worth of imports fetches 130 pesos, when these adjustments have been made, the incentive structure implies $EER_x < EER_m$. This constitutes a 'bias against exports', a concept which seems to have come independently into use in Bhagwati (1968), Little, Scitovsky, and Scott (1970), and Balassa (1971). This is also the hallmark of the IS strategy: it creates a net incentive to import-substitute relative to what international prices dictate.

Suppose, however, that EER_m yields 100 pesos per dollar's worth of imports, while EER_x is also 100 pesos. Then the home market sales will give a producer as much as exporting will: the incentive structure then implies $EER_x = EER_m$. Thus bias against exports will have been eliminated. This is defined as the EP strategy.

These definitions of EP and IS strategies are by now in common usage. But they do raise a question: how do we christen the case where there is a significant excess of EER_x over EER_m? Where the effective exchange rate is more favourable for exports than for imports, should we not call that EP instead of the one where $EER_x \approx EER_m$ as the above definitions do, and instead call the case with $EER_x \approx EER_m$ simply the trade-neutral or bias-free strategy? Perhaps that might have been the ideal way to do it. But the EP strategy came to be defined in the academic literature as the one with bias-free incentives simply because the empirical studies of the four Far Eastern economies, particularly in the NBER project, strongly suggested that these successful outward-oriented developers were in fact closer to neutrality than to a substantial positive bias in favour of exports, by and large.[13] Also, the sequencing of trade regimes, one in which the EP countries went from an IS strategy to a neutral strategy which eliminated the bias against exports, and thereby improved their export performance, prompted the researchers to define EP strategy in terms of neutrality. Given therefore the now common usage of these terms, I have suggested recently the following terminology that does least violence to what has been the practice to date:[14]

> IS strategy: $EER_x < EER_m$
> EP strategy: $EER_x \approx EER_m$
> Ultra-EP strategy: $EER_x > EER_m$

Nonetheless, it is not uncommon, especially among policy-makers, to find references to EP (or outward-oriented) trade strategy as comprehending both the neutral and the pro-export-bias strategies.[15] All one can do then is to warn the reader to be alert to see what exactly is the definition that is being implicitly used in a particular context.

These definitions clearly relate to average incentives. On the other hand, it is obvious that, within EP for instance, some activities may be import substituting in the sense that their EER_m exceeds the average EER_x. Thus, the pursuit of either the EP or the ultra-EP strategy does not preclude import substituting in selected sectors. This is, in fact, true for most of the successful Far Eastern developers. Nor does this fact render meaningless therefore the distinction among the different trade strategies, as is sometimes contended. As I have argued elsewhere (Bhagwati, 1986d):

> We also need to remember always that the average EER_x and EER_m can and do conceal very substantial variations among different exports and among different imports. In view of this fact, I have long emphasized the need to distinguish between the questions of the degree of import substitution and the pattern of import substitution. Thus, within the broad aggregates of an EP country case, there may well be activities that are being import-substituted (i.e., their EER_m exceeds the average EER_x). Indeed there often are. But one should not jump to the erroneous conclusion that there is therefore no way to think of EP versus IS and that the distinction is an artificial one – any more than one would refuse to acknowledge that the Sahara is a desert, whereas Sri Lanka is not, simply because there are some oases. (p. 93)

Nor should one equate the EP strategy with the absence of government intervention, as is often done by proponents of the IS strategy and sometimes by advocates of the EP strategy as well. It is true that a *laissez-faire* policy would satisfy the requirement that $EER_x = EER_m$. On the other hand, this is not a necessary condition for this outcome. In fact, the Far Eastern economies (with the exception of Hong Kong) and others that have come close to the EP strategy, have been characterised by considerable government activity in the economic system. In my judgement, such intervention can be of great value, and almost certainly has been so, in making the EP strategy work successfully. This is because credibility of commitment on the part of governments is necessary to induce investors to take decisions that reflect the inducements offered by the policy framework. By publicly supporting the outward-oriented strategy, by even bending in some cases towards ultra-export promotion, and by gearing the credit institutions to supporting export activities in an overt fashion, governments in these countries appear to have established the necessary confidence that their commitment to the EP strategy is serious, thus inducing firms to undertake costly investments and programmes to take advantage of the EP strategy. The *laissez-faire* model does not quite capture this aspect of the problem since its proponents implicitly assume that the policy of *laissez-faire* will be accepted at face value. But neither the establishment nor the continuation of *laissez-faire* is a realistic assumption since governments, except in the models of Friedman and Bakunin, fail to abstain or self-destruct; they will find invariably something, indeed much, to do. Therefore, explicit commitment to an activist, supportive role in pursuit of the EP strategy, providing the assurance that it will be protected from inroads in pursuit of numerous other objectives in the near future, would appear to constitute a definite advantage in reaping its benefits.

Some other caveats are also in order:

1. Development economists such as Chenery and his many associates have used the terminology of IS and EP in a wholly different fashion. They have typically used identities to decompose observed growth of output in an industry or the economy into components attributable to export promotion, import substitution and other categories.[16] Quite aside from the fact that such decompositions are, except under singular circumstances, statistical descriptions without analytical significance, they also have no relationship to the incentives-related definitions of trade strategy that have been set out here. Unfortunately, this distinction occasionally gets confused in popular discussions, especially as economists sometimes deploy both usages simultaneously (i.e. using the incentives-based definition to group countries into alternative categories and the Chenery-type terminology to explain their economic performance, as in Balassa, 1983).

2. Next, the incentives-defined EP strategy has to be distinguished from the traditional concept of 'export-led' growth with which it is again confused repeatedly. The latter relates to a situation where external growth, due to income effects centred on a country's exports, generates income expansion attributable to direct gains from trade and indirect beneficial effects. The notion of 'export-led' growth is thus closer in spirit to the notion that underlay Nurkse's and Lewis's pessimism that was dissected earlier. On the other hand, it is evident that the incentives-related EP definition has literally nothing to do with such beneficial external phenomena. Whether the success of an EP strategy, defined in terms of freedom from bias against exports, requires the presence of a beneficial external environment is of course a separate issue which has already been addressed and will be treated again in section 2.5, which focuses on the revived export pessimism.

3. Finally, it is worth stressing that the concept of EP or outward orientation relates to trade incentives (as defined by either trade policies directly or by domestic policies which impact on trade or by exchange-rate policies which have consequences for trade) but does not imply that countries with EP strategies must be equally outward oriented in regard to their policies concerning foreign investment. As it happens, Hong Kong and Singapore among the four Far Eastern economies have been more favourable in their treatment of foreign investors than the great majority of the IS countries, though the historic growth of Japan, presumably as an EP country, was characterised by extremely selective control on the entry of foreign investment. Logically and empirically, the two types of outward orientation, in trade and in foreign investment, are therefore distinct phenomena though whether one can exist efficiently without the other is an important question that has been raised in the literature and is surrounded by far more controversy than the question of the desirability of an EP strategy in trade.

2.4   Why does an export-promoting trade strategy aid successful development?

With the EP strategy defined in terms of the incentive structure, the substantive conclusion that has emerged from the major research projects listed earlier is that the EP countries have done remarkably well in terms of their economic performance. Paradoxically, the successful countries in development have therefore turned out to be those that followed this strategy but had no one rooting for their success when development efforts were being initiated in the early 1950s. Here, as elsewhere, history has turned up surprises.

In evaluating this outcome, we have to distinguish between two questions: why should the EP strategy have been helpful in accelerating economic development; and could the acceleration have been caused by factors other than the EP strategy? Prior to both questions, however, it is useful to review the evidence on the relationship between EP strategy and economic performance.

2.4.1 *The evidence*

The serious evidence on the successful impact of the EP strategy on economic performance, as measured by an improved growth rate, has to be found in the country studies of the research projects on trade and development (listed earlier). Among these, the most compelling evidence is in the analyses in the NBER project where the EP strategy was carefully defined and transitions to it from an IS strategy by various phases were systematically investigated.[17]

There is also much cited evidence that relates largely to associations between growth rates of exports and growth rates of income, as in the work of Michaely (1977a), who used data for 1950–73 for 41 countries, and the further extension of this type of work by Balassa (1978) and Feder (1983).[18]

Complementing this approach is the altogether different statistical formulation in Michalopoulos and Jay (1973). This study takes a very different approach to the problem by using exports as an argument in estimating an economy-wide production function from aggregate output and factor-use data. Using data for 39 countries, this study argued that exports are an independent input into national income.[19]

Both these Michaely–Balassa–Feder and Michalopoulos–Jay variety of findings, however, do not bear directly on the question whether the EP strategy is productive in terms of more growth. For the incentive-related EP strategy, which nearly all of these authors would embrace as the appropriate definition and concept to deploy, is not the one used to examine the question of income or growth performance. It is necessary to go behind the scenes and identify whether the superior export growth rates (or higher export magnitudes) belong to the EP countries.

This is particularly worrisome since high growth rates of exports may have been caused by high growth rates of output (which, in turn, may have resulted from other exogenous factors such as a higher savings effort), rather than the other way around. Thus, if IS does not parametrically reduce trade greatly, it is conceivable that this reverse causation could lead the rapidly expanding countries, whether EP or IS, to show higher export growth rates than less rapidly expanding economies, whether EP or IS.

Hence, while these cross-country regressions are certainly interesting, valuable and suggestive, they cannot be considered compelling on the issue in question, especially as they (and conclusions based on them) are likely to be critically dependent on the period, sample of countries and variables chosen. By contrast, the detailed country studies are methodologically superior and more persuasive. And, as noted already, they do indicate the superiority of the EP strategy.

2.4.2 *Reasons*

The reasons that the IS strategy has been generally dominated by the EP strategy, and why the countries that rapidly made the transition from the former to the latter have done better, have preoccupied economists since these findings came to light. The following hypotheses have been advanced, based on the usual mix of analytical insights, casual empiricism and econometric evidence.[20]

Resource allocation efficiency

The first set of reasons relies on the fact that the EP strategy brings incentives for domestic resource allocation closer to international opportunity costs and hence, as international economists recognise, closer to what will generally produce efficient outcomes.

This is true, not merely in the sense that there is no bias against exports and in favour of the home market (i.e. $EER_x \approx EER_m$) under the EP strategy, whereas often the researchers have observed a substantial excess of EER_m over EER_x in the IS countries. It is also valid in the sense that the IS countries seem to have generally had a chaotic dispersion of EERs among the different activities within the broader categories of export- and import-competing activities as well. That is, the degree of IS goes far and the pattern of IS reflects widely divergent incentives. By contrast, the EP strategy does better on both degree (since $EER_x \approx EER_m$) and on pattern.

The interesting further question relates to why the degree gets outsized and the pattern also goes wrong under IS. The answer seems to lie in the way in which IS is often practised and in the constraints that surround EP. Thus IS could, in principle, be contained to modest excess of EER_m over EER_x. But typically IS arises in the context of overvalued exchange rates and associated exchange controls. So there is no way in which the excess of domestic over foreign prices is being tracked by government agencies in most cases, and the excesses of EER_m over EER_x simply go unnoticed. The non-transparency is fatal. By contrast, EP typically tends to constrain itself to rough equality, and ultra-EP also seems to be moderate in practice, because policy-induced excesses of EER_x over EER_m would require subsidisation that is constrained by budgetary problems.

In the same way, the pattern of EER_m can be terribly chaotic because exchange controls and QRs on trade will typically generate differential premia and hence differential degrees of implied protection of thousands of import-competing activities, all of which are simply the side consequence of the administrative decisions on exchange allocations. By contrast, the EP strategy will rely more on unifying exchange rates which avoid these problems and, when relying on export subsidisation, will be handled both with necessary transparency and with budgetary constraints that would then prevent IS-type spectacular dispersions in resulting EERs.

The chaotic nature of differential incentives among diverse activities in IS regimes has been documented by estimates of effective rates of protection (though these estimates can be misleading in QR regimes where the import premia may reflect effects of investment controls, indicating therefore resource denial rather than resource attraction to the high-premia and therefore *ceteris paribus* high-ERP activities). The estimates of cross-sectional domestic resource costs, which provide instead a guide to differential social returns to different activities, have also underlined these lessons. The conceptual and measurement analyses of several distinguished economists, including Michael Bruno, Max Corden, Harry Johnson and Anne Krueger, have contributed greatly to this literature.

Directly unproductive profit-seeking (DUP) and rent-seeking activities

Yet another important aspect of the difference between EP and IS strategies, once we recognise that IS regimes have typically arisen in the context of exchange-rate overvaluation and associated controls on foreign exchange and trade, is that this kind of regime is more likely to trigger what economic theorists now call DUP (Bhagwati, 1982b) activities. These activities divert resources from productive use into unproductive but profitable activities designed to earn profits (or income) by lobbying to change policies or to evade them or to seek the revenue and rents they generate.[21] Rent-seeking activities (Krueger, 1974), where lobbies chase rents attached to import licences and other quantitative restrictions, are an important subset of such DUP activities. With IS

policies typically conducted within the framework of quantitative allocation systems, the diversion of entrepreneurial energies and real resources
into such DUP activities tends to add to the conventionally measured
losses from the high degree and chaotic pattern of IS[22].

It must be admitted that while economists have now begun to make
attempts at estimating these costs, they are nowhere near arriving at
plausible estimates simply because it is not yet possible to estimate
realistically the production functions for returns to different kinds of
lobbying. But, as Harrod once remarked, arguments that cannot be
quantified are not necessarily unimportant in economics; and the losses
arising from DUP and rent-seeking activities seem presently to illustrate
his observation.[23]

Foreign investment

If IS regimes have tended to use domestic resources inefficiently in the
ways that were just outlined, the same applies to the use of foreign
resources. This is perhaps self-evident. But substantial theoretical work
by Bhagwati (1973), Brecher and Diaz-Alejandro (1977), Uzawa (1969),
Hamada (1974), and others has established that foreign investment which
comes in over QRs and tariffs – the so-called 'tariff-jumping' investment –
is capable of immiserizing the recipient country under conditions that
seem uncannily close to the conditions in the IS countries in the post-war
decades. These conditions require capital flows into capital-intensive
sectors in the protected activities. It is thus plausible that, if these inflows
were not actually harmful, the social returns on them were at least low
compared to what they would be in the EP countries where the inflows
were not tariff-jumping but rather aimed at world markets, in line with
the EP strategy of the recipient countries.

In addition, I have hypothesised (Bhagwati, 1978, 1986b) that, *ceteris
paribus*, foreign investments into IS countries will be self-limiting in the
long run because they are aimed at the home market and therefore
constrained by it. If so, and there seems to be some preliminary evidence
in support of this hypothesis in ongoing econometric analysis,[24] then IS
countries would have been handicapped also by the lower amount of
foreign investment flows and not just by their lower social productivity
compared to the EP countries.

'Grey area' dynamic effects

While the arguments so far provide ample satisfaction to those who seek
to understand why the EP strategy does so well, dissatisfaction has
continued to be expressed that these are arguments of static efficiency

and that 'dynamic' factors such as savings and innovations may well be favourable under IS.

Of course, if what we are seeking to explain is the relative success of the EP countries with growth, this counter-argumentation makes little sense since, even if it were true, the favourable effects from these 'grey area' sources of dynamic efficiency would have been outweighed in practice by the static-efficiency aspects. The fact remains, however, that in the NBER project which was the only one to address these questions in some fashion, the results were not clear-cut on the issue, providing support to neither the school that maintains that IS does better on these questions, nor to the EP proponents who sometimes propose the opposite in their enthusiasm.[25] On the other hand, later evidence suggests that the EP strategy may be superior in practice on some of these dimensions.

It is simply not possible to claim that IS regimes enable a country to save more or less than EP regimes: the evidence in the NBER project, for instance, went both ways.[26]

Nor does it seem possible to maintain that EP or IS regimes are necessarily more innovative. It is possible to argue that EP regimes may lead to more competition and less sheltered markets and hence more innovation. But equally, Schumpeterian arguments suggest that the opposite might also be true.

The little empirical evidence that was available in the NBER project did not point in either direction. Since then, however, a few studies have appeared which suggest that the EP strategy may encourage greater innovation. Thus, Krueger and Tuncer (1980) have examined the 18 Turkish manufacturing industries during the 1963–76 period. They found that periods of low productivity growth roughly occurred during periods when foreign exchange controls were particularly restrictive and hence the IS strategy was being accentuated. The overall rate of productivity growth was also low throughout the period Turkey pursued an IS strategy.

Again, in an analysis of productivity change in Korea, Turkey, Yugoslavia and Japan, Nishimizu and Robinson (1984) argue that if growth is decomposed into that due to 'domestic demand expansion', 'export expansion' and 'import substitution', the inter-industrial variation in factor productivity growth reflects (except for Japan) the relative roles of export expansion and import substitution, the former causing a positive impact and the latter a negative one. This careful and painstaking research is certainly suggestive. However, as the authors recognise, export expansion may have been caused by productivity change rather than the other way around, the regressions begging the issue of causality.

What about economies of scale? Theoretically, the EP success should be increased because world markets are certainly larger than just home markets. But systematic evidence is not yet available on this question. For instance, evidence is lacking to date to indicate whether firms that turn to export markets are characterised by greater scale of output than those firms that do not. On the other hand, experience in the case of the EC suggests that trade may lead not to output-level changes so much as to product specialisation.

Suppose, however, that we do assume that economies of scale will be exploited when trade expands. The cost of protection, or the gains from trade, will then rise significantly. Thus Harris (1986) has calculated for Canada that a 3.6 per cent rise in GNP could follow from the unilateral elimination of Canadian tariffs, if economies of scale were exploited.

Finally, in the matter of X-efficiency, it is again plausible that firms under IS regimes should find themselves more frequently in sheltered and monopolistic environments than under EP regimes; in fact, a great deal of such evidence is available from the country studies in the several research projects discussed. X-efficiency therefore ought to be greater under the EP regime. However, as is well known, this is a notoriously grey area where measurement has often turned out to be elusive.

While the latter two arguments for the success of the EP strategy are therefore plausible, empirical support for them is not available. The former two arguments are a mixed bag, providing less than a compelling case for showing that EP is necessarily better on their account than IS.

2.4.3   *Growth and other objectives*

A final word is necessary on the superior economic performance of the EP strategy. Much like the die-hard monetarists who keep shifting their definitions of money as necessary in order to keep their faith, the proponents of IS have tended to shift their objections as required by the state of the art.

When it became evident that the EP strategy yielded higher growth, and that the static versus dynamic efficiency arguments were not persuasive and probably went in favour of the EP strategy, the IS proponents shifted ground. They took to arguing that the objective of development was not growth but the elimination of poverty or increasing employment; and the EP might be better for growth but was worse for these other objectives. This was part of a larger argument that became fashionable during the 1970s in certain development circles: that growth had been the objective of development to date, that the objective was wrong, and that the true objective of poverty amelioration was ill-served by development efforts directed at growth, and in fact growth even harmed the poor (in certain formulations of such critics).

Of course, in theory, economists can prove anything if they are smart enough. Conflicts among different objectives can be readily demonstrated in well-defined, suitably chosen models. What was novel, however, was the assertion that the empirical experience of the 1950s and 1960s had shown that growth did not impact on poverty and that it had even harmed it. These views, however, have not stood the test of detailed scrutiny.

The evidence does not support the views that growth was desired *per se*, that poverty elimination was not the stated objective which was pursued by means which included as a key element the acceleration of growth rates to 'pull up' the poor into gainful employment, and that growth on a sustained basis has not helped the poor. These orthodoxies are no longer regarded as plausible, as I have argued at length elsewhere.[27]

In regard to the narrower question at hand, that is, whether the EP strategy procures efficiency and growth but impacts adversely on poverty and employment, evidence has now been gathered extensively in a sequel NBER project, directed by Krueger (1982). Essentially, she and her associates document how the investment allocation under EP require the expansion of labour-intensive activities since developing countries' exports are typically labour intensive. Therefore, *ceteris paribus*, they encourage the use of labour and hence employment and hence, in countries which typically have underemployed labour, also the alleviation of poverty.

Moreover, after more than two decades of successful growth in the EP countries, especially in the four Far Eastern economies, it has become easier for economists to contemplate and comprehend the effects of compound rates and the advantages of being on rapid escalators. Even if it had been true that the EP strategy yielded currently lower employment or lower real wages, the rapid growth rates would overwhelm these disadvantages in the long run, which can be simply one generation.

It would appear therefore that both the employment-intensive nature of EP growth in developing countries and the higher growth rates in the EP countries have provided a substantial antidote to the poverty and underemployment that afflicted these countries at the start of their development process.

2.5   The second export pessimism

These lessons were important. Many developing countries learnt them the hard way: by following IS policies too long and seeing the fortunate few pursuing the EP strategy do much better. Perhaps learning by others' doing and one's own undoing is the most common form of education! But just as these lessons were widely accepted, and a 'new orthodoxy' in their favour was established, a new wave of export pessimism arrived on the scene. This second export pessimism, which is paradoxically both more serious and more tractable in principle, tends to undermine the desired shift to the EP strategy in the developing countries.

As is often the case, there are two different sets of factors generating this pessimism: (1) the objective events such as the slowing down of the world economy since the 1970s and the resurgence of powerful protectionist sentiments in the developed countries; and (2) new intellectual and academic arguments supportive of inward-looking trade policies in the developing countries. The two are not entirely unrelated since theory, especially international trade theory, does not grow in a vacuum. But they can be dealt with sequentially nonetheless.

2.5.1 *Protectionism*

In essence, the second export pessimism rests on the view that, whatever the market-defined absorptive capacity for the exports of the developing countries, the politics of protectionism in the developed countries (which still constitute the chief markets of developing-country exports) is such that the exports from developing countries face serious and crippling constraints that make the pursuit of an EP strategy (with $EER_x \approx EER_m$) inefficient, if not positively foolish.

If this assessment is correct in its empirical premises, then the EP strategy's premise that foreign markets are available at prices largely independent of one's own exports is certainly not valid. But this must be carefully understood. Concretely, for example, if the importing countries invoke market-disruption-related QRs, or frivolous countervailing duty (CVD) retaliation, if Brazil successfully exports footwear, then Brazil faces a less-than-perfectly-elastic market for footwear, and an optimal tariff (i.e. a shift to IS strategy) *in this sector* is called for. This should justify only selective protection, carefully devised and administered, not a general IS strategy. If, however, this response is feared no matter what you export, i.e. the fear of protectionism is nearly universal in scope, a *generalised* shift to IS strategy would unfortunately be legitimate.

The second pessimism, like the first, takes the latter, vastly more fearsome form, extending to exports generally. The resulting case for a general shift to the IS strategy then collapses only if one can show that the protectionist threat is not as serious as it appears or that, even though serious, there are policy options such as multilateral efforts at containing the threat effectively, that one ought to undertake while one pursues the

EP strategy. As it happens, a case can be made in support of both these responses.

2.5.2 How serious is the protectionist threat?

In assessing the extent to which the protectionist threat must be taken seriously, one may first make the prudential statement that it should never be regarded lightly. Sectional interests have always provided the political momentum through congresses and parliaments to protectionist responses to import competition. On the other hand, the post-war history of trade barriers shows the important role that executives have played in upholding the national interest, broadly served by freer trade and specialisation. Vigilance in containing protection has always been necessary. The real question is: has the threat become sufficiently more serious so that the developing countries ought to turn away from embracing the EP strategy?

First, a few facts need to be noted. As Table 2.1 briefly indicates, trade expansion has certainly slowed down considerably since the 1970s. But even then, world trade has grown faster than world income over the 1970–83 period. More compelling is the fact that the developing countries' exports of manufactures to the developed countries have grown almost twice as fast as the exports of these countries to one another, showing even during the 1970s a growth rate of over 8 per cent annually. This has happened during a period when non-tariff barriers (NTBs) such as voluntary export restraints (VERs) began to proliferate to the chagrin of everyone embracing the national interest, and during a period when the OECD countries showed sluggish growth rates and increased rates of unemployment.

That exports from the developing countries continued to grow in this fashion was first highlighted by Hughes and Krueger (1984), who thought that it was a puzzle since protectionist threats had been felt to have been translated into a large amount of actual protection already. This puzzle has stimulated Baldwin (1982, 1985) into developing an interesting thesis: that protection is far less effective than one thinks simply because there are many ways in which exporting countries can 'get around' it in continuing to increase their export earnings. Thus, Baldwin (1985) has written:

> Consider the response of exporting firms to the imposition of tighter foreign restrictions on imports of a particular product. One immediate response will be to try to ship the product in a form which is not covered by the restriction . . . . One case involves coats with removable sleeves. By importing sleeves unattached, the rest of the coat comes in as a vest, thereby qualifying for more favorable tariff treatment. (p. 110)

The use of substitute components is another common way of getting around import restrictions. The quotas on imports of sugar into the United States only apply to pure sugar, defined as 100 percent sucrose. Foreign exporters are avoiding the quotas by shipping sugar products consisting mainly of sucrose, but also containing a sugar substitute, for example dextrose . . . . At one time, exporters of running shoes to the United States avoided the high tariff on rubber footwear by using leather for most of the upper portion of the shoes, thereby qualifying for duty treatment as leather shoes. (p. 110)

Yoffie (1983) has also recently examined the VERs on footwear and textiles from a political scientist's perspective and found that the dynamic exporting economies such as South Korea and Taiwan have embraced them with considerable ingenuity, much like what Baldwin has documented and argued, to continue expanding their exports significantly.

There is also a more subtle factor at play here which relates to why VERs, which represent the method by which imports have been sought to be cut in many recent NTB actions, may have provided the mechanism by which the executives interested in maintaining freer trade despite mounting protectionism may have succeeded in keeping trade expanding. VERs are, in that view, a 'porous' form of protection that is deliberately preferred because of this non-transparent porousness. I have argued recently (Bhagwati, 1986c) that in industries such as footwear, two characteristics seem to hold that lend support to this 'porous-protection' model as an explanation for why protection is ineffective: (1) undifferentiated products (i.e. cheaper varieties of garments and footwear) make it easy to 'transship', that is, to cheat on rules of origin, passing off products of a country restricted by VERs as products of countries not covered by VERs; and (2) low start-up costs and therefore small recoupment horizons apply in shifting investment and hence products to adjacent third countries that are not covered by VERs, so that an exporting country can get around (admittedly at some cost) the VERs by 'investment-shunting' to sources unaffected by VERs. This type of strategy allows exporters to recover their investment costs since it is usually some time before the VERs get around to covering these alternative sources (or VERs are eliminated as the political pressure subsides (as was the case with US footwear).[28]

In both ways, therefore, VERs in these types of industries can yield a 'close-to-free-trade' solution for the exporting countries that are afflicted by the VERs. These countries can continue to profit from their comparative advantage by effectively exploiting, legally (through investment-shunting) and illegally (through transshipments), the fact that VERs leave 'third countries' out whereas importing-country tariffs and quotas do not.[29]

But the question then arises: why would the protecting importing countries prefer this 'porous protection'? Does it not imply that the market-disrupted industry fails to be protected as it would under a corresponding import trade restraint? Indeed it does. But that is precisely its attractiveness.

If executives want free trade in the national interest whereas legislatures respond to the sectoral interests – definitely the 'stylised' description of the 'two-headed' democracies in the United States and the United Kingdom – then it can be argued that executives will prefer to use a porous form of protection which, while assuring freer market access, will nonetheless manage to appear as a concession to the political demands for protection from the legislature or from their constituencies. Undoubtedly, these protectionist groups and their congressional spokesmen will eventually complain about continuing imports. But then the executive can always cite its VER actions, promise to look into complaints and perhaps bring other countries into the VER net, and continue to obfuscate and buy time without effectively protecting.[30]

If the foregoing arguments suggest that executives have been clever enough, both in exporting and importing countries, in keeping markets much more open than the casual reading of the newspapers would suggest, there are also additional pro-freer-trade forces that have now emerged in the world economy which need to be considered in making a reasonable assessment of the prospects for increased protectionist measures. I believe that the international political economy has changed dramatically in the last two decades to generate new and influential actors that are supportive of freer world trade.

A fairly common complaint on the part of analysts of the political economy has been the asymmetry of pressure groups in the tariff-making process. The beneficiaries of protection are often concentrated whereas its victims tend to be either diffused (as is the case with final consumers) or are unable to recognise the losses they incur as when protection indirectly affects exports and hence hurts those engaged in producing exportables.[31]

Direct foreign investment (DFI) and the growing maze of globalised production have changed this equation perceptibly. When DFI is undertaken, not for tariff-jumping in locally sheltered markets, but for exports to the home country or to third markets as is increasingly the case, protectionism threatens clearly the investments so made and tends to galvanise these influential multinationals into lobbying to keep markets open.

For example, it was noticeable that when the US semiconductor suppliers recently gathered to discuss anti-dumping legal action against Japanese producers of memory microchips known as EPROMs (or erasable programmable read-only memories), noticeably absent were Motorola Inc. and Texas Instruments Inc. who produce semiconductors in Japan and expect to be shipping some back to the United States.[32]

Almost certainly a main reason why US protectionism has not translated into a disastrous Smoot–Hawley scenario, despite high unemployment levels and the seriously 'overvalued' dollar (in the Dutch-disease sense), is that far fewer congressmen today have constituencies where DFI has not created such pro-trade, anti-protectionist presence, muddying waters where protectionists would have otherwise sailed with great ease. The 'spider's web' or 'spaghetti-bowl' phenomenon resulting from DFI that criss-crosses the world economy has thus been a stabilising force in favour of holding the protectionists at bay.

It is not just the DFI in place that provides these trade-reinforcing political pressures.[33] As I have often argued (1982a, 1986a), the response to import competition has been diluted by the possibility of using international factor mobility as a policy response. Thus, the possibility of undertaking DFI when faced with import competition also provides an alternative to a protectionist response. Since this is the capitalist response, rather than that of labour which would 'lose jobs abroad', the defusion of protectionist threat that is implied here works by breaking and hence weakening the customary alliance between both pressure groups within an industry in their protectionist lobbying, a relationship with which Magee has made us long familiar.

Interestingly, labour today seems also to have caught on to this game and is not averse to using threats of protection to induce DFI from foreign competitors instead. The United Auto Workers labour union in the United States appears to have helped induce Japanese investments in the car industry in this way. This is, in fact, quite a generic phenomenon where DFI is undertaken by the Japanese exporting firms to 'buy off' the local pressure groups of firms and/or unions who can, and often do, threaten legislative pressures for tariffs to close the import markets. This type of induced DFI has been christened as *'quid pro quo* DFI' (Bhagwati, 1985c) and appears to be a growing phenomenon (certainly on the part of Japanese firms),[34] representing a new and alternative form of response to import competition than provided by old-fashioned tariff-making.[35]

In short, both actual DFI (through the 'spider's-web' effect) and potential DFI (outward by domestic capital and *quid pro quo* inward by foreign capital) are powerful forces that are influencing the political economy of tariff-making in favour of an open economy. They surely provide some counterweight to the gloom that the protectionist noises generate today.

But all these arguments could collapse under the weight of the contention that if many countries were indeed to shift to the EP strategy, whether through conversion to the view or through conditionality such as that envisaged under the Baker Plan put forth by US Treasury Secretary James Baker III in 1985, the pressures to close markets would multiply owing to the magnitude of the absorption of exports that this would imply for the developed countries.

This takes us back partly to the Cline (1982) estimates and the several refutations of the pessimism engendered by them that were set out in section 2.2.[36] But it remains true that, even if the estimates in Cline are not to be taken seriously, the addition of any kind of trade pressure in a significant degree could touch off a wider range of sectoral, safeguard moves in the developed countries in the present climate. It is indeed possible to argue that Cline-type estimates are not plausible and exaggerate what would happen; there is a great deal of absorptive capacity in the market sense in the world economy which can readily handle improved export performance resulting from the shift of many developing countries to the EP mode of organising trade; and there are powerful new forces in the international political economy that may make the protectionist bark worse than its bite. Nonetheless, the danger of protectionism does remain acute, especially in the present macroeconomic situation of sluggish growth and continuing trade deficit in the United States. The US Executive's capacity to hold the line against protectionism has been significantly eroded by the neglect of fiscal deficits and a serious underestimate of the upsurge in the congressional sentiment in favour of protection and fair trade that would ensue from such failures and the massive adjustments they would impose on the trade sector. The US Executive is much more conscious of its earlier neglects and of their consequences for protectionism; but the fragility of the situation requires serious attention to other policy instruments such as the proposed Multinational Trade Negotiations (MTN), as discussed below.

An important consequence of the second wave of export pessimism, which is based on this protectionist threat rather than on the belief in market-determined forces that limit export prospects, is that developing countries can join in the process of trying to contain this threat and thereby change the very prospects for their trade. In turn, therefore, this suggests that they join hands with the developed countries in efforts such as the MTN to contain the threat to the world trading system and to keep markets open to expanding trade levels. Shifting to the IS strategy, therefore, based on export pessimism reflecting protectionist sentiments, simply makes no sense from an economic viewpoint unless the developing countries are convinced that protectionism is here to stay and will be translated into actuality no matter what is done – an assumption that seems to be wholly unwarranted in light of the discussion earlier in this section. A far more sensible policy approach seems rather to be to join with the executives of countries that support freer trade initiatives, among them certainly the United States, in containing the protectionist sentiments via strategies such as entering into trade negotiations.

2.5.3 New arguments for the IS strategy

It may then be useful to address some new intellectual defences of the IS strategy that have recently emerged in the academic literature.[37]

Labour market imperfections

In recent articles, especially Fields (1984), it has been argued that the EP strategy is not appropriate when there are excessively high wages in the economy and that EP countries such as Jamaica have done badly by ignoring this caveat.

The theoretical literature on market imperfections and optimal policy that emerged in the post-war period, with the independent contributions by Meade (1951) and Bhagwati and Ramswami (1963) setting off the spectacular growth of the subject during the 1960s, has shown that factor market imperfections are best addressed by domestic, rather than trade, taxes and subsidies.[38] However, it is indeed true that the second-best policy measures in such a case could be trade tariffs and subsidies, as the case may be.

There are two other problems with Fields's argument. First, he does not establish that countries such as Jamaica have in fact been following the EP strategy in the incentive-related sense that is relevant. As it happens, Jamaica certainly has not and, in fact, has for long periods been in the IS mode instead. However, this confusion of concepts and hence conclusions is, it should be noted, not confined to Fields's analysis but afflicts even the proponents of EP strategy in some cases. Second, it is not at all clear from Fields that high wages constitute a market imperfection in the sense required for departure from unified exchange rates in the form of the IS strategy.

In my view, wages are relevant in a different sense that is macro-theoretic rather than micro-theoretic as Fields suggests. If overall wages are 'too high', that can only mean that somehow they, and therefore the price level as well, are out of line with the exchange rate. That is, the country is suffering from overvaluation. In short, if that is so, we have already seen that the country is pursuing an IS strategy, whether it intends to or not. Therefore, a country simply cannot hold on to any EP strategy if it continues to experience excessive wages. The successful pursuit of EP, on a sustained basis so that investors respond to the incentives that EP defines, thus requires a sound macro policy as its foundation. Sound macro policies may then also bring, in turn, their own other rewards that supplement those that follow from the EP strategy.

Satisficing theory of IS

An interesting thesis has been proposed by the political scientist Ruggie (1983), which seems to argue that the advantage of an EP strategy cannot be enjoyed by many developing countries because they simply do not possess the flexibility of resource movements and the necessary political capacities to negotiate such flexibilities that the pursuit of EP requires. I would call this therefore the 'satisficing' theory of the IS strategy: developing countries in this predicament must make do without the gains from trade and efficiency improvements that EP strategy brings.

This is a difficult argument to judge since, even if it were valid within its premises, I do not find it compelling if such political constraints are equated with the fact of being less developed economically. In fact, given the lack of democratic structures with pressure-group politics and attendant constraints on economic action by the government, it is doubtful whether developing countries are not the ones at advantage in this matter!

Again, is it clear that tensions and distributional conflicts are necessarily more difficult under an EP strategy? An IS strategy, while insulating the economy relatively from external disturbances, may create yet more tensions and conflicts if the resulting stultification of income expansion accentuates the zero-sum nature of other policy options in the system. The correct statement of the Ruggie thesis would then seem to be that, in the pursuit of any development strategy, the compatibility of it with the political structure and resilience of the country needs to be considered. And this caveat needs to be addressed not only to the EP-strategy proponents.

Coping with external instability

A similar economic concern has been that, while EP may be better under steady-state conditions, it exposes the economy to the downside in the world economy and makes it more vulnerable to instability. Of course, the downside effects have to be set off against the upside effects. When this is done, it is not evident that countries pursuing EP strategies are necessarily worse off. As it happens, even the downside experience of EP-strategy countries during the post-oil-shock years seems to have been more favourable than the experience of the IS-strategy countries, according to statistical analysis by Balassa (1983, 1984). The reason seems to have been their greater capacity to deal with external adversity by using export expansion more successfully and thus avoiding import contraction to adapt to the world slowdown.

2.6   Conclusion

Export-promotion policies emerge with success from the detailed scrutiny offered in this chapter. Equally important is the fact that their successful adoption will indeed require collaborative and intense efforts to ensure that the protectionist threat, recently escalating, is not allowed to break out into actual protection on a massive scale.

The current Multilateral Trade Negotiations offer the only reasonable prospect for maintaining a momentum in favour of a freer world trade system. Failure in pursuing them successfully, in a spirit of accommodation and mutual understanding of constraints and needs, will only undermine what seems like the best mechanism for containing the protectionist threat.

Notes

1.   The chief studies were directed by Little, Scitovsky and Scott (1970) at the Organization for Economic Cooperation and Development (OECD), Balassa (1971) at the World Bank, Bhagwati (1978) and Krueger (1978) at the National Bureau of Economic Research (NBER) in the United States and Donges (1976) at the Kiel Institute in Germany. Complementing and overlapping each other, these studies represent a massive analysis of the central question that has preoccupied development economists from the very beginning of the discipline.
2.   Among other reviews which complement this chapter, the reader may consult Behrman (1984), Bhagwti and Srinivasan (1979), Findlay (1984a), and Srinivasan (1986a, b).
3.   On the other hand, Prebisch may have subsequently embraced the Nurkse view that primary product markets were also price inelastic, according to Balassa. I am rather referring in the text to the main Prebisch thesis as originally propounded and widely attributed to him.
4.   In technical jargon, we have here the classic case for an optimal tariff since the terms of trade vary with the level of trade.
5.   In fact, this shows how dangerous it can be to use such regressions, with little underlying rationales, for predictive purposes. I have considered this issue at great length in Bhagwati (1985a, Part II).
6.   Cf. Goldstein and Khan (1982) and Riedel (1984), who analyse this argument fully in two splendid and independent articles. Also of importance is the classic examination of the issue by Kravis (1970).

7. See again the results cited in the synthesis volumes of the research projects listed in Note 1. Also, the Goldstein–Khan (1982) analysis bears directly on this issue.
8. Cf. Riedel's (1984) discussion of this finding in his Table 4.
9. There is a substantial empirical literature on this subject, with important contributions by Balassa, Grubel, and Lloyd. In addition, recent theoretical work by Dixit, Lancaster, Krugman, Helpman, and others has provided the analytical explanation for such intra-industry trade.
10. All these arguments are effectively a rebuttal also of Dornbusch's (1986) restatement of the limited-absorptive-capacity thesis for developing countries' exports which asserts that substantial terms-of-trade losses would follow from the simultaneous resort to EP strategy by many developing countries.
11. I am indebted to Vittorio Corbo for pointing this out to me.
12. Cf. the comment on Prebisch in Bhagwati (1985a).
13. The estimated excess of EER_x over EER_m appeared to be below 10 per cent at maximum in the few careful cross-section estimates we had. This is reconfirmed for South Korea in a more recent analysis by Nam (1986).
14. The strategies are usually illustrated in terms of the simplified two-goods model of traditional trade theory.
15. See also Krueger's (1980) informal usage of the phrase in this fashion.
16. Cf. Chenery, Shishido, and Watanabe (1962) for one such decomposition. For an analytical synthesis and evaluation of alternative measures of import substitution, see Desai (1979).
17. See, in particular, the synthesis volumes by Bhagwati (1978) and Krueger (1978).
18. Krueger's (1978) synthesis volume also contains similar cross-country regressions for the ten semi-industrialised countries in the NBER project. See the extensive review in Lal and Rajapatirana (1986).
19. Balassa's (1978) re-estimation of Michaely-type regressions also incorporates the Michalopoulos–Jay approach, thus combining the two different methodologies under one rubric.
20. It is well known, of course, that factors that lead to improved efficiency and hence to income improvement need not necessarily lead to sustained higher growth rates. Thus, in the Harrod–Domar model, where labour supply is slack, a once-for-all improvement in efficiency will indeed translate into a permanent higher growth rate of income; but not so in the steady state in the Solow model where the growth rate is determined by the growth rate of labour and the rate of technical change. Over the medium-run periods, however, for which the discussion in the text is couched, where we are explaining growth rates over a period of two or three decades, these subtleties are not particularly relevant, in my judgement. Moreover, it is important to note that, for any given growth rate, a more efficient economic regime will require less savings (and hence less blood, sweat and tears) to sustain it than a less efficient economic regime.
21. See Bhagwati and Srinivasan (1983, ch. 30) for a taxonomy of such lobbying activities.
22. The conventional cost of protection, from distorted production decisions resulting from the protection, is augmented by adding the cost of tariff-seeking lobbying when the protective tariff is the result of such lobbying. Costs of other kinds of lobbying, including the effects of DUP

activities such as illegal trade (i.e. tariff evasion), can be similarly accommodated. I should also add that if the EP strategy relies, not on exchange-rate flexibility but simply on selective export subsidies to eliminate the bias against exports (as in Phase II, delineated in the Bhagwati–Krueger NBER project), the DUP activities can be expected to arise extensively in that regime as well. In fact, it was the examination of the extensive export subsidies regime prior to the June 1966 devaluation in India that reinforced my view (based on observation of licence-seeking in India) that DUP activities were important to analyse, leading to the development of that theory in my thinking and writings through the 1970s. Anne Krueger and Gordon Tullock also arrived independently at similar theories.

23. Krueger's (1974) classic article contains estimates of rent-seeking costs, that is, costs arising from resources spent in chasing premia or rents on quantitative restrictions. These high estimates up to 15 per cent of GNP are based on the assumption that rents result in an equivalent loss of resources in equilibrium (the so-called one-on-one postulate in rent-seeking theory). Recently, computable-general-equilibrium modellers such as Dervis, de Melo, Whalley, Robinson, and others have begun to incorporate such DUP and rent-seeking activities into their models and calculations, so that progress can be expected at some future date in assessing the magnitude of such costs in a plausible fashion. Cf. Dervis, de Melo and Robinson (1981) and Grais, de Melo and Urata (1986).

24. See the discussion in Balasubramanyam (1984) and in Bhagwati (1986b). In private communication, Balasubramanyam has provided further results on this hypothesis.

25. See, in particular, the extensive analysis of this question in the NBER synthesis volume by Bhagwati (1978), where some chapters are specifically addressed to summarising and evaluating these kinds of arguments with the aid of the findings in the ten country studies as also extraneous evidence and argumentation on these subjects.

26. See Bhagwati (1978, ch. 8).

27. See Bhagwati (1985d), where I review the arguments and the evidence on these issues, drawing also on the valuable contributions of Surjit Bhalla, Pranab Bardhan, Paul Isenman, Ian Little, Irma Adelman, Montek Ahluwalia, Keith Griffen, Paul Streeten and T. N. Srinivasan, among others.

28. The investment-shunting need occur only in so far as it is necessary to meet value-added rules of origin, of course, making the cost of profiting from this porousness even less than otherwise.

29. Of course, the VERs in this instance represent only a partial and suboptimal approximation to the free-trade solution which remains the desirable but infeasible alternative. Moreover, not all exporting countries are capable of the flexible and shrewd response that underlies the model of porous protection sketched above.

30. This 'two-headed' version of governments is, of course, what underlies the Feenstra–Bhagwati (1982) model of the efficient tariff. There, the model postulates that one branch of the government (pursuing special interests) interacts with a protectionist lobby to enact a political-economy tariff. Then, another branch of the government (pursuing the national interest) uses the revenue generated by this tariff to bribe the lobby into accepting a

less harmful tariff that nonetheless leaves it as well off as under the political-economy tariff. When this model was presented to a scientific conference in 1978, the general reaction was that the model had a 'schizophrenic' two-headed government! Traditional trade theory is so often modelled in terms of a monolithic government that what was obviously a realistic innovation was regarded as a bizarre feature of the model.

31. See for example, Olson (1971), Finger (1982), and Mayer (1984a).
32. See the report by Miller (1985) in the *Wall Street Journal*.
33. Of relevance here is the work of Helleiner (1977) and others. These authors, and most recently Lavergne and Helleiner (1985), have argued that multinationals have become active agents exercising political pressure in favour of free trade. The structure of trade barriers has been related to patterns of DFI by Helleiner but the later work by Lavergne finds this relationship to be fairly weak. In any event, this hypothesis and research do not extend to the potential DFI effects in favour of freer trade (through DFI becoming an alternative response to import competition) that is discussed in Bhagwati (1982b, 1986b) and in the text.
34. In fact, MITI (Ministry of International Trade and Industry) of Japan has recently completed a survey of Japanese DFI abroad and found that a large fraction of the respondents cited reasons of the *quid pro quo* variety to explain their investment decisions. I am indebted to Professor Shishido of the International University of Japan for this reference.
35. See the theoretical modelling of such *quid pro quo* DFI in Bhagwati, Brecher, Dinopoulos, and Srinivasan (1987) and in Bhagwati and Dinopoulos (1986), the former using perfectly competitive structure and the latter using monopoly and duopoly structures instead.
36. See also the critique offered by Ranis (1985). Cline (1985) basically defends his position by arguing that the high ratios of trade to GNP *à la* Far Eastern economies are likely to trigger difficulties and that he should not have been read to mean that the EP strategy would necessarily lead to such phenomenally high trade growth rates and trade ratios.
37. In the following, I select for treatment only the most important such arguments, given the central theme of this chapter. For a more comprehensive review of recent arguments for protection, including those applying to developed countries – as in Kaldor's (1966) argument for protection to prevent British deindustrialisation or Seabury's (1983) advocacy of protection to prevent American deindustrialisation for defence reasons – see my analyses in Bhagwati (1985c, 1985e, and 1986d). For a different emphasis, more sceptical of anti-protectionist arguments and EP strategy, see Streeten (1982).
38. The entire theory has been synthesised in Bhagwati (1971) and there is also a splendid short treatment by Srinivasan (1987) in his entry on distortions for *The New Palgrave*.

3

Outward orientation:
An assessment

H. David Evans

3.1 Introduction

For some time now, it has been fashionable to proclaim the benefits of various forms of a more outward-oriented development strategy, whether called export-oriented industrialisation (EOI), export-led growth, or just export promotion. The benefits of such a strategy have usually been contrasted with the export pessimism and various forms of inward-oriented or import-substituting industrialisation (ISI) strategies of the immediate post-war period, and the lacklustre performance of many developing countries in the 1970s which have been deemed inward orientated by one criterion or another.

One of the paradoxes of the world economy in the post-war period is the central place that mercantilism has held, the pursuit of a trade surplus for its own sake or the belief that a trade surplus maximises national wealth (Srinivasan, 1989). It appears in the guise of the more extreme versions of both EOI and ISI when such policies are pursued for the impact on the earning or saving of foreign exchange as an end in itself. Even the notion of reprocity in GATT itself is fundamentally mercantilist in that it makes no sense for trading nations to offer to lower their own trade barriers in return for reduction of the partner's trade barriers when each nation could reap potential gains from unilateral trade barrier reduction.[1]

In this chapter, I will argue that the theoretical and empirical evidence in favour of outward orientation, and the attribution of market liberalisation as the key policy instrument which achieved this success, is often wildly overstated. There is a strong case for the reform of trade policy regimes in many developing countries as a part of structural adjustment programmes, for a reversal of the rising tide of protectionism in the developed countries, and for multilateral trade policy reform to remove the barriers to South–South trade between developing countries. For individual developing countries, this will require trade policy reform to achieve efficient import substitution and, to some degree, export promotion. Nevertheless, given the uncertainties surrounding the evolution of the world economy and the poor prospects for multilateral trade policy reform, I think that the best mix of incentives and policy intervention after such reform will inevitably remain biased towards import substitution.

3.2 Historical background

Historically, there has been a strong empirical association between periods of rapid growth of trade and the rate of growth of GDP. The evidence shown in Table 3.1 shows that, with the exception of the period between 1870 and 1912, the statistical association between trade and growth is positive. However, the interpretation of the direction of causality is more problematic. An important part of the development literature emphasises a strong causal connection running from the growth of trade to the growth of income, captured by the metaphor suggesting that trade is the 'engine of growth'. Thus, trade is the connecting link between the rate of growth of industrial production in the developed countries and the rate of growth of output in developing countries (Lewis, 1980). This Keynesian demand-side view is in contrast to the idea that trade is the 'handmaiden of growth' (Kravis, 1970; Riedel, 1984), where trade is regarded as the facilitating rather than the driving force in the development process and where both supply- and demand-side factors are identified but no one-way causality is established. In the latter case, if the supply-side factors are sufficiently favourable, as in the case of the East Asian newly industrialised countries (NICs), there can be a very rapid rate of growth of exports from such countries against unfavourable world trade trends. As Riedel (1984) shows, the Keynesian demand-side view of trade as the 'engine of growth' works reasonably well in the aggregate when developing countries are highly specialised in primary commodity exports, but the 'engine of growth' breaks down when developing-country exports are disaggregated and when supply-side changes lead to the growth of manufactured exports from developing countries.

One of the best empirical studies of the relationship between trade orientation and growth in the post-war period is by Syrquin and Chenery (1989). Using a sample of over 100 countries over the period 1950–83,

Table 3.1   Historical rates of growth (1820–1985).

	Arithmetic average for 16 countries Average annual change (%)	
	GDP	Exports
1820–1870	2.2[a]	4.0[b]
1870–1913	2.5	3.9
1913–1950	1.9	1.0
1950–1973	4.9	8.6
1973–1979	2.5	4.8
1979–1985	1.9	3.5

[a] average for 13 countries.
[b] average for 10 countries.
Sources: Maddison (1982, Table 4.9) and World Bank (1987, Figure 3.2).

they attempt to capture the effects of economic size, the degree of openness and trade orientation, on growth. The degree of openness is measured by the deviation of each country's level of merchandise exports from the value predicted by the regressions, and the degree of primary or manufactures trade orientation captured by the index of trade orientation measures the deviation of a country's actual trade-orientation index from the one predicted by the regression equation for a country of similar income and size. Their findings suggest that small outward-oriented and manufacturing-orientated countries had the highest growth rates of per capita income over the sample period. Moreover, outward orientation, whether coupled with primary or manufactured orientation, led to faster rates of growth for large and for small countries. However, whilst such statistical studies are useful in establishing common patterns and some key differentiating aspects of country experience, they do not directly relate the degree of primary or manufactured orientation to resource endowments, or the degree of outward orientation to trade policy variables. That is, the degree of outward orientation is not measured directly by the policy variables which affect the degree of openness of an economy, but by a cross-country comparison of outcomes. Trade orientation is similarly measured by a cross-country comparison of outcomes, rather than by the underlying determinants of trade orientation.

The conditions under which developing-country exports have entered into world trade have changed a great deal since the end of the 1970s. This is evident from the dramatic change in the rate of growth of developing-country exports in relation to world trade discussed in Sarkar and Singer (1989). Using UNCTAD data, they show that, in terms of volume,

Table 3.2 Volume and unit value indices of exports of different parts of the market economy world: 1980–87.

Regions and indices:	Years							
	1980	1981	1982	1983	1984	1985	1986	1987
First World								
Volume	100	102	101	104	114	118	121	122
Unit value	100	96	92	88	86	85	97	108
Third World								
Volume	100	94	88	91	96	93	114	119
Unit value	100	105	97	88	87	85	64	71
Terms of trade*	100	109	105	100	101	100	66	66
A. Major petroleum exporters								
Volume	100	84	72	68	67	61	78	72
Unit value	100	112	106	93	91	89	52	61
Terms of trade*	100	117	115	106	106	105	54	56
B. Other Third World countries								
Volume	100	113	119	128	141	144	156	174
Unit value	100	93	84	82	83	80	78	83
Terms of trade*	100	97	91	93	96	94	80	77

*Relative unit values: unit values of exports of the different regions of the Third World deflated by the unit values of exports of the First World.

Source: UNCTAD, *Handbook of International Trade and Development Statistics*, 1987.

developing-country exports have increased much faster than world trade as a whole. At the same time, their unit values have declined very substantially for primary exports, particularly non-oil primary exports, and, to a lesser extent, a similar picture emerges for manufactured exports from developing countries. Sarkar and Singer attribute the increasingly unfavourable terms of trade for developing-country exports to a supply-side response to debt pressure on the part of developing countries in the face of a relatively sluggish growth of world demand over the same period. Although the economic mechanisms that produced this response have not been described or analysed, their empirical findings do illustrate how much the structure and characteristics of the world economy have changed in the 1980s. Whatever the case for outward orientation based on evidence from the earlier post-war period, it must be modified to take into account the new situation in the world economy today.

3.3 Outward orientation and the theory of trade policy

The theoretical argument for outward orientation depends a great deal on the strategic assumptions made. With fully employed resources, exogenously given rates of growth of the labour force and natural resources, exogenously given savings rates, and without market distortions or imperfections, protection will have a once-and-for-all effect on the level of income. In this context, the benefits of outward orientation on the rate of growth of income are usually argued to derive from the induced effects of competition on technical change, learning or savings which are not accounted for in the static case. The introduction of scale economies further strengthens the case for outward orientation, but the benefits tend to be of a once-and-for-all nature.

The most potent case for outward orientation affecting the rate of growth arises in a situation where there is some form of an institutional wage and under- or unemployed labour. In this case, the rate of profit will be higher under free trade than with protection and therefore, with a classical savings assumption, the rate of growth will rise with the introduction of free trade.[2] In the two-factor case, when the export industry is labour intensive, there will be favourable employment effects and the overall welfare benefits will tend to be favourable; when the export industry is capital intensive, the welfare effects will be more ambiguous.[3]

In the above static or dynamic contexts, the standard arguments for intervention to overcome market imperfections or distortions typically involve arguments for a direct subsidy to overcome the effects of consequences of the distortion at its source, financed with lump-sum taxation. In the case of the infant-industry argument for protection, this will typically involve situations where there are the following:

1. Market failures, such as the lack of perfect foresight in capital markets.
2. Economies of scale and the competitive outcome cannot be achieved.
3. External economies, such as in labour training.
4. Important productive inputs such as knowledge and technology with mixed characteristics of public and private goods.[4]

However, while the above arguments can underpin an interventionist industrial policy and development strategy, they do not make the case for restricting trade. The best policy response, where revenue constraints allow, is usually to direct the policy intervention as closely as possible to the market failure, thus avoiding the introduction of by-product distortions. One standard exception is the case where a country faces a less than perfectly elastic demand curve for exports, when an optimal export tax is the appropriate policy response from a single-country perspective. Another exception is when there are scale economies, in which case, depending on the nature of competition, it may be better to allow a domestic monopoly to reap the benefits of scale economies behind an import or an export subsidy.[5]

The above interventionist arguments are in the mainstream neo-classical tradition. They may be extended to encompass a view of the state as an agent with additional, if imperfect, knowledge and foresight. In this case, the appropriate response is for the state to use indicative planning so that the imperfect market signals are supplemented as far as possible through the indicative planning mechanism. However, some of the more ideological practitioners of trade policy advocacy, sometimes referred to collectively as the neo-liberal paradigm,[6] argue that where the choice is between imperfect markets and imperfect state intervention, it is better to rely on the free play of market forces.

When trade policy reform is considered either unilaterally, as in structural adjustment programmes in developing countries, or in multi-lateral trade negotiations under the auspices of GATT such as the current Uruguay round of negotiations, the ranking of trade policy instruments is very important. The standard ranking of trade policy instruments in order of least to most efficient is direct import controls, tariffs and subsidies aimed at the point of distortion.[7] However, the East Asian experience suggests that trade policy instruments cannot be ranked in terms of efficiency independently of the institutional context within which they were applied. For example, highly selective quantitative controls have been important in the South Korean case.[8] To some extent, the potential for rent-seeking behaviour has not materialised, partly because of the relative autonomy of the state and of the role of a strong national development ideology in countering these effects. More potently, quantitative controls were often tied to crude incentives in the South Korean case, for example import licences tied to the export performance of the firm. Moreover, within the state itself, performance indicators and incentives are used within the bureaucratic structures to determine promotion prospects.[9] This gave the state instruments of direct control over firms necessary for their selective industrial policies which tariffs could not achieve. In such cases, the standard ranking of tariffs as a more efficient protective instrument cannot be sustained. Quantitative controls tied to incentives, however crude, may also be superior to tariffs precisely because they provide the instruments for implementing an interventionist industrial strategy.[10] These observations have important implications for the characterisation of trade policy regimes.

Early attempts to characterise trade policy regimes as 'inward' or 'outward' oriented looked at the balance of incentives facing import-substituting industries compared with export industries.[11] Agarwala (1983) attempted to go beyond the measurement of trade policy bias by looking at the overall efficiency of the price mechanism in different countries. However, there is no clear correspondence in his study between the measured price distortion and the theoretical requirements of a distortion measure.[12] More recently, Greenaway (1986) and the World Bank (1987, ch. 5), attempted to divide a sample of forty-one countries according to the degree of inward and outward orientation using four qualitative and quantitative variables:

1. Effective rate of protection.
2. Use of direct controls such as quotas and import licensing schemes.
3. Use of export incentives.
4. The degree of exchange-rate overvaluation.

Both Greenaway and the authors of the 1987 World Development Report acknowledge that a degree of judgement inevitably enters into any such exercise where both qualitative and quantitative criteria are important. For example, as Greenaway (1986, p. 33) suggests, a narrow definition of 'strong outward orientation' based on the balance of incentives alone would leave only Hong Kong in this category. His own preference is for a weaker definition of 'strong outward orientation' which includes Singapore and South Korea as well. Another problem arises in the comparison of the classification of South Korea and Brazil. The classification of South Korea as 'strongly outward orientated' in both time periods used in the study (1963–73 and 1973–83) is based almost entirely on 1960s evidence reported in Greenaway (1986, Table 6). In contrast, with evidence from both time periods, Brazil is classified as moderately inward orientated in the earlier time period and moderately outward orientated in the second time period. Yet on the basis of a comparison of the characteristics of trade and exchange rate regimes for South Korea and Brazil in Greenaway (1986, Tables 6 and 7), the classification for Brazil in the second time period is not so clear-cut. These tables show that South Korea, with a low average rate of effective protection, a high dispersion of effective protection rates, and a realistic to undervalued exchange rate, scores as 'strongly outward orientated'. On the other hand, Brazil, with an average level of effective protection of 44 per cent, a moderate degree of dispersion of effective protection and an overvalued exchange rate, is classified as 'moderately outward orientated'. Without additional evidence on the extent of the undervaluation of the South Korean exchange rate, compared with the overvaluation of the Brazilian exchange rate, the protective effect of the two estimated rates of effective protection cannot be compared. Nor is it possible to assess the importance of differences in the degree of dispersion of the effective protective rates, or the differential effects of import controls and export incentives, on the basis of the Greenaway data.

The difficulty in estimating the impact of import controls has reinforced a recent study by Wade (1989) which suggests that there has been an overestimation of the effects of the removal of quantitative import restrictions in South Korea. He suggests that there has been much more import substitution in South Korea induced by targeted and made-to-measure protection than is captured by the available indexes of protection.[13] It would seem, therefore, that there is a real danger that the set of judgements which were made in classifying countries by trade orientation in the Greenaway study was influenced by the attribution of favourable growth performance to the degree of outward orientation. This point is reinforced by noting that there are no less than twelve alterations of country assignment by trade policy regime when the tables in Greenaway (1986, Tables 6 and 7) are compared with World Bank (1987, Figure 5.2). These doubts are further reinforced by the observation that the relative efficiency of quantitative controls, compared with tariffs, cannot be made independently of the incentive structures and institutional context within which they are used.

In contrast to the view of the 'minimalist' state, for example set out in World Bank (1987), there has been a good deal of work recently on the 'developmental state'. This new literature has contributed to building a less blinkered view of the nature of the state and the importance of state intervention in the formation and execution of a development strategy.[14] This work stresses the importance of the class base and the importance of the relative autonomy of the state, the administrative capacity of the state, the capacity for long-run decision making, and the role of intermediate levels of state intervention in the formulation and execution of a selective industrial policy. To a limited extent, this contribution is recognised in the narrow economic description of successful East Asian state intervention as providing a clearing house for information and technology in the face of market failure.[15] Yet even this narrow economic interpretation of the East Asian developmental state is resisted by neo-liberals who remain highly sceptical of any non-market policy instruments.[16]

The basis of neo-liberal scepticism of the importance of the East Asian developmental state stems from the well-documented excesses of some inward-orientated and interventionist policy regimes, captured in the generalisation of the concept of rent-seeking behaviour (Krueger, 1974) to the concept of 'directly unproductive profit-seeking activities' (DUP) by Bhagwati (1982b) and by Bhagwati and Srinivasan (1982). Clearly, the careful study of DUP activities has enriched the economic analysis of bureaucratic and state behaviour. However, the converse of DUP does not always hold: not all directly productive profit-seeking activities will be efficient. For example, Bowles (1985) documents several typical cases where inefficient productive processes may be adopted by profit-maximising competitive firms. Nor does it follow from the study of DUP activities that all interventionist state policies are likely to be inefficient.

The lesson of the East Asian developmental state experience is that interventionist activities can be highly productive. This view is reinforced by a variety of studies which stress the role of sector-level co-operation between firms and intervention by central and local government in a small-firm economy.[17] Such interventions draw on the economic rationale for an active industrial strategy outlined above, but translated to a small-firm context. In effect, the functions of the head office of a large firm are carried over to a small-firm context through interventionist policies normally associated with central government. This is achieved through networking between firms, joint ventures and cooperative arrangements between firms, and may involve significant local government involvement.

How reproducible is the East Asian developmental state experience? A glance at the conditions which make for the success of the East Asian case warns that these are not easily reproducible. In some cases, where there is no class basis for a relatively autonomous state, where administrative capacities are weak, where there is little capacity for long-run strategic decision making, and where there are no strong institutions to facilitate intermediate levels of state intervention through local governmental or parastatal organisations, the imperfect market may well be better than the imperfect state. In others, the case for the reform of state institutions along with the reform of trade policy regimes to facilitate a more efficient interventionist strategy may be more appropriate. The problem is that the final choice between arm's-length and interventionist policies depends on a great deal of judgement. The problem with neo-liberal ideology is that preferences for the 'free market' may prevail where more efficient interventionist alternatives may be possible and appropriate. Conversely, prejudice against the market mechanism may prevail where efficiency considerations suggest otherwise.

Often, writers from outside of the neo-classical tradition on the theory of trade policy fail to take into account economic efficiency considerations. However, there is no intrinsic reason why efficiency considerations should be eschewed by an 'alternative perspectives' view on trade and development, and, in fact, there are some signs that this point is being more widely recognised.[18] For example, in his review of the Brandt Report recommendations on industrialisation and world trade in the light of current trends in the world economy ten years on, Singer (1989) calls for new policies of efficient import substitution. Singer does not spell out the policy objectives or the appropriate policy instruments to be taken into account in formulating new policies of efficient import substitution. However, some elements of a framework for considering efficient import substitution can be found scattered in Singer's writings on South Korea and in other contexts.[19] His overriding policy concern is that import-substituting industries should be able to grow into exporting industries, and that existing exporters should not be disadvantaged by the cost of purchasing imports at protected rather than world prices. This implies a system of tariff drawbacks and subsidies for exporters to offset the cost of protecting import-substituting industries. The range of protective instruments he considers includes quantitative controls for the early stages of import substitution, import tariffs and preferential credit arrangements. In all cases, he favours the efficient monitoring of the costs of import-substituting industries as a part of the process of ensuring that the import-substituting industries develop a research-and-development capacity, and that the level of assistance is limited and reducing over time. Whilst these and other 'alternative perspectives' arguments for import substitution are seldom reviewed in an explicit theoretical context, arguments developed in this section provide at least part of the theoretical background against which such policies might be developed and assessed.

3.4   The empirical evidence on outward v. inward orientation

The empirical evidence against high levels of protection to sustain import-substituting industrialisation (ISI) compiled during the 1970s was based on case-study evidence covering a relatively small number of countries (see Little, Scitovsky and Scott, 1970; Krueger, 1978; Bhagwati, 1978; Balassa, 1982). This case-study evidence was used to support the theoretical case against ISI and in favour of export-oriented industrialisation (EOI). It suggested that pessimism concerning export prospects for developing countries was unfounded, particularly for non-traditional primary commodities and manufactures. Further, it suggested that, by exploiting developing countries' comparative advantage through the market mechanism, EOI was more efficient, requiring lower capital/labour ratios to achieve high rates of growth. It was also argued that additional efficiency benefits were achieved from the realisation of scale economies through sales on the world market and through induced efficiency benefits from international competition. Finally, the case-study evidence was used to support the theoretical contention that the export of labour-intensive manufactures would improve the income distribution for wage earners in labour-abundant economies.

One of the problems with using case studies is that it is difficult to generalise from this evidence. The statistical analysis of the relationship between trade orientation and growth is one way of overcoming this difficulty. Although such statistical evidence is seldom of assistance in establishing the direction of causal linkages, it can nevertheless be useful in establishing empirically the strength of the association between variables. For the most part the direction of causality must be established by theoretical argument. The work of Syrquin and Chenery (1989) already referred to shows that both outward and manufacturing orientation for small countries was associated with above-average growth performance over the post-war period. However, it does not directly relate either the degree of manufacturing orientation or the degree of outward orientation to either resource endowments or trade policies. An early attempt to establish the relationship between policy-induced market price distortions, economic efficiency and growth already commented on above can be found in World Bank (1983, ch. 6) and Agarwala (1983). This study was based on a simple cross-section regression of the average growth performance over the 1970s of a sample of over 30 countries and an unweighted average of seven indices of price distortion. Of the seven indexes of price distortion, only three related directly to trade policy regimes – an index of manufacturing protection, an index of agricultural price distortion, and an index of exchange-rate distortion. The central finding of the study was that one-third of the sample variance in growth performance of countries in the World Bank study was accounted for by the index of price distortion. It was seen at the time as providing confirmation of the earlier case-study findings in respect of the benefits of EOI (World Bank, 1983, pp. 61 and 63), that general respect for price efficiency was one of the key variables in explaining differences in the growth performance of developing countries.

The World Bank study can be criticised on a number of grounds. In addition to the lack of a clear correspondence between the measured price distortion and the underlying theoretical requirements of a distortion measure already referred to, the study also used a variety of *ad hoc* non-economic explanations of individual country behaviour for outlier observations. These criticisms suggest that there was too much weight given to the role of respect for price efficiency in general in accounting for differences in growth performance, combined with a lack of theoretical or empirical discussion of the role of omitted variables and particularly of the non-economic determinants of growth performance.

An extensive series of statistical tests reported in Aghazadeh and Evans (1988), using the 1983 World Bank study as a starting-point but adding further economic and non-economic variables, confirmed these general criticisms. Aghazadeh and Evans found that only three of the seven indexes of price distortion were important in accounting for the sample variance in growth performance, and that the least significant of these related to manufacturing protection. The more important price variables included the extent to which the sample countries had shown an appreciation of the real exchange rate over the 1970s, and the extent to which real wages moved in line with productivity. It is noteworthy that neither of the empirically important price variables relate to microeconomic efficiency, but point rather to the importance of macroeconomic management of both the exchange rate and income distribution. Other important additional variables, which together increased the variance accounted for to over two-thirds, included a cluster of economic and institutional variables centring around the capacity of an economy to sustain a rapid rate of growth of investment, including the capacity of the state for giving strategic direction to development policies.[20] The findings suggested that one of the main effects of manufacturing protection was through a negative impact on agricultural growth, a consideration which is obviously important for the design of efficient strategies of import substitution. The study also found no evidence of export-led growth, a result also found in other recent studies.[21]

None of this is to say that empirical evidence described establishes the causal linkages between the dependent and the independent variables used in the above studies. No more is claimed than the proposition that there is empirical evidence consistent with a set of theoretical explanations which give greater weight to non-price variables than appears in both mainstream and neo-liberal accounts.

The Greenaway (1986) and World Bank (1987) studies already referred to also support, at face value, the idea that the more outward-oriented countries have experienced a higher rate of growth in the 1960s and 1970s. There is also some evidence that the more outward-oriented countries have lower capital/output ratios, suggesting that outward orientation may have also been more efficient. However, on closer inspection, the case in favour of outward orientation is not so clear-cut. The problem of judgement in the classification of countries according to the degree of inward or outward orientation has already been discussed. Other doubts arise from the data used in the country classification. Direct price comparisons often do not correspond with the measures of protection, and the reasons for the discrepancies are little understood. Nor are the criteria by which the exchange rate is deemed 'realistic' at all clear.

Bearing these doubts in mind, it is not surprising that the results shown in World Bank (1987, Table 5.2) are ambiguous. It can be readily seen that, in terms of GDP, GDP per capita, domestic savings and inflation, the moderately inward-oriented countries did better than the moderately outward-oriented countries in the period 1973–85. Other factors than those captured by the moderate inward–moderate outward classification have been influencing growth performance since the world economy began to slow down in the 1970s.[22]

In contrast to the above, the results seem to be unequivocal in relation to the strongly inward-oriented category. It appears that the countries in this group did far worse than the other countries in the sample, particularly when looked at in terms of per capita GDP in the period 1973–85. Yet, when examining the criteria used for assignment of countries to the strong inward-orientation category, it is not immediately obvious how the final judgements were made in Greenaway (1986, Tables 6 and 7). In some cases, the presence of an overvalued exchange rate and extensive import controls were present; in other cases not. In any event, other unidentified factors were obviously at work as well, a point which was made in criticism of the World Bank (1983) study discussed above.

In view of these doubts, the empirical case for arguing that a change in trade policy regime from strong inward orientation to one of the other categories is not as strong as it appears on first sight. Nor does the evidence cited in Aghazadeh and Evans (1988) support the proposition that trade policy is a central determinant of growth performance. Rather, this study suggests on the basis of 1970s data that a depreciating real exchange rate in conjunction with appropriate distributive policies which allow for domestic savings, combined with investment growth and strong institutional support for this process, are the most important factors associated with rapid growth.

In empirical terms, the link between trade policy, rapid growth and economic efficiency cannot be strongly established. In this difficult and contentious area, perhaps the strongest empirical evidence is from the Syrquin and Chenery (1989) study described above, which suggested that, whatever it is that produces above-average overall trade orientation and above-average manufacturing orientation in small countries, also produces above-average growth performance. However, their findings are consistent with the argument that the aim of trade policy reform should not be to achieve strong outward orientation, but should emphasise efficient import substitution with some export promotion and growth of traditional and non-traditional exports, including manufactured exports as a part of the process of restoring health to import-substituting activities. This view is also supported by two studies using computable general equilibrium (CGE) models. Thus, Adelman (1984) found that, in the case of South Korea, a very satisfactory growth performance could be maintained with a marginal shift in the sources of final demand away from exports to domestic sources. Similarly, de Melo (1988) found that, with a stylised CGE model, a very marked increase in the degree of protection accorded to import-substituting activities would lead to a very dramatic decline in export growth, but only a marginal decline in the rate of growth of GDP.

Pursuit of a mixed strategy of efficient import substitution with some export promotion raises the obvious questions as to how much overall bias there should be towards import substitution, and what policy instruments should be used to achieve the desired 'objectives'. The conventional wisdom, that intense industry protection of 10–20 per cent for 5–8 years is the most that is justified, may have to be modified. However, there is as yet no set of empirical studies that could be used to establish a new set of 'rules of thumb' to guide infant industry-protective policies. Nor is it clear how much overall bias against exports would be justified. All that is suggested here is that, in the context of uncertain prospects for the growth of the world economy based on multilateral trading arrangements which can resist and roll back the rising tide of protectionism, further research on these questions is urgently required.[23]

The lack of overwhelming empirical evidence to support trade policy reform has not lessened the widespread recognition that such reforms should nevertheless be a part of stabilisation and adjustment policies, and should also be on the agenda for multilateral negotiations. If this conclusion is correct, a central enabling ingredient will be the creation of an appropriate political and institutional environment for industrial and trade policy reform. This is more likely to be successful if the process of reform is independent from international pressure for the implementation of inappropriate policies.

The implication that trade policy reform will inevitably involve some export expansion should not be resisted on the grounds of fallacy of composition, as is often argued by writers in the 'alternative perspectives' camp.[24] Whilst there are cases where the fallacy-of-composition argument may hold for commodities exported primarily by developing countries, it is very difficult in practice to design policies which take them into account. Worse, retention of highly restrictive trade policies by a single country or by a sub-group of producers on the grounds of the fallacy of composition runs the risk of overkill. When the export demand elasticity for the country or sub-group of countries is greater than 1, their market share falls without compensating benefits from the improvement in the terms of trade resulting from their action, as seems to have happened for sub-Saharan African countries in the 1970s.[25] One qualification to this argument is where an international agency such as the IMF, following a case-by-case approach, recommends price reform including devaluation to countries who collectively face the fallacy-of-composition problem.[26] The optimal policy in this case may be an export tax in the relevant countries administered by the IMF, with the receipts distributed as a part of the adjustment packages. An alternative might be increased generosity in the provision of transitional support for structural adjustment from the international community in return for restraint from applying an export tax. However, it is difficult to argue that, as a general principle, compensation for not exercising collective monopoly power should be a criterion for the provision of international aid.

The critical issue in the above case is that the countries affected are both poor and capital starved, and that the fallacy of composition increases the cost of adjustment which, in a more ideal world, would be financed at least in part by aid and international public capital provision. Should the affected countries resist price reform and structural adjustment even if they are unable to persuade the IMF to collect an export tax on their behalf? In the short run, additional costs would indeed be incurred as a result of lost export revenue which would arise as other exporters of the commodities concerned undertake reforms which increase the supply of exports on the world market. However, it may still be worth incurring these costs if the benefits of the structural adjustment in improving the growth performance of the economy as a whole outweigh the costs. Failure to undertake reforms essential to the long-run development prospects of the economy because of short-run costs, in this case exacerbated by the failure of institutions such as the IMF to take into account the direct way in which the policy reforms increase these short-run costs, may incur substantial costs on the economy over the medium to long run. Worse, failure to adjust now may intensify the structural adjustment problem, affecting only the timing when the reforms must inevitably take place with or without international compensation for the short-run costs arising from the fallacy of composition.

3.5 Policy responses

The circumstances, the timing and the sequencing of developing countries' trade policy reform which might be carried out will vary enormously. In the case of the 'miracle' NICs such as South Korea and Taiwan, the most important issues may relate to reform on the import side where the high and selective levels of protection operate. For these countries, a key question is how much, and for how long, should such import-substituting industries continue to receive protection. In other cases, trade policy reform is more likely to be carried out as a part of a wider process of stabilisation and structural adjustment. In such cases, the timing and sequencing of the trade policy reform may be crucial.

A recent review of the theoretical and empirical issues and difficulties involved in the timing and sequencing of trade policy (Michaely, 1986) suggests surprisingly few guidelines without strong theoretical and empirical qualification. Few would disagree with the argument that, in a world where rigidities are ubiquitous, the reform process should be multi-staged, with the speed of implementation depending on the degree of flexibility and adaptability of response. However, Michaely's description of the desirable components of the first stage of trade policy reform is more contentious. Michaely (1986, p. 56) suggests that trade liberalisation should entail a shift from quantitative restrictions to tariffs as the instrument of protection, accompanied with an appropriate exchange-rate policy and, if possible, carried out under favourable circumstances. Yet for the reasons analysed above, this first stage of the process of reform may be unmanageable and undesirable for three reasons:

1. Because of the difficulties in estimating the tariff equivalents of import controls, it is in fact very difficult to know what the reformed tariff rates should be. This may in turn make it impossible to estimate or predict what a new equilibrium exchange rate should be.
2. In the light of the first reason, it may be very difficult to prevent a very rapid draining of foreign-exchange reserves in the first stage of the reform process. This is particularly likely where it may be possible to use the removal of import restrictions to facilitate capital outflows through transfer pricing where capital market restrictions remain intact.
3. The removal rather than the reform of quantitative import controls may remove a vital trade policy instrument for selective trade and industrial policy intervention.

As argued above, it was through the reform of import controls that successful import substitution and export policies were executed in the cases of South Korea and Taiwan, rather than through the replacement of import controls by tariff equivalents. This interpretation of the South Korean and Taiwanese experience is consistent with the views of Singer outlined in section 3.3, and with those of Keesing (1979), who suggests that the first stage of the trade policy reform process should concentrate on direct intervention to stimulate exports without dismantling import controls.

Another area where there are very real prospects for trade policy reform lies in the opening up of South–South trade. In an open world economy with the rapid accumulation of capital in developing countries, standard neo-classical trade theory predicts that South–South trade could be the most dynamic component of world trade.[27] The reasons why this has not been the case are partly historical and institutional, the legacy of the colonial period which radically cut South–South trade links and opened up North–South trade,[28] and partly because of barriers to trade in the developing countries themselves. This suggests that a major part of any trade policy reform in developing countries as the debt crisis recedes should be the search for new opportunities for South–South trade. This could be achieved on the basis of bilateral negotiations either within or outside of the context of structural adjustment reforms and outside of existing regional cooperation between developing countries, as suggested by Parsan (1988) for the case of Trinidad and Tobago and Brazil. Whilst in principle the search for such trading links would be best facilitated in the context of multilateral trade reform, there is little point in waiting indefinitely for such reforms when the economic case for the opening of such trade is sufficiently powerful to suggest that it will be trade creating and not trade diverting.

Trade policy reform and the associated industrialisation strategies will inevitably involve the difficult task of 'picking the winners' in many, but not all, circumstances. Such decisions need to be made in regard to the made-to-measure import-substituting protection characteristic of the East Asian nation state success stories such as South Korea and Taiwan. They also need to be made when picking which industries are to survive trade policy reform, for example, in sub-Saharan African countries such as the Sudan, Tanzania and Zambia where the case for trade policy reform in the process of structural adjustment is very strong.

The decision-making processes by which efficient industrial strategies are established will vary from country to country, depending heavily on the political and institutional characteristics of the country concerned. The phrase 'picking the winners' is often used in a pejorative context of criticism of non-market processes of strategic choice of industries for promotion, and may therefore be misleading. Perhaps the most that can be said in general about the examples of successful interventionist strategies from the East Asian cases is that it is necessary to combine the capacity for both strategic decision making within the organs of central government with detailed implementation left to intermediate-level institutions where there is a closer interface between market and non-market decision-making processes. It would therefore seem that the provision of a more consistent political and institutional framework for economic policies will be at least as important as trade policy reform itself as the answer given to the question 'how much protection, and for how long?'.

3.6   The wider context and conclusions

Up to a point, outward orientation on the lines of the exemplary East Asian NICs has had favourable effects on the distribution of income.[29]

For these countries, there has been a measure of redistribution with very favourable growth. However, the consequences for the developed industrial countries of an open world economy may not be so favourable. With very high rates of accumulation of capital, even in a small number of successful NICs, the employment of less skilled workers in the developed countries is threatened, the distribution of income between skilled and unskilled workers is likely to deteriorate, and the returns to capital are likely to increase.[30] These trends are not in themselves arguments for protection in the industrial countries, but have certainly increased the protectionist response on both mercantilist and interest-group grounds. On this account, the prospects for a growing open world economy are not good. Indeed, the present Uruguay round of tariff negotiations under the auspices of the GATT will be deemed a success if the protectionist tide can be stemmed.[31]

This is not the place to predict the state of the world economy and the possible influences that this might have on the prospects for developing countries. Rather, the question is whether or not the principles underlying trade policy reform discussed in the previous section should be put aside in the face of continued pessimism over the prospects for developing country growth. I think not. The case for unilateral structural adjustment and trade policy reform will remain as powerful as it is today, especially if biased towards moderate levels of efficient import substitution.

Notes

1. This is not the place to analyse why such mercantilism persists. It would seem that its roots lie more in the exercise of political power and not in national economic calculus.
2. On this, see Findlay (1984b) and Bliss (1989).
3. On this, see Evans (1989b, ch.6).
4. For a recent summary of some of these arguments, see Smith (1986).
5. See Krugman (1986) and Neary (1988).
6. On this, see Colclough and Manor (1990, introduction).
7. See for example the discussion in Michaely (1977b).
8. See Leudde-Neurath (1986) and Wade (1989).
9. For a discussion of these issues, see White (1984), White and Wade (1988) and Wade (1989).
10. See also Bhagwati (1982a) for a discussion of the effect on economic efficiency of tying import licences to export performance.
11. See for example, Krueger (1978) and Balassa (1982).
12. For a critique on these lines, see Aghazadeh and Evans (1988).
13. Similar observations have been made by Wade (1989) in relation to Taiwan. Although Taiwan is not included in the statistics of World Bank studies, these observations suggest that the successful non-city-state East Asian NICs may have been less outward oriented than is often believed.

14. See in particular Bardhan (1984), White (1984), and White and Wade (1988). My own attempt to summarise this literature is in Evans (1989a, section 4.3).

15. This view is expressed in World Bank (1987, Box 4.4, p. 71). For an elaboration of the role of the East Asian developmental state in developing technological capability through a selective industrial policy, see Pack and Westphal (1986).

16. See, for example, the contrast between the discussion of industrial policy in the World Bank (1987, Box 4.4, p. 71) and the evaluation of the industrial policy debate in the surrounding text of the same publication.

17. This literature draws both on the experience of the dynamic industrial policy debate discussed in the text and on the experience of the export regions of Italy, sometimes called the Third Italy. There is also a closely related new literature on flexible specialisation summarised in Evans (1989a, section 4). For a developing-country application, see Murray *et al.* (1987).

18. For an extensive survey of non-neo-classical trade and development literature, see Evans (1989a).

19. The remarks which follow are based on a private exchange with Hans Singer.

20. See Aghazadeh and Evans (1988, equation 2.1 and Tables 3.3 and 4.2).

21. See for example the studies reported in Taylor (1986).

22. For example, Singer (1988a) finds that there is a correlation between the size of GDP per capita and the degree of outward orientation in the sample which is not controlled for in the World Bank analysis.

23. To a considerable extent, the new literature in strategic trade policy intervention, and the risk-avoidance arguments for import substitution, point in the same direction as argued here. For a recent survey of these arguments, see Stern (1989).

24. I have dealt with this argument at greater length in Evans (1990).

25. See Riedel (1984).

26. See Stewart (1987).

27. For an elaboration of this argument in the context of a trade model in which both skilled and unskilled labour are identified, see Evans (1989b, ch. 7).

28. For a discussion of this in the context of British colonial monetary systems, see Narsey (1987). See also Roemer (1977).

29. The favourable income distribution in South Korea should not all be linked to outward orientation. South Korean land reform in the post-Korean war phase already produced favourable income distribution effects in the 1950s. For some of the relevant statistics on income distribution in South Korea since the early 1960s, see the chapter by Suh and Williamson in Cornia, Jolly and Stewart (1987, p. 232).

30. See Beenstock (1984), Wood and King (1989) and Evans (1989a, ch. 7).

31. For a good summary of the rise of protectionism in the world economy and the prospects of the GATT negotiations, see MacBean (1988).

4
Empirical evidence on trade orientation and economic performance in developing countries

David Greenaway and Geoffrey Reed

4.1 Introduction and outline

The previous two chapters have been concerned with arguments for outward-looking trade policies, and a critique of these arguments. Both have been argued primarily from a theoretical standpoint drawing upon old and new arguments which have a bearing on the debate. This chapter will take these arguments as read and will refrain from any attempt either to repeat them, or to summarise them. Instead we will focus entirely on empirical aspects of the debate.

Empirical evidence on trade strategy, or trade orientation and development (however defined) is not easily summarised. This is so for several reasons. First, different analysts have addressed the issue in different ways. Second, even where the same approach has been adopted by different analysts, controversy may still remain, due for example to alternative interpretations of a given data set. Third, as the theoretical analysis has demonstrated, one can identify links between trade strategy and export growth; export growth and economic growth; trade strategy and economic growth. Empirically it is not easy to disentangle these. In order to provide a full flavour of the issues at stake and the current stock of empirical evidence, this chapter is organised as follows. Section 4.2 begins from a broad perspective, namely the relationship between trade strategy and development. This raises different kinds of methodological problems, for instance in defining trade strategy. These will be reviewed, and the empirical evidence extant at the time of writing evaluated. Section 4.3 is devoted to the narrower question of the relationship between export growth and the growth of output. As Chapter 2 indicated, the case for outward-orientated trade policies is often predicated on the

alleged growth-enhancing properties of exports. This section will examine both the methodological issues which complicate examination of
the relationship, and the results reported thus far. In section 4.4 we
address the current areas of ignorance and speculate on the kind of
questions which future empirical work might address. Finally in section
4.5 we offer some concluding comments.

4.2   Trade strategy and economic development

In the simple two-sector trade model 'trade strategy' is readily identified.
Consider Figure 4.1. P_w is the terms of trade which a given small open
economy faces. In the absence of distortions and interventions, this
would also represent the domestic relative price ratio. Although, as we
shall see later, some commentators equate this with an export-promoting
strategy, strictly speaking this price ratio represents neutrality. If an
import tariff distorted the domestic price ratio to P_T, this could be
described as import substitution. By contrast, a production subsidy
intended to increase output of A which distorted domestic prices to P_E
would describe an export-promotion strategy. These distinctions are
readily made, relying as they do on changes in a single relative price
between two clearly defined sectors.

In practice the identification of trade strategy is far more complicated.
This is so for several reasons. First, 'export' and 'import' sectors are not
always readily identifiable. The recent literature on intra-industry trade
has demonstrated how pervasive the phenomenon of industries simultaneously importing and exporting actually is (see Greenaway and
Milner, 1986). Notwithstanding the fact that intra-industry trade is
empirically less important in less developed countries (LDCs) than in
industrialised economies, this remains a complication (see Havrylyshyn
and Alikhani, 1989). Second, even when the output of particular sectors
can be reasonably clearly labelled exportable or importable, the sectors
may very well be multi-product. Different instruments of protection may
apply to each, and in calculating overall relative price effects, it may not
be obvious how different products should be weighted. Third, it is common in LDCs to find instruments of import protection simultaneously
coexisting with instruments of export promotion. Thus, in particular
cases, a given set of policy interventions which *systematically* promotes
import substitution or export promotion may not be in force. In most
developing countries policy is incrementalist in its evolution, with
policy-makers reacting to particular short-term pressures (like fiscal
constraints) with higher protection. Not only does this generate counter-
pressures for further protection in other import-substitute activities, it

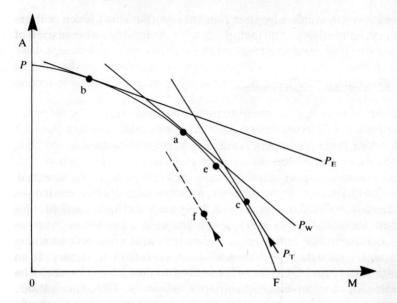

Figure 4.1   Relative prices and intervention.

may also result in the introduction of export incentives designed to offset the disincentive effects of import protection. Fourth, as the literature on the incidence of protection has shown (Clements and Sjaastad, 1985; Greenaway and Milner, 1987), the actual and intended effects of policy intervention may be quite different. The resource allocation effects of protection depend upon the substitutional relationships in the economy, something over which the policy-maker exercises little control. Thus, particular interventions may have unintended consequences. Finally, trade strategy may be time inconsistent, its emphasis altering through time. Of course this need not be the case. There are many examples of economies which have followed a particular strategy for a very long period: import substitution in India for instance. However, strategy may change. Many of the NICs which are described as following export-promoting strategies began with import-substitution regimes. In a study which used a five-way classification of policy regime, Krueger (1978) identified one case which went through all five stages over the period 1950–72. The difficulties this creates for the analyst are twofold. On the one hand, deciding which strategy is currently operative; on the other hand, identifying causality between trade strategy and subsequent economic performance.

When confronted with these complications, analysts have reacted in one of two ways, either by attempting to use a summary index of trade strategy, or by relying upon multiple criteria. As in all branches of applied economics, both involve compromises.

4.2.1 Multiple-criteria studies

This line of analysis endeavours to categorise trade strategy by reference to a number of different criteria. One can think of this approach (loosely) as focusing on policy inputs. Thus, for instance, Greenaway and Nam (1988) used information on effective rates of protection, reliance on direct controls, export incentives and exchange-rate misalignment, to classify 41 LDCs into four categories, namely strongly outward oriented, moderately outward oriented, moderately inward oriented and strongly inward oriented. Donges (1975) also relied upon a number of quantitative and qualitative indicators in a similar type of cross-section study. Although Agarwala (1983) used a 'distortion index' in his analysis of growth patterns in LDCs, the index was constructed from information on a variety of qualitative and quantitative indicators. Thus, for instance, information on, *inter alia*, tariff levels, quantitative restrictions and exchange-rate misalignment was used to distinguish between high, low and medium distortions in each. An overall inference on trade strategy could be made by reference to whether the overall degree of distortion was 'high', 'medium' or 'low'.

The advantage that this approach has is that its information content is high. No one indicator is used. The principal disadvantage, however, is that an element of judgement is inevitably at work. This is not a problem if all the indicators point in the same direction (e.g. high import tariffs, pervasive direct controls, export taxes and an overvalued exchange rate). Where, however, they point in different directions (e.g. high import tariffs, no direct controls, no exchange-rate misalignment and extensive export subsidies), it may be more problematic.

As indicated above, several studies have attempted to use multiple indicators. The most recent is Greenaway and Nam (1988). Here strong outward orientation (SOO) was identified with either a complete absence of trade controls (i.e. neutrality in Figure 4.1), or a situation where any import barriers were offset by export incentives (i.e. export promotion in Figure 4.1). Moderate outward orientation (MOO) implied limited use of direct controls, relatively low import barriers, and some provision of incentives to export, with overall incentives tending towards neutrality or a slight bias towards production for the home market. In the moderately inward-oriented (MIO) category, the overall incentive structure distinctly favours production for the domestic market and has a clear anti-export bias, with relatively high rates of effective protection, widespread use of direct controls and an overvalued exchange rate. Strong inward orienta-tion (SIO) implies very high rates of effective protection, pervasive use of direct controls, strong disincentives to the export sector, and significant overvaluation of the exchange rate.

It is self-evident that the four-way classification is to some degree judgemental, although this is really only likely to be an issue in separating the MIO and MOO sets. In the case of the SOO and SIO sets, all the indicators pointed in the same direction. Be that as it may, the principal results are summarised in Tables 4.1 and 4.2. These results are discussed in detail in Greenaway and Nam (1988) and will only be briefly summarised here. Table 4.1 suggests the following. First, manufacturing value-added appears to have grown more quickly in the outward-oriented economies between 1963 and 1985. Second, the average share of manufacturing value-added and the average share of the labour force are higher in the outward-oriented economies. The most striking differences in performance are between the SOO and SIO groups, with less striking and often less clear differences between the MOO and MIO groups. Table 4.2 suggests that capital formation and growth rates have been higher in the outward-oriented economies, incremental capital output ratios have been lower, merchandise exports higher, and the rate of per capita income growth higher. As with Table 4.1, the differences are most marked between the SOO and SIO groups, and often less clearly defined as between the MIO and SIO groups.

These results are suggestive rather than conclusive. They do suggest, however, that outward orientation has been more conducive to growth and exporting than inward orientation. The results have been criticised by, among others, Singer (1988). He argues that the findings are misleading on two counts. First, because the SOO group contains only three countries, Korea, Singapore and Hong Kong, the last two of which are city states and should be excluded. Thus the sample only really contains one country. Second, it is claimed that per capita income levels fall as we move from the SOO to the SIO countries. Thus, all the results tell us is that the poorer countries find it more difficult to grow. The first of these criticisms is at best misplaced, at worst disingenuous. If we are to claim that city states are in some sense special (and, if anything, one could readily make a case to the effect that they have special disadvantages), we might just as well begin singling out island economies, or landlocked economies, or small economies or continental economies, or whatever. The second criticism is potentially more valid, on the grounds that poorer countries are more susceptible to terms-of-trade shocks than richer countries with more diversified economies. It is worth noting, however, that, as Singer himself points out, Korea was one of the poorest countries in the world in the mid-1960s.

Table 4.1 Characteristics of industrialisation for 41 developing countries grouped by trade orientation.

Country development strategy	(1) 1963–73	(1) 1973–85	(2) 1963	(2) 1985	(3) 1963–73	(3) 1973–84	(4) 1963	(4) 1985	(5) 1965–73	(5) 1973–85
A1 Strongly outward oriented	15.6	10.0	17.1	26.3	10.6	4.9	17.5	30.0	14.8	14.2
A2 Moderately outward oriented	9.4	4.0	20.5	21.9	4.6	4.9	12.7	21.7	16.1	14.5
A Outward oriented (average)	10.3	5.2	20.1	23.0	6.1	4.9	13.2	23.0	15.2	14.3
B1 Moderately inward oriented	9.6	5.1	10.4	15.8	4.4	4.4	15.2	23.0	10.3	8.5
B2 Strongly inward oriented	5.3	3.1	17.6	15.9	3.0	4.0	12.1	12.6	5.7	3.7
B Inward oriented (average)	6.8	4.3	15.2	15.8	3.3	4.2	12.7	14.1	7.7	6.7

See Greenaway and Nam (1988) for countries grouped by trade strategy.

(1) Annual average growth of manufacturing value added.
(2) Average share of manufacturing value added in GDP.
(3) Annual average growth of manufacturing employment.
(4) Average share of labour force in industry.
(5) Annual average growth of manufacturing exports.

Table 4.2 Macoeconomic performance of countries grouped by trade orientation.

Country development strategy	(1)		(2)		(3)		(4)		(5)		(6)		(7)	
	1963–1973	1973–1985	1963–1973	1973–1985	1965–1973	1973–1985	1963	1985	1963	1985	1963–1973	1973–1985	1970	1985
A1 Strongly outward oriented	9.5	7.7	6.9	5.9	10.8	11.2	13.0	31.4	9.5	−2.0	2.5	4.5	4.1	5.9
A2 Moderately outward oriented	7.6	4.3	4.9	1.7	8.8	8.6	20.0	20.6	1.4	−2.3	2.5	5.0	7.5	20.9
A Outward oriented (average)	7.9	5.0	5.2	2.5	9.4	9.8	19.0	23.4	2.5	−2.3	2.5	4.9	6.2	13.5
B1 Moderately inward oriented	6.8	4.7	3.9	1.8	14.1	5.5	22.9	24.1	1.7	−2.2	3.3	6.2	11.3	29.0
B2 Strongly inward oriented	4.1	2.5	1.6	−0.1	2.2	−1.4	15.0	17.9	2.4	0.2	5.2	8.7	16.5	21.1
B Inward oriented (average)	5.2	3.7	2.7	1.0	8.8	2.5	17.6	21.2	2.1	−1.1	4.1	7.0	14.2	25.6

See Greenaway and Nam (1988) for countries grouped by trade strategy.

(1) Annual average growth of real GDP.
(2) Annual average growth of real per capita GNP.
(3) Annual average growth of merchandise exports.
(4) Average gross domestic savings rate.
(5) Average gross foreign savings rate.
(6) Annual average incremental capital output ratio.
(7) Average debt service as a percentage of exports.

Note: Averages are weighted by each country's share in the group total for each indicator.

4.2.2   Single-indicator studies

Several analysts have worked with single indicators of trade strategy. These attempt to summarise the relative price effects of the incentive structure in a single index or measure. Krueger (1978) proposes a measure of the bias in a trade regime as follows:

$$
B = \frac{\displaystyle\sum_{i=1}^{m} w_i \left(\frac{P_{mi}}{Q_{mi}} \right)}{\displaystyle\sum_{j=1}^{n} w_j \left(\frac{P_{xj}}{Q_{xj}} \right)}
$$

where P and Q refer to domestic and international prices respectively; m and x refer to importables and exportables respectively, w refers to weights, i and j are product groups, and the weights are defined as the share of these product groups in total imports or exports. Thus B measures the distortion of domestic prices relative to world prices in importables, compared to that in exportables. A computed value of 1 represents neutrality. Note that, of course, such a value could arise from a free-trade regime, or from a highly distorted regime, where incentives to produce in the import-substitute sector are exactly offset by incentives to produce in the export sector. An index in excess of unity indicates inward orientation; an index of less than unity indicates outward orientation.

Use of the effective exchange rate facing exportables is in the same spirit as the bias index. This is an approach which has been advocated by a number of analysts, including Balassa (1982) and Bhagwati (1986a). The basic idea is simple: one calculates the effective exchange rate facing producers in the import-substitute sector, and compares this with the effective exchange rate facing exporters in the export sector. If the former exceeds the latter, the country is said to be following an IS strategy; if the effective exchange rates are the other way around, the country is said to be following an EP strategy.

The single indicators are in principle amenable to less ambiguous calibration than multiple criteria. In principle they should also be easier to work with. Inevitably there are measurement problems, for instance with the aggregation of individual sub-groups within the tradable goods sectors. Aggregation difficulties arise not only through problems in assigning weights to individual groups, but also as a result of the fact that imports and exports may be recorded simultaneously in a given industry. Nevertheless, both of the single indicators discussed have been used.

Bias coefficients were estimated in the Krueger (1978) study. Having said this, it is important to recognise that this was but one element in a

Table 4.3 Estimates of bias in five developing countries.

Country	Year	Bias index
Brazil	1957	2.45
	1961	1.79
	1964	1.41
Chile	1956	3.69
	1959	1.94
	1965	1.95
Philippines	1960–62	2.01
	1970	1.37
South Korea	1961	0.67
	1964	0.78
Turkey	1958–59	6.31
	1970	3.01

Source: Extracted from Krueger (1978), Table 6.2.

more comprehensive analysis of trade strategy for some IO developing countries. The estimates for five of the countries concerned are reported in Table 4.3. Several points are worthy of note. First, most of the estimates exceed unity, suggesting that relative prices favour production for the import-substitute rather than the export sector. Second, for one country, Korea, the index is less than unity, implying that relative prices favour production for the export sector. Third, many of the indices exceed 2, and one case actually exceeds 6 (Turkey in the late 1950s), implying strong inward orientation. Finally, it is notable that for the 'inward-orientated' cases, the indices decline through time. This particular study is not directly comparable to those discussed above and below, since it does not attempt to correlate bias *per se* with economic performance. Rather it uses information on bias, along with other information, including effective exchange rates, to evaluate the impact of liberalisation packages.

Relative effective exchange rates have been more widely used than estimates of bias. As already noted, both Balassa (1982) and Bhagwati (1986a) make use of this indicator. So too does Krueger (1978). For purposes of comparison, we will therefore note some results from this study. These are reported in Table 4.4. The results here are consistent with those reported in Table 4.3, in that those which could be labelled inward oriented from the bias estimates, also appear to be inward oriented according to relative effective exchange rates. As with bias estimates, these indicators have not been correlated with growth performance and we merely report them as indicators of trade orientation.

An alternative single indicator which has been related to export growth and income growth is employed by Singer and Gray (1988). They use a

Table 4.4   Ratio of import to export effective exchange rates in nine developing countries

Country	Year	EER_M/EER_X
Brazil	1957	1.28
	1961	1.64
	1964	1.00
Chile	1956	1.21
	1959	1.18
	1965	1.18
Egypt	1962	0.98
Ghana	1967	1.83
India	1966	1.29
Israel	1952	0.95
	1962	0.97
Philippines	1960–62	1.64
	1970	1.37
South Korea	1961	0.68
	1964	0.78
Turkey	1958–59	1.87
	1970	1.63

Source: Extracted from Krueger (1978), Table 6.3.

measure of trade policy developed by Kavoussi (1985). Here trade orientation is defined as an interactive export term, namely

$$TO = (1 + RC)(1 + RD)$$

where RC is a 'competitiveness factor', defined as the change in value of traditional exports due to increased market share, and RD is a diversification factor, defined as the increase in the value of exports attributable to the growth of non-traditional exportables. If TO is positive, trade strategy is defined as outward oriented; if it is negative, it is defined as inward oriented. Although the definition is a narrow one, it does focus on an indicator which we would expect to be correlated with trade policy, namely export earnings. Singer and Gray (1988) show, as did Kavoussi (1985), that a correlation between export orientation and growth could be found, but that this only held in conditions when world demand was strong. When demand is slack, the correlation does not appear to hold, although the authors concede, 'outward orientation limits the fall in export earnings' (p. 400). This leads them to conclude 'that outward orientation cannot be considered as a universal recommendation for all conditions, and for all types of countries' (p. 403). No specific comment is made on inward orientation although, significantly, Kavoussi (1985), on whose findings the Singer–Gray work is based, concludes,

'The results . . . suggest that when trade policies are restrictive, export earnings are not likely to grow very rapidly even when external demand conditions are highly favourable' (p.390). Greenaway and Nam (1988) reach a somewhat similar conclusion: 'whilst the precise determinants of successful industrialisation may not be entirely clear, the determinants of unsuccessful industrialisation are much clearer. We may not be entirely clear on the precise determinants of growth; the potential for trade strategy in discouraging growth is, however, rather more apparent' (p. 433).

4.3 Export and economic growth

As noted earlier, the question of the relationship between exports and economic growth is much narrower than that discussed above. This relative narrowness should in principle make the analysis easier, but there is sufficient evidence of disagreement on both methodology and results to disprove this contention. This section begins with a brief consideration of the methodological issues, and them summarises the results reported thus far.

4.3.1 *Methodological issues*

These will be discussed under three main headings: firstly, the choice of the variables used to measure economic growth and exports or export growth (and any other variables involved); secondly, the choice between cross-sectional and time series analyses; and thirdly, the standard econometric questions of statistical technique, model specification and causality.

Analysts divide between measuring economic growth in terms of the change in either GNP or GDP, or in GNP or GDP per capita, adjusted by an appropriate price index; or that growth expressed as some percentage of a chosen base level. The most obvious measure of export (growth) is actual (change in) value of exports from time period to time period (e.g. Balassa, 1978; Jung and Marshall, 1985). However, not all writers agree that these are appropriate measures. For example, Michaely (1977a) has argued that 'Since exports are themselves part of the national product, an autocorrelation is present; and a positive correlation of the two variables is almost inevitable, whatever their true relationship to each other.' Michaely then uses the rate of change of the proportion of exports in the national product as his measure of export growth, arguing that this is a measure of export bias, and that the hypothesis that a good export performance enchances economic growth should be tested using this measure. The choice of additional variables for inclusion in estimated multivariate relationships is broad, encompassing such items as the growth in the labour force, growth in domestic and/or foreign investment, the trade or current account balance and foreign aid.

All applied economists would prefer to work with data for a large group of countries gathered over as long a time period as is consistent with the assumption of structural/institutional stability, and to carry out a joint cross-section/time series analysis. In practice, the difficulty of obtaining data and/or concern with the quality of those data often lead to either a cross-sectional study over one or two time periods for a 'large' group of countries or to a set of time series analyses for a smaller group of countries. Cross-sectional studies appear the most common, in many cases with the data for each country averaged over some time period; for example, Michaely (1977a) worked with data for 41 countries averaged over 1950–73, Balassa (1978) with averages for 43 countries over the period 1960–73, and Tyler (1981) used average values for 1964–73 for 55 countries. A major argument for the use of cross-sectional analysis is that we may reasonably assume that external influences, for example the general state of the world economy, are common to all countries and may therefore be excluded from the analysis. This is generally not possible with a time series approach. The obvious counter-argument is that it is only with time series data that we can obtain evidence of the direction of causality (discussed later); examples of studies using time series data are Williamson (1978) with data for 22 countries for 1960–74, and Jung and Marshall (1985) for 37 countries for 1950–81. Moreover, cross-sectional studies presume a similarity of structure across developing countries.

A basic problem in the choice of statistical technique is whether to use parametric or nonparametric methods. Many studies rely at least in part on a nonparametric approach, most commonly using rank correlation coefficients to measure the strength of association between economic growth and some potentially related variable such as export growth (e.g. Michaely, 1977a; Balassa, 1978). This has the advantage of not presuming a specific functional form for the relationship. Among its weaknesses, however, are the difficulties of handling multivariate relationships and the relative lack of statistical power. Parametric techniques are most often in the form of OLS regression analysis (e.g. Balassa, 1978; Tyler, 1981; Feder, 1983), but with increasing sophistication (e.g. Jung and Marshall, 1985).

The use of parametric methods brings into focus all the familiar problems of the choice of functional form and of explanatory variables, the possibilities of multicollinearity and, for time series data, serial correlation, and the vexing questions of spurious correlations, possible simultaneous determination and causality. In practice, most studies use linear functions, particularly a linearised production function. For example, Kavoussi (1984) estimates the parameters of

$$Y = aK + bL + cE$$

where Y, K, L and E are the growth rates of GNP, capital, labour and exports respectively. The rationale for the inclusion of exports in the production function is usually the specification of the basic production function as including disembodied technical progress, and then assuming that the rate of technical progress is a function of exports.

Linearity in particular may be considered doubtful in view of the marked nonlinearity of the relationships found in studies of other aspects of developing countries. For instance, Chenery and Syrquin (1975) examined a large number of structural relationships in developing countries and found most of them to be nonlinear. While the problems of choosing an appropriate functional form are rarely discussed explicitly in the literature, implicit recognition of its presence may be indicated by the identification of sub-groups of developing countries according to, say, their level of per capita income or of economic development (e.g. Michaely, 1977a; Kavoussi, 1984), or the exclusion of certain low-income countries on such grounds as 'some basic level of development is necessary for a country to most benefit from export oriented growth, particularly involving manufactured exports' (Tyler, 1981).

The exclusion of relevant explanatory variables, with the attendant risks of bias in the estimation of parameters and their standard errors, is often unavoidable given the relative paucity of data for many developing countries and the general difficulty experienced in measuring some variables given even the best data. For the reasons noted above, this may not be such a pervasive problem in cross-sectional analyses, but it must still be present. This problem is of course related to that of spurious correlation between variables, since any two variables which are correlated may well be so merely because they are both correlated with some other missing variable.

Finally, it must be remembered that correlation need not imply causality: the obvious example in economics is of two or more variables which are jointly determined in relation to some other set of variables. The causality question is of course complex, and cannot be resolved by the use of cross-sectional data alone. Even when using time series data the problems are daunting. Closely related to this question (and of course to that of functional form) is the choice of the appropriate lag structure for the explanatory variables. One of the few studies to approach these problems directly is that by Jung and Marshall (1985), who use the

Granger notion of causality to test the hypothesis that export growth causes GNP growth.

4.3.2   *A summary of results on the export growth–economic growth relationship*

Table 4.5 presents a brief summary of the data, methodology and conclusions of a set of studies conducted between 1977 and 1989. It will be seen that the majority of these find evidence of a strong assocation between exports or export growth and economic growth, shown in the table as 'Support for export growth hypothesis', and that several find evidence of a difference in the effect of exports on economic growth between countries above and below some critical level of some variable, indicated in the table as 'Threshold effect'.

Michaely's 1977 study uses rank correlation methods alone to examine the strength of the association between growth in per capita GNP and growth in exports, while Balassa (1978) and Kavoussi (1984) use rank correlations as a precursor to OLS regression analysis. Michaely is unusual in working with the growth in the share of exports in GDP as his 'export' variable, arguing, as we noted above, that since exports are part of the national product a positive correlation of the two variables is almost inevitable. This argument has been challenged by later writers, who have continued to use exports *per se* in their analyses. The general conclusion from all the rank correlation studies is that high levels of economic growth are significantly associated with high levels of export growth.

The production function methodology originated in work by Michalo-poulos and Jay (1973); the same basic approach is used by Balassa (1978, 1984), Tyler (1981), Kavoussi (1984), Moschos (1989) and Salvatore (1989). In all these studies the growth rate of either GNP or GDP is regressed upon the growth rate of exports and a set of additional explanatory variables, usually related to the labour force and investment. Balassa's 1978 study differentiates between domestic investment and foreign investment, using the ratio of each to output, and the growth in the labour force. Tyler, Kavoussi and Moschos each use the labour-force growth rate, but differ slightly in their 'investment' variable, Tyler using investment growth, Kavoussi and Salvatore the capital growth rate, and Moschos growth in real domestic investment. All demonstrate that the addition of the export variable to the estimated production functions raises their explanatory power significantly, and conclude that exports contribute significantly to the rate of economic growth of the developing countries studied. Balassa's 1984 study extends his previous work to the

Table 4.5 A selection of empirical studies on the relationship between export growth and economic growth

Study	Data set	Methodology				Conclusions
		Economic growth	Export growth	Technique	Other variables	
Michaely (1977a)	Cross-section 41 countries Ave of 1950–73	Per capita GNP growth	Growth in export share	Rank correlation	None	Support for export growth hypothesis Threshold effect
Balassa (1978)	Cross-section 10 countries Aves of 1956–67 and 1967–73	GNP growth	Export growth or real export growth	Rank correlation OLS Production function	Labour force growth Domestic investment and foreign investment/output	Support for export growth hypothesis
Williamson (1978)	Cross-section 22 countries Ave of 1960–74	Change in GDP	Lagged exports	OLS Linear models	Country dummies Direct investment Other foreign capital	Support for export growth hypothesis
Fajana (1979)	Time series 1954–74 1 country	GDP growth	Export shares or export change/output	OLS	Trade balance Current account	Support for export growth hypothesis
Tyler (1981)	Cross-section 55 countries Ave of 1960–77	GDP growth	Export growth	OLS Production function	Labour force growth Investment growth	Support for export growth hypothesis Threshold effect
Feder (1983)	Cross-section 31 countries Ave of 1964–73	GDP growth	Export growth or export change/output	OLS	Labour force growth Investment/output	Support for export growth hypothesis
Kavoussi (1984)	Cross-section 73 countries Ave of 1960–78	GDP growth	Export growth	Rank correlation OLS Production function	Labour growth rate Capital growth rate	Support for export growth hypothesis Threshold effect
Balassa (1984)[1]	Cross-section 10 countries Ave of 1973–79	GNP growth	Export growth	OLS Production function	Labour force growth Ratio to output of domestic investment	Support for export growth hypothesis
Jung & Marshall (1985)	Time series 1950–81 37 countries	Real GNP (or GDP) growth	Lagged real export growth	Maximum likelihood Simultaneous linear functions Granger causality	Lagged GNP (GDP) growth	Limited support for export growth causing economic growth
Moschos (1989)	Cross-section	Real GDP growth	Real export growth	OLS Production function	Labour force growth Real domestic investment growth	Support for export growth hypothesis Threshold effect
Salvatore (1989)	Time series 1963–73, 73–85 26 countries in 4 groups by trade policy orientation	Real GDP growth	Real export growth	OLS Production function	Labour input growth Capital input growth Growth in industrial production	Support for export growth hypothesis

[1] Also includes summary of and comparison with Balassa (1978) study.

Source: Originally derived from Jung & Marshall (1985).

1973–79 period, when the 43 countries considered were all subject to the external shocks of the quadrupling of oil prices in 1973–74 and the world recession of 1974–75. He also extends his analysis to include the policy reactions of these countries to the external shocks (drawing on his previous work in this area) and their outward or inward orientation. He concludes that: exports were an important contributor to economic growth in developing countries during this period; the contribution of exports has increased compared with the period covered in his earlier study; and an outward-oriented policy stance at the beginning of the period, and reliance on export promotion as a response to the shocks, contributed favourably to growth performance.

Evidence on the existence of a 'threshold effect' is mixed. Michaely (1977a) divided his sample of 41 countries on the basis of their per capita income levels, and found that while for the 23 countries in his higher-income group the rank correlation between economic growth and export growth was significant at the 1 per cent level, that for the low-income group was 'practically zero', and concluded that 'growth is affected by export performance only once countries achieve some minimum level of development' (p. 52). Tyler (1981), using the production function approach, concluded that 'a basic level of development is necessary for a country to most benefit from growth' (p. 124), and Kavoussi (1984), using the same approach, states that while 'in low income countries too export expansion tends to be associated with better economic performance' (p. 240), 'the contribution of exports . . . is greater among the [more advanced developing countries]' (p. 242). Balassa (1984) however comes to a different conclusion: 'for given increments of capital, labor and exports, the rate of economic growth will be higher the lower is the level of development'. Moschos (1989) criticises earlier studies for imposing an arbitrary division between more and less advanced developing countries. He searches for a critical switching-point in a cross-sectional production function analysis, and concludes that there is such a critical point, which may be best found from the data themselves rather than by reference to some arbitrary criterion, and that in the 'less advanced' group output growth is influenced mainly be export growth and capital formation, while in the 'more advanced' labour growth is also important.

Finally, we come to the question of causality – for instance, is there any evidence that a higher rate of growth in exports causes a higher rate of growth in GDP? The rank correlation analyses can of course only show covariation, while the parametric results from the various OLS studies on cross-sectional data are incapable of showing causation. Applied economists usually try to answer the question of causation by reference to a body of economic theory that suggests that one variable causes another.

However, in this area economic theory is of limited use. For example, we know from the literature that economic growth from a source quite unconnected with the economy's trade, manifested in an outward shift of the production possibilities curve, may lead to a change in the volume of exports, and that the sign of that change depends on the particular form of growth enjoyed; this suggests that causality may run from economic growth to export growth. On the other hand, we have theories suggesting that higher exports may finance greater inflows of capital goods, which may in turn lead to economic growth. Jung and Marshall (1985) have taken an approach which attempts to avoid the need to refer to economic theory, that of seeking the answer within the data by employing the test for causality put forward by Granger (1969). Working with time series data on output and export growth rates over a minimum of 15 observations from 37 countries, they conclude that 'The time series results . . . provide evidence in favour of export promotion in only 4 instances . . . . At the very least, it suggests that the statistical evidence in favor of export promotion is not as unanimous as was previously thought' (p. 11).

4.4   Where do we go from here?

That there are various gaps in our empirical knowledge, and that there is therefore considerable scope for future applied work, should be evident from the preceding sections. The interesting question for development economists is whether there is a causal connection between the trade strategy followed by a developing country and its rate of development. The major problems here are the definition and subsequent measurement of 'trade strategy', and establishing the direction of causality. While considerable work has been done on the development of measures of trade strategy, as outlined in section 4.2, it is evident that much is still left to do.

The problems of identifying trade strategy have been side-stepped in many empirical studies by concentrating on the narrower but related question of whether export growth causes economic growth. However, it should be apparent that the correlation between the trade strategy followed and the growth in exports may not be perfect. Balassa argues in his 1984 study that combination of the two approaches (trade strategy and export growth) is superior to either taken alone.

The problem of causality in the trade-strategy area has so far been tackled by reference to a body of economic theory rather than by the use of some data-based procedure such as Granger causality. Some of the questions of causality are complicated by the observation that its direction may change as a country develops, with the present rate of growth determined by a 'liberal' trade strategy that may have been made politically feasible by the attainment of a given level of development, while that level of development may have been occasioned by pursuing a protectionist policy in the past. Light may be thrown on such problems by a time series analysis of the mutual development of trade strategies and the economy for a range of countries.

The question of whether we can regard developing countries as lying on some continuum in the relationship between growth and either trade strategy or exports has yet to be resolved. Various authors suggest the presence of some threshold, above which a country may experience a relationship different to that of a country lower down the order. The threshold theory does not seem in itself to be particularly attractive (why should a marginal change in the level of development bring about a structural shift in a set of parameters?), and may be the consequence of an incorrect specification of the functional form, or the omission of relevant variables. It is possible that this could be resolved by further analysis.

4.5   Conclusions

As has been seen in Chapters 2 and 3, the link between trade orientation and economic performance has been a source of contention among economists for many years. This chapter has evaluated the empirical evidence on the issue to see whether the endeavours of applied economists can throw any light on the subject. The chapter has considered both the evidence on trade strategy and performance, and the evidence on exports and growth.

As is so often the case in applied economics, methodologically this is a difficult area. There are some fairly fundamental measurement problems, statistical pitfalls, and complications in interpretation. These have not, however, prevented a large number of economists from trying to come to grips with the issue. As we have seen, the results are not always conclusive, nor are they always straightforward to interpret. This is not peculiar to this particular economic problem, and, as always, one has to exercise an element of judgement in interpreting the evidence. Taking the evidence on trade strategy and performance, and that on exports and growth, it is difficult to avoid the conclusions that outward orientation appears to be associated more with superior economic performance than that under inward orientation, and that exports appear to be correlated with growth. Now, as we have emphasised, even if such associations are found, they do not constitute evidence on causality – that may remain an open question. It is then up to the analyst to have recourse to economic theory to help in resolving the issue. As we have already seen, this too may not be wholly conclusive. There are two responses to this predicament. One is the nihilist view – empirics can prove nothing. The second is a more agnostic view, namely that in a sense causality does not matter. If there is a correlation between outward orientation and economic performance/exports and growth, then anxiety about causality should not preclude us from recommending policies which bring about outward orientation/exports! There is in fact a third response which ties both these together – empirics may not be able to *prove* anything but it may help to *disprove* some things. In this regard, evidence linking inward orientation and growth is seriously wanting.

PART 2
Alternative instruments of export promotion

5

The role of import liberalisation in export promotion

Chris Milner

5.1 Introduction

In just the same way that import protection is a relative concept, the promotion of exports requires that exports or the production of exportables are subsidised in some way relative to other goods and services. Thus the promotion of exports can be achieved either by increasing the absolute subsidy to exports or by reducing the absolute subsidy to other goods and services. In the case of many developing countries high tariff and non-tariff barriers to imports act as a large absolute subsidy and therefore relative incentive to produce import-substitute products for the domestic market. The subsidy to import-substitute activities is directly observable in absolute terms from the price-raising effects of import restrictions. The anti-export bias generated by these import restrictions is less direct and as a result is often less evident.

The aim of this chapter is to analyse in detail the nature of the anti-export bias induced by import interventions or barriers, and to examine the role of import liberalisation in export promotion. The rest of the chapter is organised as follows. Section 5.2 sets up an analytical framework in order to identify sources of anti-export bias resulting from import interventions. This provides a basis for discussing the two analytically distinct sources of bias: the 'input tax' source of bias in section 5.3 and the 'relative incentives' source of bias in section 5.4. The policy implications of the earlier analysis and possible means of reducing anti-export bias are outlined in section 5.5. Finally, section 5.6 offers some concluding remarks.

5.2   The analytical framework

Consider a small fixed endowment and non-distorted economy with three sectors. For simplicity each sector can be regarded as producing a single composite good; one producing an exportable (X); one producing an importable (M); and a sector producing a non-tradable (N) good. Both the tradable goods require the use of an imported material (I) which is not produced domestically. It is also assumed for simplicity that the intermediate good is required in the same fixed proportion by both good X and good M. The problem of income distribution is also ignored by postulating a collective utility function. (The model, adapted from Milner, 1988, is formally set out in Appendix A at the end of this chapter.) For the present purposes we will move straight to a consideration of the equilibrium characteristics of this model, without and with import interventions.

The optimal general equilibrium situation requires consumption and production efficiency. As Appendix A shows (equations (A5.7) and (A5.8)), consumer maximisation requires that the marginal rate of substitution between any pair of final goods is equal to the relevant ratio of *gross* prices; while production efficiency (equations (A5.9) and (A5.10)) requires that the marginal rate of transformation between any pair of products be equal to the relevant net or effective prices. (In the case of the non-tradable good gross and net price are identical, since by assumption there are no intermediate inputs in its production.) If import interventions in the form of tariffs and/or non-tariff measures equivalent to a combined tariff rate of t_i on imported goods are now introduced, we can identify two interrelated but conceptually distinct forms of anti-export bias. If we define $\bar{Q}_i$ and $\bar{C}_i$ respectively as the optimal levels of production and consumption that would prevail for any good (i) under first-best conditions, then the effects of import interventions on Q_i and C_i will depend upon the extent of intervention (the magnitude of t_i), the structure of protection (whether $t_M \gtrless t_I$) and the nature of the substitutional relationships between each sector.

Consider the impact of a particular, non-uniform output and input tariff structure (i.e. $t_I > t_M > 0$). Both production and consumption distortions are induced. The rise in the gross domestic price of M relative to the gross prices X and N, will result in $C_M < \bar{C}_M$, $C_X > \bar{C}_X$ and $C_N > \bar{C}_N$. The net price of domestically produced importables (P'_M) may be unaltered by this particular non-uniform structure of input and output tariffs.[1] The net price of exportables (P'_X) must fall relative to the net price of importables and non-tradables, however, and therefore results in $Q_X < \bar{Q}_X$, $Q_M > \bar{Q}_M$ and $Q_N > \bar{Q}_N$. Thus the overall anti-export bias or effect resulting from the fact that $Q_X < \bar{Q}_X$ and $C_X > \bar{C}_X$ (where actual exports equal $Q_X - C_X$) can be conceptually decomposed into an 'input tax' effect and a 'relative price' effect. The tariff on intermediate inputs taxes both the production of importables and exportables and tends to create an anti-trade bias (or pro-non-tradables bias). This is the 'input tax' source of potential bias against both exportables and importables (which would occur if there were tariffs on intermediate goods only). In the case of importables, however, there is likely to be a compensating production subsidy which results from the existence of output (import) tariffs. Given that the cost of intermediate inputs per unit of importables produced (zP_I) is likely to be less than the total price of the final importable, then the net price of importables can be unaffected even if the rate of output subsidy (t_M) is less than the rate of input tax (t_I). If input and output tariffs are uniform or escalate with higher stages of production, then the 'input tax' effect on importables is more than offset. This offsetting subsidy effect is not available, however, for exportables from import tariffs. But even if the input tax source of anti-export bias is eliminated by exempting production of exportables from tariff duties on intermediate imports, there is still a 'relative price' bias against exportables that will be induced by the final goods or output tariffs on imports. An output tariff in isolation will raise both the gross and net price of importables relative to the relevant prices of exportables and non-tradables; shifting consumption away and production towards importables. If the prices of both exportables and non-tradables are unaffected by these consumption and production changes induced directly by an import intervention on final goods, then there is a bias induced against both exportables and non-tradables by this 'relative price' effect. As we shall see later, however, the possibility of the prices of non-tradables rising in response to the increase in P_M (if substitutability in production and/or consumption is a possibility), may mean that the pro-importables bias induced by a positive t_M constitutes a greater bias against exports than non-tradables.

Let us consider these two broad sources of anti-export bias in greater detail.

5.3   The 'input tax' source of anti-export bias

In the previous section it was established that the production effects of import interventions were dependent on the way in which nominal input (t_I) and output tariffs (t_M) influenced the net price of each type of good. The significance of the distinction between nominal and net prices can be systematically formalised with the aid of the effective protection concept. The effective rate of protection (e) for the process of producing good M is defined as:

$$e_M = \frac{P_M^{\prime t} - P_M^\prime}{P_M^\prime} \tag{5.1}$$

where $P_M^{\prime t}$ = tariff-inclusive net price of good M
$P_M^\prime$ = free-trade net price of good M

We can expand equation (5.1) if we take the expression for $P_M^\prime$ in equation (A5.6a) in Appendix A and allow tariff interventions as follows:

$$P_M^{\prime t} = P_M(1 + t_M) - zP_I(1 + t_I) \tag{5.2}$$

Since the expression zP_I can be rewritten as $a_{IM} P_M$ (where $a_{IM} = zP_I/P_M$) then the expression for the effective rate of protection becomes:

$$e_M = \frac{t_M - a_{IM} t_I}{1 - a_{IM}} \tag{5.3}$$

where $0 \le a_{IM} < 1$ (a_{IM} is the fixed technological or input/output coefficient under free-trade conditions).

In the case of the exportable (X) the definition in equation (5.1) still applies, but the gross price of the exportable cannot be raised following the imposition of an import (output) tariff, i.e.

$$P_X^{\prime t} = P_X - zP_I(1 + t_I) \tag{5.4}$$

If we substitute equations (5.4) and (A5.6b) into equation (5.1), then effective rate of protection for the exportable (e_X) is as follows:

$$e_X = \frac{-a_{IX} t_I}{1 - a_{IX}} \tag{5.5a}$$

where $a_{IM} = a_{IX}$, with export subsidisation:

$$e_X = \frac{s_X - a_{IX} t_I}{1 - a_{IX}} \tag{5.5b}$$

In the case of the importable then $e_M \gtrless t_M \gtrless t_I$, and $e_M > 0$ if $t_M > a_{IM} t_I$. Although the effective tariff rate is maximised for a given nominal output tariff when $t_I = 0$ (i.e. *ceteris paribus* an input tariff is an implicit tax on importables production), the probability of the structure of protection producing positive effective protection is high. For the escalating tariff structure $e_M > t_M$ if $t_M > t_I$, while for the uniform tariff structure $e_M = t_M$ when $t_M = t_I$. Even for the non-uniform and de-escalating tariff structure (i.e. $t_I > t_M$), effective protection can still be positive if the condition $t_M > a_{IM} t_I$ is satisfied. Negative effective protection on importables as a result of high input tariffs[2] is in general only likely to result where the tariff structure is poorly managed! Where planned or managed, the structure of protection will invariably induce positive rates of effective protection and a net or overall subsidy (e_M) for production of importables. By contrast, the effective protection rate for exportables (e_X) in the absence of subsidisation of exportables will be negative for any positive tariff on importable inputs. Thus in the absence of exportable subsidisation, negative e_X rates can only be achieved by setting t_I rates at zero rates (if $a_{ij} > 0$). But even if $e_X = 0$ there is still a high probability that $e_M > e_X$. If $t_I = 0$ for both importables and exportables, $e_X = 0$ but $e_M > t_M$. If $t_I > 0$ for importables while exportables are exempt from duties on intermediates (or can be reclaimed under a duty drawback scheme), then $e_X = 0$ but $e_M > 0$ if $t_M > a_{IM} t_I$. Thus exempting exports from duties on intermediates will remove the bias against exportables *vis-à-vis* non-tradables, but is unlikely to eliminate the bias *vis-à-vis* importables unless t_I is significantly larger than t_M (strictly $a_{IM} t_I > t_M$).

The elimination of the remaining anti-export bias where $e_X = 0$ but $e_M > 0$ (if $t_M > a_{IM} t_I$) will require some degree of export subsidisation. If t_I on exportables is effectively zero, then $e_X = s_X/(1 - a_{IX})$ (the rate of effective export subsidy or compensation). Thus s_X would have to be set equal to $e_M(1 - a_{IX})$ in order to equalise effective protection rates between importables and exportables. If exports are not exempt from intermediate duties, then s would have to be set higher; in the case considered here where $a_{IM} = a_{IX}$, then $e_M = e_X$ if $s_X = t_M$. There are of course likely to be fiscal constraints on governments equalising effective rates across tradables in this way since tariffs are fiscal enhancing and subsidies are fiscal depleting. But it would be dangerous, in any case, to encourage governments to believe that they can fashion non-uniform rates of t_M, t_I and s_X so as to equalise effective protection. The share of intermediate inputs in the value of tradables both within and between sectors is likely to vary considerably: it is a technological characteristic beyond the control of government. Thus, even in the present, simple three-good case, if the share of intermediates in exportables is lower than in importables (i.e. $a_{IX} < a_{IM}$), then $e_M = e_X$ for a common t_I (for importables and exportables) if $s_X < t_{Mj}$, the precise difference between s_X and t_M depending on the size of $a_{IM} - a_{IX}$. It becomes impossible to set rates of taxation and subsidisation in a multi-product environment to equalise net or effective rates of protection/promotion, unless all rates are uniform, i.e. $t_M = t_I = s_X$. But under balanced trade conditions (where $X = M$) the fiscal objective of trade taxation is eliminated, in the uniform intervention case. In any case, in the $e_M = e_X$ case intervention will serve (at best) to promote tradables *vis-à-vis* non-tradables (if the net = gross price of non-tradables is unaltered by these interventions).

As we will see in section 5.4 in the long run, if the price of non-tradables (P_N) also rises (in line with P_M and P_X) as a result of uniform promotion of tradables, relative prices post-intervention will be identical to pre-intervention relative prices and there will be no or zero true protection of either importables or exportables.

5.4   The 'relative incentives' source of anti-export bias

Implicit, but not explicit, in the analysis in the previous section on rates of effective protection for importables and exportables was the idea of relative incentives. Indeed the key purpose of intervention for protective or promotionable reasons is to raise the net price of the protected or promoted good or sector *relative* to the prices of other goods or sectors. It is on this aspect of commercial policy interventions (in generating anti-export bias) that we will focus in this section.[3]

We continue with a three-sector, general equilibrium model, but for purposes of expositional convenience now assume that both tradables (importables and exportables) do not require an intermediate input (i.e. $a_{IM} = a_{IX} = 0$) in their production. Gross and net price (P_M, P_X and P_N) will be identical for all goods. Certain other additional assumptions are required either to elaborate on the model or to make the analysis tractable:

1.   The initial (free-trade) internal prices of all goods are unity.
2.   The relative prices of both tradables in terms of non-tradables are flexible in order to facilitate market clearing.
3.   Trade is initially balanced, the exchange rate is fixed and any money aspects of balance-of-payments imbalance are ignored.
4.   Real income is fixed and any impact of commercial policy changes on net fiscal revenue and on the balance between income and expenditure is ignored.
5.   Substitutability in production and/or consumption between goods is possible, but complementarity is ruled out.

The equilibrium properties of the extended model can be examined in terms of equilibrium in the non-tradables market, since equilibrium in this market also implies trade balance equilibrium. A particular case is illustrated following Clements and Sjaastad (1985) in Figure 5.1, where substitutability between tradables directly is not possible, but where non-tradables may substitute with importables and/or exportables.[4] The free-trade price of importables relative to exportables is given by the world terms-of-trade ray OT. The line HH represents alternative

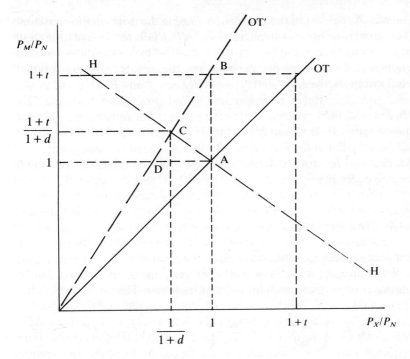

Figure 5.1 A model of true protection.

combinations of the price of importables (P_M) and of exportables (P_X) (relative to the price of non-tradables, P_N) that clear the market for non-tradables. (The negative slope reflects the fact that in this particular case non-tradables substitute in production and/or consumption with *both* importables and exportables.) Free trade equilibrium is at A where OT intersects HH; this corresponds with trade balance $(X_0 = M_0)$.

Using this framework one can examine in general terms the relative price effects of commercial policy interventions. A uniform tariff (t_M) on all importables, for instance, initially drives a wedge between the price of importables and exportables (P_M/P_X) (shifting the terms-of-trade ray from OT to OT'), and between the price of importables and non-tradables (P_M/P_N) (from unity to $1 + t$). In other words, the economy shifts initially from point A to point B; this is off the HH schedule and corresponds with disequilibrium in the non-tradables sector and a trade surplus. Equilibrating forces, however, will move the economy away from B as the excess demand for non-tradables is removed by further adjustment of relative prices. In the case of Figure 5.1 equilibrium is restored at C, as the price of non-tradables (P_N) rises to remove excess demand. As a result of the proportional rise in the price of non-tradables (d), the relative price of importables (P_M/P_N) falls to $(1 + t_M/1 + d)$ and that of exportables (P_X/P_N) to $1/(1 + d)$. The extent of these induced relative price adjustments depends on the nature of substitutional relationships between M and N, and between X and N. If X and N are very close substitutes in consumption and production then the HH schedule will be very steep, and in the extreme full equilibrium will tend towards point B. If M and N are very close substitutes the HH schedule will be very flat and the final equilibrium will tend towards point D in Figure 5.1. (For a formal derivation of the results of this extended model see Appendix B.)

5.4.1 'True protection'

Within a general equilibrium framework the 'true' effects of a tariff (t_M^*) or a subsidy (s_X^*) need to be measured in terms of their effect on the relative (rather than absolute) price of tradables. Thus:

$$t_M^* = \Delta\left(\frac{P_M}{P_N}\right) \quad \left(= \frac{t_M - d}{1 + d} \text{ in terms of Figure 5.1}\right) \quad \textbf{(5.6)}$$

$$s_X^* = \Delta\left(\frac{P_X}{P_N}\right) \quad \left(= \frac{s_X - d}{1 + d} \text{ in terms of Figure 5.1}\right) \quad \textbf{(5.7)}$$

Except for the case where X and N are perfect substitutes (i.e. where the HH schedule is vertical at a relative price P_X/P_N of unity and equilibrium at B in Figure 5.1), the true tariff will be less than the nominal tariff. The divergence between true and nominal rates depends upon the extent of the proportionate induced price rise in non-tradables (d). Given a high degree of substitutability between M and N then $d \to t$, and $t_M^* \to 0$ (with equilibrium restored at D in Figure 5.1). In the absence of export subsidies, there is actual (relative) disprotection of exports as P_X/P_N falls to $1/(1 + d)$. The true subsidy is negative in this case (see Figure 5.2). In the uniform nominal protection case, i.e. $t_M = s_X$, true protection will be uniform across sectors but at a zero rate (for any pattern of substitutional arrangements). No sector is protected because relative prices are unaltered.

Perhaps of more practical interest is the case where there is nominal protection of both importables and exportables, but where the rate of subsidisation of importables exceeds the rate of export subsidisation (i.e. $t_M > s_X > 0$). The distribution or division of true protection across sectors

True protection
(t_m^*, s_x^*)

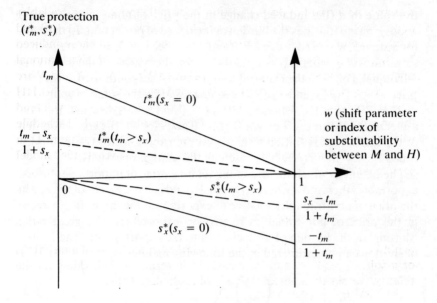

Figure 5.2 True protection and the structure of protection.

depends entirely on substitutional relationships in the economy (see Figure 5.2). If non-tradables and exportables are such close substitutes that their relative prices cannot be altered, i.e. $d = s_X$, then from equations (5.6) and (5.7) we can see that the true subsidy is zero, and although the true tariff is positive it is less than the nominal tariff. Alternatively, if non-tradables and importables are perfect substitutes then $d = t_M$. In this case the true tariff is zero and the true subsidy is negative. Thus the protection of import-competing activities in isolation tends to disprotect export sectors, and the subsidisation of exports tends to disprotect import-substitution activities. If import and export protection are simultaneously applied, the effects in this type of economy tend to be mutually offsetting. The net effects of commercial policy interventions on domestic relative prices are in fact likely to be very different from their intended effects.

5.4.2 *The incidence of protection*

The divergence between true and nominal rates of protection depends therefore on the structure of intervention (on whether $t_M \geq s_X \geq 0$) and on the value of d (the induced change in the price of home or non-traded goods); but so too does the burden or incidence of protection. In the case, for instance, where $t_M > 0, s_X = 0$ and $d = 0$ because X and N are perfect substitutes (i.e. where $t_M^* = t_M$ and $s_X^* = 0$), the burden of the import tax falls equally on both the exportable and non-traded goods sectors (i.e. the price ratios P_M/P_N and P_M/P_X have increased by the same proportion). At the other extreme, where $t_M > 0, s_X = 0$ and $d = t_M$ because M and N are perfect substitutes (i.e. where $t_M^* = 0$ and $s_X^* < 0$), the cost or burden of the import tax is shifted totally onto the export sector (i.e. the price ratios P_M/P_X and P_N/P_X have risen by the same proportion).

The extent to which the rise in the relative price of importables 'taxes' exportables therefore (where $t_M > s_X$) depends on the extent of the rise in the price of non-tradables relative to exportables: the larger the increase in the price of non-tradables relative to exportables, the greater the 'shifting' of the burden of protection onto the export sector. The degree of shifting can be estimated in the following manner:

$$\Delta\left(\frac{P_N}{P_X}\right) = w\Delta\left(\frac{P_M}{P_X}\right) \tag{5.8}$$

where w = shift or incidence parameter $(0 \le w \le 1)$.

Where $w = 1$, M and N are very close substitutes and the price of home goods rises by the full amount of the import tariff (i.e. $t_M = d$). The burden of import protection falls wholly on the export sector. At the other extreme where $w = 0$, X and N are such close substitutes that the relative price of non-tradables and exportables cannot be altered. In this case the burden of import protection is shared between the non-import sectors.

This tariff-cum-subsidy case (where $t_M > s_X$) is an appropriate one to consider in the context of many developing countries. It demonstrates clearly the problems of trying to pursue mixed commercial policy strategies. In particular it illustrates forcibly the 'costs' or anti-export bias that import protection imposes on the export sector and the importance of relative incentives. Export subsidies are likely only to reduce the relative disincentives induced by import protection, and not to provide the intended/desired relative incentives to induce resources out of the non-tradables sector into export production. If $s_X = t_M$ and the potential relative disincentive induced by import protection is fully offset or compensated by export promotion measures, the price of non-tradables will in long-run equilibrium also rise by the amount of $t_M (s_X)$ resulting in zero true protection of tradables. Relative prices will return to the free-trade position with uniform import protection and export promotion.

5.5 Policy implications and the reduction of anti-export bias

The previous sections have identified two aspects or potential sources of anti-export bias induced by commercial policy interventions. The first, the reduction or even elimination of the 'input tax' source of anti-export bias, is, apparently, more straightforward to deal with. As equations (5.3) and (5.5b) show, tariffs on intermediate inputs 'tax' both importables and exportables. This problem could be dealt with in principle by either exempting both importables and exportables from tariffs on intermediate inputs, or by compensating both importables and exportables with equivalent output subsidies (in the case where $a_{IM} = a_{IX}$ this is achieved with uniform intervention, i.e. $t_M = s_X$). But duty exemption or zero rating for intermediate imports[5] would only be a solution if the rates for t_M and s_X were also set at zero or uniform positive rates. In the former case there would be free trade (i.e. no commercial policy interventions) and trade interventions would have no fiscal role or implications. In the latter case, uniform intervention (i.e $t_M = s_X$ would merely replicate the free-trade structure of relative (net) prices – with the price of non-tradables rising in response to positive (nominal or effective) protection of tradables to leave true protection (t^*, s^*) at zero rates – and would also result in a zero net fiscal impact given trade balance.[6] Thus uniform intervention results in no anti-export bias, but also eliminates any rationale under first-best conditions for commercial policy interventions since there is no true protection/promotion and no net fiscal yield. Indeed the zero-intervention case is presumably preferable to the uniform intervention case, since the resource costs of administering the uniform intervention case are avoided.

It is impossible therefore to isolate the 'input tax' source of anti-export bias from a consideration of the relative incentives effects of the whole structure of protection and intervention. On grounds of allocative efficiency the economist should be happy to recommend the free-trade solution to eliminating anti-export bias, given efficient markets. It may be more useful for operational purposes, however, to assume that we start from a position of non-uniform intervention $(t_M > t_I > s_X = 0)$ with constraints on imposing the zero or uniform intervention solution. These constraints might arise as a result of economic arguments for import protection or for using border taxes for revenue purposes. We may reject the argument or advocate alternative means of achieving legitimate aims. But failure to recognise these constraints is likely to reduce the credibility of policy recommendations aimed at reducing anti-export bias, in situations where the immediate free-trade solution is politically unfeasible.

5.5.1 *Policy options for reducing anti-export bias*

The analysis has established that in the appropriate context of relative incentives:

$$\text{Anti-export bias} = f(\bar{s}_X, \overset{+}{t}_I, \overset{+}{e}_M)$$

We have therefore a framework for analysing the policy options for reducing anti-export bias.

Raise export subsidies (s_X)

In an absolute sense we can eliminate the 'input tax' source of anti-export bias by setting the nominal subsidy $s_X = a_{IX}t_I$ such that $e_X = 0$. This will reduce but not eliminate the relative disincentive to produce exportables, since with $e_X = 0$ and $e_M > 0$ (if $t_M > t_I$) there is an effective subsidy for importables production only. But why opt for a fiscal-depleting solution in the shorter and longer run, which involves more intervention rather than less? As argued earlier, in the extreme as the nominal subsidy is raised further so that the effective subsidy differential $(e_M - e_X)$ becomes smaller, true protection and net fiscal yield decline. The administration and policing costs of the intervention system, and the political economy barriers to dismantling the intervention bureaucracy, are merely increased.

Lower intermediate import tariffs (t_I) on exports

It is the case that with $t_I = 0$ for exportables only, the $e_X = 0$ (if $s_X = 0$) and the $(e_M - e_X)$ differential is reduced. But there are disadvantages with this solution. It is again revenue-depleting, directly given the fall in import duties and indirectly in so much as there will be costs associated with administrating duty-drawback arrangements or with policing exemptions applying to exports only. It is also the case that zero tariffs on imported intermediate inputs may conflict with other objectives or requirements: by raising the import-intensity of exportables, export competitiveness may be reduced, or by lowering the protection of intermediate relative to final importables, the incentive to produce intermediates locally may be reduced. Given, however, that developing countries typically are price-takers in world markets, and multinationals may be significant in their export sectors, the pressure to eliminate the absolute net price reduction due to intermediate duties is likely to be high. This option should be viewed at most as a complementary measure. If a_{IX} and the scheduled t_I are relatively small then the absolute (effective) disprotection of exportables will be small. Without export subsidisation the upper limit on e_X is zero, in which case there is more scope to reduce the $(e_M - e_X)$ differential by reducing e_M.

Lower the effective protection of importables (e_M)

In the case of many developing countries the (average) effective protection of importables is relatively high, since there is in general tariff escalation $(t_M > t_I)$.[7] Lowering effective protection on importables in order to reduce anti-export bias requires therefore either that t_M falls or t_I rises, or both. Raising t_I for importables will in fact be revenue-enhancing if tariff exemptions applied previously to a significant proportion of imported inputs into importables or if duty rates are in general below their revenue-maximising levels. It will also tend to reduce the disincentives to produce intermediates locally. If exports cannot be isolated from an increase in t_I, then it may be more appropriate to lower e_M by lowering t_M, i.e. by lowering nominal tariffs on (final) imports. Again this adjustment in nominal tariffs may be revenue-enhancing if final or output tariffs are in general above revenue-maximising levels. Even if the fall in t_M is revenue-depleting, total import duties may still increase if the rise in t_I is sufficiently revenue-enhancing. Import liberalisation does not necessarily conflict therefore with short-term revenue objectives (see Greenaway and Milner, 1990b).[8] Indeed, given the significant share of intermediate goods in many developing countries' imports, lowering the (average) rate of effective protection of importables can be achieved whilst raising the average rate of duty collection on imports. If, for example, 'pre-liberalisation' tariff rates are $t_M = 0.35$ and $t_I = 0.1$, then $e_M > 0.35$ (if $a_{ij} = 0.4$ then $e_M \approx 0.517$) and with equal shares in total imports the average collection rate on final and intermediate inputs is 0.225. With reform of the tariff schedule such that $t_M = t_I = 0.25$, then e_M falls to 0.25 but the average duty rate is also 0.25. The lowering of nominal output protection may also be achieved by the lowering of non-tariff import restrictions. Indeed higher import tariffs are consistent with lower overall nominal and effective protection. Thus, in the short term, replacement of quantitative import restrictions with partial tariff equivalents can be both import-liberalising and fiscal-enhancing. In the longer term the further reduction of anti-export bias will involve lowering the average level of import tariffs; at levels below maximum revenue rates this will be revenue-depleting at least in terms of the import taxes/GDP ratio. This may necessitate other fiscal reforms to maintain the overall tax/GDP ratio. (Reducing dependency on trade taxes is likely to be desirable on efficiency grounds.) The other major constraint on reducing anti-export bias first by import rationalisation (i.e. inducing greater uniformity) and then by genuine import liberalisation, is of course associated with the reduced protection of the importables sector. That is, however, an unavoidable adjustment cost facing the reduction of anti-export bias. It has to be faced whichever of the options is employed. The removal of anti-export bias and the maintenance of (true) protection for the import-substitute sector are mutually exclusive options!

5.6   Conclusions

If we allow for the possibility of substitutability (in consumption and production) between the products of different sectors of the economy, then, in the long run, uniform intervention (e.g. subsidisation) produces the same structure of relative prices as does free trade. It is impossible therefore for developing countries to sustain, simultaneously, general strategies of import protection and export promotion. Given the high levels of import protection currently to be found in many developing countries, a broadly based strategy of export promotion requires therefore that the structure of relative prices (between importables and exportables) is significantly altered. Raising the absolute price of exportables sufficiently through subsidisation is not a very feasible or desirable option, given the increased consumer costs and tax burden associated with this. A more desirable and feasible means of *relative* export promotion is the general lowering of import barriers. Partial import liberalisation may well be tax-revenue enhancing, and thus additional revenue might be used to ease the adjustment problems associated with the liberalisation of imports. More significantly, perhaps, gains in the form of lower prices and greater choice for consumers and of increased external stimulus to producer efficiency are achieved with this policy option.

Of course policy-makers in developing countries always have the option to try *selectively* to import-protect and export-promote in specific activities, i.e. to raise the prices of some tradables relative to those of other tradables. Substitutability between subsidised and non-subsidised products may of course reduce the scope for such selectivity. Even if selective adjustment of the structure of relative prices is possible, however, the experience of selective intervention during many developing countries' import-substitute episodes does not encourage one to believe that policy-makers are likely to be very good at picking goods with the greatest export potential. The consumer would merely continue to pay for this selective approach to export promotion in the form of higher prices.

Notes

1. The net price of importables is unaltered if $P_M t_M = P_I z t_I$, since from equation (A5.6a) in Appendix A the tariff-inclusive net price of importables (P_M'') is given by:

    $$\overline{P}_M(1 + t_M) - z P_I(1 + t_I)$$

2. Negative rates of effective protection are often observed in studies of the structure of protection in developing countries, but invariably for a minority of industries (see, for instance, Milner, 1990). The incidence may be accounted for by the fact that some protected importables are both final goods and intermediate inputs for other industries. This is more likely to be a problem in industrialised countries than in developing countries with less comprehensive and complex inter-industry linkages.

3. A number of recent papers on commercial policy (Sjaastad, 1980; Sjaastad and Clements, 1981; Clements and Sjaastad, 1985; Greenaway and Milner, 1987; Milner, 1989) have focused on the relative price or 'true' protection impact of policy interventions.

4. This pattern of substitutability is consistent with the following sector arrangements of factor intensities: $(K/L)_M < (K/L)_N < (K/L)_X$ or $(K/L)_M > (K/L)_N > (K/L)_X$. A labour-abundant developing economy may be appropriately described by the latter of these two arrangements. For the implications of alternative substitutional arrangements see Greenaway and Milner (1988) and Milner (1989).

5. Zero rating of intermediate imports (implicitly or explicitly) may be difficult to reconcile with import protection, if there is a domestic capability in the intermediates used by the final tradables. In the present model this problem is abstracted from.

6. The fiscal loss from export subsidisation can be reduced of course by subsidising only non-traditional exports, for instance.

7. High rates of effective protection on importables often result also from non-tariff import restrictions (quotas, bans, etc.). In the analysis it has been assumed that t_M is a composite measure of all the price-raising effects of all import interventions. No distinction was needed to identify the nature of anti-export bias. A distinction needs to be drawn, however, for policy-reform purposes, since there is no direct fiscal loss with the lowering of non-tariff barriers.

8. In the long run further tariff reductions for both t_M and t_I may be revenue-depleting for a given value of M. Income and import growth may offset this of course. But in the extreme if t_M and t_I are eliminated then import duties will be zero.

Appendix A

The following assumptions describe the model in detail:

1. There are three sectors or goods, M (importable), X (exportable) and N (non-tradable).

2.   Each unit of M and X requires z units of I (imported input), i.e.

$$I = z(Q_M + Q_X) \qquad \text{(A5.1)}$$

3.   The gross transformation curve, which defines production possibilities, is concave to the origin and is given by:

$$T(M, X, N) = 0 \qquad \text{(A5.2)}$$

4.   The prices of X, M and I are fixed on world markets, i.e. $\bar{P}_X$, $\bar{P}_M$ and $\bar{P}_I$.

5.   Preferences in the home country are represented by a collective utility function:

$$U = U(M, X, N) \qquad \text{(A5.3)}$$

The collective indifference curves are convex to the origin.

Consider the technical problem of maximising utility (equation (A5.3)) subject to constraints, and in the absence of import interventions. For any output mix we must satisfy the gross transformation function (equation (A5.2)), and the economy must satisfy the budget constraint of balanced trade, namely

$$\bar{P}_M Q_M + \bar{P}_X Q_X - \bar{P}_I I + P_N Q_N = \bar{P}_M C_M + \bar{P}_X C_X + P_N C_N \qquad \text{(A5.4)}$$

where Q_i = production of good i
$\qquad\quad C_i$ = consumption of good i
and $P_N Q_N = P_N C_N$ (by definition)

Since $I = z(Q_M + Q_X)$, equation (A5.4) can be rewritten as:

$$P'_M Q_M + P'_X Q_X + P_N Q_N = \bar{P}_M C_M + \bar{P}_X C_X + P_N C_N \qquad \text{(A5.5)}$$

where $P'_M = \bar{P}_M - z\bar{P}_I \qquad\qquad\qquad\qquad\qquad\quad$ (A5.6a)

and $\quad P'_X = \bar{P}_X - z\bar{P}_I \qquad\qquad\qquad\qquad\qquad\quad$ (A5.6b)

(Equations (A5.6a) and (A5.6b) define net prices of the two tradable goods.)

The necessary conditions for a maximum are:

$$\frac{U_M}{U_X} = \frac{\bar{P}_M}{\bar{P}_X} \qquad \text{(A5.7)}$$

$$\frac{U_M}{U_N} = \frac{\bar{P}_M}{P_N} \qquad \text{(A5.8)}$$

$$\frac{T_M}{T_X} = \frac{P'_M}{P'_X} \qquad\qquad\qquad\qquad \text{(A5.9)}$$

$$\frac{T_M}{T_N} = \frac{P'_M}{P_N} \qquad\qquad\qquad\qquad \text{(A5.10)}$$

where T_i = denotes first-order partial derivative of the gross transformation function with respect to good i.

and U_i = denotes first-order partial derivative of the collective utility
function with respect to good i.

Appendix B

The equilibrium properties of the model can be examined in terms of
equilibrium in either market: equilibrium in the non-traded goods sector
implies trade balance, and trade balance implies equilibrium in the
non-traded sector. Thus full equilibrium following a commercial policy
intervention requires that:

$$\hat{D}_N = \hat{S}_N \qquad\qquad\qquad\qquad \text{(B5.1)}$$

where $\hat{D}_N = h_X^D \hat{P}_X + h_N^D \hat{P}_N + h_M^D \hat{P}_M \qquad\qquad \text{(B5.2)}$

and $\hat{S}_N = h_X^S \hat{P}_X + h_N^S \hat{P}_N + h_M^S \hat{P}_M \qquad\qquad \text{(B5.3)}$

(h^S and h^D are compensated supply and demand price elasticities for
home goods with respect to i, $i = X, N$ and M).

The elasticities are subject also to the homogeneity constraint:

$$\sum_i h_i^S = \sum_i h_i^D = 0 \qquad\qquad\qquad \text{(B5.4)}$$

Substituting equations (B5.2) and (B5.3) into equation (B5.1) gives:

$$h_X^S \hat{P}_X + h_N^S \hat{P}_N + h_M^S \hat{P}_M = h_X^D \hat{P}_X + h_N^D \hat{P}_N + h_M^D \hat{P}_M \qquad \text{(B5.5)}$$

In this case non-tradables (N) are the intermediate goods which
substitute with either of the tradables (X and M). Thus we may rearrange
equation (B5.5) so that:

$$\hat{P}_N(=d) = \left(\frac{h_M^D - h_M^S}{h_N^S - h_N^D}\right)\hat{P}_M + \left(\frac{h_X^D - h_X^S}{h_N^S - h_N^D}\right)\hat{P}_X \qquad \text{(B5.6)}$$

or $\hat{P}_N(=d) = w\hat{P}_M + (1-w)\hat{P}_X$ **(B5.7a)**

or $d = wt_M + (1-w)s_X$ **(B5.7b)**

where $w = \dfrac{h_M^D - h_M^S}{h_N^S - h_N^D}$ **(B5.8)**

The shift parameter w is in fact an index of substitutability between home goods and importables. Equation (B5.5) can be rewritten as:

$$w = b \left| \frac{h_M^S}{h_N^S} \right| = (1-b) \left| \frac{h_M^D}{h_N^D} \right| \qquad \textbf{(B5.9)}$$

where $b = \dfrac{h_N^S}{h_N^S - h_N^D}$ $(0 \le b \le 1)$

and shows that w is a weighted average of the degree of substitutability between N and M in production $(|h_M^S/h_N^S|)$ and in consumption $(|h_M^D/h_N^D|)$

For expositional convenience we assume symmetry in substitutability, i.e. $|h_M^S/h_N^S| = |h_M^D/h_N^D|$. Thus:

$$0 \le w \le 1 \qquad \textbf{(B5.10)}$$

(For a more general derivation see Greenaway and Milner, 1987.)

6

The role of the exchange rate and other macroeconomic instruments in encouraging exports

Peter Montiel

6.1 Introduction

Advocates of outward-oriented trade reform have long recognised the importance of the macroeconomic setting to the success or failure of this strategy. A number of attempted trade liberalisations in developing countries have floundered on account of inappropriate accompanying macroeconomic policies. Since heavily indebted countries are being encouraged by the international economic community to adopt outward-oriented strategies to grow their way out of their current problems (see, for example, Balassa *et al.*, 1986), the issue of the appropriate macroeconomic environment in which to carry out such reforms has assumed increased relevance.

This chapter examines a number of issues concerning the types of macroeconomic policies that are suitable for sustaining an outward-oriented trade strategy. Since exchange-rate management plays a key role in this context, this topic is addressed in the next section. Although the role of the exchange rate is probably central, stability of the general macroeconomic environment is also conducive to the success of outward-oriented trade reform. The reasons for this are spelled out in section 6.3, which also addresses the still unsettled and controversial issue of whether macro-stabilisation is necessary *before* trade reform can be undertaken. Even with macro-stability in hand, the economy's long-run outward orientation depends on general macroeconomic policies not directly related to the external sector, because such policies affect the long-run equilibrium real exchange rate, which, as Mussa (1986) points out, can in this sense serve as an 'instrument of commercial policy'. This issue is treated in section 6.4. The chapter closes with a brief summary.

6.2   Exchange-rate management

With few exceptions, developing countries have continued to maintain fixed exchange-rate regimes in the period since floating rates became the norm for industrial countries. According to the International Monetary Fund, as of 30 June 1988, 90 out of 131 developing-country members of the Fund maintained official exchange rates for their currencies (IMF, 1988). The nominal exchange rate therefore remains an important tool of macroeconomic policy for these countries. Moreover, the official exchange rate continues to play an important role in determining export profitability. Even in the common case where the official parity coexists with exchange controls on current and/or capital transactions, giving rise to a parallel market in foreign exchange, such controls tend to be supplemented with export surrender requirements designed to prevent exporters from transacting in the parallel market. Although smuggling and under-invoicing are not unknown in the developing world, it is reasonable to suppose that, except in pathological cases and in the case of illegal exports, the bulk of developing-country export earnings are converted to domestic currency at an official exchange rate.[1]

The management of the official exchange rate has received increased attention over the past several years in developing countries, and official devaluations have come to occupy a more prominent role in programmes of stabilisation and adjustment for such countries. The adequacy of the official exchange rate is typically assessed with the use of real exchange-rate calculations. For present purposes, the real exchange rate can be defined as the price of non-traded goods measured in units of traded goods. This is a key macroeconomic relative price, since it affects the traded–non-traded composition both of domestic demand through substitution effects and of domestic production by affecting the relative short-run and long-run profitability of production in the two sectors.

The short-run relationship between the real exchange rate and the profitability of production in the exportable and importable sectors can be readily demonstrated using a simple framework. Consider an economy consisting of three production sectors: exportables (X), importables (Z), and non-traded goods (N). Production requires labour and capital, but in the short run sectoral capital endowments are given. The profitability of output in each sector (the marginal product of capital) as well as the short-run sectoral output levels are thus inversely related to the product wage in that sector. Letting W denote the product wage in the exportable sector, ζ the terms of trade (the price of exportables in terms of importables), and e the real exchange rate (the price of non-traded goods in terms of importables),[2] labour-market clearing requires:

$$L_X^D(W) + L_Z^D(W\zeta) + L_N^D(W\zeta/e) = \bar{L}$$

where $L_i^D(\ )$ is the demand for labour in sector i, with $L_i^{D\prime} < 0$, and $\bar{L}$ is the (fixed) supply of labour.[3] This condition implies:

$$\frac{dW}{de} = \frac{L_N^{D\prime} W\zeta/e^2}{L_X^{D\prime} + L_Z^{D\prime}\zeta + L_N^{D\prime}\zeta/e} > 0$$

Thus, a real exchange-rate depreciation (decrease in e) reduces the product wage in the exportables sector and thus increases the short-run profitability of export production at the same time that it increases production of exportables. Moreover, since it increases the marginal product of capital in this sector, a *sustained* real exchange-rate depreciation is conducive to investment in this sector and thus the long-run expansion of capacity for the production of exportables.

This key macroeconomic role of the real exchange rate has focused attention on the importance of employing nominal exchange-rate policy to ensure that the real exchange rate does not become overvalued. This is particularly important in the context of trade reform. The removal of anti-export bias by eliminating quantitative restrictions (QRs) and lowering tariffs on imports, as well as possibly subsidising exports, creates incentives to increase both exports and imports. However, the short run elasticity of exports is likely to be substantially smaller than the long-run one, due to the need to expand capacity in the export sector. In the short-run, then, trade deficits may increase unless a real exchange-rate depreciation encourages domestic production, and discourages domestic consumption, of both exportables and importables *vis-à-vis* non-traded goods. By increasing trade deficits, overvaluation has directly undermined several attempted trade liberalisations (see Corbo and de Melo, 1987), for a discussion of the role of the real exchange rate in Southern Cone liberalisations). It has also done so less directly by contributing to a pattern of stop–go devaluation crises, resulting in general macroeconomic instability which is inimical to successful trade reform (see section 6.3).

Unfortunately, for many developing countries such episodes have become endemic, and the instability they have imparted to microeconomic incentives cannot have been conducive to long-term growth. Evidence regarding the links among real exchange-rate behaviour, macroeconomic stability, and long-term growth emerges from studies of certain successful East Asian economies and some less successful ones in Latin America. Lin (1987), for example, compares the experience of Taiwan and Korea with that of Argentina and Chile and finds that, along with the explicit fiscal and other measures promoting exports in the former, an important role was played by exchange-rate management. The official exchange rate was administered flexibly to prevent the real exchange rate from becoming overvalued in Taiwan and Korea, while

Argentina and Chile were plagued by inflationary episodes in which the nominal exchange rate failed to be adjusted sufficiently to keep up with the increase in the domestic price level, leading to periods of severe overvaluation. Sachs (1985), in comparing the macroeconomic performances of a larger sample of countries in Latin America and East Asia, finds that the former experienced a real appreciation (amounting to about 10.5 per cent) on average over the period 1976–78 to 1979–81, compared with a real depreciation of about the same magnitude in the latter. He concludes that 'of all the causes of poor Latin American economic performance considered so far, the most significant seem to be trade and exchange rate policies' (p. 547).[4] To these and other comparative studies could be added a number of individual country studies that carry the same message – macroeconomic performance can be much enhanced if repeated overvaluation of the real exchange is avoided.

The implementation of this advice is not trivial, however. It is not enough merely to adopt a crawling peg in which the rate of change of the nominal exchange rate is adjusted to the difference between the domestic and foreign rates of inflation, thereby pegging the real exchange rate. Two additional considerations must also be taken into account.

First, exchange-rate policy and fiscal policy are closely linked through the public sector's budget constraint. Given an upper bound on the debt–GDP ratio, the steady-state public-sector deficit must be financed through seignorage. Thus the ratio of the fiscal deficit to GDP and the rate of inflation are linked in steady state.[5] Since the real exchange rate must also be constant in steady state, the rate of crawl of the nominal exchange rate must equal the domestic inflation rate minus the world rate of inflation. Thus, if the rate of crawl is an exogenous policy variable, it determines the steady-state domestic inflation rate and this in turn determines the financing available for the government through seignorage, thereby fixing the sustainable fiscal deficit ratio.[6] In this case, the exchange rate functions as the economy's nominal anchor. Under a 'passive crawl' rule that pegs the nominal exchange rate, however, continuing to adjust the fiscal deficit to the rate of crawl leaves the economy without a nominal anchor, thereby destabilising the price level (see Adams and Gros, 1986, for some simple examples). Thus, an exchange-rate policy that attempts to peg the real exchange rate requires that fiscal policy be explicitly assigned to the task of stabilising the steady-state inflation rate.

Second, although fiscal policy can determine the steady-state inflation rate while a passive crawl pegs the real exchange rate, this does not imply that active exchange-rate management can be abandoned. The real exchange rate is an endogenous macroeconomic variable – at least in the long run. Attempts to fix it at some constant initial value in the face of permanent shocks that alter its long-run equilibrium value – such as permanent changes in the terms of trade or world real interest rates – will simply prove destabilising. Thus, some flexibility must be introduced into the 'passive crawl' to allow the real exchange rate to adjust to changes in its long-run equilibrium level. This could take the form of discrete nominal exchange-rate changes accompanying unexpected permanent shocks or variations in the rate of crawl that permit a gradual adjustment of the real exchange rate.[7]

6.3 Stabilisation and liberalisation

While there is general agreement on the proposition that a stable macroeconomic environment is conducive to the success of trade liberalisation, it is less clear that macroeconomic stability is a *necessary* condition for successful trade liberalisation, i.e., that trade liberalisation should be held in abeyance until macroeconomic stability is restored. This section examines the reasons why macroeconomic instability makes successful trade liberalisation less likely and then addresses the arguments that have been presented in support of the view that stabilisation should precede liberalisation in developing countries.

Macroeconomic instability in a developing country often results in a series of 'devaluation crises' typically characterised by successive episodes of rising prices, slow growth, current account and overall balance-of-payments deficits, rising premia in parallel foreign exchange markets, and increasingly tighter trade and foreign exchange controls (Edwards and Montiel, 1988). These tend to culminate in massive capital flight in anticipation of devaluation and/or the diversion of foreign-exchange receipts into unofficial markets, causing a severe drain in official foreign exchange reserves. Eventually the anticipated devaluation comes, accompanied by at least a temporary tightening of monetary and fiscal policies and possibly some relief of quantitative restrictions on external transactions.

An important characteristic of such episodes is the instability of key relative prices and other microeconomic incentives. Real exchange rates tend to appreciate sharply prior to devaluation, then experience a discrete depreciation as a result of the nominal devaluation. Trade taxes and quantitative restrictions imposed for balance-of-payments reasons are repeatedly changed, and interest-rate ceilings cause real interest rates to mirror the instability of the inflation rate.

Such a setting simultaneously makes the trade system more restrictive and the benefits of liberalisation harder to achieve. The trade system is made more restrictive both because of the imposition of trade taxes for fiscal and balance-of-payments reasons and because of the effects on the trade regime of an overvalued exchange rate in the presence of quantitative restrictions on imports. As Krueger (1981a) has emphasised, when quotas are in effect, exchange-rate overvaluation increases the domestic relative price of importables, thus aggravating the anti-export bias of the trade regime.

At the same time, trade reform is less likely to be effective in this setting, for a number of reasons:

1. The instability of relative prices reduces their information content, weakening the incentive effects on which the efficiency-enhancing resource reallocations associated with trade reforms rely (Fischer, 1987).
2. The fiscal and balance-of-payments effects of liberalisation may be negative in the short run, and this may induce private agents to expect the reversal of trade reforms in the context of large fiscal and balance-of-payments deficits. If the sustainability of such reforms is not credible, costly investments in resource reallocation will not be undertaken.
3. Fiscal deficits tend to reduce the availability of credit for private investment at the same time that capital flight absorbs part of private saving. For both reasons, the resources available for the new private investment needed to reallocate production in response to the incentives created by trade reform may be severely curtailed. Fiscal stringency will also have an adverse impact on new public infrastructure investments that may be required by prospective new export industries.
4. Price-level instability tends to promote wage indexation, and such indexation makes the real exchange-rate depreciation that supports an attempted trade reform much harder to achieve. In the presence of indexation, a large part of nominal exchange-rate devaluation may be dissipated in the form of an increase in the price level, rather than a real exchange-rate depreciation.

In view of the well-known difficulty of achieving stabilisation in countries with long histories of macroeconomic instability, however, the operative question is whether the adoption of an outward-oriented strategy must await the success of stabilisation or whether both initiatives should be undertaken simultaneously. A number of observers (see Lin, 1987; Sachs, 1987) have cited the experiences of successful East Asian countries to argue that stabilisation should take precedence. The failure of Southern-Cone attempts at stabilisation-cum-liberalisation has also raised questions about the wisdom of undertaking both initiatives simultaneously. Nevertheless, other analysts (see Balassa *et al.*, 1986) have advocated the adoption of an outward-oriented strategy for heavily indebted countries still suffering from severe macroeconomic imbalances.

Perhaps the most compelling argument for reducing severe macroeconomic instabilities before embarking on trade reforms is that in the presence of such problems trade liberalisation simply may not achieve its intended results. If the enhanced profitability of the export sector is perceived not to be sustainable because the private sector expects export taxes to be reimposed, subsidies to be temporary, or the real exchange rate quickly to become overvalued again; if limited funds are available for private investment in the export sector because of fiscal deficits and capital flight; and if complementary public infrastructure investments are not forthcoming, then the costly reallocation of resources towards production for export will not be undertaken. With minimal export growth coupled with rapid import expansion, incipient trade deficits may emerge. Moreover, in the absence of investment in the export sectors, workers released by the import-competing sectors will not be absorbed elsewhere. The combination of trade-balance deterioration and increased unemployment may soon doom the liberalisation effort.

A second consideration, emphasised by Sachs (1987), is that the instruments of stabilisation may conflict with those of trade liberalisation and outward orientation. Several examples can be cited: exchange-rate depreciation may promote exports, but will contribute to domestic inflation – especially, as mentioned above, when price instability has led to widespread indexation. While the removal of import tariffs may be anti-inflationary, fiscal incentives to exports will raise domestic prices. Moreover, both enlarged export subsidies and reduced import tariffs may increase fiscal deficits. Similarly, stabilisation calls for reduced public-sector spending, while trade reform may require increased public-sector infrastructure investments. Finally, if reforms prove to be 'incredible' (Calvo, 1986), they may severely aggravate macroeconomic disequilibria by triggering a flood of imports of durables in anticipation of the reimposition of tariffs and quantitative restrictions.

Finally, the government in question may possess limited political capital and administrative resources. It is clear that both orthodox stabilisation and trade liberalisation typically face powerful domestic political opposition. While the political economy of stabilisation-cum-liberalisation has not (to my knowledge) been worked out, it is hard to believe that the political obstacles that confront stabilisation and liberalisation separately would be diminished by combining the two.

The conclusion seems unavoidable that thoroughgoing outward-oriented trade reforms should not be undertaken in the context of severe and recurring macroeconomic crises. It is equally clear, however, that if reform is to await the achievement of internal and external balance, then the time to undertake such reforms may never come in many cases. What remains an important topic for research, therefore, is how much macroeconomic stability is necessary before what types of reforms can be implemented with a reasonable chance of success.

6.4   Outward orientation in the long run

An outward-oriented trade reform is designed to shift resources from the production of importables to that of exportables while domestic demand shifts in the opposite direction, the net result being an increase in both exports and imports. But since a third sector is also involved – the non-traded goods sector – both the short-run and long-run outcomes for exports and imports will depend on the behaviour of the real exchange rate. As indicated in section 6.2, a short-run real exchange-rate depreciation is conducive to the success of the reform since it favours the production of both exportables and importables while discouraging domestic demand for both, thereby preventing the emergence of excessive trade deficits. In the short run, the nominal exchange rate can be adjusted with this end in mind. In the long run, however, the real exchange rate is an endogenous macroeconomic variable that cannot be controlled via nominal exchange-rate changes. This section describes policies that can be employed to influence the long-run real exchange rate and thus sustain the economy's outward orientation.

The equilibrium real exchange rate is affected both by variables which are exogenous to the domestic economy and by domestic policy variables. Among the former are the terms of trade, international transfers and world real interest rates (already mentioned in section 6.2). The latter include commercial policies as well as fiscal and financial policies.

Since commercial policy is itself one of the factors that affects the equilibrium real exchange rate, an important result from this literature is that the amount of incentive given to exports by a once-and-for-all outward-oriented trade reform will in general change over time. For example, a number of authors have derived the result that a reduction in import tariffs may result in an appreciation of the equilibrium real exchange rate.[8] In this case, if trade reform is accompanied by a nominal devaluation such that the real exchange rate depreciates on impact, export incentives would diminish as the initial real depreciation is reversed over time. This can be avoided only by the adoption of other macroeconomic policies that tend to depreciate the long-run equilibrium exchange rate.

Among the policy tools available for this purpose are changes in the size and composition of the government budget. A change in the mix of government spending from non-traded to traded goods will result in an equilibrium real depreciation, since the reduction in demand for non-traded goods will require a decrease in their relative price. A permanent increase in lump-sum taxes on the private sector will have similar effects, provided that the revenues are not used to finance an increase in government spending on non-traded goods. Finally, a reduction in the overall size of the government budget would also result in a real depreciation, provided that enough of the spending cut fell on non-traded goods. In the case where a reduction in import tariffs leads to an equilibrium real appreciation, fiscal policies of this type could be relied upon to maintain the original incentives to exports in the long run.

Mussa (1986) and Edwards (1987) have examined the effects of certain financial policies on the equilibrium real exchange rate. Mussa finds that a permanent increase in the real rate of return available to private asset holders results in long-run real appreciation, while Edwards concludes that capital account liberalisation also has this effect. These results suggest that financial liberalisation may at least partially undermine the export-promoting effects of outward-oriented trade reform. Depending on the priority attached to financial liberalisation, they suggest the need either to postpone financial liberalisation or intensify fiscal measures designed to minimise any equilibrium real exchange-rate appreciation.

6.5 Summary

This chapter has examined the nature of the macroeconomic environment that is conducive to the success of outward-oriented trade reforms. A key role is played by the real exchange rate. In the short run, real exchange-rate depreciation will prevent the emergence of trade deficits of a magnitude that would threaten the reform effort. While a crawling peg may prevent the real exchange rate from becoming overvalued after an initial nominal devaluation, such a policy must be adopted with care. Fiscal discipline becomes important in this case to keep the rate of inflation under control, and active exchange-rate management continues to be necessary to permit the real exchange rate to adjust to changes in 'fundamentals'.

Outward-oriented trade reform is most likely to succeed in an environment of macroeconomic stability in which perceived changes in key relative prices can be regarded as sustainable. This suggests that at least some degree of stabilisation is a necessary condition for successful outward-oriented trade reform, but precisely how much remains an unresolved issue.

Finally, export promotion also has a dynamic dimension. In the long run, the real exchange rate is an endogenous variable, affected by 'fundamentals' such as the trade regime itself. If the level of export incentives achieved in the immediate post-reform period is to be maintained in the longer term, supporting fiscal and financial policies may be required.

Notes

1. Trade data discrepancies suggest that smuggling and under-invoicing may account for up to a third of all legal exports in some developing countries, although the figure is much smaller in the majority of cases. For some caveats on the use of such data to measure the importance of smuggled exports, see McDonald (1985).
2. With fixed terms of trade, the real exchange rate could equivalently be defined as the price of non-traded goods in terms of exportables.
3. The supply of labour could be expressed as a function of the real wage measured in terms of some consumption bundle without altering the nature of the relationship between W and e derived in the text.
4. For a similar comparison of Western Hemisphere and Asian countries (and similar conclusions) with broader country coverage, see Khan (1986).
5. For full discussion see Sargent and Wallace (1981) and Buiter (1986).
6. I abstract away from multiple equilibria on this point; see Bruno and Fischer (1986).
7. For models of equilibrium real exchange-rate determination see Mussa (1986) and Khan and Montiel (1987).
8. See, for example, Edwards (1987), Khan and Zhaler (1985), and Khan and Montiel (1987).

7

Compensatory financial and fiscal incentives to exports

Rodney E. Falvey and Norman Gemmell

7.1 Introduction

It is widely recognised that the import restrictions and currency over-valuations common to many developing countries lead to a 'bias' against exports (see Chapters 5 and 6). In addition to these 'policy-induced' biases or distortions, it is often argued that developing countries suffer from 'natural' or 'endogenous' distortions (Bhagwati, 1971) – such as underdeveloped domestic product and factor markets – which undermine the competitiveness of their exports relative to those from developed countries.

The proximate objectives or 'targets' for which import restrictions and currency overvaluation are the 'instruments' are usually the promotion of domestic import-competing industries and the raising of government revenue. It is important to recognise that protection of a range of import-substituting industries is common, even in developing countries pursuing generally outward (export)-oriented development strategies. For some (e.g. Korea) import substitution appears to form a continuing part of their longer-term development strategy, while for others (e.g. Singapore) import restrictions have been slowly dismantled during a transition period from an 'inward' to an 'outward' orientation.

Import restrictions are rarely considered 'first-best' instruments, although where alternative policy instruments are limited, and where governments have other (e.g. revenue) constraints, a case can be made for import tariffs as 'second-best' instruments.[1] It is clear, however, that in the short to medium term policy-makers are often unwilling to abandon import restrictions, and even where they are, dismantling them takes some time. It is then the case, as Bliss (1988) notes, that existing import restrictions must essentially be taken as given in the search for welfare-improving policy instruments. In addition, while pegging the domestic currency to some foreign currency (such as the US dollar) may sometimes represent the best means of ensuring a stable and predictable exchange rate in the long run, it can lead to temporary over- (or under-) valuation in the short run (Rhee, 1985). Policies that counter any 'real' effects of these temporary deviations may be seen as preferable to continually adjusting the exchange rate itself.

Import protection harms exports through two channels: (a) it reduces domestic exporters' competitiveness in world markets by raising the cost of imported (or import-competing) inputs into export production; and (b) it reduces the incentive for the production of exportables relative to importables. Similarly, currency overvaluation keeps the domestic price of 'essential' imported inputs low, with import restrictions typically designed to raise the price of inessential imports, but simultaneously reduces the domestic price of exports. Export-promotion policies might therefore be justified as an attempt to 'compensate' for or to 'neutralise' the effects of these biases against exports.

The existence of 'externalities' associated with exporting itself has been suggested as additional grounds for export-promotion policies. There may be potential economy-wide benefits from 'intensifying competitive pressures and managerial efficiency, accelerating technical progress by greater contact with foreign institutions and ideas' (Findlay, 1984b, p. 11).[2] Infant-exporter arguments for temporary assistance have also been put forward, based on the notion that entry into new export markets is a difficult and costly activity with the cumulative volume of exports having a favourable effect on the unit costs of exporting (Findlay, 1984b, p. 12). A similar argument emerges in markets where exports have a quality dimension and purchasers can only obtain information on quality post-purchase. In markets for such 'experience goods', exporters' quality reputations are established through a process of consumer 'learning' analogous to that for production. Temporary and selective export subsidies can then be used to exploit this 'consumer learning' externality.[3] It is hardly surprising therefore that various developing countries, as part of an 'outward-oriented strategy', have adopted a number of 'compensatory' financial and fiscal instruments specific to the export sector.[4]

This chapter first considers (section 7.2) the range of export incentives used by developing countries, particularly those in South East Asia where such incentives are important. It then examines how well these incentives can 'compensate' for the distortions they are designed to overcome (section 7.3). Our approach is to examine the welfare impact of policy instruments in circumstances where 'actual' domestic prices differ from their shadow values. This helps to identify the targets which export-promotion policies should aim at if they are successfully to counteract the unintended distorting effects of other policy instruments, and allows us to comment on the 'optimality' or otherwise of the type of export incentives currently in use. Our conclusions are then drawn together in section 7.4.

7.2 Compensatory export incentives in practice

Export incentives designed to limit or compensate for unintended distortions from import-substituting policies have been used by Korea and Taiwan, for example, since the early 1950s. The 1960s and 1970s, however, saw an expansion in the range of incentives used, their generosity, and the number of countries adopting them. The developing economies of South East Asia – mainly Korea, Taiwan, Hong Kong, Singapore, Thailand, Malaysia, the Philippines and Indonesia – have perhaps made the most intensive use of such measures, though various other countries (e.g. Ivory Coast, Brazil) have adopted similar export-promotion devices.[5]

This section concentrates on the measures used in the South East Asian economies. Some examples of the types of incentives provided at various times by these governments are given in Table 7.1, while Table 7.2 gives an indication of the magnitudes of these incentives in Korea, Malaysia, the Philippines and Thailand. The incentives listed in Table 7.1,[6] which represent implicit or explicit production subsidies to exporters, are categorised according to whether they are 'input' or 'output' related. The significance of this distinction is that subsidies to particular inputs (intermediate or primary) are likely to create different 'by-product' distortions from subsidies to output (production or export).[7] Several features of the incentives in Tables 7.1 and 7.2 may be noted.

Firstly, many of the measures are *implicit* (rather than direct) subsidies. This largely reflects an attempt to choose incentives that will minimise the probability of retaliatory action (countervailing duties) on the part of (importing) trading partners. In particular, retaliation is less likely if these incentives fall within the GATT rules on 'subsidies'.[8] These rules distinguish between export and 'other' subsidies, and also between export subsidies on primary and non-primary products. 'Other' subsidies and export subsidies on primary products are permitted unless they are demonstrated to have adverse effects on the trade or production of trading partners. Export subsidies on manufactured goods are prohibited for developed countries, but are permitted for developing countries provided they do not cause 'serious prejudice to the trade or production' of trading partners. However, given that it is largely left up to the importing government to determine whether 'adverse effects' and

Table 7.1   Types of export incentives used in various developing countries.

Type of export promotion scheme[a]

A. *'Input-related' incentives:*[b]
   (i) Intermediate input-related
       Tariff and tax exemptions/rebates on imported inputs for exporters and their
           domestic suppliers
       Import credits for exports
       Wastage allowance subsidies
       Reduced prices of public utility inputs
   (ii) Primary input-related
       Accelerated depreciation
       Reduced interest rates for exporters
       Investment loans (preferential access)

B. *'Output-related' incentives:*[b]
   (i) Direct
       Production loans for exporters (preferential access/interest rate subsidy)
       Domestic indirect and direct tax exemptions/rebates
       Import entitlement/licences linked to exports
       Export credits (preferential access/interest rate subsidy)
       Foreign exchange deposits held by central banks for use by individual exporters
       Foreign exchange loans (preferential access)
       Subsidised shipment insurance
       Direct export subsidies
   (ii) Indirect
       Infrastructure provision
       Credits for, and government provision of, overseas marketing activites, R & D
           expenses, etc.

C. *'Externality-related' incentives*
       Export 'quality' inspection and incentives
       Monopoly rights granted in new export markets

Notes: [a]These measures have operated at various dates in at least one of: Hong Kong,
Indonesia, Korea, Malaysia, Philippines, Singapore, Taiwan, Thailand.
[b]The 'output-related' – 'input-related' division is based on whether the amount of 'subsidy'
received is determined primarily by levels of output or input use.

Source: Adapted from Yusuf and Peters (1985).

'serious prejudice' have occurred, export promotion through overt
subsidies, particularly export subsidies, tends to be discouraged by the
threat of countervailing action.

Unfortunately GATT has no comprehensive definition of 'subsidy'.
Instead illustrative, but not exhaustive, lists of export and other subsidies
have been established, and the rules tend to emphasise the 'effects' rather
than the 'form' of policies. Some principles have evolved from GATT
practice, however. *Indirect taxes*, which include duties, sales taxes,
value-added taxes and excise taxes, falling on physically incorporated
inputs or on the product itself may be refunded at the border (i.e. upon
exportation of the product) without being considered a subsidy. Import-

charge refunds are also permitted on domestically produced inputs having the same quality and characteristics as imported inputs. But the refunding of *direct taxes*, that is any tax on a factor of production (e.g. income and wages taxes), at the border will be considered subsidisation.

These rules leave two obvious anomalies. Refunds of taxes on goods and services used in the production process but not physically incorporated into the product, e.g. taxes on capital equipment and fuel, are considered subsidies. In fact countervailing actions have been taken against countries using export-rebate schemes with respect to taxes on overhead production costs. Also, while the import charges which can be refunded include 'tariffs, duties and other fiscal charges', no allowance is made for refunding the implicit charges paid on quota-restricted items.

These considerations clearly influence the selection of incentives from those listed in Table 7.1. Indirect tax exemptions and rebates are likely to be preferred to direct tax exemptions and rebates. As long as import substitution is confined to consumption goods and intermediate inputs, its direct effects on exporters' costs can be offset by import-duty rebates under GATT rules. However, if import substitution moves beyond this to capital goods, the implicit tax on exportable production cannot be offset so readily. Developed countries seem prepared to take a fairly liberal view of developing-country policies, but only to the extent that their own producers are not adversely affected.

Secondly, some incentives are targeted at 'exporters' while others depend on the volume (or value) of exports. Firms typically qualify as 'exporters' by having some minimum proportion of output which is exported, and therefore incentives which are targeted at *exporters*, rather than exports, also provide an implicit subsidy to *domestic* sales by these firms.

Finally, the way in which particular types of export incentives are administered can influence their effectiveness. Consider, for example, the various means of giving exporters relief from import duties on their inputs – duty exemptions, rebates ('drawbacks'), bonded warehouses and factories, and the use of 'domestic letters of credit' (DLC). The advantage of an exemption-based over a drawback-based system is that the former avoids the inevitable time-lags involved in bureaucratically administered reimbursement.[9] On the other hand, exemption systems can be administratively complex to set up and difficult to monitor. Bonded warehouses and factories allow domestic firms to be treated similarly to those located in export-processing zones (see Chapter 8) in terms of their access to imported inputs. The main disadvantages of this arrangement are the requirement, typically, that firms are exclusively engaged in exporting and the costs of customs' inspection of each warehouse or factory.

Table 7.2 Export incentives in Korea, Malaysia, the Philippines and Thailand.

(A) Tax incentives for priority industries

Type of incentive	Country Malaysia	Philippines	Thailand	Korea
Priority industries	'Pioneer' (exports; also socially desired goods not already produced on commercial terms	'Preferred' (demand exists, not supply); 'Pioneer' (demand and supply must both be generated)	'Promoted' (development-oriented industries based on decisions by the Board of Investment)	'Key' (government determined)
Tax holidays	5–10 years based on investment, location, and employment: cit, dit, dt (2–8 years); indefinite loss carryover	All taxes, except cit, are exempt on a diminishing basis up to 1981; loss carry forward to a maximum of 10 years	3–8 years plus 50% reduction for 5 more years; includes bt, cit	All taxes: cit, it on unincorporated units; dit, pt; pat – for 5 years plus 50% reduction for 3 additional years
Deductions	Does not apply due to exemptions	Organisational and pre-operating costs from taxable income	25% of installation costs from net profits	Does not apply due to exemptions
Tax credit: (i) Equipment	Post-exemption period: 25–40% of capital expenses incurred during exemption period	100% on domestic and imported equipment; penalty of twice the credit for unauthorised resales	100% exemption of bt on equipment	100% on domestic and imported equipment; no penalty law
(ii) Interest payments	Information unavailable	Conditionally, on foreign loan interest	Information unavailable	Full exemption from tax on interest on foreign loans
Accelerated depreciation	Conditionally available	Allowed to a maximum of twice the usual rate of 20%	Conditionally available	Domestic equipment may receive up to 4 times usual rate
Tariffs on machinery and raw materials	cd exemption on raw materials and machinery not available locally	cd exemption on machinery locally not available; not so for materials	cd exemption on raw materials and machinery not available locally	cd exemption on 'capital goods' interpreted to include raw materials

(B) Tax incentives specific to export industries

Export industries	All export industries are included in the 'pioneer' category; the following incentives are additional	Export Incentives Act does not specify whether the following incentives are additive	All export areas are not 'promoted'. Following incentives related to exports (promoted as well as traditional exports)	All foreign exchange-earning industries are defined within 'key' sectors; the following are additional incentives
Tax holidays	4–7 years' holiday for capital investments (instead of usual 2–5 years for pioneer industries)	et exemption if revenues exceed US$5 million within 5 years from the registration	Exemption from bt and et on exportation of manufactures	bt exemption
Deductions	Expenses such as foreign advertising, export market research, transport costs deductible from tax base	it base reduced by a certain portion of export revenue, based also on domestic content	Not available	Not applicable due to total exemptions
Tax credit	Not available	Export producers: tax credit equivalent to the sales, compensating and specific taxes and raw material duties	7/8 of cd on raw materials	50% for it and cit
Accelerated depreciation	Additional 40% of the residual value of capital assets	Same as in priority sectors	Same as in priority sectors	Same as in priority sectors

Note: Abbreviations used: it = income tax; cit = corporation income tax; dit = dividend income tax; bt = business tax; dt = development tax; pt = property tax; pat = property acquisition tax; cd = customs duty; et = export tax.

Source: Shome (1986).

Perhaps the most comprehensive and cost-effective administrative device for import duty relief is based on the DLC. A DLC is a 'promise-to-pay' document which an exporter's bank issues to domestic firms supplying the exporter (including import agents). The government can then use the DLC as a qualification for import duty relief, thereby gaining an exemption system that extends to 'indirect exporters', is funded by the private sector, and is easily monitored through the banking system (see Rhee, 1985, pp. 111–18). The DLC has been extensively and successfully used for this purpose in Korea where it has been found to be particularly effective in offering assistance to small-scale exporters who often would not qualify for relief under other systems (due to administrative costs).

However administered, relief from import tariffs and domestic sales taxes does appear to be important for the profitability of exporting. In Taiwan, for example, Scott (1979) found that 'for the average manufacturing establishment engaged in producing exports, rebates on import duty, commodity tax, and other indirect taxes on exports in 1971 equalled nearly three-quarters of its estimated value added and more than double its estimated operating surplus' (p. 325). Though Scott recognises that these estimates may slightly exaggerate the importance of rebates, they nevertheless suggest that exporting could hardly have been worth while for domestic producers in the absence of a rebate scheme.

7.3 Compensatory export incentives in theory

The use of policy-induced distortions in some markets partially to offset the adverse effects of unalterable distortions in other markets forms the central core of the analysis of the 'second best'. Here we use this analysis to illustrate the potential strengths and limitations of export-promotion policies in improving welfare, where some importables' markets are distorted by unalterable tariffs. For this purpose we adopt a simple standard model of a small trading economy.[10]

The 'budget constraint' facing this country on world markets is that the value of its consumption of traded goods less the value of its production of traded goods, both valued at world prices, equals its trade deficit, i.e.

$$\sum_{i=1}^{n} p_i^*(D_i - x_i) = B \qquad (7.1)$$

where p_i^* is the given world price, D_i is the domestic compensated demand, and x_i the domestic net output of product i, $i = 1, \ldots, n$, and B

is the trade deficit. This constraint can be rewritten in terms of gross outputs (X_i) by using

$$x_i = X_i - \sum_{j=1}^{n} a_{ij} X_j \tag{7.2}$$

where a_{ij} denotes the number of units of intermediate input i used to produce domestically one unit of gross output of commodity j. Then equation (7.1) becomes

$$\sum_{i=1}^{n} (p_i^* D_i - v_i^* X_i) = B \tag{7.3}$$

where $v_i^* = p_i^* - \sum_{j=1}^{n} a_{ji} p_j^*$ denotes the value added per unit of gross output of commodity i evaluated at world prices.

Equation (7.3) can be used to derive a convenient measure of the welfare effects of various policy interventions. Assume all goods are traded.[11] Since D_i is a function of domestic final goods prices ($p = (p_1, \ldots, p_n)$) and aggregate real income (U) only, the total derivative of $D_i(p, U)$ is

$$\mathrm{d}D_i = \sum_{i=1}^{n} D_{ij} \mathrm{d}p_j + D_{iu} \mathrm{d}U = \mathrm{d}\bar{D}_i + D_{iu} \mathrm{d}U \tag{7.4}$$

where $D_{ij} = \partial D_i / \partial p_j$, $D_{iu} = \partial D_i / \partial U$ and $\mathrm{d}\bar{D}_i$ measures the real-income compensated change in the final demand for commodity i. Totally differentiating (7.3) and substituting (7.4) yields (assuming $\mathrm{d}B = 0$)

$$m \, \mathrm{d}U = -\sum_{i=1}^{n} p_i^* \mathrm{d}\bar{D}_i + \sum_{i=1}^{n} \mathrm{d}(v_i^* X_i) \tag{7.5}$$

where $m = \sum_{i=1}^{n} p_i^* D_{iu}$ is positive and has a standard interpretation as the 'marginal propensity to spend evaluated at shadow prices'. Since all goods are, by assumption, tradable at fixed world prices, these prices represent their 'shadow prices' to this economy. In particular, p_i^* is the shadow price of a unit of product i in final demand, and v_i^* is the shadow value added of a unit of gross output of i – representing the shadow price of the output (p_i^*) less the shadow cost of the intermediate inputs used in its domestic production ($\sum_j a_{ji} p_j^*$). Equation (7.5) also illustrates that when all goods are tradable at fixed world prices, the effects of policy changes on final demand and production can be considered separately. This simplifies any analysis of compensatory export incentives, but also highlights the potential disadvantage in their tendency to concentrate on only the production side of the market.

Using the definition of v_i^*, $d(v_i^* X_i)$ can be expressed as

$$d(v_i^* X_i) = v_i^* dX_i + X_i dv_i^* = v_i^* dX_i - X_i\left(\sum_j p_i^* da_{ji}\right) \quad (7.6)$$

The gross output changes (dX_i) can be further decomposed into two components – one corresponding to movements along a given production possibility frontier $(d\bar{X}_i)$ and the other the result of any movements off the frontier itself (dX_i^0). Thus

$$dX_i \equiv d\bar{X}_i + dX_i^0 \quad (7.7)$$

Policies that change domestic (relative) value-added prices (v_i) induce shifts around the production frontier. Policies that impact directly on primary factor markets (e.g. taxes or subsidies on wages in a particular sector) will induce a shift off the frontier.

If (7.7) is substituted in (7.6), and the homogeneity properties of the compensated demand functions $(\sum_{i=1}^n p_i d\bar{D}_i = 0)$ and gross output movements along the frontier $(\sum_{i=1}^n v_i d\bar{X}_i = 0)$ are used, plus cost minimisation with respect to the intermediate input mix $(\sum_j \Pi_{ji} da_{ji} < 0$, where Π_{ji} is the cost of a unit of intermediate input j to industry i),[12] then (7.5) can be expressed as

$$m dU = \sum_{i=1}^n \left\{ (p_i - p_i^*) d\bar{D}_i - (v_i - v_i^*) d\bar{X}_i \right.$$
$$\left. + v_i^* dX_i^0 + X_i\left(\sum_j (\Pi_{ji} - p_j^*)(da_{ji})\right) \right\} \quad (7.8)$$

Equation (7.8) isolates the potential sources of welfare gains given the existence of some divergences between domestic market and shadow prices. If the domestic price of product k exceeds its shadow price, then welfare can be increased $(dU > 0)$ by (a) an increase in final consumption of k ($d\bar{D}_k > 0$ when $p_k > p_k^*$); (b) a reduction in gross output of k ($d\bar{X}_k < 0$ when $v_k > v_k^*$); and (c) an increase in the use of k as an intermediate input ($da_{ki} > 0$ when $\Pi_{ki} > p_k^*$). This corresponds to the sense in which product k is being 'under-consumed' – both in final demand (because its price to consumers is above the shadow price) and as an intermediate (because its intermediate price is above its shadow price) – and 'overproduced' (because its value-added price is above its shadow value-added price). Also, shifts off the production frontier may be welfare-improving if they result in an increase in the value of domestic output at shadow prices (i.e. $\sum_{i=1}^n v_i^* dX_i^0 > 0$), although clearly they must result in a decline in the value of domestic output at domestic prices ($\Sigma_{i=1}^{n} v_i \, \mathrm{d} X_i^0 < 0$), if the shift is inside the frontier.

To investigate the implications of these results for compensatory export incentives, it is useful to consider the components of equation (7.8) separately.

7.3.1 Final demand-related policies

From the definition of $\mathrm{d}\bar{D}_i$, we have that.

$$\sum_{i=1}^{n} (p_i - p_i^*) \mathrm{d}\bar{D}_i = \sum_{j=1}^{n} \left(\sum_{i=1}^{n} (p_i - p_i^*) D_{ij} \right) \mathrm{d} p_j \qquad (7.9)$$

Equation (7.9) reveals standard 'second-best' results. If $p_i > p_i^*$, then welfare can be improved by a tax on the consumption substitutes of i, and a subsidy on the consumption complements of i (i.e. $\mathrm{d} p_j \gtrless 0$ as $D_{ij} \gtrless 0$). This notion generalises to cases where many markets have fixed distortions. Indeed, one can solve for the second-best 'optimal' intervention in the final demand for j by setting the coefficient on $\mathrm{d} p_j$ in (7.9) equal to zero to obtain

$$\frac{p_j - p_j^*}{p_j} = \sum_{i \neq j} \alpha_{ij} \left(\frac{p_i - p_i^*}{p_i} \right) \qquad (7.10)$$

where $\alpha_{ij} = p_i D_{ij} / \Sigma_{k \neq j} p_k D_{kj}$, so that $\Sigma_{i \neq j} \alpha_{ij} = 1$.[13] The optimal consumption intervention in sector j is therefore a weighted average of the existing consumption distortions in the other sectors, where the weight on the distortion in the market for product i is positive or negative as j is a substitute or complement for the product in final demand.

Since a given set of tariffs on (some) imports effectively taxes consumption of these goods, a pattern of taxes and subsidies on the consumption of exportables (and other) goods can be welfare-improving. But as (7.10) reveals, the optimal pattern of consumption taxes and subsidies on the consumption of exportables depends in a complex way on the substitution and complementarity relationships among the goods involved.

In practice it seems unlikely that the direct taxes or subsidies on domestic consumption of exportable final goods are chosen in this way. Domestic sales taxes generally do not discriminate between goods on this basis, and export taxes on final goods (which implicitly subsidise domestic consumption) appear to be directed primarily at raising revenue.

However, where export incentives subsidise exports *per se*, they do effectively tax domestic exportables consumption. Of course such explicit consumption taxes can only be justified by (7.9) for exportables that are consumption substitutes for the restricted importables.

7.3.2 *Direct production-related policies*

Analogous results apply on the production side. One can write

$$- \sum_{i=1}^{n} (v_i - v_i^*) \, d\bar{X}_i = - \sum_{i=1}^{n} (v_i - v_i^*) \left(\sum_{j=1}^{n} X_{ij} dv_j \right)$$

$$= - \sum_{j=1}^{n} \left(\sum_{i=1}^{n} (v_i - v_i^*) X_{ij} \right) dv_j \qquad (7.11)$$

where $X_{ij} = \partial X_i / \partial v_j$. Suppose intermediate input coefficients (a_{ji}) are fixed, and there are no changes in factor market distortions. Then if $v_i > v_i^*$ welfare can be improved by an increase (decrease) in the unit value added of the production substitutes (complements) of i (i.e. $dv_j \gtrless 0$ as $X_{ij} \gtrless 0$). At the second-best 'optimum',

$$\frac{v_j - v_j^*}{v_j} = \sum_{i \neq j} \beta_{ij} \left(\frac{v_i - v_i^*}{v_i} \right) \qquad (7.12)$$

where $\beta_{ij} = v_i X_{ij} / \Sigma_{k \neq j} v_k X_{kj}$, so that $\Sigma_{i \neq j} \beta_{ij} = 1$.[14] The optimal value-added intervention for sector j is then a weighted average of the value-added distortions in the other sectors, where the weight on i is positive if i and j are production substitutes $(X_{ij} < 0)$ and negative if i and j are production complements $(X_{ij} > 0)$.[15]

Unlike final demand, however, the relationship between production taxes and subsidies and unit value addeds involves both direct and indirect effects. A tariff on product i, for instance, distorts not only the unit value added of product i itself, but also the unit value addeds of all goods that use i as an intermediate input. Similarly, potentially offsetting production interventions applied with respect to product j can involve: (direct) taxes or subsidies on the output of j; (indirect) taxes or subsidies on intermediate inputs used in the production of j; or (indirect) taxes or subsidies on the use of j itself as an intermediate input into other products.

The concept of *effective protection* is intended to capture these direct and indirect effects.[16] To illustrate the issues involved, consider the effective rate of protection on commodity j (E_j) which is measured by

$$E_j \equiv \frac{v_j - v_j^*}{v_j} = \frac{(q_j - p_j^*) - \sum_{k \neq j} a_{kj}(\Pi_{kj} - p_k^*)}{q_j - \sum_{k \neq j} a_{kj}\Pi_{kj}} \qquad (7.13)$$

where q_j is the domestic producer price of a unit of output j. Suppose j is an exportable. Then in the absence of any direct tax or subsidy on the production of j itself (i.e. $q_j = p_j^*$), tariffs on importables used as intermediate inputs into j reduce the unit value added of j and result in negative effective protection for j production (i.e. $E_j = -\Sigma_{k \neq j} a_{kj}(\Pi_{kj} - p_k^*)/v_j < 0$). One can view some of the policies examined in section 7.2 as aimed at removing this negative effective protection on exportables, and thereby achieving 'neutral' status (i.e. $E_j = 0$). This outcome can be achieved either by the appropriate direct production subsidy on j (i.e. $q_j - p_j^* = \Sigma_{k \neq j}^n a_{kj}(\Pi_{kj} - p_k^*)$) or by allowing j producers access to importable intermediate inputs at world (shadow) prices (i.e. $\Pi_{kj} = p_k^*$).

If intermediate input coefficients can be varied, then differences between the domestic and shadow prices of these inputs will also distort the intermediate input mix chosen by producers. This provides another argument for allowing producers access to intermediate inputs at world (rather than domestic) prices, although the same outcome (i.e. an optimal input mix) can be achieved as long as domestic intermediate prices are all equiproportional to their shadow prices.

As noted in section 7.2, the combination of GATT rules and administrative convenience typically results in duty exemption or draw-back systems, rather than direct subsidies, being employed to achieve $E_j = 0$. Although the use of domestic letters of credit and other rebate or exemption systems seems to have worked fairly well in most South East Asian countries, the complex intermediate supply chains in well-developed production systems make it extremely difficult to compensate entirely for the distortions due to import restrictions by this method.[17] Nevertheless, the adoption of 'intermediate-input-related' incentives such as those listed in Table 7.1 is an important step towards providing exporters with inputs at world prices.

Since $E_i > 0$ for import-competing products, neutrality with respect to exportables still leaves an overall production bias against exportables.[18] The provision of further incentives could then be viewed as 'extended neutral' policies which attempt to remove this production bias against exportables. If importables are protected at different effective rates, and some likely not at all, then (7.12) indicates that the optimal structure of intervention in other goods is again a weighted average of these effective rates, including any zero rates and with the possibility that the weighting on some rates will be negative. Selecting the 'optimum' policy for exportable j is then likely to be an informationally and administratively difficult task, and simpler procedures are likely to be sought.

It is not surprising, therefore, that most of the 'direct-output-related' incentives listed in Table 7.1 are not targeted differentially at the production substitutes and complements of importables. Rather there is a general tendency to subsidise exportable production of manufactures. This can be justified if such exportables are production substitutes to the protected importables 'on average'. Here it is useful to distinguish between production subsidies to exportables, which leave the domestic and world prices of the output equal for intermediate users, and export subsidies, which raise the domestic price of the output to intermediate users. Only in the latter case is the production of user industries taxed as a result. Indeed, some taxes on intermediate-good exports are used in this way to promote domestic processing industries.[19] The 'indirect-output-related' incentives listed in Table 7.1 are likely to provide a mixture of export and general trade incentives. Thus while government provision of bonded warehouses and factory buildings can usually be targeted at exporters, the provision of road networks and docks will tend to facilitate trade in general.

7.3.3   Factor market-related policies

The final, and least direct, channel through which export incentives can be provided lies in the markets for the primary factors. By subsidising the use of primary factors in some sectors, or taxing their use in others, welfare can be raised if the outcome is $\Sigma_{i=1}^{n} v_i^* \, \mathrm{d}X_i^0 > 0$ in (7.8). Determining an appropriate pattern of factor taxes and subsidies requires a detailed knowledge of the production structure, however.

To illustrate the basic issues involved, consider the simple specific factor model,[20] where production in each sector requires the use of two primary factors – one specific to that sector (F_i) and the other mobile between sectors (K). Suppose that the government imposes a per unit tax on the use of the mobile factor in sector i of t_i (which becomes a subsidy if $t_i < 0$). Then, in equilibrium, the primary factor unit cost in sector i can be written as

$$v_i = b_{Ki} r T_i + b_{Fi} R_i \qquad (7.14)$$

where b_{ji} measures the number of units of primary factor j required per unit of output i, $T_i = 1 + t_i$, and r and R_i are the returns per unit to the mobile and specific factors respectively.

Following standard derivation (e.g. Caves and Jones, 1985, supplement to ch. 6) one can show that the effects of changes in these factor taxes or subsidies at constant product prices and for given total factor employments are

$$\hat{r} = - \sum_{i=1}^{n} \delta_i \hat{T}_i \tag{7.15}$$

and

$$dX_i^0 = - X_i \theta_{ki} \gamma_{ki} \left(\hat{T}_i - \sum_{j=1}^{n} \delta_j \hat{T}_j \right) \tag{7.16}$$

where $\delta_i \equiv \lambda_{ki} \gamma_{ki} / \gamma$, λ_{ki} is the proportion of the total mobile factor in the ith sector, γ_{ki} is the elasticity of the mobile factor's marginal product in sector i, $\gamma \equiv \Sigma_{i=1}^{n} \lambda_{ki} \gamma_{ki}$, θ_{ki} is the share of the mobile factor in the unit value added of sector i (i.e. $\theta_{ki} \equiv b_{Ki} r T_i / v_i$), and a '^' denotes a proportional change.

Using (7.16), the third term in equation (7.8) then becomes

$$\sum_{i=1}^{n} v_i^* dX_i^0 = \sum_{i=1}^{n} rK\lambda_{ki}\gamma_{ki} \left[\sum_{j=1}^{n} \delta_j \frac{v_j^*}{v_j} T_j - \frac{v_i^*}{v_i} T_i \right] \hat{T}_i \tag{7.17}$$

where K is the total employment of the mobile factor. If initially there are no factor distortions (i.e. $T_j = 1$ for all j), then the sign of the coefficient on T_i in (7.17) is just

$$\text{sign} \left[\sum_{j=1}^{n} \delta_j \frac{v_j^*}{v_j} - \frac{v_i^*}{v_i} \right] \tag{7.18}$$

The appropriate pattern of factor taxes and subsidies therefore depends on the relative distortions in product value-addeds. If the distortion in the value added of sector i exceeds the overall average (weighted by the δ_j) distortion in value addeds (i.e. (7.18) is positive), then it is welfare-improving to impose a tax on the use of the mobile factor in industry i (i.e. $T_i > 1$); and conversely if the distortion in i is less than the average. At the optimum,[21]

$$\frac{v_i^*}{v_i} T_i = \sum_{j=1}^{n} \delta_j \frac{v_j^*}{v_j} T_j \tag{7.19}$$

If importable i is subject to a tariff, then $v_i^*/v_i < 1$ and $v_j^*/v_j > 1$ for all other goods which use i as an intermediate input. Equation (7.18) then implies a welfare gain from taxing the use of the mobile factor in i. The appropriate policies in the other sectors depend on the relative size of the distortion in their value addeds – that is, on the importance of i as an intermediate input in their production. Clearly it will be welfare-improving to subsidise the use of the mobile factor in at least one sector (that for which v_j^*/v_j is the largest). Again the optimal pattern of intervention in exportable markets may involve either taxes or subsidies, depending on the precise production interrelationships involved. But if all exportable producers have access to intermediate inputs at world prices (i.e. $v_j^*/v_j = 1$ where j is an exportable), then a general pattern of subsidising the use of the mobile factor in exportable production will be welfare-improving (since $v_i^*/v_i < 1$ for protected importables).

As was shown in section 7.2, subsidising capital use in export industries has been a common policy in outward-oriented developing countries. Whether this will be welfare-improving, however, depends on a number of considerations. Firstly, in the short run capital may be a sector-specific factor in production, and subsidising its use will not improve welfare, or encourage exports, since this specific factor will already be employed to the maximum. In the medium to long term, however, investment can be expected to respond to such incentives. Secondly, even in the simple specific factor model considered above, the second-best optimal pattern of taxes and subsidies on mobile factor use depends in a quite complex way on the distortions in value added of importables and exportables. Welfare gains from a general subsidy to mobile capital use in exportables depend on exportables being relatively large intermediate users of the protected importables, though the existence of duty rebate or exemption schemes makes welfare gains more likely for such subsidies. Thirdly, our illustration used a single mobile factor only. In the presence of additional mobile factors (e.g. labour), taxes and subsidies on the use of only one of them will also distort relative mobile factor proportions, inducing further by-product inefficiencies which will tend to reduce welfare. Direct factor subsidies of this type are also likely to be subject to countervailing duties by trading partners.

7.3.4 *Externality-related policies*

While the analysis of this section has concentrated on examining policies to compensate for endogenous or 'policy-induced' distortions affecting export industries, section 7.2 also noted 'externality' arguments for subsidising exports independently of any anti-export biases. The 'externality related' incentives in Table 7.1 may be viewed as policies designed to exploit the 'infant exporter' and 'consumer learning' externalities. Monopoly rights granted to exporters in new markets internalise both any cost-reduction benefits available in the early phases of exporting and any externalities associated with the establishment of reputations for quality. The monopoly element refers to an exclusive right to export rather than any monopoly power that is likely to be exercised in the importing market. Quality inspections can perform a similar role, particularly where consumers may generalise a reputation of poor quality for particular products of a given national origin, to a wider range of exports from the same country.

7.4 Conclusions

This chapter has been concerned with the ways in which various developing-country governments have used fiscal and financial instruments to help compensate for particular, but common, 'biases' against exporting. These 'biases' result both from 'natural' features of the domestic economy (such as informational deficiencies, imperfect markets), and from unintended effects of other government policies (such as import tariffs). Within the outward-oriented economies of South East Asia 'compensatory' export incentives have been especially prominent and a wide range of measures has been adopted, mainly in the form of indirect production subsidies to exports and on intermediate inputs and factors used by exporters.

In assessing how well these incentives meet their objectives two approaches may be followed:

1. We might examine what policies should be adopted to counteract distortions affecting exportables, if governments are interested in maximising social welfare but cannot remove these distortions. Actual incentives can then be assessed by reference to these 'second-best' policies. This is generally the approach adopted in this chapter.
2. We might assume that export expansion improves social welfare and examine whether exports have been increased by the various measures used. A major problem with this latter approach is that identifying the *ceteris paribus* effects of compensatory fiscal/financial policies within a broader export-promotion strategy is extremely difficult and, perhaps for this reason, reliable studies of this type are few. Korean incentives have been the most intensively studied in this regard, where the evidence generally points to significant stimulating effects of various export-promoting instruments.[22]

In adopting the first approach we have not compared actual and optimal policies in detail but rather have sought to identify the principles involved and to illustrate their application with reference to some of the incentives commonly used. The analysis also helps to make explicit the assumptions that are required for export incentives to be regarded as welfare-improving.

In the light of this analysis a number of limited, general conclusions would seem to be appropriate. Firstly, since it is likely generally to be the case that restricted importables and exportables are substitutes (in demand, and especially in production), then some subsidisation to counteract distortions is probably appropriate. Evidence of effective disprotection of exportables in several developing countries confirms such distortions. As section 7.2 indicated, the development of administrative devices to counteract these distortions has rendered such subsidisation policies more effective in recent years.

Secondly, failure to target some incentives only at the *exports*, and not at the domestic sales of exporting firms, will likely encourage domestic consumption which should rather be taxed either directly or indirectly by subsidising exported output only. Thirdly, capital and labour factors are probably best considered mobile in most cases so that the widespread use of capital, but not labour, subsidies will potentially create by-product distortions in technology and input choice. Fourthly, if there are externalities associated with exporting then export subsidies beyond 'neutrality' will help to internalise these and achieve wider benefits to the economy provided retaliation can be avoided. It is often the case that such externalities are confined to the entry phase into new markets and apply only to a limited range of products, however. Export subsidisation with a wide coverage and a long duration could not then be justified on these grounds. Fifthly, the distinction that the GATT rules draw between exemptions and rebates on direct and indirect taxes, implies clear advantages for the use of indirect incentives if countervailing action is to be avoided.

To these conclusions should be added at least two warnings. Firstly, general (implicit or explicit) subsidies to exports run the risk of subsidising complements of importables (in demand or production) which should rather be taxed. This suggests the need for a careful examination of the pattern of complements and substitutes for distorted importables to ensure that such distortions are not exacerbated rather than compensated by export subsidies. A similar point relates to the extent of factor mobility.

Secondly, the analysis in section 7.3 identified certain conditions under which net taxation or subsidisation of exportables might be recommended. It did not in general, however, specify the *magnitude* of such taxes or subsidies. This clearly requires detailed knowledge of specific demand and production parameters and the precise effects of individual policy instruments. In addition, since various demand-, production- and factor-related policies may be used simultaneously, these cannot be determined in isolation. An important point to emerge, however, is that, because attempts to correct one distortion by the introduction of another will typically also introduce some by-product distortion(s), complete compensation for the initial distortion may not be desirable. A pertinent example is likely to be the use of import-tariff rebate systems which fail to 'subsidise' domestic indirect exporters. If the system's coverage cannot be improved, an attempt fully to compensate direct exporters may not be optimal.

Notes

1. See Stern (1988), especially pp. 82–3.
2. These 'externality' effects have been formally modelled by Feder (1983).
3. See Mayer (1984b).
4. Rhee (1985) categorises these 'compensatory' export incentives into two levels: (1) 'neutral' incentives which 'seek to enable exporters to compete with foreign competitors in world markets on an equal footing in regard to undistorted markets and policies' (Rhee, 1985, p. 8). This appears to involve achieving a zero effective protective rate for exportables, thus countering the anti-export bias in (a) above; (2) 'extended neutral' incentives which seek, in addition, to remove the anti-export bias in (b) above by providing equal incentives for exporting as for import-substituting activities. This appears to involve achieving equal effective protective rates for exportables and importables, thereby also creating a 'positive bias' in favour of exports relative to 'free trade' competitors. Rhee assumes here that foreign competitors are not similarly affected by policy and endogenous distortions.
5. See some of the individual studies in Part III.
6. One incentive in Table 7.1 requiring some elaboration is 'wastage allowance' subsidies. In some developing countries (e.g. Korea) the permitted tax-free imported input requirements for exporters are determined on the basis of input/output coefficients agreed upon between the government (or tax authority) and each exporting industry. Even if, on average, no subsidy is involved, the relatively more efficient exporting firms in each industry, who can economise on their use of imported inputs, may be allowed to sell their surplus duty-free imports (i.e. 'wastage') on the domestic market, sometimes making a substantial profit.
7. The concept of 'by-product' distortion is discussed in Corden (1974).
8. See Low (1982) for a discussion of export subsidies and the GATT.
9. However, Hill (1987) found that under a recent (May 1986) Indonesian scheme 'requests for duty-free imports are being handled in three working days . . . ; drawback payments are taking seven to nine days, as compared to a statutory limit of one month' (p. 19).
10. For a more general discussion of the second-best in small open economies see Corden (1974) and Lloyd (1974).

11. This allows us to illustrate the key relationships in the simplest possible way. Besides greatly complicating the analysis, including non-traded goods (or traded goods subject to quantitative restrictions) modifies the results derived below in two important ways. First, the production and final consumption sides of the market can no longer be treated separately. A change in any consumption tax or subsidy, for example, will affect the demand for and hence price of non-traded goods. The impact of a distortion in one tradable's market on another tradable's market will now include not only the direct effects captured below but also indirect effects operating through the induced changes in non-traded goods prices. These latter effects will depend on the substitution and complementarity relationships between these traded goods and the non-traded goods. Second, import-substitution policies will tend to expand production (reduce consumption) of importables at the expense of both exportables and non-tradables in general. Since the prices of non-tradables are determined in the domestic market, they will adjust further taxing exports where prices are fixed at their world levels. Neutral export incentives can then be viewed as removing some of this bias against exports, while extended neutral incentives appear intended to ensure that increased import-substituting production occurs at the expense of non-tradables, and perhaps traditional exports, rather than manufactured exports. For a discussion and references see Dixit (1985).
12. Here we also assume that intermediate input proportions depend only on relative intermediate input prices and not also on primary factor prices.
13. This solution uses the homogeneity property of compensated demand functions, i.e. $\Sigma_{i=j}^{n} p_i D_{ij} = 0$ for all $j = 1, \ldots, n$; so that $p_j D_{jj} = -\Sigma_{i \neq j} p_i D_{ij}$.
14. This solution uses $\Sigma_{i=1}^{n} v_i X_{ij} = 0$ for all $j = 1, \ldots, n$; so that $v_j X_{jj} = -\Sigma_{i \neq j} v_i X_{ij}$.
15. Note that since $X_{jj} > 0$, $\Sigma_{i \neq j} v_i X_{ij} < 0$.
16. Effective protection is discussed in more detail in Chapter 5.
17. Ahmad (1987, p. 18), for example, argues that the Indian drawback system in the 1970s only partially compensated exporters using taxed intermediates (including imports).
18. Clearly only by coincidence would the optimal effective rate of protection on exportables be zero in (7.12).
19. Examples are the export taxes on lumber in Indonesia and lumber and copra in the Philippines.
20. See, for example, Caves and Jones (1985, ch. 6).
21. Further interpretation can be given to this expression if one notes that the shadow return to the mobile factor in this framework is given by

$$r^* = r \sum_{j=1}^{n} \delta_j \frac{v_i^*}{v_j} T_j.$$

Then (7.19) can be written as

$$T_i = \frac{v_i}{v_i^*} \frac{r^*}{r}.$$

In a sense the deviation of the mobile factor's return from its shadow value (r^*/r) summarises the average level of distortion in the mobile factor market.

22. See, for example, van Wijnbergen (1981), Yusuf and Peters (1985), and Jung and Lee (1986). The first two studies generally find Korean investment does respond to variables open to government influence (e.g. extent of credit), and exports may be presumed to be affected by such investment. Jung and Lee study export performance explicitly and find a positive role for export subsidies and related incentives.

8

Export processing zones

Peter Warr

8.1   Introduction: Export processing zones and economic welfare

Since the mid-1960s, many less developed countries (LDCs) have implemented policies designed to stimulate exports of non-traditional manufactured goods. One form this 'export promotion' effort has taken is the establishment of export processing zones (EPZs). Many of these zones were constructed in the early 1970s and by the early 1980s around 35 existed in Asia alone, with an aggregate employment of at least a quarter of a million (United Nations, 1985). Globally, their importance was probably more than double this.

EPZs are special enclaves, outside a nation's normal customs barriers, within which investing firms, mostly foreign, enjoy favoured treatment with respect to imports of intermediate goods, company taxation, provision of infrastructure and freedom from industrial regulations applying elsewhere in the country. Although details vary, a universal feature is the almost complete absence of either taxation or regulation of imports of intermediate goods into the zones. These privileges are subject to the conditions that almost all of the output produced is exported and that all imported intermediate goods are utilised fully within the zones or re-exported.

This is an extended version of a paper published in edited form in *The World Bank Research Observer* (Warr, 1989). Thanks are due to the World Bank for allowing the material to be reproduced in this volume. The World Bank does not accept responsibility for the views expressed herein. The chapter has benefited from comments from W. M. Corden, Demetris Papageorgiou and Michael Selowsky. The author is responsible for the views presented and any errors.

Despite the large public investment required to establish an EPZ, perusal of government documents accompanying decisions to do so invariably reveals confusion about the economic effects that can be expected and their welfare significance. Much of this confusion is also present in the economic literature dealing with EPZs. The present chapter aims to clarify these matters and to draw out the crucial relationship between the benefits and costs of establishing EPZs and the overall trading regime of the country establishing them. The frame of reference is the economic welfare of citizens of the country establishing the zone. We begin with a simple theoretical analysis which is then illustrated by case studies drawn from four East Asian countries.

The economic activities occurring within EPZs have primarily been labour-intensive light manufacturing processes such as electronics assembly, garment production, assembly of light electrical goods, etc. A notable feature of the firms producing within the zones is their international mobility. Turnover is high and firms leaving an EPZ in one country often migrate to an EPZ in another, in which conditions are more favourable.

The 'footloose' character of firms operating within EPZs – their international mobility and capacity to adjust output rapidly in response to changing conditions – has been overlooked in most of the small amount of theoretical work that has appeared. This literature has drawn upon the classical Heckscher–Ohlin model of production for analysing the impact of EPZs.[1] Insofar as this analysis treats capital as being internationally mobile, it fails to capture the international mobility of capital goods which is central to the functioning of EPZs. The central conclusion of most of this literature – that EPZs are necessarily welfare-reducing for the countries establishing them – is heavily dependent on the Heckscher–Ohlin framework being used and is thus largely irrelevant for EPZs as they actually operate.

Empirical work on EPZs has also tended to overlook the footloose character of EPZ firms, leading to a misplaced preoccupation with the factor intensity of production within the zones. In an otherwise useful descriptive study of EPZs, Spinanger (1984, p. 65) writes that their establishment tends to produce positive welfare effects analogous to those resulting from a movement towards free trade because the elimination of tariffs and other distortions causes factor intensities of production 'to correspond more closely with the factor endowment of the host country'. This conception of an EPZ rests on the traditional assumption that capital is internationally immobile. It assumes implicitly that the capital used in the EPZ is domestic capital in fixed total supply, which has moved to the EPZ from elsewhere in the host country. Once this assumption is discarded, the factor intensity of production within

EPZs is of limited relevance for an assessment of the welfare impact of the zones.

Most of the economic literature on EPZs has been concerned with their benefits and costs, but has stopped short of formal benefit–cost analysis. The explanation is usually that the data on the zones under study are inadequate for the purpose. EPZs are closely monitored by host governments and, when compared with the data available for other public projects in LDCs, the statistical information is unusually complete. These data normally include detailed time series of zone exports, imports, employment, use of utilities, infrastructure and administrative costs, etc. What the empirical studies have lacked has been an analytical framework within which the benefits and costs of EPZs can be identified conceptually and quantified empirically.

Section 8.2 begins with some elaboration on the footloose character of EPZ firms. Section 8.3 provides a brief description of the incentive package and other facilities in a 'typical' EPZ. Section 8.4 describes the economic performance of EPZs in four Asian countries: Indonesia, Korea, Malaysia and the Philippines. Section 8.5 introduces a simple conceptual framework – the 'enclave model' – within which the benefits and costs of an EPZ can be analysed, and discusses the various components of such an analysis. This model is then applied in section 8.6, which presents the results of detailed benefit–cost analyses of the four Asian EPZs. Finally, section 8.7 discusses the relationship between EPZs and trade policy in general.

8.2   The economics of the footloose manufacturer

In its standard forms, international trade theory treats 'factors of production' – capital, labour, land – as immobile internationally but mobile domestically. In contrast, final commodities are considered mobile across as well as within international boundaries. EPZs exploit the international mobility of capital goods owned by internationally 'footloose' manufacturing firms. EPZs are essentially devices for attracting these firms and their capital equipment into the host country where these capital goods are combined with domestic labour – relatively immobile internationally – to produce traded goods which the firm exports. The firm tries to move its capital equipment to countries in which it can earn the highest rate of return.

In essence this process can be viewed as an indirect form of labour export. The foreign firm producing within the EPZ receives the services of domestic labour. In return, the domestic workers receive wages and some training. Not surprisingly, many of the countries establishing EPZs have also engaged in the direct export of temporary labour to the Middle East and elsewhere.[2] In the case of EPZs, the capital goods move where the labour is; with direct labour export, the movements are reversed.

A simple model to represent the international mobility of capital goods was recently developed by Jones (1980) and Caves and Jones (1985). An amended version of the Caves and Jones model is presented below in order to bring out the economic features which are most relevant for understanding EPZs.

The processing activity within the zone produces final traded goods using three kinds of inputs: traded intermediate inputs, capital goods and labour. The traded intermediate inputs include the electronic components, plastic casings, electrical circuitry, etc., used in producing electronic goods, and the textiles, buttons, cotton thread, etc., used in producing garments. The prices of these goods, the wages paid, and the return to the capital goods used are formally related by

$$Pj = \sum_i a_{ij} P_i + a_{Kj} R_j + a_{Lj} w \qquad (8.1)$$

where P_j is the price of the final goods j, P_i is the price of the intermediate input i, a_{ij}, a_{Kj} and a_{Lj} are the amounts of intermediate good i, capital goods and labour, respectively, required to produce a unit of good j, and w is the wage rate. These variables determine R_j, the rate of return to capital goods resulting from the production of good j in this country's EPZ.

It is convenient to define the value-added generated per unit of production of good j, V_j, by writing

$$V_j = P_j - \sum_i a_{ij} P_i \qquad (8.2)$$

and (8.1) now becomes

$$V_j = a_{Kj} R_j + a_{Lj} w \qquad (8.3)$$

Figure 8.1 now represents equation (8.3) for each of two countries, labelled 'poor' and 'rich'. In the rich country unit labour costs, $a_{Lj} w$, are higher than in the poor country, but unit requirements of capital goods, a_{Kj}, are lower. The rich country's schedule thus has a higher vertical intercept (unit labour costs), i.e. point B lies above point C, and a lower slope (unit capital good requirement) than the poor country's.

The footloose manufacturer moves to the country where the highest value of R_j can be realised and this is represented by the shaded surface in the diagram. When unit value-added is high, implying high rates of return to the capital goods specific to commodity j, the rich country is able to

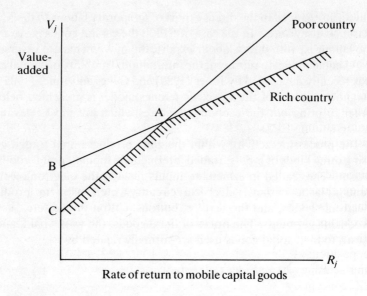

Figure 8.1 Movement of the footloose manufacturer.

attract the processing activity. In the rich country the scarce capital goods are used more efficiently – unit capital good requirements per unit of output are lower – and in this case unit labour costs are relatively unimportant. But if unit value-added falls, implying a squeeze on returns to its commodity-specific capital goods, unit labour costs become relatively more important. Below point A the process migrates to the poor country.

This chain of events is consistent with the 'product cycle' process identified by Vernon (1966). It suggests a gradual migration of newly developed manufacturing processes from rich countries – where scarce capital goods are used more efficiently – to poor countries – where unit labour costs are lower – as international competition forces the unit value-added generated by these processes downwards.

8.3 The economic environment of the EPZ

8.3.1 The economic background

In the early 1970s, Japan's relaxation of restrictions on investment abroad led to competition among Asian countries hoping to attract these and similar foreign investments. Light manufacturing activities, intensive in the use of unskilled and/or semi-skilled labour, were identified as targets. These are activities in which low-wage countries possess a potential cost advantage and which are capable of being transported internationally at low cost. The EPZ was an economic environment specially designed to attract these 'footloose' activities.

Most of the potential host countries already possessed protected manufacturing sectors and had experimented unsuccessfully with import substitution-based industrialisation policies. It was becoming clear that these inward-looking policies had discouraged export-oriented manufacturing and foreign investment. The potential gains of exchange earnings and employment creation from a more export-oriented strategy were being forgone.

Export processing zones appeared to provide the opportunity for some of the advantages of export promotion to be realised without threatening the position of the existing manufacturing and politically powerful manufacturing sectors. This provided the second major attraction of the EPZ concept: it left the protection of domestic industries intact. Export-oriented firms were offered an economic environment free of many of the barriers to trade and industrial regulations characterising the domestic environment, on condition that all their output was to be sold abroad. Production would take place within enclaves designed both to attract export-oriented light manufacturing firms and to shield domestic firms from competition.

8.3.2 *Characteristics of EPZs*

The detailed characteristics of EPZs vary, but four features are almost universal. The following account provides a simplified description of the 'typical' EPZ.

Duty-free import of raw materials

Raw materials required for the production of exports may be imported duty-free and without regard to any quantitative restrictions applying within the domestic economy. Products may be exported without payment of export taxes, sales duties, etc. EPZs may be physically located anywhere within the host country, but the processing activities undertaken within them occur 'outside' the country insofar as the jurisdiction of normal customs provisions is concerned.

Although goods produced within EPZs may not normally be sold within the domestic economy, when consignments are rejected by foreign buyers or fail to meet delivery deadlines, permission can be given for domestic sale. Sales of this kind simply displace imports which would have occurred from other sources and they usually attract normal customs duties.

EPZs firms' purchases of raw materials and intermediate goods from within the domestic economy are frequently subsidised in an attempt to encourage backward linkages between EPZ firms and the domestic economy. The subsidies, commonly called 'rebates' or 'drawbacks', are intended to counteract the effects of domestic protection. The rates of subsidy are in principle equal to the tax (import duty, excise tax, sales tax, etc.) component of the domestic prices of these goods. In the early 1970s it was hoped that linkages of this kind would generate substantial benefits to the local economy both because the social cost of producing these goods was below their market prices and because commercial contact between domestic suppliers and EPZ firms would benefit the former through 'technology transfer'.

Company income-tax holidays

Temporary exemptions from normal income-tax provisions are frequently offered, with an official duration of from three to ten years. It is common for EPZ firms to negotiate successfully for continuation of these tax holidays long beyond their official expiration by threatening to relocate in another country. Once relocated, the firm's tax-free holiday begins again.

The Philippines offers a generous schedule of deductions instead of income-tax holidays. Very little tax revenue has been raised from Philippines' EPZs because most firms declare overall trading losses.[3] Some firms have declared annual losses for over a decade while still producing and even expanding operations considerably. It is understood that vertically integrated firms utilise transfer pricing to relocate their profits internationally. Minimisation of global tax burdens and the avoidance of political risk are motives for this behaviour. The Philippines experience suggests that check-pricing methods to monitor transfer pricing are ineffective and that tax holidays are less important than they may appear.

Streamlined administration

EPZ firms are usually provided with streamlined customs documentation requirements for imported raw materials and capital goods and exported final products. A separate branch of the administration has often been created to mediate between EPZ firms and the government. The aim is to reduce EPZ firms' administrative costs and to prevent unnecessary and costly delays. The degree to which these bodies are empowered to act on behalf of the government varies, but other departments can resent interference with their 'normal' functions and become uncooperative with the EPZ bodies.

Regulations applying within the domestic economy but from which EPZ firms are exempted typically include: restrictions on foreign ownership of firms (EPZ firms are usually allowed to be fully foreign owned); restrictions on repatriation of profits; restrictions on the employment of foreign nationals in managerial, supervisory and technical roles; and requirements for special approvals for the importation and installation of labour-saving capital equipment. EPZ firms may also be granted access to the host country's allocation of import quotas. This is very important for garment producers wishing to export to the European Economic Community.

Superior physical infrastructure and subsidised utilities

An EPZ usually consists of a fenced area with a perimeter and gates policed by customs officials to prevent duty-free materials from being smuggled into the domestic economy. While infrastructure facilities such as roads, and telephone and telex communications are normally superior to those outside, they are generally inferior to those found in the industrial areas of developed countries.

Utilities are often subsidised. Electricity tariffs are especially important in this regard because light manufacturing enterprises are heavy users of electrical power. Rates charged within EPZs are frequently below, and never above, industrial rates elsewhere in the host country.

EPZs usually include standard-construction factory buildings, constructed and managed by government authorities, within which investing firms may rent floor space. Rental rates are generally lower than commerical industrial rates elsewhere within the country. Alternatively, firms may lease land within the zone and construct their own buildings. If they leave the zone, firms may sell or lease these buildings.

8.4 The economic record of EPZs in four Asian countries

8.4.1 *Aggregate economic performance*

This section summarises the results of detailed studies of EPZs in the following four Asian countries:

Indonesia: The Jakarta Export Processing Zone.
Korea: Tha Masan Free Export Zone.

Malaysia: The Penang Free Trade Zone.
Philippines: The Bataan Export Processing Zone.

These zones all began operations in the early 1970s. Each is the largest and longest-operating EPZ in the country concerned. This section draws on detailed case studies of these four zones previously conducted by the present author.[4]

Tables 8.1 to 8.4 summarise the aggregate economic performance of these four zones up to 1982. Among them, they employed roughly 90,000 people in 1982. This is not especially impressive, but these four zones are representative of many others in Asia with a total employment of at least three times this amount. The Indonesian zone is less representative of EPZs in general than the other three. It is small and has a number of unusual characteristics but is worthy of examination in that it was begun as an experimental project and, partly on the basis of its performance, the Indonesian government has decided to establish several more EPZs.

A feature of the zones not revealed by the tables is their industrial composition. In the earliest years of the zones garment production frequently dominates, but electronics assembly subsequently becomes more important. Indonesia and Malaysia are exceptions in that garments have always been the dominant industry in the former and electronics in the latter. These two industries are quite different. Garment production is generally far more labour-intensive and utilises a technology which has remained static for many years. Some production processes in electronics production and assembly are also labour-intensive, but generally both

Table 8.1   Indonesia: aggregate economic performance of Jakarta EPZ (1977–82).

Indicator	1977	1978	1979	1980	1981	1982
Number of firms	4	7	15	18	18	18
Number of persons employed	773	1,653	4,317	6,374	7,520	7,742
Value (millions of US dollars)						
Exports	0.9	12.8	5.9	18.7	28.7	37.5
Imports of raw materials	1.2	11.8	6.4	13.0	13.5	13.8
Local raw materials	0	0.01	0.6	1.9	5.2	9.5
Imports of capital goods	0.1	1.0	1.0	1.2	0.8	0.3
Local capital goods	0	0	0.03	0.01	0.03	0.01
Total official taxes	0.01	0.15	0.33	0.40	0.56	0.56
Estimated unofficial taxes	0.23	3.11	1.32	2.76	3.60	3.60
Percentage						
Local to total raw materials	0	0.80	9	13	28	41
Local to total capital goods	0	0	2.9	0.8	4.6	3.2

Note: All monetary quantities are in current prices.

Sources: Bonded Warehouses Indonesia, Jakarta; International Monetary Fund, *International Financial Statistics*, various issues; and Warr (1983).

Table 8.2 Korea: aggregate economic performance of Masan EPZ (1972–82).

Indicator	1972	1973	1974	1975	1976	1977	1978	1979	1980	1981	1982
Number of firms	70	115	110	105	99	99	97	94	88	89	83
Number of persons employed	7,072	21,240	20,822	22,248	29,615	28,401	30,960	31,153	28,532	28,016	26,012
Value (millions of US dollars)											
Exports	23.9	145.5	298.0	257.1	441.0	496.5	579.2	621.7	577.3	664.4	601.3
Local sales	0	0	6.2	7.9	25.2	28.1	81.7	90.7	82.5	99.0	92.1
Imports of raw materials	16.5	91.7	176.7	137.8	216.7	239.3	270.7	293.0	266.2	295.9	281.7
Local raw materials	1.0	23.1	48.6	44.6	92.7	120.0	130.0	149.4	131.3	144.0	142.7
Total wages and equipment	5.9	17.9	18.9	23.2	36.2	41.4	47.5	51.5	49.4	59.0	59.6
Total electricity used	0.2	1.3	2.3	2.0	3.4	3.8	4.5	4.8	4.5	5.1	5.3
Total taxes	0	1.44	1.79	1.55	1.71	1.50	1.85	1.78	1.74	2.31	2.17
Percentage of local to total raw materials	6	20	22	24	30	33	32	34	33	33	34

Note: All monetary quantities are in current prices.

Sources: Administration Office, Masan Free Export Zone, Masan; International Monetary Fund, *International Financial Statistics*, various issues; and Warr (1984a).

Table 8.3   Malaysia: aggregate economic performance of Penang EPZ (1972–82).

Indicator	1972	1973	1974	1975	1976	1977	1978	1979	1980	1981	1982
Number of firms	10	21	31	32	33	34	35	35	41	49	50
Number of persons employed	–	15,627	18,569	22,412	25,780	27,895	30,372	35,379	38,355	38,078	36,298
Value (millions of US dollars)											
Exports	2.1	53.6	94.2	192.2	274.3	226.1	591.5	1,085.2	972.9	717.5	714.9
Local sales	–	0.1	2.3	1.7	6.9	4.6	9.4	2.6	0.06	14.5	47.1
Imported raw materials	1.3	55.0	127.8	185.1	237.2	193.6	425.6	492.4	707.0	523.1	520.6
Local raw materials	0.07	0.9	2.8	7.1	6.7	10.5	13.3	14.5	14.5	16.9	22.8
Raw material from EPZs	–	–	–	5.8	12.0	13.1	40.3	64.5	76.6	48.9	82.3
Imported capital goods	0.4	13.4	54.7	29.7	9.5	15.2	120.0	53.9	36.6	36.7	36.6
Local capital goods	0	1.8	18.9	27.0	2.2	3.6	2.6	21.7	3.3	4.0	3.9
Total wages paid	0.9	6.3	5.2	14.0	17.4	25.0	43.2	56.6	72.3	80.5	83.4
Total electricity used	0.4	0.7	1.7	5.7	6.9	0	8.6	12.1	17.8	23.5	23.2
Total taxes paid	0	0	0	0	0	0	0.14	0.15	0.09	0.74	1.29
Percentage											
Local to total raw materials	5	2	2	4	3	5	3	3	2	3	4
Local to total capital equipment	0	12	26	48	19	19	18	29	8	10	10

– Not available.

Note: All monetary quantities are in current prices.

Sources: Penang Development Corporation, Penang; International Monetary Fund, *International Financial Statistics*, various issues; and Warr (1987b)

Table 8.4 The Philippines: aggregate economic performance of Bataan EPZ (1972–82).

Indicator	1972	1973	1974	1975	1976	1977	1978	1979	1980	1981	1982
Number of firms	1	5	14	16	39	38	47	51	51	52	52
Number of persons employed	–	1,298	3,321	5,502	8,962	12,821	17,495	18,877	19,204	19,858	19,410
Value (millions of US dollars)											
Exports	0.4	0.9	2.1	7.3	22.4	39.7	73.1	98.2	122.7	134.0	159.6
Local sales	–	3.9	6.8	4.3	11.7	13.6	14.8	16.5	13.3	8.2	5.0
Imports of raw materials	0.2	0.5	2.9	7.8	15.8	38.5	47.3	66.4	77.3	81.2	122.3
Local raw materials	0.07	0.2	0.3	0.8	4.2	9.9	3.8	7.9	9.5	7.4	8.5
Total wages paid	–	0.6	1.5	2.5	4.3	6.6	9.3	14.4	20.4	22.4	21.8
Total electricity used	–	0.1	0.3	0.5	0.7	0.9	1.2	1.6	1.5	1.7	1.6
Total taxes paid	–	–	0.07	0	0.4	0.6	1.5	2.2	1.9	1.7	1.4
Total domestic borrowings	1.8	22.8	61.4	117.8	85.9	89.4	3.3	2.8	2.3	1.9	1.5
Percentage of local to total raw materials	30	30	8	10	21	20	7	11	14	9	6

– Not available.

Note: All monetary quantities are in current prices.

Sources: Export Processing Zone Authority, Manila; International Monetary Fund, *International Financial Statistics*, various issues; and Warr (1985).

capital intensity and the rate of technological change are much higher than in garment production.

The data on total numbers of firms present in the zones in Tables 8.1 to 8.4 also fail to reveal the 'footloose' character of EPZ firms. The case of the Philippines' Bataan EPZ provides a good example. From Table 8.4, the total number of firms occupying the zone at the beginning of the years 1979 to 1982 remained almost constant, increasing from 51 to 52 firms during 1980. But during 1979, four firms entered the zone and four others left. In 1980, five entered and four left. During 1981, three entered and three left and during 1982, two entered and four left.

Aggregate data on export volumes and employment also disguise the high degree of year-to-year variation that characterises individual EPZ firms. Table 8.4 shows that between 1981 and 1982, total exports from the Bataan EPZ rose by 19 per cent. When the data are examined at the level of individual firms, exports rose in only 29 of the 52 firms which were present at the beginning of 1981 and declined in 26, including the three which left the zone during that year. The average increase in firm-level exports among the first group, weighted by exports in 1981, was 42 per cent, while the weighted average decline among the second group, excluding the three which left the zone, was 29 per cent. These large variations in output partly reflect the adjustments of the larger corporations to which EPZ firms belong, in response to perceived changes in demand for their products. But they also reflect the international relocations of production within these corporations, in response to perceived changes in the profitability of its firms in particular locations.

8.4.2   *Local raw material use and technology transfer*

When the zones were established one of the anticipated benefits was that EPZ firms would gradually increase their purchase of local raw materials and that the commercial contacts accompanying these backward linkages would benefit domestic firms through 'technology transfer'. However, except for Indonesia, where local textiles are purchased significantly by the zone's garment producers, local raw materials comprise no more than a third of total raw material use. In Malaysia, local raw materials comprise only a few per cent of total raw material use. Purchases of raw materials and intermediate goods produced by other EPZ firms is more than three times as important. In the Philippines, the share of local raw materials had declined to less than 10 per cent by 1982.

Managers of EPZ firms report that the main obstacle to purchase of local raw materials is their low and unreliable quality. Entire shipments of finished goods may be rejected if the raw materials or intermediate goods used were inferior. The changing industrial composition of the EPZs is another explanation for declining use of local raw materials. Garment and footwear manufacture uses a much higher proportion of local raw materials than electronics assembly. As the composition of the EPZ shifts towards electronics, the proportion of local raw materials declines.

Reluctance to rely upon local raw materials also derives from the global strategies of the corporations involved. Parent firms wish to preserve a high level of international mobility for their processing operations and developing long-term commercial relationships with local suppliers in the host countries does not serve this goal. Subsidies to local raw material purchases will end once the firm leaves the country, requiring it to find new suppliers elsewhere. If the corporation wishes to retain the capacity to relocate its processing activities internationally at short notice it is more expedient to purchase these inputs at the cheapest reliable international source.

It has generally come to be recognised that the 'technology transfer' initially hoped for has not occurred. Of course, many of the industries in EPZs possess no technology that is not universally available. Labour-intensive garment production is a good example. Those that do, of which electronics firms are the best example, guard this information carefully, even from their own workforces. Technical information is a valuable corporate asset and some of the firms' competitors are generally producing within the same EPZ. To hand technological knowledge to the locals is also to hand it to one's competitors. It is hardly surprising that valuable technological knowledge is not readily given away; it has to be purchased.

8.4.3 *Working conditions and wages*

Working conditions in EPZs have been widely criticised by writers from industrialised countries. This criticism has commonly rested on an exaggerated picture of harsh working conditions and low wages in EPZs contrasted with more favourable conditions in industrialised countries. This perspective is often combined with the claim that EPZ firms 'exploit' their workers and enjoy enormous profits, at the expense of potential employment in similar labour-intensive industries in the industrialised countries. This type of discussion has usually not reflected familiarity with the employment conditions and wages existing outside the EPZs in the developing countries concerned and has ignored the obvious fact that unless workers were better off being 'exploited' in an EPZ than otherwise, EPZ firms would find it impossible to hire.

Useful information on working conditions, wages and worker

characteristics in the Philippines' Bataan EPZ, and in similar industries elsewhere in that country, was provided by Castro (1982). Zone workers are typically female (74 per cent of total employment), unmarried with no previous factory experience (two-thirds of Castro's sample) and between the ages of 17 and 24 years. Turnover rates are high. The average duration of zone employment is around three years. Most of the workers in Castro's sample were temporarily absent members of larger households (average size six members) and the income of the zone worker represented roughly half the combined cash incomes of these households.

According to Castro's survey, almost half of all zone workers worked overtime and the average working week was 54 hours. Of those who had worked previously in paid employment, their average EPZ earnings were 35 per cent higher than these previous earnings. Castro concludes that there was a clear income gain from moving to a job in the EPZ.

Data provided in a survey conducted by the Philippines' Ministry of Trade and Industry[5] suggest that – allowing for differences in living costs – real wages of unskilled workers are roughly the same in the EPZ as in similar employment in the capital city. Real wages for skilled workers were somewhat higher in the EPZ. Whereas unskilled workers may be drawn from any part of the country, including rural areas, skilled workers must be recruited from the capital city, requiring a premium to attract them.

EPZ firms appear generally to adhere to minimum-wage laws, where these exist. Firms operating within the domestic manufacturing sector may often avoid these regulations but the greater visibility of EPZs and their politically sensitive position make violations of minimum-wage restrictions more difficult.

8.5   The enclave model and the welfare economics of EPZs

8.5.1   *The enclave model*

The benefits and costs resulting from an EPZ's existence, as experienced by citizens of the host country,[6] will now be considered. The aim is to compare the observed situation in which the zone is present with the hypothetical one in which it is absent. The foreign ownership of firms and the 'offshore' nature of the zones themselves suggest a simple framework within which their impact on the domestic economy can be analysed. This framework can be termed the 'enclave approach', following Corden (1974b and 1985). It is depicted in Figure 8.2.

Consider (1) the flows of goods and services and the financial flows which occur between the EPZ and the rest of the world, and (2) the flows

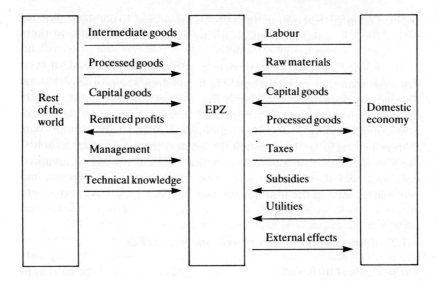

Figure 8.2 The enclave model.

occurring between the EPZ and the host country. The essence of the enclave approach is that flows of the second kind are relevant to the evaluation of the welfare impact of the zone on citizens of the host country but that flows of the first kind are not.

EPZ firms purchase intermediate and capital goods from abroad and these flows are accompanied by financial flows in foreign currency in the opposite direction.[7] In vertically integrated firms these transactions occur within the firm, giving rise to questions of transfer pricing. The firm may also repatriate profits to parent companies abroad. The thrust of the enclave approach is that all these transactions between the EPZ firms and the outside world are irrelevant for an evaluation of the effects of the zone on economic welfare within the host country, except insofar as they impinge on linkages between the EPZ and the domestic economy.

The issue of transfer pricing provides a good illustration. Suppose there is no company income taxation applying to EPZ firms within the host country – an accurate assumption for many countries possessing EPZs. Transfer pricing influences whether a firm's profits will be realised, in accounting terms, in the host country or elsewhere. But, so long as these profits are earned by the (foreign) EPZ firm, whether they are realised in the host country or abroad, and whether they are repatriated or retained by the EPZ subsidiary, is essentially irrelevant for economic welfare in the host country. But now, if these profits are subject to domestic taxation within the host country, transfer pricing affects the magnitude of these taxes and becomes highly relevant.

The economic environment existing within an EPZ is generally less distorted than that existing elsewhere in the domestic economy. Nevertheless, this does not in itself imply that the net outcome of the real and financial flows represented in Figure 8.2 necessarily raises welfare in the host country. Only a detailed examination of the benefits and costs involved can resolve this question. In the next section we discuss each of the main forms of economic linkage between EPZ firms and the domestic economy and its welfare significance. This discussion explains the procedures used in the four benefit–cost analyses presented next.

8.5.2   *Components of a benefit–cost analysis of EPZs*

Firms' profits and losses

Most firms occupying EPZs are foreign owned. Their profits or losses, to the extent that they are retained or incurred by the firms themselves, do not enter our calculations directly. The *domestically* owned portion of profits and losses, if any, properly belongs in a national economic evaluation of the zone but these profits can seldom be estimated satisfactorily from the available data. To the extent that they are collected, data on firms' profits and losses are unreliable but suggest that if the profits of domestic firms were to be measured accurately they would comprise only a minuscule proportion of the overall benefits from EPZs.

In the benefit–cost analysis component of this study, firms in the zones will be treated, for the most part, as if they were fully foreign owned. Therefore, the profits of domestically owned firms will be omitted. This is generally unavoidable, given data limitations, but in view of the small proportion of overall investment in the EPZs that these firms typically represent, this omission is minor.

Foreign-exchange earnings

Public discussion of the benefits of EPZs has placed considerable stress on the foreign-exchange earnings derived from the zones. This discussion has tended to reflect the presumption that these earnings have direct welfare relevance for the host country. For example, the possible effect that the transfer pricing practices of multinational corporations may have on the country's foreign-exchange earnings from the zones has been widely discussed. But to a first order of approximation the foreign-exchange earnings of foreign-owned EPZ firms merely constitute transactions between these firms and firms abroad. These transactions have no direct effects on the economic welfare of domestic nationals and are therefore irrelevant for the calculation of the host country's net gain from the EPZ.

It must be realised that, regardless of the difference between a firm's officially declared exports and imports for a given year, the corresponding amount of foreign exchange remains the property of the firm itself (leaving possible taxation aside for the moment). It would be incorrect to call this amount the host country's foreign-exchange earnings. These funds may be treated in three ways:

1. They can be held in liquid form in foreign-exchange accounts, whether inside or outside the host country.
2. They can be used for the purchase of imported capital equipment.
3. They can be converted into the domestic currency to be spent on wages and purchases from the local economy.

Item 1 is of little welfare importance and reduces to a decision as to where the firm chooses to do its banking. Item 2 can also be disregarded if the imported capital equipment is ultimately disposed of abroad or scrapped. Item 3 does have welfare importance because there may be a net benefit to the host country from these purchases. Thus, providing these benefits are estimated separately, the foreign-exchange earnings of EPZ firms are not in themselves important.

To purchase domestic raw materials and services from the domestic economy and to hire local workers, EPZ firms must convert sufficient foreign-exchange earnings into the domestic currency. This is done through the central bank at the official exchange rate. The question therefore arises whether the social value of the foreign exchange received by the host country's central bank exceeds the value of the domestic currency the firms are given in exchange.

The value of the foreign exchange received must be understood to mean the domestic value of the additional traded goods and services the host country may absorb as a result of the addition to its foreign-exchange holdings. The value of the domestic currency given in exchange to EPZ firms means the domestic value (opportunity cost) of the domestic factors of production and intermediate goods and services purchased by EPZ firms with these funds. In the circumstances where exchange controls and domestic protection imply that the social value of foreign exchange in terms of the domestic currency exceeds the official exchange rate, the requirement that these currency conversions must be made through the central bank at the official exchange rate constitutes, in effect, a form of taxation.

It is helpful to think of this calculation in two separate steps. The first step is the calculation of the value in domestic currency of the additional traded goods the host country is able to absorb as a result of foreign currency received from EPZ firms relative to the amount of domestic currency given up. This ratio is equivalent to the shadow price of foreign exchange divided by the official exchange rate. The second step is the calculation of the social opportunity cost of the domestic factors and intermediate goods purchased by the firms relative to the market prices of these items, also in domestic currency. This part of the calculation, involving the shadow prices of domestic factors and raw materials, is best handled separately.

Of course, the firms' true foreign-exchange earnings will presumably differ from their conversion of foreign exchange into domestic currency. Transfer pricing may be one of the mechanisms by which this profit is realised, but for an *ex post* measurement of the host country's actual gains, the firm's actual foreign-exchange conversion is the relevant statistic.

Employment

Host-country governments' concern for the employment generated by the zone presumably reflects the view that the social benefits derived from generating an additional job outweigh the costs. In economic terms, therefore, the wage received by the worker is considered to exceed the social opportunity cost of employment in the zone. Difficulty arises when attempting to measure the relevant opportunity cost. Wages paid in the zones are normally equal to, or slightly above, wages paid in comparable employment outside the EPZ. Nevertheless, estimates of the social opportunity cost (shadow price) of unskilled and semi-skilled labour commonly suggest that it is less than wages paid in the manufacturing sector.

Such estimates can be found for most LDCs. A difficulty in applying these estimates arises in relation to the transfer of skills to EPZ employees. Their estimated value could in principle be incorporated either by reducing the estimated parameter of the opportunity costs of labour, or by increasing appropriately the wage-received parameter. But, in the absence of detailed estimates of the value of these transfers there is no solid basis for making such an adjustment. Consequently, some arbitrariness cannot be avoided.

Technology transfer

Zone administrators generally agree that significant transfers of technology and skills from EPZ firms to the domestic economy have seldom occurred. Those firms possessing technological knowledge from which local firms could benefit (most notably electronics and electrical firms) have been isolated from the domestic economy. Little of their raw materials and capital equipment has come from local sources. Nevertheless, these backward linkages had been cited as a major potential source of technology transfer. In retrospect, the earlier expectations were naive. To the extent that intermediate products are internationally traded, EPZ firms should be expected to continue to purchase from the cheapest source which is reliable as to delivery date and quality.

Managerial techniques and methods of product quality control are inevitably transferred to the local middle-level managers employed by EPZ firms. These managers can eventually obtain significantly higher salaries in domestic industry than they could have after a similar period of employment elsewhere. This suggests that the managerial training they have received confers a benefit to the domestic economy. This may not be fully captured in the wages these workers receive in the EPZs. One way of treating this is to say that the social opportunity cost of the employment of these workers in the EPZ is lowered by such training. These externality effects can be incorporated in principle by adjusting (downwards) the parameter of the opportunity cost of labour.

Domestic sales

Almost all of the output of EPZs must be sold abroad, but domestic sales are sometimes permitted when, for example, finished consumer goods are rejected by foreign buyers. These sales are typically treated as imports into the host country and duty must be paid at the normal rate. They substitute for imports which would otherwise have occurred. The net value to the host country of the goods consumed is the value at c.i.f. prices of the imports which are displaced, but this is also the net price actually paid to the EPZ firm for the goods. The net price paid is the tariff-inclusive domestic price minus the duty. Thus, as these sales have no net welfare effects, they can be ignored in the benefit–cost analysis.

Purchase of domestic raw materials and capital goods

Governments typically encourage the use of domestically produced raw materials, intermediate inputs and capital goods by EPZ firms. This can be interpreted as meaning that governments believe that prices paid by firms for these materials exceed the marginal social costs of supplying them. Locally produced raw materials and capital goods generally compete with imported substitutes and the rates of duty applied to these imports provide the basis for estimation of the difference between the social opportunity cost of providing these imports (their border c.i.f. prices) and the prices paid (tariff inclusive). When EPZ firms receive a rebate (drawback) from the host government equivalent to the duty which would have been paid on these imported inputs, there remains no net welfare effect from their purchase by EPZ firms.

Electricity use

EPZ firms, especially garment and textile producers, are major users of electricity. The benefit–cost analysis must compare the tariff rates paid with estimates of the long-run marginal cost (LRMC) of supplying additional power. If the average tariff exceeded the LRMC, the use of electricity by EPZ firms would entail a net tax. In the reverse case, there would be a net subsidy.

Domestic borrowing

One of the inducements sometimes offered to foreign investors has been the freedom to borrow on local capital markets, sometimes combined with government guarantees of the repayment of these loans. Local borrowing would be unimportant if the capital markets of the host country were open to international capital flows. These loans would then simply induce private capital inflows from abroad and would not displace local investment. However, when local capital markets are closed, and interest rates deliberately suppressed, the analysis is quite different. This combination of factors is common among Latin American countries (Diaz-Alejandro, 1970) and also occurs in the Philippines.

The implication of the suppression of domestic interest rates is that the value of domestic output forgone as a result of additional borrowings by (foreign) firms operating in an EPZ exceeds the value of the compensation ultimately received from these firms in the form of interest and principal repayments. Another way of stating this is that the shadow price of capital exceeds its market price.

Taxes

While taxes raised from EPZ firms are generally quite small, they nevertheless represent a clear source of economic benefit for the domestic economy. They would not be received if the firms were not present. Firms that transfer to the zones from elsewhere in the host country, or foreign firms that would have entered even if the zones were not present, are exceptions, but seem certain to be unimportant. Most investment is foreign and, according to firm managers, very few of these firms would have entered the host countries in the absence of the package of incentives represented by the EPZs: The full value of taxes received is therefore counted as a net benefit to the host country.

The low rates of company income tax offered by host-country governments to attract foreign firms into the EPZs sometimes achieve this goal. In the case of firms that would have located in the country without these tax incentives, they result in a shift of tax revenue from the host country to elsewhere, usually the firm's parent country. Despite this, an *ex post* evaluation of the EPZ must look at the actual amount of revenue raised.

Development and recurrent costs

The establishment of the zone site, its maintenance and administration all represent economic costs and in principle should be evaluated at shadow prices. Reliance on financial costs is to some extent inevitable in the absence of disaggregated data. Against these costs must be placed the payments made for land leasing and any other charges levied on zone firms, not counted elsewhere in the analysis.

8.5.3 Net benefits from an EPZ

It is now possible to present a simplified algebraic expression for the net economic benefit derived from an EPZ, evaluated from the point of view of the host country. In a given year, t, the net benefit can be written

$$N_t = (L_t w + M_t P_M + E_t P_E + R_t + T_t) S_F^*$$
$$- (L_t w^* + M_t P_M^* + E_t^* P_E^* + B_t S_K^*) - A_t - K_t \tag{8.4}$$

where: L_t denotes employment in year t;
$\quad w$ denotes wage paid;
$\quad M_t$ denotes domestic raw material used in year t;
$\quad P_M$ denotes the price paid for this raw material;
$\quad E_t$ denotes the utilities (e.g. electricity) used in year t;
$\quad P_E$ denotes the price paid for these utilities;
$\quad R_t$ denotes interest and principal repayments of domestic loans in year t;
$\quad T_t$ denotes taxes paid in year t;
$\quad S_F^*$ denotes the ratio of the social value of foreign exchange to the official exchange rate;
$\quad w^*$ denotes the shadow price of labour;

P_M^* denotes the shadow price of domestic raw material;

P_E^* denotes the shadow price of utilities;

B_t denotes domestic borrowing in year t;

S_K^* denotes the ratio of the shadow price of capital to its market price;

A_t denotes the administrative costs of the zone in year t;

K_t denotes the capital cost (including maintenance) of the physical infrastructure of the EPZ provided by the host government in year t.

For simplicity of notation, the above expression assumes all market and shadow prices to be constant over time.

The first bracketed term represents the payments made by the EPZ firm to employ labour, purchase raw materials and electricity, to repay domestic loans and to pay taxes. Sufficient foreign exchange must be converted to domestic currency, at the official exchange rate, to finance these payments. This accounts for the term S_F^* outside the brackets, the ratio of the social value of foreign exchange to the official exchange rate.

The second bracketed term represents the social opportunity cost of the labour, raw materials, utilities and financial capital absorbed by the EPZ firms. The final two terms, A_t and K_t, denote the administrative and construction costs of the zone. During the construction of the zone these may be the only non-zero items. The net present value of the zone is then calculated by discounting N_t over the life of the zone.

8.6   Benefits and costs of EPZs: Evidence from four Asian countries

In this section the results of detailed benefit–cost analyses of EPZs conducted for each of the four Asian countries discussed earlier are summarised. First (section 8.6.1), the basis for the cost–benefit analyses is summarised, particularly the sources of the shadow prices used. Next (section 8.6.2), the results of the benefit–cost analyses are presented, and these results are then compared and analysed in section 8.6.3.

8.6.1   Sources of shadow prices

Estimates of the shadow prices of labour; foreign exchange, capital, etc., are available for most developing countries. Their quality varies widely. In some cases, they lie buried in consultants' reports, government studies and other unpublished manuscripts. The best available estimates of the major shadow prices and other relevant parameters for each country were as follows:

Indonesia: Hughes (1983), Pitt (1981) and Munasinghe (1980).
Korea: Koo (1981) and Nam (1981a,b).
Malaysia: Veitch (1977, 1979 and 1984).
Philippines: Medalla and Power (1984) and Manalaysay (1979).

The above studies provided the basis for the shadow prices, but variations were made in some cases to update or correct the estimates they contain or to amend them to a form more suitable for the evaluation of EPZs. In several cases uncertainty remains in the estimates of the relevant shadow prices, so a range of values was used. We summarise below the values used for the most important shadow prices in the 'base case' calculations. These are the seemingly 'most likely' values in each case. They are summarised in Table 8.5 as ratios of the estimated shadow prices to market prices.

8.6.2   *Results of the benefit–cost analyses*

Table 8.6 summarises the contributions of each of the major benefit–cost categories to the calculated aggregate net present value (NPV) of the EPZs. Costs appear as negative items. For consistency, the calculations each assume a real discount rate of 7.5 per cent and a total life for the EPZ of 25 years. The final row of Table 8.6 displays the calculated internal rate of return (IRR) for each of the EPZs. Table 8.7 presents the NPV computations in somewhat more convenient form by expressing the various components as a percentage of the *gross* benefits of the EPZ (the sum of all positive NPV items appearing in Table 8.6).

8.6.3   *Components of computed net benefits and costs*

A methodological digression on foreign exchange earnings

Before discussing the results in Tables 8.6 and 8.7 in detail it is useful to focus attention on a methodological point: the distinction between the benefits deriving from 'foreign-exchange earnings' and those deriving from other sources. As explained above, the benefits attributed to

Table 8.5   Estimated ratios of shadow prices to market prices: four Asian countries.

Category	Indonesia	Korea	Malaysia	Philippines
Labour	0.75	0.91	0.83	0.64
Foreign exchange	1.00[a]	1.08	1.11	1.25
Domestic raw material	0.85	0.92	0.90	0.96
Domestic capital equipment	0.85	0.98	0.91	0.96
Electricity	1.05	1.33	0.93	1.30
Domestic financial capital	n.a.	n.a.	n.a.	1.58

n.a. Not applicable.

[a] Hughes (1983) concluded that the effects of Indonesia's import barriers (tariffs and quotas), which raise domestic prices above border prices, and subsidies on the consumption of traded goods (such as rice and petroleum products) roughly cancelled, implying that the shadow price of foreign exchange was approximately equal to the official rate.

Sources: Indonesia: Hughes (1983), Pitt (1981) and Munasinghe (1980). Korea: Koo (1981) and Nam (1981a, 1981b). Malaysia: Veitch (1977, 1979, and 1984). Philippines: Medalla and Power (1984) and Manalaysay (1979).

foreign-exchange earnings arise from the fact that EPZ firms must convert foreign exchange into domestic currency to meet their domestic costs. These costs include their wage bills, purchases of domestic raw materials and capital equipment, taxes, utility bills, factory rentals, etc.

It is analytically possible to separate the net gains arising from the conversion of foreign exchange into domestic currency from those arising from the subsequent domestic payments, as reflected in Tables 8.6 and 8.7. Alternatively, the two can be combined, and it makes economic sense to do so. Indirectly, foreign exchange is being paid to domestic workers, raw-material suppliers, etc. The separation of the benefits deriving from 'foreign-exchange earnings' from those arising from the subsequent domestic payments is somewhat artificial and potentially misleading.

Consider a hypothetical example: the conversion of US$1m. into Philippines pesos at the official (1982) exchange rate of P9.17 = US$1 for the payment of local wages. When the US$1m. is converted into pesos, there is a net gain to the Philippines arising from the difference between the official exchange rate and the shadow price of foreign exchange – the social value of this foreign exchange. The estimated value of 1.25 for the ratio of the shadow price to the official rate implies a net gain of P2.29m. Now when the P9.17m. is paid to Philippine workers there is a second net gain arising from the difference between the social opportunity cost of labour and the market wage. The estimated value of 0.64 for the ratio of these two sources of gain arises from the way our shadow prices have been

Table 8.6 Welfare impact of EPZs: net present value for four Asian countries (millions of 1982 US dollars).

Category	Indonesia	Korea	Malaysia	Philippines
Employment	4	39	111	59
Foreign exchange earnings	0	65	94	72
Local raw materials	5	16	18	3
Local capital equipment	0	0	10	0
Taxes and other revenue	23	18	10	11
Electricity use	−1	−13	−53	−4
Administrative costs	−13	−17	−4	−23
Infrastructure costs and subsidies	−3	−68	−43	−196
Domestic borrowing	0	0	0	−147
Total net present value	15	40	143	−225
Internal rate of return (percent)	26	15	28	−3

Table 8.7 Composition of net present value: four Asian countries (per cent of gross benefits).

Category	Indonesia	Korea	Malaysia	Philippines
Employment	13	28	46	41
Foreign exchange earnings	0	47	39	50
Local raw materials	16	12	7	2
Local capital equipment	0	0	4	0
Taxes and other revenue	72	13	4	8
Electricity use	−3	−9	−22	−3
Administrative costs	−41	−12	−2	−16
Infrastructure costs and subsidies	−9	−49	−18	−135
Domestic borrowing	0	0	0	−101
Total	47	29	59	−155

defined. But the two are aspects of the one phenomenon: the (indirect) payment of US$1m. to hire domestic workers. Philippine workers are indirectly earning for the Philippines US$1m. in foreign exchange, generating a net gain to the Philippines of P4.59m.[8]

Table 8.8 now shows the re-estimated distribution of net benefits taking the above argument into account. This table substitutes for the first five rows of Table 8.7. The gains from 'foreign-exchange earnings' have been redistributed among the other benefit–cost categories. The results for Indonesia are unchanged from Table 8.7 because the estimated net gains from foreign-exchange earnings were zero in that case (see footnote to Table 8.5). The percentage totals do not add to 100 because only part of the firms' foreign-exchange conversions can be attributed to the four categories appearing in the table.

Table 8.8 Composition of net present value with foreign exchange earnings distributed: four Asian countries (per cent of gross benefits).

Category	Indonesia	Korea	Malaysia	Philippines
Employment	13	55	68	69
Local raw materials	16	14	15	3
Local capital equipment	0	0	8	0
Taxes and other revenue	72	14	5	9

Benefits

We shall discuss first the composition of the estimated benefits from EPZs (the positive elements of Tables 8.6 to 8.8) and then turn to the cost items. Since the results for Indonesia require special explanation it is convenient to begin with the results for the other three countries.

From Table 8.7 it is clear that the major sources of gain in Korea, Malaysia and the Philippines derive from employment and foreign-exchange earnings. With the gain from foreign-exchange earnings distributed as in Table 8.8, employment accounts for more than half the gross benefits in each case. Local raw material use and tax revenue are of much smaller importance and across the three countries the overall importance of these two sources of gain is roughly similar. For these three countries, it is a useful approximation to say that the EPZs represent a form of indirect labour export; other sources of benefit are of minor importance.

Turning to the result for Indonesia, two unusual features must be stressed. First, an unusually high proportion of raw materials is obtained within Indonesia. These are primarily Indonesian textiles used in garments. By 1982 over 40 per cent of all raw materials used were purchased from within Indonesia. The estimated net gains from this source actually outweigh the estimated net gains from employment generation.

The second unusual feature is the importance of the 'tax and other revenue' category. The composition of the US$22.6m net gain from this source appearing in Table 8.6 is: property tax $2.9m.; other official taxes $0.9m.; 'unofficial' taxes $25.9m.; and expenditure on the drawback scheme –$7.1m.[9] The 'unofficial' tax item, discussed in detail elsewhere (Warr, 1983; Gray, 1979), represents the outcome of rent-seeking behaviour by government officials.

Although it seems appropriate to include the 'unofficial' tax item as a net benefit to Indonesia, it is important to draw attention to it both because of what it reveals about the way the net benefits from the zone are distributed among individuals, and also because the collection of these rents is achieved at considerable social cost. A labyrinth of regulations and a highly 'personalised' administration of both these regulations and the normal customs provisions provide the opportunity for heavy costs to be imposed on uncooperative firms. The outcome is a somewhat wasteful form of revenue collection. If these revenues are excluded from the benefit–cost analysis, the NPV of $15m. appearing in Table 8.6 becomes −$11m., and the IRR becomes negative (Warr, 1983).

The $7.1m. expenditure on the 'drawback' scheme is a subsidy to the use of domestic raw material. This is intended to counteract the effects of protection on the costs of the imported items used in the production of these raw materials. Insofar as the estimated net gain from the use of these raw materials is smaller than this amount ($4.9m), it appears that the 'drawback' provisions are costing Indonesia more than they are worth.

Costs

The costs of achieving the benefits discussed above are summarised by the negative elements of Tables 8.6 and 8.7. In Table 8.7 they are expressed as a percentage of the sum of all net benefit items. The striking features of this table are the enormous infrastructure cost of the Philippines' Bataan EPZ and also the heavy cost resulting from the granting to EPZ firms of (subsidised) access to the Philippine capital market. Either of these items is itself large enough to outweigh the sum of all benefits derived by the Philippines from its EPZ.

Another feature of Table 8.7 is the low administrative and infrastructure cost of Malaysia's Penang Free Trade Zone. On the other hand, it is notable that the cost of Malaysia's subsidisation of electricity effectively outweighs the combined benefits derived from the use of local raw materials and local capital equipment and all tax revenues raised from EPZ firms.

8.7 Summary and conclusion: EPZs and trade policy

EPZs are vehicles for attracting foreign investment in export-oriented, light manufacturing. At the time the zones were becoming popular, in the early 1970s, the governments establishing them almost invariably mentioned three objectives for the zones: foreign-exchange earnings, employment and technology transfer. The competition among host countries for 'footloose' processing activities meant than individual countries generally found it more difficult than they had expected to attract this kind of investment. Nevertheless, to the extent that firms were attracted, the first two objectives of the zones were met.

The zones have contributed significantly to the employment of unskilled and semi-skilled workers. Moreover, the conversions of foreign exchange into the domestic currency that were necessary to pay these workers contributed to the host countries' foreign-exchange earnings. Indirectly, EPZ workers were being paid in foreign exchange and in this respect EPZs were similar to the direct export of labour. Many of the countries establishing EPZs have also been exporting temporary labour directly, to the Middle East in particular.

The EPZs are generally isolated from the domestic economy. The substantial gains from 'technology transfer' that were initially sought have not occurred. It had been hoped that the commercial contacts between EPZ firms and domestic firms that would accompany backward linkages from the zones to the domestic economy would lead to externalities of this sort, to the benefit of domestic firms. However, the use of domestic raw materials by EPZs has not been significant, and these linkages have generally been in areas where 'technology transfer' is not particularly likely.

EPZ firms have made little contribution to tax revenue. This has been equally true in countries which have granted company income-tax holidays and those which have not. In the latter case (e.g. the Philippines) transfer pricing practices have been used to minimise the firms' global tax burdens. Many firms have declared operating losses every year for over a decade while expanding production. In those countries where tax holidays have been granted, the threat to leave the EPZ has enabled firms to extend the holidays well beyond their official expiration dates.

The example of the Philippines shows that the limited benefits from EPZs can be extremely costly. The Philippines' first and largest EPZ, the Bataan EPZ, was a vehicle for regional decentralisation. The infrastructure costs of constructing an EPZ in the isolated site chosen were very high. Moreover, to attract foreign firms into the zone, the government granted EPZ firms preferential access to the Philippines' capital market at suppressed interest rates and with government guarantees of the loans. Not surprisingly, most of the firms' investments in the zone – over 90 per cent – were financed in this way (Warr, 1985, 1987a). The subsidy that was implicit in this policy led to a heavy social cost for the Philippines.

In contrast, the example of Malaysia shows that EPZs can be established and operated at relatively low cost. The Malaysian and Korean examples show that, viewed as public investments, EPZs can yield acceptable social rates of return. Of course, in these benefit–cost calculations all other policy instruments, and in particular all other instruments of trade policy, are held constant. It is possible to look at the EPZs in this partial manner, but this exercise raises the question of whether it would have been possible to achieve the benefits available from EPZs in another, more cost-effective way.

Export processing zones always permit the duty-free importation of raw materials and intermediate goods. In recent years, several of the countries that established EPZs in the 1970s have extended this provision to firms producing for export but located outside the EPZs. The duty-free raw materials are held in bond on the factory site until required for production. The Philippines, Malaysia and Korea each provide good examples. This change of policy undermined the advantages of EPZs to some extent and showed that construction of expensive special zones was not necessary for the duty-free characteristic of EPZs to be made available to other firms, whether producing for export or not.

Duty-free importation of raw materials and intermediate goods is not the only attraction of EPZs. Reduced 'red tape', through the simplification of customs procedures, clarification or elimination of regulations, and the upgrading of industrial infrastructure are also important. There is no necessity to confine these provisions to EPZs. A point that managers of foreign firms mention frequently is the importance of stable and clear policies to attract foreign investment. This obviously applies as much outside the EPZs as within. Most of the features that have enabled EPZs to attract foreign investment could be applied outside the zones, with similar effectiveness, and without establishing new special enclaves.

The features of the domestic economy which impede foreign investment, and which EPZs are intended partly to counteract, also impede the development of efficient domestic industries. To the extent that a liberalised environment within the EPZs deflects attention from these matters, the net outcome could be worse than what would have occurred in the absence of the zones.

The benefits from EPZs are limited. They are definitely not 'engines of development'. For countries in the early stages of development, the zones can provide an efficient and productive means of absorbing surplus labour. Even then, the zones could never be expected to provide more than a modest part of the solution to the vast employment problems of these countries. EPZs also expose the domestic business community to examples of internationally competitive industrial enterprises and this demonstration effect is undoubtedly valuable, especially in the early stages of industrialisation, as are the externalities arising from the on-the-job training of local middle-level managers. In the early 1970s, when the zones were being founded, high expectations were often voiced for these kinds of external benefits. It is difficult to assemble hard evidence on these matters but close observers of EPZs, including zone administrators themselves, generally consider that these expectations have been only partially realised at best.

As industrial development proceeds, and the surplus labour which characterised the earlier stages of industrialisation is absorbed, interest in EPZs tends to wane. Taiwan and Korea, having been pioneers in the establishment of EPZs in the late 1960s and early 1970s, have more recently become considerably less interested in this type of enclave development. Perhaps in the next couple of decades a similar change of attitude can be expected in many of the LDCs now actively promoting EPZs. Other LDCs, currently thought of as being pre-industrial, will presumably replace them.

The success of the liberal economic environment existing within EPZs says a great deal about the nature of the economic environment outside the zones in the countries establishing them. In cases where EPZs have been successful in attracting new foreign investment, earning foreign exchange, generating employment, etc., two kinds of lessons can be drawn. Within a partial context, something is revealed about the utility of the export processing zone concept itself: EPZs can make a limited contribution to economic development, especially in the early stages of industrialisation. But within a broader context, something more important is revealed about the degree to which restraints on trade, unnecessary bureaucracy and restrictive regulations have inhibited and continue to inhibit economic activity outside the zones: the very success of EPZs points to the benefits that a more liberal economic environment could make possible within the domestic economy. It may well be that this demonstration of the economic gains that could be achieved from a more general liberalisation is the most significant contribution that EPZs can make to the development process.

Notes

1. See Hamada (1974), Rodriguez (1976), Hamilton and Svensson (1982). Hamilton and Svensson (1983) is a partial exception to this description. See also Balasubramanyam (1988) for a useful discussion of this literature.
2. Examples in East and South East Asia include Korea, the Philippines, Thailand and Indonesia.
3. For example, the proportions of firms in the Philippines' Bataan EPZ (discussed in section 8.4) who declared overall trading losses in their annual financial statements were: 1980, 58 per cent; 1981, 81 per cent; 1982, 75 per cent; and 1983, 64 per cent (Warr, 1985, p. 12).
4. These case studies are: Indonesia, Warr (1983); Korea, Warr (1984a); Malaysia, Warr (1987b); and the Philippines, Warr (1985, 1987a). Readers wishing more detail on individual cases may refer to these studies.

5. Details are provided in Warr (1985).
6. Our discussion will disregard income distributional considerations within the host country.
7. To keep Figure 8.2 simple these financial flows are not indicated in the diagram. Most of the flows shown in the diagram are accompanied by financial flows in the opposite direction, but exceptions are taxes and subsidies and external effects such as transfers of managerial and technical knowledge.
8. The aggregate welfare outcome for the Philippines would have been essentially no different if the US$1m. had been paid directly to Philippine workers who then converted it into the domestic currency through the Central Bank.
9. The negative sign draws attention to the fact that this item is a revenue outlay – a subsidy – rather than a tax receipt.

PART 3
Case studies in export promotion

9

Export promotion strategy and economic development in Korea

Chong-Hyun Nam

9.1 Introduction

Few would question Korea's outstanding success in its drive to achieve rapid economic growth and industrialisation ever since it adopted an outward-oriented trade strategy in the early 1960s. But many seem to question – both inside and outside Korea – whether such a phenomenal success has been made possible because of, or in spite of, a very activist role of government both in trade and investment activities throughout most of its recent economic development period.

Until very recently, for instance, domestic markets remained rather highly protected in a supposedly outward-oriented economy, and during the 1970s, the government was actively involved in promoting the so-called heavy and chemical industries (HC industries henceforth),[1] with package assistance programmes for these 'strategic' industries. So a very complex system of trade and industrial incentives has been at work in Korea. We may distinguish three categories: incentives for import substitution, incentives for export promotion, and incentives for the promotion of specific industries (perhaps both for import substitution and export promotion simultaneously).

This chapter attempts to identify the major trade and industrial incentives that have been at work in Korea for the past three decades or so, and to evaluate their effects on economic as well as industrial development. We will then be able to derive major lessons from these experiences.

9.2 Trade and industrial policies, and industrial transformation: A brief overview (1954–86)

Korea is a relatively small country in terms of area (97,000 km^2) but is one of the world's most densely populated countries, standing only next to Bangladesh. The land is mostly mountainous with less than a quarter being arable. Korea's mineral resource endowment is also extremely poor with no known oil reserves. Furthermore, at the end of the war in 1953, Korea was left devastated with virtually no industrial base.

Korea is endowed, however, with a relatively well-educated and industrious labour force which is often referred to as Korea's only major resource. Indeed, the labour force was a major factor behind the outstanding economic performance of export-led growth based on the manufacturing of labour-intensive products. This 'success story' has been studied extensively and is now well known.

Table 9.1 provides basic data on the overall economic performance for the 1954–86 period. As can be seen, real GNP in Korea increased more than ninefold between 1954 and 1986, with an average annual growth rate of 6.9 per cent. The growth performance was not even, however, over this period. Real GNP grew at an average annual rate of 8.1 per cent for the last two decades (1964–86) of the outward-oriented developing period, contrasting sharply with the average growth rate of 4.7 per cent during the preceding decade (1954–64) of the inward-oriented developing period. As a result, real per capita income rose from $587 in 1954 to $723 in 1964, but thereafter rapidly increased to $2,300 in 1986 when measured by 1980 US constant prices. The gradual decline in the rate of population growth, from about 2.5 per cent for 1954–64 to 1.5 per cent for 1974–86, also contributed to this rapid increase in per capita GNP (Korea's population increased from 21.8 million in 1954 to 41.6 million by 1986).

9.2.1 *Policies prior to 1960*

Prior to 1960, the Korean economy was subjected to a number of problems which could be easily anticipated in an immediate post-war period. The economy suffered from severe macroeconomic imbalances such as high unemployment, budget deficits, and balance-of-payments deficits under the high pressure of inflation. During the latter half of the 1950s, the inflation rate averaged more than 30 per cent and the balance-of-payments deficit averaged between 5 and 10 per cent of GNP.

The government's effort was therefore largely directed to alleviating the economic pressures that resulted from the price levels and the balance of payments. As a part of the anti-inflationary measures, nominal

Table 9.1 Major economic indicators for Korea: 1954–86.

	1954	1964	1974	1986	Average annual growth rate		
					1954–64	1964–74	1974–86
Population (million persons)	21.8	28.0	34.7	41.6	2.5	2.2	1.5
GNP (billion won)[1]	6,183	9,790	24,425	59,289	4.7	9.6	7.0
Per capita GNP (thousand won)[1]	284	349	704	1,468	2.1	7.3	5.8
Per capita GNP (US dollars)[1]	587	723	1,463	2,300			
Sectoral value added (share of GNP, %)							
Primary industry	50.2	45.9	24.6	13.8	3.8	3.0	2.4
Manufacturing	5.3	9.7	20.6	33.3	11.2	18.1	11.1
Social overhead	44.4	44.4	54.8	52.9	4.7	11.9	6.8
Sectoral employment (share of total labour force, %)							
Primary industry	–	61.9	48.2	23.6	–	0.8	-2.7
Manufacturing	–	8.8	17.8	25.9	–	10.8	5.1
Social overhead	–	26.9	34.0	50.0	–	6.2	5.4
Exports and imports[2]							
Commodity exports, f.o.b. (million US dollars)	24	119	4,460	34,714	17.4	43.7	17.1
(Ratio of exports to GNP, %)	(0.8)	(4.1)	(24.0)	(35.7)			
Commodity imports, c.i.f. (million US dollars)	243	404	6,852	31,584	5.2	32.7	12.5
(Ratio of imports to GNP, %)	(7.2)	(14.0)	(37.0)	(32.5)			
Share of manufactures in exports (%)	–	51.2	87.5	94.2			
Investment and saving[2]							
Share of investment in GNP (%)	11.9	14.0	31.7	30.2			
Domestic savings rate (%)	6.6	8.7	19.9	32.8			
Foreign savings rate	5.3	6.9	12.1	-2.5			
External debt[2]		(1965)	(1975)	(1986)			
Gross (million US dollars)	–	177	8,456	44,510			
Net (million US dollars)	–	50	6,750	–			
GNP deflator (%, 1980 = 100)	1.0	7.2	30.7	141.4	21.8	15.6	12.4

Notes: [1] Based on 1980 prices.
[2] Based on current prices.

Source: Bank of Korea, *Economic Statistics Yearbook*.

exchange rates were kept fixed and allowed only insufficient adjustments, resulting in chronically overvalued exchange rates, despite periodic devaluations. On the other hand, to bring the balance-of-payments problem under control, the authorities resorted heavily to import restriction measures such as multiple exchange rates, import licensing, and high tariffs on selected items. The net result of these policies was discrimination against exports, since incentives towards import substitution were substantial. Thus one could safely argue that Korea was a typical inward-oriented developing economy until the late 1950s, with a relatively large labour pool in the agricultural sector.

9.2.2   Policy reforms of the 1960s

In contrast to the lack of balanced economic policies, except for the emphasis on import substitution, during the 1950s, numerous economic reforms and plans directed to economic development goals were put forth during the 1960s. The First Five-Year Economic Plan (1962–66) was implemented in 1962 and the sixth one (1987–91) is currently under way. Issues such as development of key industries, modernisation of industrial structure, and creation of an adequate supply of social overhead capital were especially stressed in each plan.

The major policy shift, however, began with the reforms of the payment regime and the financial sector during the period 1964–65. The Korean currency was devalued from 190 won against the US dollar to 255 won in May 1964, and the interest rate on ordinary loans of banking institutions was raised from 16 to 26 per cent per annum in September 1965. Other important policies introduced simultaneously or immediately after these reforms were the introduction of comprehensive export-promotion schemes, gradual attempts to liberalise import controls, and the encouragement of inflow of foreign loans to fill the domestic savings gap.

The 1965 interest-rate reform was intended to enhance the efficiency of domestic resource allocation and to provide incentives to save. Remarkable progress was made in mobilising domestic savings and facilitating the inflow of foreign capital. This high-interest-rate policy, however, lasted only through 1971 when a low-interest-rate policy was taken up again.

The attempt to relax import controls beginning in the mid-1960s proceeded only to a limited degree, however, and was by no means as vigorous as export promotion mainly because of chronic balance-of-payments problems. Furthermore, very complicated industrial incentives were offered to the agricultural sector beginning in the late 1960s.

9.2.3 HC industry promotion in the 1970s

After a decade of successful growth under an outward-oriented development strategy covering the first two Five-Year Economic Plans (1962–71), Korea seemed to be losing its comparative advantage in labour-intensive exports, largely due to the rapid increase in domestic wage–rental ratios as a result of the accumulation of capital relative to labour. Rising protectionism abroad against imports of light industrial products was also viewed as a limit to the continuation of export expansion. Thus, it was believed that major shifts in production and exports to more skill- and technology-intensive industries were necessary. The need for that was also accentuated by the exceptionally strong aspiration and zeal of the late Park's regime to shorten the time needed to reach an 'advanced industrial state'.

This change in industrial strategy was first put into practice in the late 1960s when the government introduced a series of special laws to promote the so-called HC industries. It was not until 1973, however, that the apparatus of the new strategy was substantially established. In 1973, the HC Industry Promotion Committee was established within the government to provide necessary support for the largely government-sponsored investment projects. This policy was pursued vigorously for the next seven years. This government-led industrial restructuring attempt, however, proved to be very costly for the economy. The attempt encountered from the beginning a number of obstacles, both internal and external.

The external obstacles were the oil-price hikes, delay in industrial adjustments in industrialised countries, rising protectionism, and the world-wide recession in general. More importantly, however, Korea suffered from a 'too fast and too much' investment attitude in the industries whose comparative advantages were not quite warranted by Korea's factor endowments. Korea's technological and skill base, as well as the domestic savings capacity, were not adequate to support such massive capital-intensive investments. The result was the creation of excess capacities in some unprofitable industries, depleting investment funds that would have been otherwise available to other export industries.

This massive investment programme in the HC industries and stagnation in export performance coupled with a declining savings rate forced the Korean economy to rely heavily on foreign borrowing to finance its domestic savings gap. As a result, the external debt, which stood at $16.8 billion in 1978, rose to $40.1 billion by 1983, making Korea the fourth largest debtor country in the world.

9.2.4   *Recent attempts at liberalisation for the 1980s*

As the Korean economy underwent a period of stagnation, in particular
from 1979 to 1981, the Korean economic planners and advisers were fully
convinced that the economic downturn was not due solely to the
unfavourable external development or domestic political instability. The
government-led growth during the 1960s and 1970s had, in fact, produced
a number of signs of structural imbalances in the economy by the late
1970s, such as underdevelopment of the financial sector, insufficient
development of small and medium firms, and an unjustifiable protection
structure of the home markets. In particular, investments encouraged by
the government in the HC industries in the 1970s began to produce a large
number of failures.

The reaction of the government to these developments was to increase
its reliance on the market mechanism by gradually reducing the
government's role in the management of the banking sector as well as in
the investment decision-making process. The government also stepped
up its efforts to liberalise import controls and thereby to increase
competition in the domestic markets as well as to reduce the cost of
protection. By any standard, the recent liberalisation plan appears to be
by far the most bold initiative the Korean Government has ever made in
opening up the domestic market with such a strong political commitment.
A Tariff Reform Committee was set up within the government early in
1983, and a package of import liberalisation plans was formulated.
According to the government's time-phased plan announced in 1983,
Korea's import liberalisation rate was to be increased from 80.3 per cent
in 1983 to 91.6 per cent and 95.2 per cent in 1986 and 1988 (see Table 9.2).
The plan also included a tariff reform schedule by 1988. The main feature
of the tariff reform is to reduce over time the range of basic tariff rates
differentiated from 0 to 100 per cent depending on commodities as of
1983 to 0 to 30 per cent in 1988. As a result, the average basic tariff rate is
to be lowered from 23.7 per cent in 1983 to 19.9 per cent in 1986 then to
18.1 per cent with a range from 0 to 30 per cent by 1988.

One of the important features of the 1983 liberalisation package was to
set up a time-phased plan for each import item to be liberalised, giving
higher priority of liberalisation to overly protected commodities and
items that enjoyed a monopolistic market structure in domestic markets.
An exception, however, was made for the agricultural sector: the
liberalisation plan for this sector was largely reserved for further special
study, particularly in relation to the farm income-support policy.

After the successful completion of the 1983 liberalisation plan as
scheduled, a new tariff reform plan for 1989–93 has been prepared.
According to this new plan, the average tariff rate is to be decreased from

Table 9.2 Import liberalisation plan for Korea: 1983–88.

Industry	No. of import items (1983)	Import liberalisation rate (%)			
		1983	1984	1986	1988
Primary and processed food	1,386	73.2	75.8	80.1	–
Chemical products	2,182	94.4	95.0	97.8	–
Basic metals	802	90.9	92.8	98.8	–
Machinery	1,414	68.7	77.9	89.5	99.9
Electronics and electrical	495	53.6	62.6	86.9	100
Textile	1,089	80.4	90.4	96.1	–
Others	547	81.2	82.1	86.8	–
Total	7,915	80.4	84.8	91.6	95.2

Source: Ministry of Trade and Industry.

18.1 per cent in 1988 to 7.9 per cent in 1993, and the average tariff rate for manufactures from 16.9 per cent to 6.2 per cent for the same period.

Along with the import liberalisation scheme, the government also introduced a series of policy reforms in the 1980s. For instance, the major commercial banks were privatised, and all the interest subsidies were eliminated from the 'policy' loans in 1982. All the industry-specific promotion laws were abolished and a more general Industry Promotion Law was introduced in 1986. Industrial incentives in the new laws took a more indirect form of assistance such as fiscal incentives that are to be applied to manpower training and R&D activities in an industry-neutral manner. On the other hand, the government implemented a series of tight monetary and fiscal measures with currency devaluations throughout the first half of the 1980s. These policy reforms have undoubtedly contributed to the recent success of the Korean economy in curbing inflation, in resuming a high growth rate, and in turning the balance of payments from red to black beginning in 1986 (see Table 9.1).

9.2.5 *Industrial transformation*

The policy shift in the early 1960s, followed by the rapid economic growth, has brought fundamental changes in all sectors of the economy. First of all, rapid expansion of exports was achieved, initially through rapid increase of labour-intensive production, followed by the expansion of capital- and skill-intensive production as the factor endowments shifted with capital and skill accumulation. As can be seen in Table 9.1, the ratio of exports to GNP was only 4.1 per cent as of 1964, but it rose rapidly to 24.0 per cent by 1974 and to 35.7 per cent by 1986. Moreover, manufactured goods have been the dominant element in the growth of exports since the early 1960s: exports of manufactured goods accounted for only 51.2 per cent of total exports in 1964, but increased to 87.5 per cent by 1974 and 94.2 per cent by 1986. As a result, the share of the manufacturing sector increased from 9.7 per cent in 1964 to 33.3 per cent in 1986, whereas the share of agriculture decreased from 45.9 per cent to 13.8 per cent in the same period.

The rapid expansion of labour-intensive production since the early 1960s has also helped to improve the employment situation: the official unemployment rate, which stood at 8.2 per cent in 1963, decreased to less than 5 per cent in 1969 and to less than 4 per cent in 1976. The labour market has remained near full employment since then except for the period of economic stagnation in the early 1980s.

Table 9.3 shows the changes in the industrial structure of the Korean manufacturing sector over the 1954–83 period. A few notable features are evident from the table. First, there was a substantial structural change since the early 1950s: the share of heavy industries increased from 16.5 per cent in 1954 to 55.1 per cent in 1983, while the share of light industries declined sharply from 83.5 to 44.9 per cent for the same period. Second, among light industrial products, the share of exportable goods – textiles, leather and footwear – remained stable: therefore all the decline in the share of light industries resulted from the slow growth of importables and non-traded consumer goods – food, wood and printing. Finally, the heavy industries that grew most rapidly include chemical products, iron and steel, electrical machinery and transport equipment which have received special concessions during the 1970s.

Despite the impressive performance of the Korean economy since the early 1960s, the underlying policy management has been by no means flawless. Aside from the episode of the HC industry drive of the 1970s, a few aspects have to be mentioned. First, ever since the First Five-Year Economic Plan was launched in 1962, development planners often tended to put forward a very ambitious investment programme, far exceeding the expected level of domestic savings and inflow of foreign capital. The resulting excess demand was met by a rapid increase in monetary growth, and this in turn raised domestic prices, worsening the balance of payments. For the 1964–86 period, the inflation rate by GNP deflators averaged over 13 per cent. Certainly this inflationary financing of investment could have helped to achieve immediate growth targets, but the long-run undesirable side-effects were also considerable. Worsening income distribution,[2] reduced efficiency in the allocation of resources, discouragement of domestic savings and greater need of foreign loans were the main side-effects of such inflationary financing.

Second, despite the higher rates of domestic inflation relative to the

Table 9.3 The structure and growth of manufacturing industries in Korea: 1954–83 (at constant 1980 prices).

	Composition as percent of total manufacturing value added				Growth rate		
	1954 (1)	1964 (2)	1974 (3)	1983 (4)	54–64 (5)	64–74 (6)	74–83 (7)
Light industries	83.5	67.3	54.4	44.9	7.7	15.9	8.9
Food, beverages and tobacco	50.6	38.2	25.0	19.0	7.1	13.4	7.2
Textiles and wearing apparel	18.7	15.7	17.8	15.2	8.3	19.4	8.4
Leather and leather products	0.8	1.5	0.6	0.5	5.3	20.4	8.8
Footwear	0.8	0.8	0.8	0.8	10.1	16.7	11.2
Wood and furniture	4.4	2.2	1.6	1.1	4.1	14.4	6.3
Rubber products	1.3	1.5	1.6	2.1	11.6	18.8	12.6
Printing, publishing and allied industries	4.8	5.0	2.1	1.7	10.5	9.1	7.5
Plastic products	0.2	0.6	1.3	1.5	21.4	25.8	11.1
Professional and scientific measuring and controlling equipment	0.3	0.3	0.7	1.0	9.4	26.4	13.5
Miscellaneous manufacturing industries	1.6	1.7	2.9	2.0	10.7	24.3	6.2
Heavy industries	16.5	32.7	45.6	55.1	17.3	21.5	13.7
Paper and paper products	1.1	2.6	2.0	1.9	19.4	14.6	9.5
Industrial and other chemical products	2.8	5.6	9.4	10.7	18.0	23.5	11.4
Non-metallic mineral products	2.9	5.6	5.5	5.3	17.8	17.5	9.7
Iron and steel	0.1	1.5	4.6	6.1	39.0	30.8	13.4
Non-ferrous metal	0.6	0.8	0.5	1.5	15.7	11.2	23.7
Metal products	1.6	1.8	1.5	2.5	12.7	15.8	16.3
Machinery	3.2	3.7	2.6	4.8	11.8	14.4	17.1
Electrical machinery	0.4	1.4	6.5	10.0	24.6	35.6	15.0
Petroleum products	2.0	8.2	8.5	6.7	32.0	18.3	7.5
Transport equipment	1.8	1.5	4.5	5.6	12.2	30.5	12.7

Source: Bank of Korea, National Income Accounts, 1984, pp. 190–3.

rates experieinced by Korea's major trading partners during the 1970s, the exchange rate had been kept at 484 won per US dollar between 1974 and 1980, resulting in a real appreciation of the Korean won by nearly 30 per cent for the corresponding period.[3]

It is believed that the significant decline in the export growth rate in the late 1970s was partly due to this exchange-rate mismanagement. The slow growth of exports was also affected by the largely government-led inefficient investments and adverse external conditions that developed during the 1970s.

Third and finally, export-promoting policies have been implemented in Korea without the dismantling of import restrictions of the 1960s. Moreover, the protection structure of the home markets has become increasingly complex during the 1970s due to agricultural price supports and industry-specific promotion efforts. It is, therefore, not entirely clear *a priori* whether or not exports have in fact been favoured over import substitution as a result of the overall incentive system. More detailed information on the structure of incentives is therefore needed to make a comparison between the extent of protection provided to exports and to import substitution. This is discussed further in detail in section 9.3.

9.3   The anatomy of trade policies

9.3.1   *Incentives for export activities*

Export incentives introduced since the early 1960s in general took the form of a preferential tax system, a preferential loan system and various administrative support systems. More specifically, the preferential tax system included tariff exemptions on imported raw materials and intermediate and capital goods for export production, exemptions from indirect taxes on intermediate inputs and export sales, a reduction of direct taxes on profits made through export activities, reserve funds created from taxable income to develop new foreign markets and to defray export losses, and an accelerated depreciation allowance for fixed capital used directly in export production. The preferential loan system provided exporters with access to subsidised short- and long-term credits for their purchase of inputs and for the financing of their fixed investments. Besides, generous wastage allowances were granted on imported duty-free raw materials over and above the requirements of actual export production. An export–import linkage system permitting access to otherwise prohibited imports was in operation, and preferential rates on several overhead inputs, such as electricity and railroad transportation, was made available.

Some of these incentives should not be regarded as genuine subsidies. For example, exemption of intermediate inputs and export sales from indirect taxes, and exemption from duties on imported inputs allowed exporters to operate under a virtually free-trade regime. They were allowed to buy their inputs and sell their outputs at world market prices.

The system of export incentives remained virtually unchanged through the early 1970s. Beginning in 1973, however, some of these incentives were abolished in an effort to reduce the scope of export subsidies. The 50 per cent reduction in profit taxes on export earnings was abolished in 1973. In July 1975, the system of prior tariff exemptions on imported inputs used in export production was changed into a drawback system. The discount on electricity was abolished in 1976, and wastage allowances have been repeatedly reduced, bringing them closer to the market rate during the 1970s.

As a result, since the mid-1970s, interest-rate subsidies and credit availability associated with export-related loans have become the major export incentives. Preferential loans for export activities consist of short-term loans tied to the gross value of export sales with a term, in general, of less than 90 days, and long-term loans for fixed investment in export industries and for exports on credit. The government has steadily increased preferential loans to export industries. For instance, the share of preferential short- and long-term loans to export industries in the total domestic credits increased from 5.1 per cent in 1960 to 20.5 per cent in 1978. The weighted average interest rate on all preferential loans to export industries was 7.7 per cent in 1966 and 10.6 per cent in 1978, whereas the lending rate on ordinary loans of commercial banks was 26.4 per cent in 1966 and 19.0 per cent in 1978.[4] This interest rate differential between preferential and ordinary loans had been gradually reduced and was abolished with the June 1982 interest-rate reform. The availability of short- and long-term loans tied to export sales was also removed for all but the small firms by 1988.

In discussing important factors underlying the successful export expansion in Korea since the early 1960s, one should not fail to recognise the significant role of the informal incentives that the government provided to exporters, namely, the administrative support. These include the special attention of the highest officials given to any difficulties met by exporters: rapid processing of the government's paperwork, and the promise of governmental support in the future, etc. Although no one can estimate the value of such informal incentives, the extent to which the administrative effort was geared to encourage exports is well known.

9.3.2 *Incentives for export versus domestic sale*

As far as instruments of import controls are concerned, legal tariffs, to a large extent, appear to be inoperative in Korea. Many imports are exempt from duties and a number of commodities are subject to prohibitive tariffs. Table 9.4 presents the data on tariffs actually collected and exempted, with the implicit tariff rates calculated on the basis of these data. According to the data, the legal tariff rates for all commodity imports far exceeded the actual tariff rates during the period of 1968–86: on average the legal tariff rate was 16.2 per cent whereas the actual rate was 6.7 per cent. As expected, the trend of actual tariff rates had little to do with the trend of legal tariff rates. These figures of tariff rates, however, should by no means be taken as a measure of incentives given to import-substitution industries in Korea. This is because quantitative import restrictions have been far more important than tariffs in controlling imports in Korea.

Along with the liberalisation attempts undertaken in the mid-1960s, the so-called 'positive' list system was changed into a 'negative' list system, in which all commodities not listed were automatically approved for imports (AA items). Generally, the items and their quantities to be restricted were determined twice a year by the government on the basis of import needs, the balance-of-payments situation, and the protection requirements of domestic industries. The quantitative restrictions were mostly applied to import-competing items and imports of non-essential or luxury goods, whereas import of raw materials and non-competitive intermediate goods were normally approved automatically.

In the second half of 1967 when the negative system was adopted, more than 60 per cent of the 1,312 basic import items (CCCN 4-digit) became AA commodities (see Table 9.5). But since then, the import liberalisation rate measured by the ratio of AA items to the basic import items has declined steadily, reaching a low of 49 per cent in 1975. It was only in 1977 that the government began to relax import controls again, mainly as a result of favourable developments in the trade balance. This liberalisation attempt was interrupted by the second oil shock of 1979 and the worsening of the balance-of-payments situation in subsequent years. But as soon as the balance of payments improved in the early 1980s, the government introduced a package of import liberalisation plans in 1983.

In conclusion, non-tariff restrictions seem to have played an important role in the protection of Korea's import-substitution industries. Therefore, to measure with any degree of accuracy the extent of effective protection given to domestic sales, one would have to rely on price comparisons between domestic and international markets. Such an attempt was made by Nam (1981b) for 1978.

Table 9.4 Operative import tariff rates in Korea: 1968–86.

	1969	1974	1980	1982	1984	1986
A. Tariff collected and exempted						
1. Tariff collected (billion won)	37.2	126.7	766.1	1,012.6	1,594.0	1,942.6
2. Tariff exempted (billion won)	66.4	302.8	789.5	1,040.9	1,211.3	1,476.0
3. Total legal tariffs (A.1 + A.2)	104.3	329.5	1,555.6	2,053.5	2,805.3	3,418.6
4. Total imports (million US dollars)	1,462.9	6,581.8	21,598.0	23,474.0	30,631.4	31,583.9
5. Total imports (billion won)	404.2	2,781.8	13,737.0	17,533.7	25,344.4	27,206.4
B. Tariff rates						
1. Actual tariff rates (A.1 ÷ A.5)	9.4	4.6	5.6	5.8	6.3	7.1
2. Legal tariff rates (A.3 ÷ A.5)	25.8	15.4	11.3	11.7	11.1	12.6

Source: Ministry of Finance, Office of Taxation *Economic Statistics Yearbook* (1987).

Table 9.5   Non-tariff import restrictions in Korea: 1967–88.

	Prohibited	Restricted	Automatic approval (A)	Total (B)	Rate of import liberalisation (=A/B) (%)
1967	118	402	792	1,312	60.4
1969	75	514	723	1,312	55.1
1971	73	518	721	1,312	55.0
1973	73	556	683	1,312	52.1
1975	66	602	644	1,312	49.1
1977	61	560	691	1,312	52.7
1979	–	328	682	1,010	67.5
1981	–	1,911	5,649	7,560	74.7
1983	–	1,482	6,078	7,560	80.3
1985	·–	970	6,945	7,915	87.7
1987	–	499	7,412	7,911	93.6
1988	–	358	7,553	7,911	95.4

Source: Ministry of Trade and Industry.

Note: The classification of import items was based on the 4-digit CCCN codes through 1980, but 8-digit CCCN codes since then.

Table 9.6 gives estimates of effective subsidy rates granted to export sales in contrast to effective protection rates given to domestic sales for 1978. Implicit subsidies to export sales were estimated on the basis of interest-rate differentials between export loans and ordinary bank loans and reduction in direct taxes, under the assumption that other incentives were either not genuine subsidies or negligibly small in amount. The calculations show that, unlike effective protection rates on domestic sales with some high positive rates and some negative ones, effective subsidy rates for export are quite even across industries, averaging about 16 per cent. Thus, export incentives appear to have been at least less distortionary then import-substitution incentives. The estimates also show that, for the manufacturing sector, excluding beverages, tobacco and processed food, the subsidy rate for export sales was 15.9 per cent, whereas that for domestic sales was 3.5 per cent implying that, on average, there were greater incentives to sell abroad than to sell in the domestic market.

There is a possibility, however, that the above estimates for the effective subsidy rates to export activities are only a considerable understatement, for the following reasons: first, the subsidy due to credits at below-market interest rates was calculated on the basis of the interest-rate differentials between export loans and non-preferential bank loans. But the interest rates on non-preferential bank loans were also, in general, set by the government at rates much lower than those obtainable under free-market conditions in Korea. Thus the interest subsidy measured here may be a substantial underestimate, perhaps in the order of 100 per cent. Second, in many new export industries, export

Table 9.6 Relative incentive rates on export and domestic sales in Korea: 1978 (%).

	Effective subsidy rate for export sales		Effective protection rate for domestic sales		Effective incentive rate for total sales	
	Balassa[a]	Corden[a]	Balassa	Corden	Balassa	Corden
I. Agriculture, forestry and fishing	15.9	15.1	77.1	73.4	72.6	69.1
IV. Mining and energy	11.4	10.6	-25.7	-23.8	-23.6	-21.8
Primary production, total	15.3	14.5	61.9	58.7	58.6	55.5
II. Processed food	31.7	16.7	-29.4	-16.0	-23.0	-12.6
III. Beverage and tobacco	13.2	10.8	28.0	22.8	27.8	22.6
V. Construction materials	19.1	15.1	-15.0	-11.9	-10.5	-8.4
VI-A. Intermediate products I	23.6	17.1	-37.9	-27.4	-31.4	-22.7
VI-B. Intermediate products II	26.3	17.6	7.9	5.3	12.0	8.1
VII. Non-durable consumer goods	17.3	12.1	31.5	21.9	24.0	16.7
VIII. Consumer durables	38.0	23.1	131.2	81.0	83.2	51.2
IX. Machinery	24.4	16.9	47.4	33.2	43.2	30.3
X. Transport equipment	26.1	16.9	135.4	73.8	87.2	48.7
Manufacturing, total	22.8	15.8	5.3	3.7	9.7	6.7
All industries	17.9	13.9	30.6	24.1	27.8	21.9
Primary production plus processed food	15.6	14.0	55.5	50.0	52.3	47.1
Manufacturing, excl. bev. and tob.	23.6	16.2	2.7	1.9	8.2	5.6
Manufacturing, excl. bev. and tob. and processed food	22.9	15.9	5.1	3.5	10.0	7.0
All industries, excl. bev. and tob.	18.1	14.0	30.8	24.2	27.9	21.9

Source: Nam (1981, p. 206).

[a] These names relate to alternative estimation procedures; see Balassa (1982) for an explanation of the distinction.

expansion did not accompany import liberalisation. Domestic markets were often reserved for those firms that were in their early stage of exporting under the infant-industry argument, resulting in export expansion at the expense of domestic consumers. Finally, it is difficult to estimate the value of informal incentives that the government provided to exporters, but no one can doubt that they affected considerably the relative benefits from exporting compared with production for the domestic market.

Based on these facts, one may safely conclude that the Korean trade incentives in 1978 were in general biased towards export activities. Despite this incentive bias to exports, the export growth rate declined significantly in the late 1970s, worsening the balance of payments. The mismanagement of exchange rates and investment policies during the 1970s are believed to be largely responsibile for that.

It is also evident that the Korean structure of protection for domestic sales became increasingly complex and inefficient during the 1970s. This situation led to the serious attempt at liberalising imports with a series of currency devaluations in the early 1980s. At the same time, formal export subsidies had almost been eliminated by the early 1980s.

9.3.3   *The efficacy of alternative trade routes*

As seen, the shift to outward from inward orientation in trade policies was not achieved in Korea through an outright liberalisation of trade with currency adjustments but rather by introducing a set of export incentives to offset anti-export bias without wholesale dismantling of import barriers.

In theory, the scheme of export subsidies without removing import barriers (an 'export-subsidy' route to outward orientation) could be a close substitute for import liberalisation with currency realignment (a 'free-trade' route to outward orientation) since a 10 per cent tariff on all imports together with a 10 per cent subsidy on all exports would be equivalent to no tariff and no subsidy and a 10 per cent depreciated exchange rate. In practice, however, the export subsidy route is inferior to the free-trade route since not only does the former involve administrative costs but also export subsidies or import controls are rarely applied in a manner that would be neutral among industries or products. Furthermore, quantitative restrictions of any kind tend to generate large premia for which rent-seeking activities are triggered. Many able entrepreneurs may devote much of their energy and resources to privately profitable, but socially wasteful, rent-seeking activities.

Nonetheless, Korea had to resort to the 'export subsidy' rather than the 'free-trade' route for a few reasons. First, import liberalisation could only have occurred slowly due to the political pressure of those vested interest groups benefiting from import protection. Second, the currency devaluation that may have been required to reduce import barriers was feared as a source of inflationary pressure. Third, import taxes constituted a major source of government revenue. Finally, policy-makers were guided by the erroneous belief that both exports and import substitution can be better promoted by the scheme of export subsidies with import barriers.

The 'export-subsidy' route to outward orientation had become increasingly costly, however, by the early 1980s for Korea in two major respects. One is that the export subsidies through preferential loans at below-market rates became increasingly burdensome to Korea's monetary authority due to an ever-increasing export volume. Another is that subsidies by developing countries in general have increasingly become subject to countervailing duties by industrial countries, notably the United States. Korea became one of the four developing countries that were most frequently countervailed by the United States in the early 1980s.[5] For these reasons, most export subsidy measures had been removed in Korea by the early 1980s. At the same time import liberalisation was progressing rapidly so that a 'free-trade' route could successfully replace the 'export-subsidy' route.

9.4 Concluding remarks

As seen, an outward-oriented strategy was successfully implemented through the 'export-subsidy' rather than the 'free-trade' route until very recently in Korea. Despite somewhat chaotic government interventions both on the exports as well as on the import-substitution side, the net effects largely offset each other, resulting in a good deal less discrimination – or more neutrality – between import substitution and export production than in most of the other developing countries.

Outward orientation on trade policies, however, was not the sole factor behind the relatively successful performance of the Korean economy. In order for trade policies to function effectively, it is imperative to have the essential infrastructure in place. Education, transport and communication; the maintenance of macroeconomic stability; and a well-defined legal system aimed at reducing transaction costs of all economic activities are all part of an economic framework conducive to efficient market processes. Although the Korean Government fumbled in some areas, such as in HC industry promotion and the management of the financial sector, it was a relatively efficient provider of other essential services mostly through the implementation of the successive Five-Year Economic Plans.

The net result of trade policies combined with other complementary policies, therefore, helped to open up the Korean economy, resulting in the rapid expansion of trade. The rapid expansion of manufactured exports in particular has been the major feature of the dramatic growth of the Korean economy over the past two decades or so.

While the export-subsidy route to outward orientation has been rather effectively used in bringing about the desired economic transformation in Korea with rapid economic growth and industrialisation, it was not entirely without costs for the economy. In fact, the costs are so dear in some respects that reservations need to be made for other developing countries blindly to emulate such an incentive system. A few lessons are in order.

First, as mentioned before, the rapid expansion of exports has been greatly facilitated through the ready availability of credits at below-market interest rates,[6] but such an export-financing system and the credit-rationing system as a whole are largely held responsible for the relatively underdeveloped financial sector in Korea. The financial sector has been used more often as an instrument for channelling funds into favoured industries or investment projects rather than as an intermediary between savers and investors. The results were the development of rent-seeking activities, capital-intensive investments unwarranted by Korea's comparative advantage, and frequent loss of control over credit expansion. Still the financial sector remains as the most underdeveloped area in Korea, presenting a serious bottleneck in furthering economic growth.

Second, another undesirable consequence caused by past trade policies is the inefficient protection structure of the domestic markets. The wide dispersion of effective protection rates across industries, resulting primarily from quantitative import restrictions, clearly indicates that further improvement in allocative efficiency can be achieved. The highly protected industries include agriculture, certain chemical products and luxury consumer goods.

Third, an 'export-subsidy' route to outward orientation was successfully implemented in Korea, but this was possible mainly because protection of import substitution was relatively low initially. Thus, the anti-export bias due to import barriers was easily offset by export subsidies. Large export subsidies, however, did not suffice to offset the high protection of import substitution in countries such as Brazil and Mexico. Furthermore, export subsidies and import barriers increasingly risk countervailing actions and other retaliations by some industrial countries. This tilts the balance even more in favour of a 'free-trade' route over an 'export-subsidy' route to outward orientation.

Finally, despite the recent threat of new protectionism by some industrial countries, the export pessimism arising in some developing countries, including Korea, should not be overly exaggerated. As of 1983, developing-country exports account for only a tiny share – 2.3 per cent – of the markets for manufactures in the industrial economies.[7] Also, there is no sign of a slowdown in the contribution of exports to GNP growth in the developing countries in recent years as compared with that observed during the 1960s.[8] At the same time, even if the threat of the new protectionism becomes a more imminent reality, the best trade strategy for developing countries as well as for Korea is still to maintain an outward orientation from an economic standpoint.

Notes

1. HC industries include such industries as basic metals, petrochemicals, machinery, electrical and electronics, and transport equipment.
2. According to Park (1981, p. 289), the Gini index improved slightly between 1965 and 1970 from 0.34 to 0.33, but worsened to 0.38 by 1976 in Korea.
3. See Edwards (1985) for estimates of real exchange rates.
4. See Nam (1981a, p. 193).
5. See Nam (1987).
6. In fact, Hong's (1979) estimate has shown that all loans through financial institutions in the 1970s were extended, on average, at a negative real rate of interest.
7. See World Bank (1987, p. 81).
8. The relative growth rate of manufactured exports to GNP growth rate in developing countries is estimated at 2.3 for 1980–86 compared with 1.8 for 1965–73. See World Bank (1987, p. 26).

10

Indonesia: Export promotion after the oil boom

Hal Hill

10.1 Introduction

Indonesia is the third most populous developing country and the world's largest archipelago. It has a strong natural resource endowment, but the geographic distribution of these resources and of the population is most uneven. For example, the central island of Java (plus Madura) has over 100 million inhabitants – 60 per cent of the total population – on only 7 per cent of the land area. Its population density of about 750 (persons per sq km) is one of the highest in the world, and about 20 times that of the rest of the country.

Indonesia's economic performance during the twentieth century has been equally varied. Under Dutch rule until the Japanese invasion of 1942, the country's economy over this period resembled the classic colonial structure of an export-oriented, foreign-dominated, extractive and cash-crop enclave alongside the underdeveloped indigenous economy. Independence from Holland was declared in 1945 but the full transfer of political authority was not effected until 1949. Political instability and a daunting array of economic challenges resulted in sluggish economic performance during the 1950s culminating, towards the end of the decade, in extensive nationalisation of foreign (mainly Dutch) property. Adventurous economic and foreign policies ushered in a period of economic decline and rampant inflation in the first half of the 1960s. An unsuccessful leftish coup in 1965 produced a decisive regime change in the following year, and a government committed to economic orthodoxy at home and political moderation abroad. The adoption of

I am indebted to H. W. Arndt for many useful comments on an earlier draft of this chapter.

pragmatic economic policies, substantial aid and private capital inflows, and the massive windfall gains after the OPEC-inspired oil price increases all contributed to rapid economic development during the 1970s unparalleled in the country's history. However, following the sharp decline in oil prices during the 1980s the country has had to cope with subdued economic growth and a serious balance-of-payments situation.[1]

Except for the most recent period, developments in the manufacturing sector have largely mirrored those general economic trends. In the mid-1960s Indonesia possessed one of the smallest manufacturing sectors in the world's major developing countries, smaller than that of, for example, the Philippines and even Hong Kong. From the late 1960s, however, output grew very rapidly, fuelled by rapid economic growth, by the backlog in consumer demand accumulated during the earlier period of stagnation, and by a heavily protectionist regime which excluded much import competition (McCawley, 1981). Such rapid growth was maintained throughout the 1970s, a phenomenon at least in principle in conflict with the theoretical predictions of the 'Dutch disease' literature. Over this period, manufacturing remained almost entirely domestic-market oriented. In sharp contrast to neighbouring East Asian developing market economies, manufacturing exports remained negligible until the early 1980s. Thereafter, however, Indonesia's manufactured exports began to grow rapidly, for the first time overtaking the nation's traditional agricultural exports and comparable in magnitude to some other (albeit smaller) middle-income developing countries.

How was Indonesia able to achieve such rapid export growth so quickly? Is the growth sustainable? What were the principal policy instruments? And are there any lessons for other developing countries? These are the questions addressed in this chapter. We begin with a brief overview of Indonesian industry, followed by an examination of the circumstances leading up to the export-oriented phase. We then investigate the policy tools adopted in the transition phase of the 1980s, and the outcome in terms of industrial and export growth. Our main conclusion is that, notwithstanding the size of the country's external debt and the importance of maintaining the momentum of policy reform, Indonesia's experiment in industrial export promotion during the 1980s has been a success. By and large the 'right' policy instruments were selected, they were implemented effectively, and the results have been impressive.

10.2 An overview of Indonesian industrialisation[2]

There are five salient features of Indonesian manufacturing industry which need to be emphasised in any assessment of the country's export-promotion strategies and performance.

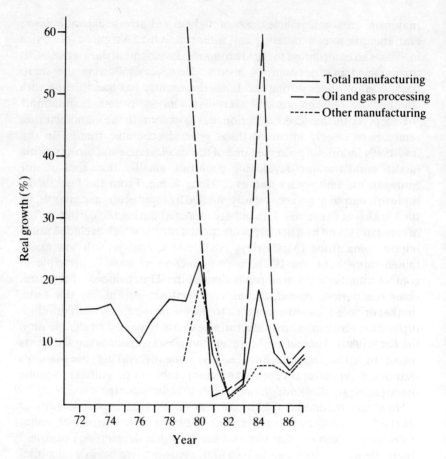

Note: 1978–87 at constant 1983 prices; 1972–78 at constant 1973 prices.

Figure 10.1   Manufacturing growth in Indonesia: 1972–87. (Source: BPS, *Pendapatan Nasional Indonesia (National Accounts of Indonesia)*, Jakarta, various issues)

First, output has grown very rapidly since the early 1970s, though with a marked slowdown after 1980 (Figure 10.1). The double-digit growth virtually throughout the 1970s was supported by the 'expenditure-recycling' effects of the windfall oil revenues, rapidly rising domestic demand and high rates of effective protection for many manufactures. Huge government investments in oil processing and gas refining – a sector which has accounted for between one-third and one-quarter of total manufacturing value added – contributed to rapid growth in several years, and to the sluggish performance in the early 1980s; the 'lumpy' nature of such investments also explains the considerable year-to-year variations in growth rates.[3]

The second feature is a strong concentration in resource-based processing industries and, to a lesser extent, labour-intensive consumer goods, both reflecting the country's resource endowment. According to the *1986 Economic Census* (which actually refers to 1985), for example, heavy processing industries generated 49 per cent of the value-added; oil and gas processing alone contributed 29 per cent. By contrast, 'light' industry – mainly simple resource-based and labour-intensive consumer goods industries – produced 41 per cent, and the small but rapidly growing capital goods industry 11 per cent.[4] The heavy processing industries have also been growing most rapidly: production of oil and gas products (see Figure 10.1), iron and steel, cement, and fertiliser has far exceeded the average for manufacturing as a whole (Table 10.1). By contrast, the growth of consumer and capital goods industries has been a good deal more subdued, particularly during the 1980s.

Third, ownership patterns are unusual, at least compared with other East Asian developing market economies (Hill, 1988; Thee and Yoshihara, 1987). While policy has generally adhered to principles of economic orthodoxy and pragmatism, state-owned enterprises dominate key areas of the 'commanding heights' of manufacturing, including oil and gas processing, fertiliser, cement, steel, alumina, sugar processing and aircraft manufacture. State enterprises also constitute a substantial minority in many other industries. The pivotal role of such enterprises has been shaped by three main factors: history, ideology and the availability of funds. The Soeharto regime inherited many state-owned enterprises from the previous regime, and for various reasons not all were returned to their previous foreign owners. Notwithstanding a broad commitment to a market economy, elements of the current regime have a deep mistrust of market forces, and of foreign (including local Chinese) ownership of key sectors of the economy. And the oil bonanza in the decade after 1973 provided the financial resources to fund huge state enterprises. In contrast to the large state enterprises, domestic private firms, while providing the bulk of manufacturing employment, are a good deal smaller and more labour-intensive than the industry average. Equally, foreign firms play only a modest role as measured by their ownership, although they are much more important as suppliers of new technology.

A fourth feature is the almost wholly inward-looking nature of manufacturing until the early 1980s, driven almost entirely by import substitution and domestic demand growth. For most of the 1970s, manufactures constituted just 1 or 2 per cent of total merchandise exports, before rising sharply after 1982 (Figure 10.2). In many respects, the factors underlying this dismal record were the very obverse of those

Table 10.1 Index of manufacturing production for Indonesia: selected industry groups (1980–88) (1975=100).

	Number of establishments[a]	1980	1981	1982	1983	1984	1985	1986	1987	1988 Q1
Consumer goods										
White cigarettes	13	130	124	115	120	117	97	86	74	69
Clove cigarettes	20	151	180	186	196	224	246	266	296	323
Yarn	20	118	126	121	114	123	110	115	125	146
Weaving	193	126	138	130	121	125	127	132	154	177
Intermediate goods										
Plywood	6	392	471	424	438	418	387	429	557	582
Paper	8	153	152	148	129	164	182	206	219	225
Basic chemicals	13	128	127	130	132	147	149	154	170	159
Fertiliser	3	466	492	496	560	706	850	930	927	885
Tyres and tubes	12	257	301	294	300	300	311	329	356	297
Glass	17	208	257	259	227	247	249	245	348	323
Cement	7	367	391	419	566	616	686	767	806	781
Iron and steel	15	1,034	1,247	970	1,147	1,165	1,158	1,359	1,422	900
Capital goods										
Structural metal products	24	172	188	196	203	197	214	218	252	360
Electrical appliances	16	340	349	333	351	279	243	219	208	n.a.
Motor vehicles	17	194	248	226	198	179	183	211	233	206
Motor cycles	5	114	164	187	130	93	100	128	117	n.a.
All groups		194	213	213	226	240	258	275	290	287

[a] As at 1988.

Source: BPS, *Indikator Ekonomi* [*Economic Indicator*], Jakarta, various issues.

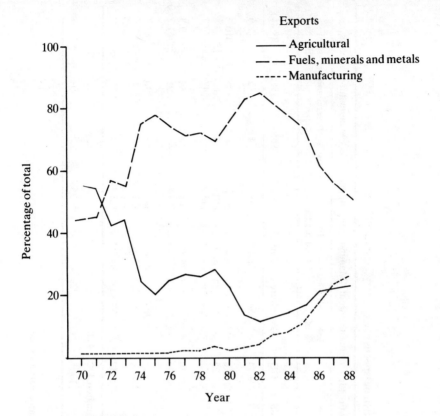

Note: Defined as follows:
   Agricultural – SITC 0,1,2 (excl. 27 and 28), 4
   Fuels, minerals and metals – 27,28,3,68
   Manufacturing – SITC 5-8 (excl. 68).

Figure 10.2. Composition of Indonesian exports: 1970–88. (Source: BPS, *Ekspor (Exports)*, Jakarta, various issues)

contributing to the remarkable transformation in the 1980s, to be discussed shortly: high oil prices resulted in a squeeze on other tradable goods activities, as well as postponing any serious government effort to reform the quite chaotic systems of regulation and protection which impeded non-oil exports. Low levels of technology and skills, and poor infrastructure, also contributed to the inward orientation of most firms.

Finally, Indonesia's industrial structure and performance differ significantly from that of neighbouring Asian countries and other oil exporters (Table 10.2). Its manufacturing growth before 1980 exceeded that of

Table 10.2 Indonesian industrialisation in comparative perspective.

	GNP	Manufacturing growth real annual average, as % of		Manufacturing output 1986 as % of		Manufacturing output 1985		Manufactured exports		
	total per capita					total	per capita	as % of merchandise exports		total per capita
	1986 ($)	1965–80	1980–86	GDP	Agriculture	($m)	($)	1965	1986	1986($)
Indonesia	490	12.0	7.7	14	54	11,447	68.8	4	22	19.6
Other ASEAN										
Malaysia	1,830	n.a.	5.8	n.a.	n.a.	n.a.	n.a.	6	36	310.2
Philippines	560	7.5	–1.7	25	96	8,048	140.5	6	61	50.8
Thailand	810	10.9	5.2	21	124	7,696	146.3	4	42	70.2
Other Asian										
India	290	4.3	8.2	19	59	35,597	45.6	49	62	9.3
Korea	2,370	18.7	9.8	30	250	24,466	589.5	59	91	761.2
Other oil exporters										
Mexico	1,860	7.4	0	26	289	43,613	543.8	16	30	60.7
Nigeria	640	14.6	1.0	8	20	7,373	71.5	2	1	0.6
Lower middle-income countries	750	7.4	3.0	17	77	85,260	123.4	8	27	32.9

Source: World Bank, *World Development Report 1988*, Washington, DC, 1988.

most countries (but not Korea), and continued to compare well after 1980, most notably against the two other oil exporters. In spite of the growth, its manufacturing sector remains comparatively small. Aggregate output is much smaller than in Korea, India and Mexico, and only about 40 per cent larger than in neighbouring Philippines and Thailand, countries with populations only one-third of Indonesia's. In terms of its per capita output and share of GDP, Indonesia is much closer to India than to Thailand, Mexico or Korea. And its manufactured exports remain quite small. Indonesia's industrial orientation is therefore rather unusual: it has something in common with Mexico and Nigeria through the inter-sectoral effects of a resource boom (and bust); in other respects it is more akin to India in having a 'large, domestic-oriented' manufacturing sector and extensive state ownership; and in recent years it has finally followed its East Asian neighbours in the vigorous promotion of manufacturing exports.

10.3 The origins of export promotion: Crisis and response in the 1980s

At the peak of the second oil boom, Indonesia's dependence on its exports of oil and gas and related products was extraordinarily high: in 1981, for example, oil and gas generated over three-quarters of merchandise exports (and the 'fuels, metals and minerals' group almost 85 per cent; see Figure 10.2) and two-thirds of government revenue. The decline in commodity – and especially fuel – prices which began about 1982 therefore affected the Indonesian economy profoundly. Although Indonesia's terms of trade held up fairly well initially (Figure 10.3), owing mainly to some buoyant agricultural commodity prices, the immediate effects of the weakening OPEC cartel were twofold.

First, GDP growth fell sharply, from an annual average of 7.5 per cent over the period 1973–81 to just 3.0 per cent from 1981 to 1986.[5] Second, a serious balance-of-payments problem emerged. Particularly after the very sharp decline in oil prices in early 1986, large current-account deficits rapidly raised external indebtedness. This rose by almost 250 per cent in nominal US dollar terms between 1981 and 1987, partly because about one-third of the total was denominated in the strongly appreciating yen. As a consequence, the debt-service ratio also rose sharply, by more than 300 per cent over the same period.

The Soeharto regime's legitimacy has always rested primarily on its economic management credentials. The sluggish growth and rising debt therefore posed the most serious economic policy challenge since the period of hyper inflation and stagnation in the mid-1960s. Eschewing a

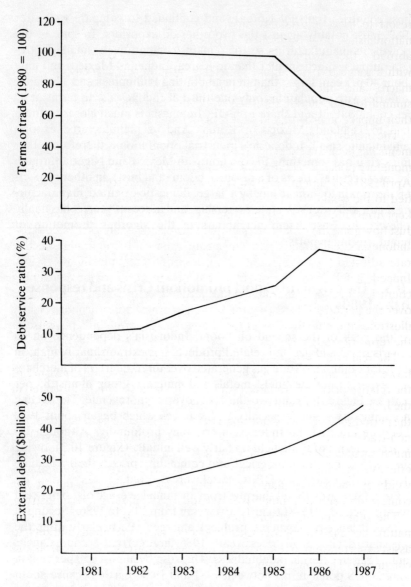

Notes: Debt is disbursed and outstanding long and medium-term debt, as at end of year.
The debt service ratio is debt repayments (principal plus interest) as a percentage of gross exports of goods and services.

Figure 10.3 Indonesia's terms of trade and external indebtedness: 1981–87. (Sources: Department of Finance, Jakarta, and World Bank)

resort to fiscal imprudence or a retreat to inward-looking economic nationalism – both counselled in some influential quarters at home and abroad – the government responded along broadly conventional lines with a range of expenditure switching and absorption measures, both macro- and microeconomic. The remainder of this section briefly summarises the major reforms, while the following section examines their impact on growth and export performance.

The major macroeconomic instrument to hasten structural adjustments has been the exchange rate, combined with conservative fiscal and monetary policies. There were two large devaluations of the rupiah, in April 1983 and September 1986,[6] in addition to the currency being loosely tied to the weakening US dollar. On both occasions inflation has been kept firmly under control, resulting in substantial effective devaluations. Just how great the orders of magnitude have been is a matter of debate.[7] Indonesia's real effective exchange rate – that is, the nominal effective rate adjusted for relative inflation rates – fell dramatically after 1982. Indeed, it fell more sharply than that of almost all major developing countries, including the debt-ridden economies of Brazil and Mexico, over the period 1981–88 (Figure 10.4). No other indicator more clearly illustrates the effectiveness of the Indonesian government's response to the terms-of-trade decline.

The real effective rate is an imperfect indicator of 'competitiveness', however, because it does not necessarily provide an accurate measure of the relative prices of 'tradables' and 'non-tradables'. This is illustrated in the Indonesian case by the construction of such a relative price index over the period 1980–87, using housing as an (albeit imperfect) indicator of the non-tradables category (Figure 10.5). The resulting index suggests a much smaller change in relative prices than that indicated by the real effective exchange rate.[8] Nevertheless, the general conclusion remains valid: exchange-rate management has been effective, in that it has conferred a decisive competitive advantage on tradable goods industries.

The other major reforms have been principally microeconomic in nature, designed to improve the efficiency of factor and goods markets, to assist exporters and to remove the dead hand of bureaucratic controls and corruption. They include the following measures.

10.3.1 *Putting exporters on a free market footing*

To ameliorate the effects of Indonesia's complex and highly interventionist system of protection, the government experimented with several 'compensatory financial' measures. Initially these took the form of a

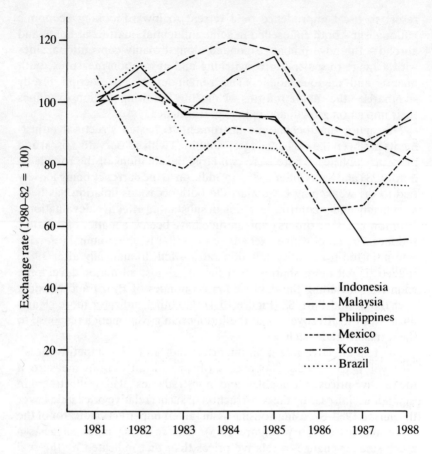

Figure 10.4 Real effective exchange rates: Indonesia and selected developing countries (1980–88). (Source: Morgan Guaranty, *World Financial Markets*, various issues)

straight-out payment to exporters under the *Sertifikat Ekspor* (Export Certificate) scheme. However, in 1985 it was dropped, on the grounds that it was a blunt and costly system, and because it was regarded as a subsidy and therefore unacceptable when Indonesia joined the GATT. In its place in May 1986 the government introduced a new arrangement, administered through a body known by its Indonesian acronym as P4BM, offering exporters a combination of duty drawbacks and exemptions on imported inputs. Managed by an able administrator who interpreted the scheme's regulations liberally, these arrangements proved very effective. By the middle of 1987, following some additional minor modifications,

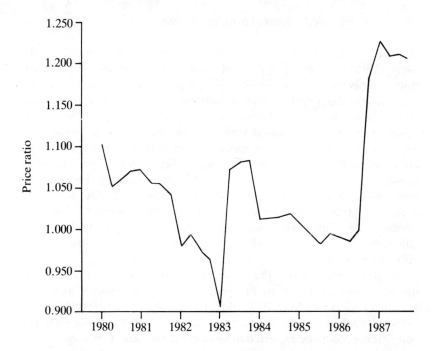

Note: 'Tradables' are denoted by the wholesale price index for imports, while
'non-tradables' are represented by the 17-city price index for housing.

Figure 10.5   Tradable/non-tradable price ratio in Indonesia: 1980–87. (Source:
BPS, *Indikator Ekonomi (Economic Indicator)*, Jakarta, various issues)

the scheme was accessible to virtually any Indonesian exporting firm,
regardless of size, location, industry or ownership.[9]

10.3.2   *Reform of the customs service*

In April 1985 the government transferred the entire responsibility for
customs surveillance to the Swiss company, SGS, removing all discretionary authority from the customs bureaucrats. The service had previously
been regarded as one of the most corrupt sections of the Indonesian
government, with high-level military involvement. An astonishing array
of bureaucratic requirements had resulted in long delays for both exports
and imports. The new system both removed corruption (with the
incidental side-effect of substantially increasing government revenue)
and facilitated the smooth flow of goods through the ports.

10.3.3   *A simplified system of trade protection*

Flushed with a second round of windfall revenue gains from oil, by the early 1980s Indonesia's system of manufacturing protection was extraordinarily complex and inefficient.[10] A plethora of non-tariff barriers (NTBs) was the major protective instrument, and many of these were administered in a highly politicised fashion. (For example, state enterprises or interests associated with powerful political individuals were awarded exclusive import licences; it was not uncommon for major domestic producers also to hold the import licence for the products they produced.) Moreover, effective rates of protection varied enormously, from instances of negative value added at international prices to rates in excess of 100 per cent. The system thus had the well-known distorting effects on resource allocation, exacerbated by the fact that many labour-intensive and potential export industries had low or even negative effective protection.

As described above, the government substantially reduced the implicit anti-export bias in the protection regime through its export reform measures of May 1986. But this left domestic-market-oriented firms untouched – including those which, through gradually acquired competence, could be expected to find export markets. This anomaly was addressed in an increasingly broad-ranging set of policy reform packages, introduced in October 1986, January and December 1987, and November 1988, which have progressively converted many of the NTBs to approximate tariff equivalents, or at least reduced the 'intensity' of the existing NTBs (for example, a shift from sole importer to general importer licensing). With tariffs once again becoming a more important instrument of protection, their structure has been simplified, though hardly unified, in order to reduce the huge inter-industry variations in effective protection. As a consequence, the proportion of manufacturing output covered by NTBs fell from almost one-half in mid 1986 to a little over one-third in early 1988 (Table 10.3). Significantly, the sharpest relative decline occurred in the textiles, clothing and footwear group, the major contributor to Indonesia's growing exports of footloose manufactures. Nevertheless, the coverage of NTBs after the reforms remains disturbingly high.

10.3.4   *A simplified system of licensing and regulation*

Although less amenable to quantification than the protection regime, the effects of the system of licensing and regulation on industrial performance and efficiency may have been even more damaging. By the early

Table 10.3 Effective protection and policy reform in Indonesian manufacturing.

Industry	Effective protection, 1985[a]	Coverage of NTBs[b]	
		Mid 1986	Early 1988
Textiles, clothing, footwear	49	64.0	38.2
Wood products	14	0	0
Paper and printing	14	69.6	50.4
Chemical products	45	59.9	51.1
Non-metallic minerals	43	28.2	21.7
Basic metals	31	45.5	29.2
Engineering products	48	86.7	60.3
Other manufactures[c]	40	28.9	24.6
Manufacturing[c]	n.a.	49.1	34.8

Source and Notes:
[a]Fane and Phillips (1987).
[b]Percentage of domestic production covered by import licences, as estimated by the World Bank.
[c]Excludes food, beverage and tobacco manufacture.

1980s, enterprises – particularly in the 'formal' sector – were subject to a daunting array of bureaucratic requirements from a wide range of government departments and agencies and different tiers of government (see McCawley, 1983, for an excellent description of the system). Practically every major – and many minor – commercial decisions by firms entailed complex negotiations with the bureaucracy, resulting in at least two general effects. One was simply the resource cost of the system: the sheer costs of bureaucratic compliance, and the centralising effects of such a regime (especially at a time when the government was actively attempting to promote a dispersed industrial structure). The second was the more general effect on the business environment. Complex and unworkable regulations not only produced a 'rent-seeking' environment in which genuine commercial expertise became a less important arbiter of performance, but also engendered a climate of business uncertainty owing to the unpredictable policy implementation of a system which conferred considerable discretionary authority on government officials.

Regulatory reform has proceeded more slowly than changes to the trade regime. The government's Capital Investment Coordinating Board (known as BKPM) has simplified its licensing requirements in a series of annual reforms since 1985. Foreign investment entry provisions are also more straightforward. But these largely piecemeal measures have been comparatively minor for a regime in need of fundamental reform.

10.3.5 *Other reforms*

Three other major sets of reforms have been introduced over the same period, with important implications for trade performance. First, beginning in 1984 sweeping modifications to the taxation system were enacted. Along with sharp cuts in prescribed rates of company and income tax, these included the abolition of virtually all fiscal incentives for investors, domestic and foreign alike (see Gillis, 1985, for a description of these reforms). Apart from the beneficial effects of removing the relative factor prices (principally capital-cheapening) distortions in the old system, the new arrangements do not appear to have deterred foreign investment, which rose significantly in 1987 and 1988. The second important reform, introduced progressively between 1983 and 1988, liberalised the banking industry, reducing the strangle-hold of the large state banks, removing many central bank subsidies, and encouraging greater competition. The reforms should be of major benefit to Indonesian firms, since banking 'spreads' (that is, between deposit and lending rates) are among the highest in East Asia. Finally, in late 1988 the government announced steps to improve efficiency in the state enterprise sector, an important reform not only because of sheer size of these firms, but also because many are producing key upstream inputs for downstream, more labour-intensive and export-oriented industries.

The reforms since 1983 have thus been comprehensive and effectively implemented, indicating in the process the extent of distortionary government intervention at the beginning of the decade. Before examining the effects of the reforms on export performance, in the next section, three general observations are pertinent.

First, there are several interesting 'political economy' lessons which emerge from the Indonesian reforms. Since the early 1970s the country's industrial policy climate has been shaped by the interaction between three loosely defined groups of senior officials favouring divergent sets of policies. At the risk of great oversimplification, these comprise the 'technocrats', favouring a more market-oriented, less *dirigiste* approach; the 'nationalists', who advocate more controls and intervention, and a broadly inward-looking strategy; and what might be termed a 'high tech' group, which, while in general agreement with the first group on broad industry policy, accords high priority to government promotion of a range of technologically sophisticated industries (aircraft, shipping, telecommunications). The first group has been firmly in control of the macroeconomic policy levers since the mid-1960s. Yet the lesson from the Indonesian experience is that these individuals were virtually powerless to tackle the soft micro 'under-belly' of the policy environment as long as oil prices remained high. Their political power derives almost exclusively from their credentials as competent economic managers. During the era of rapid, oil-induced growth, they made very little headway on micro-policy reform.

Declining oil prices changed this political economy equation quite fundamentally, placing greatly increased authority in the hands of these technocrats. As a corollary, Indonesia's powerful, centralised – and some would say authoritarian – political structure was able to ensure that most of the reforms have been effectively implemented. The government swept aside vested interests adversely affected by the banking, customs and trade policy reforms, not to mention any worker disaffection (including the huge civil-service workforce) arising from the cuts in real wages which were an inevitable consequence of the real devaluations. The Indonesian political economy experience may not be easily general-ised, nor may the combination of austerity and control be sustainable in the long run. But it is doubtful if any other political system could have delivered the same successful economic outcome as effectively.

The second observation is that, serious as Indonesia's growth decelera-tion and external indebtedness are, the country's economic problems do not resemble the crises of Latin American inflation nor African economic decline. Even during the most severe period of terms-of-trade decline, Indonesia still recorded real growth in per capita GDP, and inflation has been kept firmly under control. Despite periodic capital flight and speculative pressure on the rupiah – both, oddly, in 1987, well *after* the large 1986 devaluation and the worst of the terms-of-trade deterioration - there was never a 'crisis' atmosphere in Indonesian policy-making. This factor, combined with the quality of senior economic leadership and powerful presidential support, undoubtedly contributed to policy out-comes superior to those in many other countries. Moreover, owing to Indonesia's generally prudent macroeconomic management after 1966, to the fact that distortionary interventions, however harmful to growth and efficiency, were still comparatively mild, and to the country's liberal foreign-exchange regime, the government did not have to confront the difficult 'sequencing' issue[11] with which many other regimes had to grapple.

Finally, how do the Indonesian reforms rate in comparative interna-tional perspective? It is very difficult to obtain such accurate, cross-country data. One standard reference point is the schema employed in the 1970s, by the NBER's trade liberalisation project (see Bhagwati, 1978; Krueger, 1978), although this is not particularly useful for Indonesia which has maintained a very open exchange-rate regime since 1966. According to this five-phase classification, Indonesia probably would have been in phase II in the early 1980s (that is, intense reliance on quantitative restrictions), progressing to phase IV (substantial relaxation of such restrictions) towards the end of the decade. Such a substantial achievement should have contributed to export and (*ceteris paribus*) GDP growth. We now look at the actual record.

10.4 Outcome: Reforms which worked

There is little doubt that the reforms have been successful. Exports of manufactures, which had been negligible in the 1970s, rose dramatically after 1983. Manufactures rose from just 2 per cent of merchandise exports in 1980 to a projected 20 per cent in 1988, in the process overtaking traditional agricultural commodity exports, which had accounted for over 50 per cent of the total before 1970 (Figure 10.2). The sharply rising share was, of course, partly attributable to falling oil prices. But, equally, the value of manufactures rose impressively, from $500 million in 1980 to almost $4 billion in 1987, implying a nominal annual growth of 34 per cent (Table 10.5).[12] The increase was particularly marked after 1982, as successive reform measures began to take effect.

Several comments on this export expansion are in order. First, there has been strong reliance on a very small range of products. Plywood alone has generated up to 50 per cent of the total, following the government's progressive prohibition on the export of logs in the early 1980s. Such exports could hardly be considered 'manufactures' in any genuine sense, since they were simply the result of government-enforced export substitution, buttressed by the country's power in the international markets for tropical timber. Among the footloose industries, garments and textiles have been by far the most important exports, in most years producing over half this sub-total. Consequently, just three items have accounted for up to three-quarters of all manufactured exports during most years. Such a heavy concentration has rendered the country vulnerable to trends in these international markets. Nevertheless, Indonesia has followed the usual pattern among developing countries of initially penetrating world markets in a narrow range of products. Moreover, since about 1986 there have been indications of much greater export diversification, especially among the labour-intensive items (Table 10.5).[13]

Second, the composition of Indonesia's manufactured exports has broadly reflected the country's relative factor endowments, in that resource-based and labour-intensive manufactures have been dominant items. Such a trend is consistent with the hypothesis that export patterns are a better indication of revealed comparative advantage than those of production, since for most countries the latter are subject to more intensive government intervention, much of it often 'anti-market' in nature. Throughout the 1980s, Indonesia's strong export growth has been propelled by resource- and labour-intensive goods, which in most years have generated over 80 per cent of the total (Table 10.5). Moreover, even the small capital-intensive group has been dominated by exports such as fertiliser, paper products, steel products and tyres, all of which have a strong natural-resource component.

Indonesia's export specialisation is illustrated more clearly with reference to indices of revealed comparative advantage (RCA) for the three factor intensity groupings (Table 10.4). The country's poor export performance during the 1970s is reflected in uniformly low RCA indices for all categories. Those for the resource-intensive group began to rise sharply in the early 1980s, owing mainly to the ban on log exports. The index for the labour-intensive group also rose, although less spectacularly, and it remains much lower than that for neighbouring countries. By contrast, the RCA for capital-intensive exports has remained consistently low, with the special case of fertiliser the only major exception to this conclusion.

Table 10.4 Revealed comparative advantage (RCA) indices for Indonesian manufactured exports: 1970–86

	Total	Labour-intensive	Resource-intensive	Capital-intensive
1970	.02	.03	.02	.02
1975	.02	.02	.01	.02
1980	.04	.10	.20	.01
1981	.06	.09	.49	.02
1982	.07	.11	.70	.02
1983	.13	.22	1.53	.02
1984	.18	.26	1.61	.07
1985	.12	.20	1.51	.02
1986	.27	.38	3.13	.10

Notes: RCA index, commonly associated with Balassa (1965), is defined as:

$$\frac{X_{ij}}{X_i} \bigg/ \frac{X_{wj}}{X_w}$$

where: X_{ij} = country i's exports of commodity j
X_i = country i's total exports
X_{wj} = world exports of commodity j
X_w = world exports
For details of classification, see notes to Table 10.5.

Source: International Economic Data Bank, Research School of Pacific Studies, Australian National University, based on United Nations trade data. I am most grateful to Prue Phillips for the preparation of these data.

Table 10.5   Major manufactured exports of Indonesia: 1980–88 ($ million).

	1980	1981	1982	1983	1984	1985	1986	1987	1988	Average annual growth, 1980–87	
										Nominal value	Volume
Resource-intensive											
Total	119	257	354	770	832	992	1,209	2,036	1,404	50.0	n.a.
% of all manufactures	24	38	44	56	45	49	46	52	48		n.a.
Major items:											
plywood	68	195	316	738	791	941	1,127	1,901	1,291	60.9	35.9
cement	26	20	8	7	13	22	41	57	42	11.9	24.4
leather	6	6	7	6	7	8	15	45	41	33.4	40.7
Labour-intensive											
Total	287	249	323	486	826	785	1,054	1,303	1,024	24.1	n.a.
% of all manufactures	57	37	40	35	45	38	40	33	35		n.a.
Major items:											
clothing	98	95	116	157	296	339	522	596	418	29.4	28.9
woven fabrics	43	34	43	107	183	227	287	385	304	36.8	42.3
yarn	3	2	1	14	17	13	20	84	64	61.0	59.9
oils and perfumes	21	15	17	19	29	23	27	34	20	7.1	1.0
glass and glassware	3	2	3	9	10	8	13	31	46	39.6	41.9
electronics	94	74	117	125	214	77	29	15	17	–23.1	32.5
musical instruments	n	9	11	21	26	39	43	28	19	n	n
furniture	3	2	2	4	5	7	9	27	33	36.9	50.1
footwear	1	3	3	3	5	8	8	22	36	n	n

Capital intensive

Total	97	166	131	116	181	266	377	556	467	28.3	n.a.
% of all manufactures	19	25	16	8	10	13	14	14	16		
Major items:											
fertiliser	35	4	10	47	37	80	127	86	67	13.7	94.6
paper products	5	n	2	6	20	21	33	96	73	52.5	61.4
steel products	8	8	8	n	7	28	58	136	89	49.9	55.8
inorganic chemicals	n	5	2	4	33	35	27	25	12	n	48.5
rubber tyres	n	n	n	1	2	7	11	23	24	n	n
Total, all manufactures	501	673	809	1,373	1,839	2,044	2,639	3,895	2,895	34.1	n.a.
Three largest as % of total	52	54	68	74	71	74	73	74	70		

Notes: 1. The following definitions are used:

Resource-intensive – SITC items 61, 63, 66 (excluding 664–666), 671.

Labour-intensive – SITC items 54, 55, 65, 664–666, 695–697, 749, 776, 778, 793, 81–85, 89 (excluding 896–897).

Capital-intensive – SITC items 5 (excluding 54 and 55), 62, 64, 67 (excluding 671), 69 (excluding 695–697), 7 (excluding 749, 776, 778, 793), 86–88, 896–897.

This classification was developed by Krause (1982), as subsequently modified by Ariff and Hill (1985).

2. The following SITC codes are used for the major exports (corresponding ISIC codes in parentheses): plywood 634 (33113); cement 661 (3631); leather 611 (323); clothing 84 (322); yarn 651 (32112); woven fabrics 652–9 (32112); oils and perfumes 551 (35233); glass and glassware 664-5 (362); electronics 749, 776, 778 (3833); musical instruments 898 (3902); furniture 821 (332); footwear 851 (324); fertiliser 562 (3512); paper products 641 (341); steel products 672-3 (371); inorganic chemicals 522 (3511); rubber tyres 625 (3551).

3. 'n' indicates less than $1 million, and growth rates rendered irrelevant by very small initial base. 1988 data refer to January–July only.

Source: BPS, *Ekspor* [*Exports*], Jakarta, various issues.

Table 10.6 Characteristics of major manufacturing export industries in Indonesia.[a]

Industry	Exports, 1987 ($million) (1)	Factor intensity, 1985[b] (2)	Employment 1985 ('000) (3)	Index of production 1987 (1975=100) (4)	Average employees per firm, 1985 (5)
Plywood	1,901	95	88.0	557	907
Clothing	596	39	69.7	n.a.	108
Woven fabrics	385	50	156.3	154	152
Steel products	136	778	15.6	1,422	522
Paper products	96	133	21.6	219	160
Fertiliser	86	499	16.8	927	1,200
Yarn	84	102	65.6	125	698
Cement	57	284	13.7	806	1,247
Leather	45	80	4.4	n.a.	54
Oils and perfumes	34	114	6.5	n.a.	112
Glass and glassware	31	241	10.5	348	263
Musical instruments	28	378	0.4	n.a.	74
Furniture	27	37	12.6	n.a.	44
Inorganic chemicals	25	130	12.1	n.a.	105
Rubber tyres	23	48	12.6	356	419
Footwear	22	89	8.9	176	77
Electronics	15	200	19.7	208	179
Total/average for all industries		100	1,684.7	290	130

Notes: [a]Data in columns (2), (3), (5), (7)–(11) refer to firms with at least 20 employees.
[b]Defined as value added per employee as a percentage of this ratio for all manufacturing.
[c]Since the protection estimates are calculated from input–output classification, these are not always identical to the industry listed.
[d]Share of value added of four largest firms in the industry.
[e]Share of value added; private–foreign joint ventures classified as foreign; 'Govt JV' refers to state enterprises in joint ventures with foreign firms; 'Govt' includes private–government joint ventures.
n.a. Not applicable

Sources: BPS, *Ekspor* [*Export*], *Indikator Ekonomi* [*Economic Indicators*], Jakarta, various issues, and *Sensus Ekonomi 1986* [*1986 Economic Census*], Jakarta, 1988. Protection estimates from Fane and Phillips (1987).

Table 10.6 Continued.

Industry	Effective protection, 1985[c] (6)	Four-firm concentration rates, 1982[d] (7)	Ownership Shares, 1983[e]			
			Private (8)	Foreign (9)	Govt (10)	Govt (JV) (11)
Plywood	10	22	77.2	21.2	1.6	0
Clothing	26	46	97.2	2.6	0.2	0
Woven fabrics	61	35	62.2	27.4	9.2	1.2
Steel products	22	78	8.9	8.3	36.0	46.8
Paper products	147	51	50.5	23.7	25.8	0
Fertiliser	74	68	0	0	100	0
Yarn	52	35	53.6	35.4	9.9	1.1
Cement	36	68	15.2	8.5	55.3	21.0
Leather	8	64	70.9	0	29.1	0
Oils and perfumes	34	63	35.4	64.6	0	0
Glass and glassware	65	78	26.0	70.2	3.8	0
Musical instruments	43	100	2.1	97.9	0	0
Furniture	67	25	87.1	12.4	0.5	0
Inorganic chemicals	4	48	25.5	28.0	28.7	17.8
Rubber tyres	66	81	30.8	55.7	13.5	0
Footwear	79	71	17.9	75.6	6.6	0
Electronics	43	54	32.4	54.0	5.6	8.0
Total/average for all industries		n.a.				

Third, what of the characteristics of the major exporting industries? These cover such a diverse range of attributes as almost to defy generalisation (Table 10.6), but some common threads are evident. For one thing, the export drive has been led primarily by (domestic) private and government-owned firms (columns 8–11); industries dominated by foreign investors have played a comparatively minor role. Among the 'big three' exports (plywood, garments and textiles), private firms are dominant, while in two of the next three (steel products and fertiliser) state firms are the major actors. Indonesia's experience, therefore, does not support the frequent assertion that foreign investors are likely to play a crucial role in the early stages of developing countries' export-promotion strategies. Another feature of the export industries is that in most the average firm size is greater than the manufacturing average (column 5), suggesting the presence of pecuniary economies of scale which are necessary to take advantage of international market opportunities. Many of these industries are quite small employers of labour, however (column 3); again the 'big three' stand out. The impact of the trade regime on these industries has been varied, at least prior to the recent trade reform packages which placed exporting firms on an effective free-trade footing; all major export industries received at least some protection in 1985 (column 6), but the dispersion in effective rates was very considerable. Similarly, there was a substantial variation in seller concentration in these industries (column 7), with most being broadly competitive in nature.

Finally, Indonesia appears to have been more successful at export market diversification than at product diversification (Table 10.7). Notwithstanding strong nationalist sentiment concerning the dangers of 'dependence', particularly in the country's economic relations with Japan, in most major export industries there appears to be little basis for the exertion of monopolistic power on the part of overseas buyers. In only two of the seven major export industries – clothing and steel – does the largest market absorb over half of Indonesia's exports. And it is only in clothing that Indonesia displays an unhealthy reliance on a single market, a factor of special importance in view of a likely decline in aggregate American imports as the government attempts to reduce that country's current-account deficit.

In sum, Indonesia's move into export promotion has been reasonably successful. A number of effective reforms were introduced. In response, manufactured exports have grown rapidly. Although these exports have been concentrated in a narrow range of products, six years after the commencement of the boom there are firm signs that the growth has become more broad-based. Moreover, the exports have been dominated by industries in which Indonesia possesses a strong comparative advan-

Table 10.7 Major markets for selected manufactured exports of Indonesia: 1987 (3 major export markets, $million).

						Three markets as % of total
Plywood Japan	515	United States	405	China	232	60.6
Clothing United States	370	West Germany	44	Holland	35	75.3
Woven fabrics United States	60	Japan	46	Italy	38	37.4
Steel Japan	83	United States	35	Malaysia	8	92.7
Paper products Singapore	21	Hong Kong	21	Malaysia	21	64.9
Fertiliser China	29	Thailand	13	Japan	4	53.8
Yarn Singapore	18	Korea	16	Thailand	11	53.8

Source: BPS, *Ekspor 1987 [1987 Exports]*, Jakarta, 1988.

tage, international markets have been reasonably diversified and the export drive appears to have been led in the main by domestic (private and government) firms.

10.5 Beyond export promotion

Indonesia's trade policy reforms have been both necessary, in the face of a dramatic decline in the country's terms of trade resulting from falling oil prices, and desirable, on economic welfare grounds. Notwithstanding its creditable record, however, Indonesia's experience also highlights a number of critical considerations in the formulation and execution of successful export-promotion strategies. Some of these issues have tended to be neglected in the export-promotion literature.

First, and obvious, export-oriented trade policy reform involves much more than simply placing exporting firms on a free-trade footing. Three years into the reforms, Indonesian exporters were able to source their traded inputs at international prices with little difficulty. But beneath the 'hard state' record on macroeconomic reforms, there is still a soft micro 'under-belly' in the current regime. With regard to government contracts, and the non-traded sector more generally, much still needs to be done, since high costs in these areas inhibit the competitiveness of the tradable goods industries.[14] Despite the removal of many NTBs, much of Indonesian manufacturing still receives very high levels of effective protection; undoubtedly, many cases of high protection are politically inspired. The government has hardly begun to tackle the problems of inefficiency in the huge state-enterprise sector. And, as noted, reforms in the field of regulation and licensing have been a good deal less effective than the trade policy measures. For all these reasons, the partial removal of efficiency-retarding biases once firms have reached the 'export threshold' leaves many of the constraints to international competitiveness untouched. Moreover, underlying the whole reform process is a pervasive anti-market ideology in many influential sections of the Indonesian government. Not unreasonably, investors fear that a removal of the externally induced imperatives for reform could usher in a return to the past, inward-looking strategies.

The difficult balance between macro- and microeconomic reforms has also produced other problems. One obvious example is the poor state of Indonesia's physical and social infrastructure. Neglected during the decade of war and revolution in the 1940s, and for the first two decades of independence, by the late 1960s these were in an appalling state. Virtually all major services required for the functioning of a modern economy – roads, power, harbours, telecommunications, skilled labour – were in woefully inadequate supply, and basic needs such as health and education were being met at a very low standard. An immediate effect of the oil boom in the 1970s was a large increase in government revenue, much of which was immediately recycled in the form of development expenditures on such infrastructure requirements. Over the period 1972–83 these rose more than fourfold in real per capita terms, also doubling as a share of GDP (Table 10.8). Such a 're-stocking' of infrastructure undoubtedly contributed to the rapid growth of this period.

However, falling oil prices resulted in an equally sharp contraction. The government, understandably anxious to restore macroeconomic balance and facing a drastic squeeze on its 'discretionary' expenditures owing to rising debt-service commitments, cut its capital expenditures dramatically. But in the process a major dilemma has emerged: the primary objective of its reforms has been the promotion of the non-oil sector, particularly manufacturing, but these activities require an efficient infrastructure support base to be competitive. There is no simple resolution of this problem. Fiscal austerity must continue as a cornerstone of policy. But this will have to be supplemented increasingly by a range of innovative initiatives in the provision of infrastructure, such as

Table 10.8 Public finance in Indonesia: 1972–87.

	Domestic revenue		Development expenditure	
	as % of GDP	Real per capita (Rp '000)	as % of GDP	Real per capita (Rp '000)
1972	12.8	21.6	6.4	10.7
1973	14.5	27.0	7.0	13.1
1974	16.4	33.5	9.0	18.4
1975	17.7	35.2	11.1	22.0
1976	18.8	37.2	13.3	26.3
1977	18.6	39.8	11.3	24.3
1978	17.8	43.3	10.6	26.0
1979	19.5	55.1	11.7	33.0
1980	20.9	69.3	12.1	40.1
1981	20.9	72.2	11.9	41.1
1982	19.8	65.7	11.7	38.9
1983	19.6	66.8	13.4	45.8
1984	18.3	65.3	11.4	40.9
1985	20.4	73.9	11.5	41.7
1986	16.7	57.3	8.6	29.6
1987	15.8	54.8	7.1	24.7

Source: Republik Indonesia, *Nota Keuangan* [*Financial Note*], Jakarta, various issues.

leasing, user-cost provision, more aggressive utilisation of foreign aid and investment, and perhaps even some stimulus in the form of greater rural public works, especially if it can be demonstrated that the import leakages are low.

The Indonesian experience also illustrates that countries can easily overdo the export-promotion strategy. One example, referred to earlier, was the country's Export Certificate scheme, a blunt and second-best compensatory promotional instrument. Two more recent and important cases concern prohibitions on unprocessed commodity exports, and the export-pricing strategies of state enterprises.

Motivated by a desire to develop downstream processing linkages, to increase fiscal returns and to exert its power in international markets, the Indonesian government has progressively banned the export of unprocessed logs, rattan, leather and hides. Of these, the former has been by far the most significant, explaining the spectacular increase in plywood exports, from $120 million in 1980 to a probable $2.5 billion in 1988 (Table 10.5). The objective of resource-rent maximisation is laudable: research during the 1970s suggested that Indonesia probably extracted less than one-third of the potential revenue from its timber exports (Ruzicka, 1979), for a variety of reasons ranging from commercial and administrative inexperience to outright corruption. But the ban has certainly been a sub-optimal instrument for rent appropriation. Timber concessions have been tied to investments in processing, resulting in excess capacity and inefficiency in the latter sector. Felling has been indiscriminate, owing to very poor-quality resource management and political abuses, and has resulted in the depletion of valuable timber stands at an excessive rate on both economic and environmental grounds. And the ban has contributed little to the objective of improved agro-industry linkages, since firms need only invest in the most minimal low-quality processing facilities to obtain access to valuable concessions. For all these reasons, the returns from forest exports have been disappointing, and the growth of plywood exports – by far the largest item among manufactures – a poor indicator of genuine export-oriented industrialisation.[15]

The exports of state enterprises raise a different issue. These firms play a significant role in a number of newly emerging export industries, mainly in heavy processing activities such as steel, paper products, fertiliser, cement and inorganic chemicals (Table 10.6). While Indonesia has a competitive advantage in such resource-based industries, the pricing structures of these firms suggest that in some instances the real returns from exporting are questionable. While financial data on Indonesian state enterprises are notoriously difficult to obtain, most receive substantial state subsidies, in the form of cheap credit and loan guarantees, direct grants and a range of other facilities (free land is a common example). Moreover, as energy-intensive operations, these firms benefit from the subsidised pricing which is presumed to exist between the huge state-owned oil and gas conglomerate, Pertamina, and other state affiliates. None of this is to deny the significance of these firms' recent export performance, nor to suggest that Indonesia does not possess a comparative advantage in such activities. Rather, there appear to be implicit subsidies in some exports, possibly to compensate for inefficiencies elsewhere in the system.

A final factor in Indonesia's export strategy, and perhaps the most important determinant of its long-run success, is political sustainability. The reforms underpinning the export drive have, like all attempts at significant structural adjustment, generated an array of political tensions and challenges. Most of these derive not so much from the export strategy *per se*, as from the sharp deterioration in the country's terms of trade in the mid-1980s. But political pressures have the capacity to disrupt the course of economic reform. Successful real devaluations, for example, inevitably imply a reduction in real wage rates – though not necessarily in the real wage bill for manufacturing – and this has almost certainly occurred (Jayasuriya and Manning, 1988). The removal of special licensing facilities and other concessions, equally, creates disenchantment among the former beneficiaries. Increased reliance on the market and the private sector results in an expanded role for foreign and non-indigenous (principally Chinese) firms, to the dismay of nationalist groupings.

Thus far, Indonesia's political structures have weathered the transition to an export-oriented strategy successfully, for a variety of reasons not adequately understood (Mackie, 1989). A measure of heavy-handedness, an appreciation in the general community of the need for restraint and reform, and the partial insulation of much of the rural population from external shocks may be part of the explanation, but none is entirely convincing. Inevitably for a regime in power for almost one-quarter of a century, attention now focuses on the post-Soeharto era, and on whether future political systems will be able to maintain the pace of reform.

Notes

1. For a more detailed account of economic developments since 1965 see the four-monthly 'Survey of recent developments' published in the *Bulletin of Indonesian Economic Studies*, Australian National University. The best general reference on the economy, though now rather dated, is Booth and McCawley (1981).
2. For such an important country, the literature on Indonesian industrialisation is surprisingly sparse. The best reference up to the late 1970s is McCawley (1981). Important recent material includes Poot *et al.* (forthcoming) and Thee (1988). See also the industry sections in the recent 'Surveys' for the *Bulletin of Indonesian Economic Studies* (Note 1), especially Pangestu (1987), Hill (1987), and Jayasuriya and Manning (1988). Other studies include Rocpstorff (1985) and Beals (1987). Soehoed (1988) contains an interesting account of industrialisation, by one of the chief architects of industrial policy after 1966.
3. Recent and as yet unpublished research suggests that the recorded slow-down after 1980 might have been exaggerated by the fact that growth rates in the late 1970s were overestimated. But the broad picture of rapid growth since 1970 and a deceleration after 1980 is probably still correct.
4. The following definitions are used for these categories, according to ISIC (International Standard Industrial Classification) codes:
   Light industry: ISIC 31, 32, 33, 342, 355, 356, 39
   Heavy processing industry: ISIC 341, 351, 352, 353, 354, 36, 37
   Capital goods industry: ISIC 38
5. For a detailed analysis of the sudden reduction in growth, see Sundrum (1986, 1988).
6. An earlier devaluation, in November 1978, was quickly overtaken by the effects of the (unanticipated) second round of oil price increases.
7. See Arndt and Sundrum (1984) and Warr (1984b, 1986) for discussion of this issue.
8. Note that an increase in the index in Figure 10.5 indicates a devaluation, whereas the reverse is the case in Figure 10.4.

9. It might be noted in passing that the government did not take the next step and establish export-processing zones. Indonesia is alone among East Asian developing countries in not establishing such zones on any scale, apart from a small zone in Jakarta (Warr, 1983). The major explanation appears to have been that the government has not been prepared to permit 100 per cent foreign ownership, a usual feature of such zones, nor provide the basic infrastructure requirements.
10. Major studies of Indonesia's protection policies in the decade up to the early 1980s include Pangestu and Boediono (1986), Parker (1985), Pitt (1981), and an unpublished World Bank report for the year 1975. Fane and Phillips (1987) provide the most complete and up-to-date study.
11. That is, the question of whether to liberalise first in the capital or current account of the balance of payments. See Edwards (1984) for a discussion of the issues involved here.
12. A note on definitions is appropriate here. In Tables 10.4–10.7 the conventional definition of 'manufactured exports' is employed, namely SITC 5–8 less SITC 68. However, such a classification can be misleading since it does not correspond exactly to the national-accounts definition of 'manufacturing' (that is, ISIC 3). The former excludes many resource-based activities, a non-trivial omission as illustrated by the following 1987 export data for Indonesia (in $ million):

Trade definition (SITC 5–8 less 68)	$3,895
Production definition (ISIC 3) – total	$10,182
– non-oil (+gas)	$6,666

The conventional trade definition is employed throughout this chapter, since data using the latter method are not easily available. For more discussion of this issue see Hill (1986).
13. This diversification is only barely evident in the shares of the three largest exports (bottom row, Table 10.5) because of the rapid growth in plywood exports after 1986; however, the trend is clear in the 'non-plywood' categories.
14. For a dramatic exposé of business and politics in Indonesia and the complex networks of political patronage, see the three-part report in the *Asian Wall Street Journal*, 24–26 November 1986. Robison (1986) provides a more historical and scholarly perspective.
15. There has been a considerable debate on the costs and benefits of the log export ban. See, for example, Fitzgerald (1987) and Lindsay (forthcoming). Pangestu (1989) provides a local perspective on one of the major timber regions of the country.

11

India: Export promotion policies and export performance

V. N. Balusubramanyam and Dipak R. Basu

11.1 Introduction

The story of India's export performance and policies has often been told. It is a story of missed opportunities and neglect of exports during the decade of the 1950s and early 1960s, and of haphazard and uncoordinated efforts at export promotion since then. The story also offers valuable insights into many of the controversial issues relating to exports and development. The first of these relates to the relative impact of domestic supply factors and external demand constraints on the export perform- ance of developing countries. Ingrained in this area are issues relating to the influence of economic size of countries, commodity composition and market orientation on exports. Second is the issue of the scope and relevance of various sorts of incentives for exports in an economic environment fraught with policy-induced distortions. Third is the broad issue of whether or not an outward-looking strategy of development is desirable for a country of India's size and long history of inward-looking development, and whether or not such a country could in fact make a successful transition from an inward-looking to an outward-looking strategy even if it were desirable to do so.

This chapter reviews India's export performance and policies since the 1950s to the present in the light of these issues. The second section reviews India's export performance and policies during the decade of the 1950s, a phase which can be described as one of benign or even wanton neglect of the export sector. The third section analyses the performance and policies from the early to the mid-1960s, a period during which a wide variety of export incentive schemes were adopted. The fourth section analyses the post-1966 devaluation-cum-export incentive schemes and their impact on India's export performance. The final section pulls together the main conclusions of the essay.

11.2 Export performance and policies during the 1950s

This period in India's economic history coincides with the first two of her Five-Year Plans. Much of the academic debate on India's economic performance and policies during this period is centred on the design and economic philosophy of the Second Five-Year Plan (1956–61); for the second plan not only heralded the beginning of a process of centralised economic planning in India but also set in motion the inward-looking strategy of development with import-substituting industrialisation as the centre-piece of the strategy. The theoretical underpinning of the plan (christened in the literature as the Mahalanobis model after its architect, the reputable Indian statistician Professor Mahalanobis), with its emphasis on investments in heavy industry, and the allocation of planned investments biased in favour of the public sector of the economy, have all been the subject of a number of studies (Bhagwati and Chakravarthy, 1969; Bhagwati and Desai, 1970; Rudra, 1973). The issue of relevance to this essay, though, is the role allotted to exports in the Plan. It is by now well known that the thrust of the Second Five-Year Plan was on the domestic transformation of savings into investment with an in-built investment allocation strategy which emphasised investments in capital goods industries as opposed to consumer goods industries, and hence provided for a maximisation of investment in the short run. In this scheme exports or the transformation of domestic savings into investment via foreign trade was largely ignored.

Various explanations abound in the literature for this neglect. One explanation is that the comfortable balance-of-payments position and the fairly impressive performance of the export sector during the period of the First Five-Year Plan (1951–56) imbued a sense of complacency on the part of the planners, and they settled for whatever contribution exports were likely to make to overall resource availability without any conscious efforts at promoting exports. This may be a much too charitable explanation of the neglect of exports in the grand design of the Second Five-Year Plan. Admittedly the accumulated foreign currency reserves at the time of India's independence in 1947 cushioned the balance of payments, and the average growth in the volume of exports during the First Plan period showed an improvement over that achieved during the three preceding years 1948 to 1950. During the period 1951–56 the volume of India's exports grew at an annual average rate of 5.4 per cent.

But the growth in volume was more than offset by the post-Korean war decline in prices resulting in a negative growth rate of exports at 6.8 per cent per annum (Table 11.1). However, as several studies on India's export performance have noted, the country's share in world exports precipitously declined from 2.5 per cent in 1947 to 1.4 per cent by the end of 1956. Indeed this decline in India's share of world exports continued unabated well into the 1960s and 1970s, with the share being a mere 0.41 per cent by the end of the year 1979 (Singh, 1964; Bhagwati and Desai, 1970; Wolf, 1982). During the 1950s India lost ground to her competitors in most of the commodities in which she had a sizeable share of the world market. In the case of tea her share of world exports declined from a high of 50 per cent in the early 1950s to 30 per cent by the end of 1960; in the case of the jute manufactures it declined from 86 per cent to 73 per cent; and in the case of the cotton textiles India's share in world exports declined from 13 per cent to well below 11 per cent. The story was much the same in the case of several other items of traditional exports such as vegetable oils, oil seeds and tobacco. In the face of these facts policy-makers could hardly have been complacent about India's export performance. Why then the neglect of exports and the opportunity to transform domestic savings into investment through foreign trade?

Another explanation for the neglect of exports in the early years of planning is that India's policy-makers were influenced by the prevalent thesis of export pessimism, a major theme in development economics during the 1950s. Briefly put, the thesis is that primary commodity exports, of the sort India's exports consisted of during the 1950s, were faced with a stagnant world demand as a consequence of both relatively low income elasticities of demand for such commodities, and the growth of substitution of synthetic materials for raw materials in the production process of manufactured products in the developed countries (Nurkse, 1959). Analogous is the Prebisch–Singer thesis that developing countries specialising in the production and exports of primary products experienced a long-run deterioration in the terms of trade. Primary products were faced with relatively low income and price elasticities of demand, and increased supplies of such commodities would serve only to depress their prices relative to those of manufactured goods imported by the developing countries (Singer, 1950; Prebisch, 1959). Thus, while the traditional doctrine of comparative cost advantage points to potential gains from trade, there was no guarantee that the developing countries specialising in the production and exports of primary commodities could reap a fair share of the gains.

This explanation for the neglect of exports on the part of India's policy-makers in the early years of planning is also not convincing. For, as stated earlier, since the 1950s India has lost ground to her competitors

Table 11.1   India's exports: annual average growth rates (1951–88).

Year	Total value of exports (Rs million)	Growth rate (%)	Volume index of exports (1968–69=100)	Growth rate (%)
1951–2	7,289		58	
1952–3	5,273		65	
1953–4	5,262	−6.8	65	5.4
1954–5	5,885		68	
1955–6	6,039		75	
1956–7	6,130		71	
1957–8	5,845		77	
1958–9	5,532	0.9	70	−0.2
1959–60	6,299		75	
1960–1	6,329		70	
1961–2	6,606		74	
1962–3	6,853		79	
1963–4	7,932	4.2	89	3.7
1964–5	8,163		93	
1965–6	8,065		87	
1966–7	10,949		84	
1967–8	11,987		86	
1968–9	13,579	7.1	100	4.9
1969–70	14,133		100	
1970–1	15,352		106	
1971–2	16,080		107	
1972–3	19,708		120	
1973–4	25,230	21.0	125	6.3
1974–5	33,288		133	
1975–6	40,430		147	
1976–7	51,460		174	
1977–8	54,040		168	
1978–9	57,260	5.4	139	5.2
1979–80	64,590		199	
1980–1	66,750		135	
1981–2	77,423		139	
1982–3	83,091		135	
1983–4	88,096		141	
1984–5	99,812	8.2	145	2.2
1985–6	104,279		145	
1986–7	114,896		154	
1987–8	151,790		154	

Sources: Estimated on the basis of data in *Basic Statistics Relating to the Indian Economy*, *1950–51 to 1968–69* (Planning Commission), *Report on Currency and Finance*, 1980–81 Vol. II, Reserve Bank of India, and the *Reserve Bank of India Bulletin* (various issues).

in many of her traditional exports in which she possessed a comparative advantage, mainly because of the increase in the price of her exports relative to that of her competitors. As several studies have noted, the poor export performance of India during this period was largely a consequence of increasing domestic pressures, lack of attention to product quality, and a trade policy which in many cases hampered rather than promoted exports by levying export duties and imposing controls on exports (Singh, 1964; Bhagwati and Desai, 1970). These facts suggest that loss of competitiveness on the external markets rather than an external demand constraint was a significant factor in India's poor export performance during the 1950s. In any case, as Bhagwati suggests, the argument that a significant expansion of exports was unlikely to materialise was not spelt out in the early draft Plan documents. It is also worth noting that the celebrated theses of Nurkse and Prebisch concerning export pessimism were fully adumbrated only in the late 1950s long after the Second Five-Year Plan was in operation. These facts lend credence to Bhagwati and Desai's suggestion that the thesis of export pessimism was an *ex post* rationalisation of the inward-looking investment in industrialisation strategy underlying the Second Five-Year Plan. It is also worth noting that the observed growth in world trade during the 1950s and 1960s provides little support to the export pessimism thesis. As Bhagwati notes, world trade did not merely grow rapidly during the 1950s and 1960s, it grew even faster than world income. While world output grew at an annual average rate of 4.2 per cent during the period 1953–63, world trade increased at a rate of 6.1 per cent (Bhagwati, 1988).

The only plausible explanation for the neglect of exports and the opportunity to transform domestic savings into investment through foreign trade during the 1950s and early 1960s appears to be the policy-makers' allegiance to the principle of 'self-reliance', an enduring theme in India's economic philosophy. Successive Five-Year Plans have endorsed 'self-reliance' as an objective of development planning. This in itself may be unexceptionable. Broadly interpreted, self-reliance means no more than relying on one's endowments and resources with a view to maximising one's economic gains. And such maximisation of gains may require exchanging those goods and services which one is relatively efficient at producing for goods and services which others are efficient at producing. Indeed, the doctrine of comparative cost advantage of international trade theory is no more than an enunciation of the principle of self-reliance. Simply put, the doctrine states that countries should specialise in those goods whose opportunity costs at home are low relative to those of other countries and exchange them through trade for goods whose opportunity costs of production at home are relatively high.

In India, however, self-reliance appears to have been equated with self-sufficiency. As Lipton and Firn (1975) succinctly put it, self-reliance in the Indian context does not mean 'let us do what we are good at doing', but rather, 'leave us all we are in principle able to do'. This adherence of the policy-makers to the principle of self-sufficiency may have been influenced to a large extent by the sheer size of the economy with its endowment of relatively abundant labour and natural resources, both of which permit in principle the production and sale of a wide range of goods on the domestic market. It is also likely that in the early heady days of independence from a colonial power economic nationalism was running high, with the objective of a speedy reduction of economic dependence on the former colonial power and economic self-reliance being a manifestation of such nationalism. It should be of little surprise that in the prevailing circumstances with the principle of self-sufficiency being the dominant economic objective, exports and the foreign-trade route of transforming domestic savings into investment were largely ignored.

11.3   Export performance and policies up to the mid-1960s

The growth in volume of exports achieved during the First Five-Year Plan years was short-lived. During the years of the Second Plan (1956–61) both the volume of exports and average price of exports stagnated. The growth in the value of exports during this period was a mere 0.8 per cent per annum (Table 11.1). Indeed, if we disregard the contribution of the Korean-war boom to the growth in the volume of exports during the first half of the First Five-Year Plan, India's export earnings stagnated during the entire decade of the 1950s.

As argued earlier, domestic policies which neglected and in many cases discouraged exports rather than an overall demand constraint were responsible for the stagnation of India's exports during the 1950s. It is by now received wisdom that the import-substituting industrialisation strategy had provided entrepreneurs with highly lucrative domestic markets sheltered from international competition in the presence of which they had little incentive to turn to the highly competitive export markets. The policy-oriented bias in favour of production for domestic as opposed to export markets is indicated by the estimates of 'purchasing-power parity effective exchange rates' (PPP-EER) for imports and exports. The effective exchange rate (EER) indicates the number of units of rupees actually paid or received for a unit of foreign exchange. This could exceed the nominal or official exchange rate at which a unit of foreign exchange is converted into rupees, if international transactions are subject to various forms of restrictions and incentives. If there are subsidies on exports, the EER would exceed the official rate by the extent of subsidies. Likewise if there are tariffs and various sorts of surcharge on imports, the EER for imports could exceed the official rate by the extent of tariffs and surcharges. The EER, adjusted for changes in international prices of traded goods relative to their domestic prices, yields the PPP-EER. Depending on the rates of tariffs and subsidies, the PPP-EER could differ between commodities and different sectors. In general, if the PPP-EER for imports exceeds that for exports, production of import substitutes would be relatively profitable. In other words, the number of rupees earned by producing import substitutes would exceed that which can be earned by producing for the export market, because the domestic price of import substitutes would exceed that of comparable imports by the extent of tariffs and quotas on imports.

Available estimates indicate that the PPP-EER for imports was consistently higher than that for exports throughout the 1950s and 1960s, although the gap tended to narrow after 1962 (Table 11.2). This observed differential between the PPP-EER for imports and exports indicates the policy-induced bias in favour of production for the domestic market and against that for exports.

Exports, however, could not be ignored for long. The capital goods-oriented industrialisation strategy of the Second Five-Year Plan had not conferred all the hoped-for benefits. Far from easing the balance of payments, the import-intensive nature of the industrialisation process had imposed a strain on the balance of payments. Foreign aid, which had enabled the economy to ride out the exchange crisis in 1956, could not be relied upon for ever to ease the payments positions; in any case, one of the objectives of the development progress was to relieve the country from dependence on foreign aid. The policy-makers were thus forced into the realisation that increased export earnings were an imperative necessity. The wide-ranging schemes of export promotion instituted with the beginning of the Third Five-Year Plan were in effect an attempt at redressing the bias against exports. We proceed to describe briefly the nature and extent of these schemes prior to analysing their impact on India's exports.

11.3.1   *Export incentives (1962–66)*

Two distinct periods can be identified in the history of India's export incentive schemes: the period up to the year 1966 when the rupee was devalued, and the post-devaluation period. Although various sorts of export-incentive schemes were in operation even during the 1950s, a vigorous effort at export promotion was undertaken only in the early 1960s beginning with the institution of various sorts of export-

Table 11.2 Purchasing power parity: effective exchange rates (Rs/US $) for India (1950–86)

Year	Imports (EER$_m$)	Exports (EER$_x$)	Import/Export (EER$_m$/EER$_x$)
1950	5.25	4.14	1.27
1955	7.30	5.74	1.27
1960	5.67	4.86	1.17
1961	5.83	4.84	1.20
1962	5.97	5.04	1.18
1963	6.06	4.93	1.23
1964	5.66	4.71	1.20
1965	5.73	4.79	1.20
1966	7.31	5.68	1.29
1967	6.23	4.86	1.28
1968	6.32	5.20	1.22
1969	6.50	5.31	1.22
1970	6.65	5.38	1.24
1971	10.25	7.66	1.34
1972	11.39	8.08	1.41
1973	10.51	8.20	1.28
1974	10.09	8.13	1.24
1975	12.13	10.08	1.20
1976	13.00	10.69	1.22
1977	13.01	10.77	1.21
1978	15.18	12.44	1.22
1979	14.41	11.89	1.21
1980	12.68	10.42	1.21
1981	13.96	11.47	1.21
1982	16.37	13.45	1.22
1983	17.33	14.24	1.22
1984	18.59	15.44	1.20
1985	19.80	17.06	1.16
1986	19.92	17.16	1.16

Note: $EER = R(1 + S_j) I_{wj}/I_{ij}$
where EER = Purchasing power parity exchange rate
   R = Nominal exchange rate (Rs/US$)
   S_j = Net subsidy rate on the jth category of exports and imports
   I_{wj} = World inflation index in imports in jth category of exports and imports
   I_{ij} = Indian inflation index in jth category of exports and imports.

Sources: Estimates for 1950–71 from Bhagwati and Srinivasan (1975). Estimates for 1972–81 from Wolf (1982). Estimates for 1981–86 based on data in IMF *Exchange Rate and Inflation Indices.*

subsidisation policies. The export-subsidisation policies prior to the devaluation in 1966 can be broadly grouped into two: (1) fiscal measures, and (2) import entitlement schemes. The first of these consisted of a variety of measures including exemptions from sales tax, refunds of indirect taxes paid on inputs, direct tax concessions, outright subsidies, and rail freight concessions. The complex nature of these schemes and the bureaucratic delays and inefficiencies associated with their administration have often been recounted (Bhagwati and Desai, 1970; Bhagwati and Srinivasan, 1975; Bagchi, 1981). Suffice it to note that the scope and content of these schemes were frequently changed and the schemes imposed a considerable cost on the exchequer. For instance, as Bhagwati and Srinivasan note, the refund of excise duties to exporters alone amounted to Rs58 million in the year 1963–64.

Import entitlement sch⌐ ⌐es, however, constituted the principal method of export promotion. These schemes have attracted considerable attention in the literature both because of their complex nature and the interesting analytical issues they pose. In essence the scheme entitled eligible exporters to receive import licences, fetching high import premia, in proportion to the exports effected. More specifically the scheme allowed a specified percentage of the f.o.b. value of exports to be retained and used for the importation of raw materials and components required in the production of exports. The general rule was that the import entitlement would not exceed 75 per cent of f.o.b. export value, and the import entitlement would equal only twice the value of import content. Bhagwati and Srinivasan (1975) have graphically described the complex nature of the scheme and the observed non-adherence to the stated general rule in the operation of the scheme. Given the overriding objective of maximising the value of exports, the twin principles governing the general rule were more often than not ignored. In addition, subject to certain constraints, exporters were allowed to sell their entitlements to other exporters, and earn whatever premia the entitlements fetched on the market. It is also worth noting that the rule that entitlements were for the importation of raw materials and components required in the production of exports was also relaxed with the introduction of the so-called special dry-fruits scheme. Under the scheme exporters of items such as engineering goods and chemicals were given import licences to import dry fruit, which hardly counts as an input in the production of chemicals and engineering goods, and allowed to earn the high premia they fetched on the market. According to Bhagwati and Srinivasan the value of exports covered by the entitlement schemes amounted to around 60 to 80 per cent of total Indian exports.

The import entitlement schemes were replaced with the import replenishment scheme soon after the devaluation of the rupee in 1966. It is, however, worth noting the economic effects of the scheme. The scheme along with the other fiscal measures no doubt contributed to the growth of export earnings at around 3.7 per cent per annum during the period 1961–66 (Table 11.1). This growth in exports was in large measure due to the addition of a number of relatively fast-growing items in world trade such as chemicals, engineering goods, clothing, handicrafts and leather manufactures to India's exports (Table 11.3). Most of these goods were covered by the export incentive schemes, and the incentives they provided appears to have had the desired effect of rendering exports a profitable activity relative to domestic sales. Even so, it is pertinent to ask whether the complicated bureaucratically administered schemes were the most efficacious method of promoting exports as opposed to either an outright devaluation of the rupee or an across-the-board *ad valorem* subsidy on exports. Bhagwati and Srinivasan's incisive analysis of the issue comes to the conclusion that while the Third Plan witnessed a major shift towards export subsidisation, export-promotion policies were inefficiently designed and implemented. The major factor contributing to the inefficient design of the scheme of import entitlements was the lack of uniformity. The subsidisation schemes, as Bhagwati and Srinivasan argue, involved policy intervention in a selective manner, with little economic rationale. There was obviously little by way of economic rationale for the stipulation that exporters were entitled to imports of inputs amounting to twice the value of their requirements. The one more unit of import in addition to 'replacement' was obviously designed to offset the attractions of the profitable domestic markets. But the scheme inevitably resulted in differing rates of *ad valorem* subsidies for different commodities, as the rate of subsidies under the scheme was tied to the import content of exports. Moreover, the premia that the entitlements fetched on the domestic market also differed between commodities because of the restrictions placed on their sale. It is this selectivity and non-uniform nature of the scheme that resulted in indiscriminate export promotion with little economic basis. The import entitlements which were tied to the f.o.b. value of exports also provided an incentive to over-invoice exports, and send out shoddy goods in search of short-run profits. Another built-in inefficiency of the import entitlement scheme relates to the self-limiting nature of the subsidy it provided to exporters. One of the incentives to export which the scheme provided was the premiums on import entitlements the exporters could earn on the domestic market. But if the export values increased as a result of the scheme, entitlements entering the market would increase proportionately, thus driving down the premiums. And the lower the premium, the lower also the incentive to export at the margin.

Many of these inefficiencies could have been avoided by implementing a scheme of across-the-board *ad valorem* subsidies for all exports or a suitable devaluation designed to offset the overvaluation of the effective exchange rate for exports. But as in most areas of economic policy the Indian policy-makers appear to have opted for a cumbersome, bureaucratically administered scheme. The devaluation of the rupee in 1966 appears to have been, in part, a response to the problems posed by the complicated system of export incentives.

11.4   The 1966 devaluation and export incentive schemes in the post-devaluation period

The devaluation of the rupee in 1966 was in part an attempt at offsetting the overvaluation of the effective exchange rate for exports which the complex scheme of subsidies had begun to create. It was also forced upon the government by the Aid-India consortium which made devaluation a precondition for the resumption of aid following the India–Pakistan war, during which period aid had been suspended. The rupee was devalued by 57.5 per cent on 6 June 1966, with the official rate for the dollar increasing from Rs4.76 to Rs7.50. The devaluation was accompanied by various other measures including the removal of the import entitlement schemes for exporters, abolition of a number of cash subsidy schemes for exports, imposition of countervailing export duties on a number of traditional exports in which India was supposed to enjoy monopoly power, and a significant reduction in import duties. This policy package was then conceived as an attempt at streamlining the existing complicated set of export incentive schemes. The supposed rationale for the removal of various sorts of subsidies on exports, including the import entitlements, was that the devaluation would be an efficient and adequate substitute for the subsidies. The countervailing duties on traditional exports were designed to offset the effects of devaluation on exports which faced an inelastic demand with respect to price on external markets. The significant reduction in tariffs on a number of imports was again an attempt at offsetting the effect of the devaluation on the domestic price of imported items. These policies accompanying the devaluation, however, served to lower the effective degree of devaluation implied by the nominal change in parity. Bhagwati and Srinivasan's detailed estimates of the impact of the various measures accompanying the formal devaluation of the effective exchange rates for exports and imports show that the net devaluation was around 21.6 per cent for exports and 42.3 per cent for imports. This compares with the formal devaluation of the rupee by 57.5 per cent. The reduction in the effective devaluation for exports from that implied by the nominal devaluation was due to the imposition of countervailing duties on nearly 62 per cent of the total value of traditional

Table 11.3 Commodity composition of India's exports (1950–85) (percentage of total exports).

	1950-1	1955-6	1960-1	1965-6	1970-1	1975-6	1976-7
Traditional exports	70.6	68.9	64.4	60.0	42.6	28.9	26.9
Tea	13.4	17.9	18.7	14.3	9.7	5.9	5.7
Jute manufactures	18.9	19.4	20.5	22.7	12.4	6.2	3.9
Cotton	19.7	9.3	8.7	6.9	4.9	4.0	5.2
Non-traditional exports	6.5	7.0	15.2	24.5	40.0	53.7	53.3
Iron ore	–	1.0	2.6	5.2	7.5	5.3	4.6
Silver	n.a.	n.a.	n.a.	n.a.	n.a.	4.3	3.3
Gems	n.a.	n.a.	–	1.8	2.7	3.7	5.6
Leather and leather							
manufactures	4.3	3.8	4.1	4.3	5.3	5.6	4.6
Iron and steel	0.3	n.a.	1.5	1.6	5.9	1.7	5.6
Engineering goods	0.1	n.a.	2.7	2.5	7.6	10.2	11.0
Chemicals	1.4	0.9	0.5	1.1	1.9	2.1	2.2
Clothing	–	–	0.1	0.8	2.0	5.0	6.5

Table 11.3 Continued.

	1977–8	1979–80	1980–1	1981–2	1982–3	1983–4	1984–5
Traditional exports	31.6	39.0	33.0	29.9	28.1	29.6	29.1
Tea	10.3	5.6	5.8	4.8	4.2	6.2	6.7
Jute manufactures	4.5	5.2	4.7	2.9	2.3	2.1	3.2
Cotton	4.1	6.3	6.4	5.4	4.5	3.7	3.6
Non-traditional exports	50.5	61.0	67.0	70.1	71.9	70.4	70.9
Iron ore	4.5	4.4	3.9	3.9	3.8	4.3	4.6
Silver	1.5	8.0	–	–	–	–	–
Gems	10.1	–	9.5	8.6	10.1	12.2	11.6
Leather and leather manufactures	4.9	8.6	4.9	5.1	4.3	4.0	5.6
Iron and Steel	3.5	1.6	1.0	1.0	0.04	1.4	1.0
Engineering goods	11.5	10.1	15.1	15.0	13.5	12.7	11.9
Chemicals	2.2	3.2	3.4	4.3	4.4	4.7	5.2
Clothing	6.1	7.5	8.3	9.5	10.3	6.9	8.4

Sources: *Monthly Statistics of the Foreign Trade of India* (Director General of Commercial Intelligence, Government of India), various issues, and *The Reserve Bank of India Bulletin*, Bombay, various issues.

exports, and the abolition of import entitlements and other subsidies on a range of non-traditional exports which virtually offset the nominal devaluation. It is worth noting in this context that the premia on import entitlements, which were abolished in 1966, had risen dramatically on a number of entitlements, reaching the order of 100 per cent in many cases. It should, therefore, be of little surprise that the abolition of the entitlements following the devaluation reduced the effective degree of devaluation appreciably in the case of most exports. The obvious conclusion that this suggests is that the export incentive schemes in force prior to the devaluation were, in fact, not only chaotic but also in many cases over-generous.

The abolition of the various export incentives was, however, short-lived. Most of the incentive schemes in existence prior to the devaluation were re-introduced, albeit in a modified form, in August 1966. These consisted of cash subsidies for a number of exports including the bulk of engineering goods, chemicals, processed foods, paper products and cotton textiles; duty drawbacks and tax rebates; import replenishment schemes in place of the import entitlement schemes; and preferential issue of import licences for exporters. Cash subsidies were a given percentage of the f.o.b. value of exports, with specific rates for different goods. These generally ranged from 4 to 25 per cent of the f.o.b. value of exports. The import replenishment scheme resembled the import entitle-ment schemes in all respects but two. First, import replenishments were restricted to the replacement of import content of exports whereas the import entitlement scheme allowed for the importation of twice the amount of inputs used. Second, unlike in the case of the entitlement schemes the rates of entitlements were relatively stable. The import replenishment licences were issued on the basis of a fixed proportion of the f.o.b. value of exports and the rates ranged from 5 per cent to 70 per cent. The scheme, however, preserved most other features of the pre-1966 scheme entitlements including transferability of entitlements, and the laxity with which many of the conditions governing the scheme were enforced. Constraints of space preclude a detailed discussion of the varied and complex nature of the post-devaluation incentive schemes. The interested reader is referred to the detailed analysis of these schemes provided by Bhagwati and Srinivasan (1975). We reproduce here Bhagwati and Srinivasan's estimates of the approximate range of effective equivalent subsidies resulting from the various schemes in order to convey an idea of the extent of the incentives provided (Table 11.4). These estimates suggest that in a wide range of non-traditional exports including engineering goods, chemicals, plastics, sports goods, paper products and processed foods, export incentives since devaluation averaged around 50 to 90 per cent on an effective *ad valorem* basis.

Table 11.4 Approximate range of average subsidy to selected Indian exports since the 1966 devaluation.

Scheme	Range of effective, equivalent export subsidy (% of f.o.b.)
Cash subsidies	15–20
Import replenishment licences	15–30
Domestic materials in international prices	5–15
Drawbacks and rebates	10–20
Preferential licensing	10–20
Total range	50–90

Source: Bhagwati and Srinivasan (1975).

11.4.1 Economic impact of the schemes

The first point to note in evaluating the post-devaluation schemes is that they were no less complicated and bureaucratically administered than the schemes in operation prior to the devaluation. Bhagwati and Srinivasan's strictures concerning the inefficiencies associated with the pre-devaluation schemes apply to these schemes also. The relevant issues, however, are threefold: (1) the impact of the schemes on the growth of India's exports, (2) the fiscal burden of the schemes, and (3) the economic rationale underlying the schemes.

Since the mid-1960s India's exports recorded an impressive performance. The annual average growth in the value of exports was around 7 per cent during the period 1966–71; during the first half of the 1970s they grew at an unprecedented rate of 21 per cent per annum; and in the ensuing five-year period the rate of growth of the total value of exports exceeded 5 per cent per annum (Table 11.1). It is also worth noting that since the mid-1960s the composition of India's exports has significantly changed in favour of non-traditional items (Table 11.3). What precisely was the contribution of the incentive schemes to the growth in exports during the latter half of the 1960s and the 1970s? It is difficult to unravel the influence of incentive schemes from a number of other factors including external demand conditions on the growth of exports. Bhagwati and Srinivasan, however, attempt such an analysis by estimating multiple regression equations for three principal non-traditional exports – engineering goods, chemicals, and iron and steel products. The dependent variable in each case is exports measured in US dollars and the independent variables include domestic output of the relevant commodities designed to capture the availability of imported inputs, real domestic investment designed to capture the effect of domestic demand pressures on exports, and the dummy variable which takes the value of 0 for the years prior to the devaluation and 1 for the years following. The coefficient of the dummy variable if positive and significant would suggest that the devaluation-cum-subsidy schemes were successful in increasing exports. The time period for which the regressions are estimated cover the years 1951–52 to 1970–71. Although the estimated equations are not robust they do suggest that in the case of iron and steel and engineering goods devaluation-cum-subsidies did alter the export performance for the better. It is, however, to be noted that a scheme of subsidies was in place even prior to the devaluation and the assignment of a value of 0 for the dummy variable prior to the devaluation may have biased the results. It cannot, however, be denied that in the absence of the devaluation-cum-subsidy package India's export performance would have been much less impressive than it actually was during the latter half of the 1960s. The results of the statistical analysis also bring into dispute the thesis that devaluations would be counterproductive in the case of developing countries which are supposedly faced with price-inelastic demand and supplies for their exports.

It should be noted, however, that India's impressive export performance since the mid-1960s cannot be attributed entirely to export-promotion policies. There were also a number of fortuitous factors which contributed to the acceleration of growth in the value of exports. The closure of the Suez Canal in 1967 improved India's competitive position in Asian and East African markets relative to her European and American competitors. The domestic recession during 1965–67 was also a factor in the growth of exports during the late 1960s. Faced with a stagnant domestic market during the recession, firms may have turned to external markets, often selling goods at prices below their average costs of production in an attempt to recoup as much of their fixed costs of production as possible. Other factors which contributed to the acceleration of India's exports during the first half of the 1970s included the growth in grant-aided exports to Bangladesh, the commodity price boom in the world markets during the early 1970s, the phenomenal increase in the value of exports of sugar during 1972–76 following a world shortage of sugar, and the depreciation of the rupee exchange rate during the years 1973–75 when the rupee was pegged to the pound sterling. As Verghese's (1978) estimates show, when the impact of these fortuitous factors is taken into account the rate of growth of India's exports during the period 1971–76 turns out to be 6.6 per cent per annum as opposed to the recorded rate of growth of 21 per cent per annum in value terms. Since then the growth rate of India's exports has averaged around 5 to 8 per cent per annum (Table 11.1). Admittedly a growth rate in excess of 5 per cent is a distinct improvement on the earlier dismal record during the 1950s and early 1960s. And it is likely that in the absence of the export-promotion policies the country would not have been able to sustain the observed growth rate.

Even so, it is legitimate to ask if the country has paid too high a price for the export achievement in terms of the resources expended on the incentive schemes. The data on the extent of subsidisation of India's exports cited in Table 11.4 suggest that the resource costs of the subsidy programmes could be considerable. Bagchi (1981) estimates that during the period 1973–74 to 1977–78 the total amount spent on subsidies amounted to Rs1,040 million a year, reaching Rs4,670 million a year by the end of the year 1977–78. These expenditures amounted to 5 to 9 per cent of the total value of export earnings, and nearly 12 to 13 per cent of the value added of the export industries. These expenditures are not inconsiderable. In this context the comment of the Public Accounts Committee of the Parliament on the cash assistance of nearly Rs1,100 million paid to exporters of engineering goods against an export value of Rs4,470 million during the period 1971–74, quoted by Bagchi, is revealing:

> While the votaries of the cash assistance scheme may argue that this is not too high a price for maintaining a steady growth in exports, which is vital for the economy, if the value of the other concessions and facilities, like import replenishment, concessional railway freight, concessional bank finance, supply of raw materials at subsidised prices, grants-in-aid etc., extended to exporters is also quantified and taken into account, the total cost of the export promotion effort may well turn out to be not quite proportionate to the net gain accruing to the country as foreign exchange.

Another telling criticism of the schemes relates to the indiscriminate and often bizarre fashion in which they were disbursed. In many cases the cash assistance provided to exporters was disproportionately high relative to their foreign-exchange earnings. In the case of three commodities the Public Accounts Committee found that in the early 1970s the cash assistance provided as a proportion of net foreign-exchange earnings was 93 per cent, 151 per cent, and 131 per cent. Again Deepak Lal reports that in the case of ten engineering goods the cash subsidies paid bore no relationship to the difference between the f.o.b. price of exports and their domestic prices. The professed rationale for the payment of cash subsidies is that they bridge the difference between the f.o.b. realisation price of exports and the marginal cost of production. Lal's estimates show that in the case of most of the ten engineering goods the rates of cash subsidies paid as a percentage of the f.o.b. value of exports bore little relation to the estimated rates required to bridge the difference between domestic costs and export prices. What is more intriguing is that in several instances the domestic costs were actually below the f.o.b. prices and yet the items in question were recipients of subsidies (Lal, 1979). Indeed, Lal's analysis of the subsidy schemes relating to the ten engineering firms shows that in general the schemes had little success in raising the effective exchange rate for exports with a relatively high social rate of return; and the schemes had altered the relative divergences between private and social rates of return in essentially arbitrary ways, for which no clear economic justification can be provided. In sum, India's export incentive schemes, though they may have sustained the growth of exports, appear to have been not only expensive relative to what they have achieved but many of the schemes also appear to lack any sort of economic rationale.

All this should be of little surprise, especially to those trained in the neo-classical mould of economics. They would argue that the root cause of India's export problem is the indiscriminate import-substitution policy the country has pursued. Symptomatic of the problem are the existence of highly profitable domestic markets, lack of imported inputs, high costs of production, the high capital intensity of exports and poor quality of products exported – all of which have constrained exports. As the estimates of effective exchange rate for imports and exports, reported earlier, show, the import-substituting industrialisation policies have imparted a bias against exports.

It could, though, be argued that import substitution is a policy datum which cannot be dislodged, and export promotion schemes are required to offset some of the unavoidable constraints the policy imposes on exports. These include the high cost of imported inputs required for the production of exportables, the existence of highly profitable domestic markets, and the policy-induced difference between domestic costs of production and export prices. Hence the cash subsidies, import replenishment scheme and various sorts of concessions offered to exporters. But as Lal's analysis referred to earlier shows, the export incentive schemes have been operated with little regard to the social profitability of exporting firms they have assisted, and in many cases the schemes have altered the relationship between social and private profitability in an arbitrary fashion. The problem here appears to be not so much one of administrative incompetence but an inability to estimate social and private costs of production in an economy fraught with factor and product market distortions arising from the panoply of controls on foreign trade in particular and economic activity in general. Most of the perceived problems which the export incentive schemes are designed to solve are only symptoms of the disease, the disease being the indiscriminate and exorbitantly high levels of protection coupled with attempts at replacing the price mechanism with bureaucratic decision making exemplified by the complex system of industrial licensing policies in force in India. In such an economic environment export-promotion policies, which are in the nature of second- or third-best policies, may not only have little impact on the growth of exports but also exacerbate the distortions.

In recent years, though, there has been a perceptible change in attitudes towards foreign trade planning in India's development process. The Tandon Committee Report on export strategy, published in 1980, for instance, recognised that there is a case for allocating productive resources optimally between import-substituting production and export-oriented production. Such an optimal allocation policy would require the adoption of trade and resource-allocation policies which would equate the effective exchange rate for the domestic production of importables with that of exportables. According to Bhagwati, such a policy would eliminate the bias against exports and amount to an export-promotion policy. In essence the policy would allow resource allocation between sectors to proceed on the basis of relative costs and economic efficiency. It should be noted that the policy does not emphasise export promotion based on an armoury of export incentive schemes. It equates an export-promotion policy with one which removes the discrepancy between the effective exchange rate for imports and that for exports and removes the bias against exports. But instituting such a policy in an economy which has for long pursued an import-substituting strategy of industrialisation grounded in a battery of controls over trade and resource allocation may not be easy. Relaxation of controls over imports coupled with subsidies on exports may not necessarily equate the two exchange rates: for they may not eliminate the bias against exports imparted by the domestic industrial licensing policies and other controls over resource allocation. As is well known, such policies are instrumental in generating widespread rents to the fortunate few who are able to acquire the licences. Estimation of the impact of such rents on effective exchange rates may prove to be exceedingly difficult: and even if it were possible to do so it may be neither feasible nor desirable to offset their impact on relative effective exchange rates through a system of subsidies. For, as stated earlier, a bureaucratically administered system of subsidies may more often than not turn out to be counterproductive. For these reasons a genuine attempt at liberalisation of the foreign trade regime cannot be confined to the relaxation of import controls and the institution of export subsidies. It should also have to do away with the cumbersome system of industrial licensing policies if any real gains from liberalisation are to be achieved. This is, in fact, the conclusion of a recent study by Lucas (1988) which, on the basis of a simulation model, attempts to evaluate the effects of trade liberalisation on the performance of the Indian manufacturing sector. The simulation exercise shows that trade liberalisation, which allows domestic prices to track world prices, alone would actually result in a small decline in industrial production. But a policy of trade liberalisation combined with a policy of sectoral allocation of investments based on private rates of return rather than administrative controls is seen to result in substantial gains in value added. In this context it is heartening to note that recent attempts at liberalisation of the economic regime have emphasised not only liberalisation of imports but also relaxation of the industrial licensing system. Whether or not the liberalisation attempts will be sustained is hard to say.

11.5   Conclusions

This chapter has reviewed India's export performance and policies from the early 1950s to recent years. It has attempted to analyse the rationale for the neglect of the export sector in the early years of economic planning, and concluded that a desire for 'self-sufficiency', grounded in economic nationalism, rather than various economic explanations including the thesis of export pessimism in fashion at the time, was responsible for the neglect. The chapter has also reviewed the literature on the design and economic impact of the export incentive schemes in operation since the early 1960s. It underscores the conclusion of many of the studies on the subject that most of the schemes lack any sort of economic rationale, they have been inefficiently administered, and in many cases they have resulted in excessive and indiscriminate subsidisation of exports. It has also argued that a strategy of export promotion which relies on a bureaucratically administered system of export incentives could be counterproductive. The chapter also doubts the wisdom of piecemeal liberalisation of the hitherto bureaucratically controlled economic regime, based on relaxation of import controls and export incentives. A genuine attempt at liberalisation designed to promote output and exports may have to liberalise not only the foreign trade regime but also the complex system of industrial licensing and other controls over sectoral investment allocation.

12

Export promotion and trade liberalisation in Latin America

Tim Congdon

12.1   Introduction

Latin America has had a particularly urgent need to raise exports in the 1980s. Because of the rise in dollar interest rates between 1977 and 1981, its countries had to increase their export receipts sharply in order to service their debts. The pressure was intensified after the onset of the debt crisis in 1982, when the virtual cessation of new loans from the international banking system required most Latin American nations to engineer a massive resource switch into improving their external payments. It has been estimated that a net resource transfer to Latin America from the rest of the world equivalent to 3.7 per cent of the region's GDP in 1981 became a net resource outflow equivalent to 4.7 per cent of GDP in 1983.[1] The abruptness of the resource switch was exaggerated by adverse import and export price trends, with an index of the region's terms of trade deteriorating from 125.9 in 1977 (1972 = 100) to 99.3 in 1982.[2]

Since large cuts in imports would have endangered development programmes, exports had to be encouraged. On the whole, export growth has been good over the last decade and the majority of Latin American countries have made surprisingly large sacrifices to maintain credit-worthiness. Between 1980 and 1987 the volume of Latin American exports rose by 4.4 per cent a year, whereas the volume of world trade increased by 2.6 per cent a year. However, the statistics for the region as a whole disguise marked divergences between countries. Between 1980 and 1987 the volume of Latin American exports climbed by 35 per cent, but five countries, Mexico (97 per cent), Colombia (68 per cent), Brazil (54 per cent), Uruguay (52 per cent) and Chile (48 per cent) showed rises of about 50 per cent or more, whereas six countries (Bolivia, El Salvador, Nicaragua, Guatemala, Venezuela and Peru) had significant contractions.[3]

The argument of this chapter is that the disparity between the successful and unsuccessful exporters reflects differences in policy approach. In general, the successful exporters adopted outward-looking economic policies involving significant trade liberalisation, whereas the unsuccessful exporters tried to cocoon themselves from the international economy and to protect their industries from foreign competition. The chapter also discusses one of the key issues to emerge from Latin American liberalisation attempts, namely the difficulty of reconciling trade liberalisation with inflation control.

The nature of the potential dilemma here is easy to describe, if not to resolve. Trade liberalisation is eased when the country concerned maintains a competitive exchange rate. But the pursuit of a competitive exchange rate often involves heavy currency depreciation which aggravates inflationary pressures. If policy-makers instead fix the exchange rate (or the rate at which it depreciates) in order to combat inflationary expectations, they risk impeding export growth. The loss of export dynamism is unfortunate not only because it is inconsistent with long-term policy goals, but also because it may alienate influential producer groups who would otherwise have benefited from outward-looking policies. Of course, without the support of at least some producer groups trade liberalisation is unlikely to prove politically sustainable. These questions are considered by comparing the Chilean liberalisation of the late 1970s with the more recent Mexican liberalisation.

12.2 Export promotion and economic liberalisation

In the Latin American context the official attitude towards export promotion must not be seen in isolation, but as only one aspect of the relationship between government and the external sector. In the 1950s and 1960s many Latin American governments were strongly influenced by the doctrines of Raul Prebisch, who argued that technical progress would lead to a long-run deterioration in the terms of trade of commodity-producing nations relative to the industrial countries. He therefore urged deliberate programmes of import substitution, including high import barriers to keep out foreign manufactured goods.[4] The result was that the growth of both imports *and exports* was constrained, and that much of Latin America failed to share in the gains from greater international specialisation enjoyed by the industrial countries in the first 30 years after the Second World War. Largely because of the protectionist and nationalistic orientation of their intellectual élites, Latin American countries did not participate in the tariff rounds, under the aegis of the General Agreement on Tariffs and Trade, which were the key to rapid trade growth among the industrial countries.

The connection between import restrictions and poor export performance is readily understood, at a general level, in terms of the implications for resource allocation. Import restrictions require countries to allocate more resources to the production of goods that would otherwise have been imported. In consequence, fewer resources are available for the production of exports and exports are lower than they would be with a more open trade regime. But there are other links. If companies cannot import the most up-to-date capital equipment from abroad, they are less competitive on world markets; if they cannot buy components from the cheapest international supplier, their own products are more expensive than those of companies in other countries who can. As remarked by Diaz-Alejandro in a 1965 paper 'On the import intensity of import substitution', experience in Latin America had given new emphasis to 'the fact that the domestic manufacture of many types of previously imported finished goods often requires substantial importation of raw materials and intermediate products . . . so that the net import substitution (the value added domestically) is often a relatively small percentage of the value of the finished product' (Velasco, 1988, p.11).[5]

Less noticed as a disincentive for exporting, but undoubtedly also important, are exchange controls and the inefficiency of financial systems. Latin American countries have had long histories of exchange restrictions of various kinds, which have discouraged (or forbidden) their residents from holding foreign currency. Businessmen naturally have less interest in exporting in order to earn foreign exchange. This effect might not be particularly significant if the domestic currencies of Latin American countries were attractive in their own right and gave returns similar to those in foreign currencies. But, traditionally, interest rates in Latin America have been low relative to inflation rates and often negative in real terms. Businessmen's keenness to export therefore depends not only on the ready availability of the resources and inputs (including the imported inputs) needed for the production of exports, but also on a favourable financial environment. They want to know that export proceeds can be held in a remunerative form. Exchange derestriction and reduction in inflation (in order to raise real interest rates) may contribute vitally to the success of exports.

Many Latin American countries have apparently elaborate export-promotion programmes, with explicit subsidies such as grants or fiscal rebates for certain types of export, cheap credits to help finance exports and state-supported organisations to assist foreign marketing. Sometimes export incentives are extremely generous. For example, in Peru an institution called CERTEX was set up in 1975 in order to stimulate exports of textiles. At one stage it gave an effective rate of subsidy of 70 or 80 per cent because it was assessed in relation to the value of production, not of value added.[6] Such arrangements are not usually effective in raising exports as a·whole, however'much they may benefit particular kinds of export and particular exporters. A high subsidy for one export product has to be financed by taxation on other sectors of the economy, some of which might have become exporters if they had faced less adverse fiscal treatment. Even worse, the government may be tempted to cover the cost of export subsidies by borrowing from the central bank, which adds to the money supply, aggravates inflation pressure, strengthens the political argument for exchange controls and creates a financial malaise inimical to exporting. Too often in protectionist, import-substituting Latin American countries attempts to encourage more exports also mean more bureaucracy, more taxation and more inflation.

One way to minimise the fiscal cost of export promotion, and also to meet industrialists' pleas to be able to import capital goods and inputs freely, is to create special free-trade zones. A number of countries have experimented with such zones, but undoubtedly the most significant has been the Mexican in-bond plant (*maquiladora*) programme, approved in 1965 and initiated in 1967. Under the programme machinery, equipment and materials can be imported duty-free to a strip of territory within 20 km of the border with the USA, as long as the products are exported.[7] The *maquila* concept has certainly attracted a considerable amount of foreign, mostly American, capital and created a large number of jobs. It has been estimated that the total number of workers in *maquila* plants was 11,000 in 1968, only a year after the inception of the programme, and reached 290,579 in 1987.[8] However, research indicates that the *maquilas* are effectively low-wage enclaves of the US economy and that linkages with the rest of Mexico are 'very meagre', amounting to only 1 or 2 per cent of their input purchases. '*Maquila* factories make almost no contribution to the growth of local industry or, indeed, industry elsewhere in Mexico.' (Skair, 1988, p. 293) Arguably, it is rather ridiculous to believe that a nation makes itself better off by erecting barbed-wire fences within its own territory. Such fences are, of course, necessary to differentiate the *maquiladora* zone from Mexico as such.

In the mid-1960s it had become widely recognised that import-substitution policies were not working. Latin American countries continued to suffer from balance-of-payments problems, even though industrialisation was supposed to have reduced their dependence on expensive manufactured imports. Morever, import restrictions had reduced the growth rates of their trade ·and so their share of world markets, and seemed to be partly responsible for disappointing rates of overall economic growth. In a 1974 paper Diaz-Alejandro showed that the share of Argentina, Brazil, Colombia and Mexico in world exports had fallen from 6.15 per cent in 1948–49 to 2.28 per cent in 1970–71.[9] Import substitution became increasingly unfashionable. With growing awareness that disappointing export performance was attributable not just to restrictive commercial policies, but also to distortions and inefficiencies caused by excessive state intervention generally, some economists declared themselves in favour of comprehensive liberalisation programmes. Particularly strong and articulate support for economic liberalisation came from economists connected with the University of Chicago, where the cause of free markets and responsible monetary policy had been championed by Professor Milton Friedman.

It would be wrong to give the impression that the intellectual shift was uniform across Latin America or that policy-makers moved away from import-substitution strategies at roughly the same time in all the major countries. Brazil, for example, had a major liberalisation episode between 1964 and 1967, which was followed by several years of rapid growth of both output and exports, but then reverted to the import-substitution model in the mid-1970s. Import substitution was favoured by influential groups in the Ministry of Planning and the National Development Bank (BNDE), who pointed to sharply rising import penetration in intermediate inputs and capital goods as evidence of market opportunities which could be exploited by domestic producers.[10] Although Brazilian trade policy has been erratic since then, with government officials frequently paying lip-service to the merits of trade liberalisation, the reality is that Brazil is still a highly protectionist country. Under a New Industrial Policy announced in April 1988 bans on the import of about 5,000 items were supposed to have been abolished by the end of the year. In November 1988 the timetable was put back twelve months and at the time of writing (October 1989) progress remains uncertain.[11]

Whereas the mid-1970s saw Brazil becoming more inward-looking and autarkic, it was the heyday of Chicago School economists in Chile. Their programme of economic reforms, implemented after 1973 during the military regime of General Pinochet, was to prove of immense significance for the rest of Latin America. It represented the most radical departure from the statist and protectionist trend which had been entrenched in much of the region since the 1930s. It proposed a model which, however objectionable in certain respects, was difficult to ignore.

In fact, Chile was not the first Southern Cone country to embark on economic liberalisation. A military coup in Uruguay in February 1973 was followed by the publication of a *Plan Nacional de Desarrollo* (National Development Plan) in April 1973 which called for the restoration of the price system as the principal guide to resource allocation. Increased openness to international economic influences, involving the abolition of import quotas and the reduction of tariffs, was an integral part of the programme.[12] The changes in Uruguay pre-dated those in Chile by several months. However, they did not go so far and are less noteworthy.

12.3   Trade liberalisation and inflation control in Chile

The central features of the Chilean economic liberalisation in the mid- and late 1970s have been discussed in a number of places and are well known. When General Pinochet seized power in September 1973 the Chilean economy was in a shambles. The new government, advised by its Chicago-trained economic team, undertook drastic remedial action. It completely reversed the interventionist and financially irresponsible policies of the previous Allende government, and regarded inflation control and the restoration of market mechanisms as its main economic priorities. After some initial uncertainty about how far the economy should be opened to international competition, it undertook one of the most sweeping programmes of trade liberalisation ever seen.

At the end of 1973 many imported products were subject to quotas, the maximum tariff was 220 per cent and the average tariff was 90 per cent. By early 1977 all quotas had been scrapped, the maximum tariff was 65 per cent and the average tariff was 27 per cent. In December 1977, after Chile had left the Andean Pact customs union which had restricted its freedom of action, de Castro, the Minister of Finance, announced that a tariff of 10 per cent was to be applied to all imports, except cars, from June 1979. As the early stages of trade liberalisation proceeded, the government carried out a conventional anti-inflation strategy, with the emphasis on eliminating the budget deficit and restraining monetary growth.

The transformation of the economy in this period was spectacular. Inflation, which had exceeded 500 per cent in 1973, came down to more reasonable levels. The increase in the consumer price index in the year to December 1977 was 63.5 per cent and in the year to December 1978, 30.3 per cent. Both imports and exports boomed, partly because of more sensible exchange-rate policies but also, and more importantly, because of trade liberalisation. Export volume trebled between 1973 and 1980.[13] The growth of so-called 'non-traditional exports' (i.e., products which Chile had not been known to export in any quantity before) was particularly dramatic, with their nominal value soaring from $71.2m. in 1973 to $1,820.8m. in 1981. Because of the explosion in exports, import liberalisation was not followed – as its critics had expected – by a deterioration in the balance of payments. On the contrary, a dire external payments crisis in late 1973 was substantially cured by the achievement of a small current-account surplus in 1976.

These successes seemed a clear endorsement of the policy changes recommended by the Chicago economists. In particular, the dynamism of non-traditional exports implied that high levels of protection before 1973 had misdirected resources away from potential export sectors. This experience was important for other countries and encouraged them to accept the argument of economic theory, that import liberalisation was equivalent to export promotion. Partly influenced by events in Chile, Argentina adopted a major trade liberalisation programme (*Plan de Apertura*) in December 1978. The programme – to be implemented, like its Chilean predecessor, under a sympathetic military government – envisaged a progressive reduction in tariffs from January 1979 to January 1984, by which stage the maximum rate would be 35 per cent.

But between 1980 and 1982 much went wrong with the Chilean and Argentinian liberalisations. In retrospect, the main weakness of policy in both countries has been identified as the attempt to limit inflation by exchange-rate manipulation. In February 1978 de Castro announced that Chile's currency (the peso), which from September 1973 until then had been devalued constantly in order to offset domestic inflation and maintain export competitiveness, would instead be devalued according to a fixed schedule known as the *tablita* (or 'little table'). The schedule envisaged that the rate of devaluation would gradually diminish. This was intended to signal the sincerity of the government's anti-inflation resolve and force domestic inflation to come into line with international inflation. The shift in approach, with the exchange rate a determinant of the inflation rate rather than determined by it, was well defined and deliberate. So also was a similar policy development in Argentina, which introduced a *tablita* virtually in conjunction with the *Plan de Apertura* in January 1979.

The Argentine programme broke down much earlier than Chile's. During 1979 and 1980 the rate of devaluation fell in line with the schedule set out in the *tablita*. Inflation also fell, from 140 per cent in 1978 to 40 per cent (at an annualised rate) in the fourth quarter of 1980. But the slowdown in inflation was much less than the reduction in the rate of devaluation and the Argentine price level rose far above international levels. The overvaluation of the Argentine currency encouraged massive imports and hampered exports in foreign markets. Unhappily, the overvaluation was so serious that non-traditional exports did not show any dynamism at all and no significant producer groups emerged to defend the trade liberalisation. In effect, the programme of inflation control became inconsistent with the aim of integrating the Argentine economy more fully into the international economy. A drastic weakening in the balance of payments in late 1980, accompanied by a heavy drain of foreign exchange reserves, was followed by the abandonment of the *tablita* in early 1981, large devaluations in March and June, and a return to rapid inflation of well over 100 per cent. The *Plan de Apertura* was stigmatised by its association with the failed anti-inflation policies and was suspended. The constitutional government that replaced the military regime in November 1983 re-imposed quantitative restrictions on imports. In the words of the 1985 Inter-American Development Bank report on *Economic and Social Progress in Latin America*, these restrictions 'largely reduced the relative openness of the economy in earlier years' (Inter-American Development Bank, 1985, p. 181).

In contrast to the Argentine trade liberalisation, which was virtually stillborn, the Chilean attempt was to last for many years. But there was a similar tension between inflation control and *apertura* policies. The *tablita* culminated in the fixing of the Chilean peso's exchange rate (at 39 to the US dollar) in July 1979. As in Argentina, official control over the exchange rate led to exchange-rate overvaluation, but the problems were not apparent immediately. There was sufficient dynamism in the export sector to keep exports growing in 1979 and 1980, while inflation also fell sharply and in late 1981 even became low by the standards of the industrial countries.

It was only towards the end of 1981 that the Chilean economy began to show signs of strain. The overvaluation of the exchange rate stopped the growth of non-traditional exports and a slowdown in the world economy reduced the price of copper, which remained the largest export product. With the cessation of new bank credits after the onset of the debt crisis in mid-1982, Chile faced a grave adjustment problem. To maintain its external credit-worthiness it had to shift – in a period of little more than a year – about 15 per cent of GDP from domestic absorption into the external balance. This shift could be accomplished only by a full-scale slump which caused GDP to fall by over 14 per cent in 1982. In the public mind the liberalisation programme became associated with, and to some extent discredited by, the traumatic falls in output and employment. Despite the severity of the recession, the fixed exchange rate against the dollar could not be maintained. After a devaluation on 14 June 1982, it was allowed to float in August and depreciated quickly. The inevitable acceleration of inflation soon followed.

The need for such an abrupt and radical resource switch can be blamed on the *tablita* and the subsequent fixed exchange-rate policy. If the currency had been devalued steadily in late 1979, 1980 and early 1981, inflation might not have fallen so much in late 1981, but non-traditional exports might have kept on growing and macroeconomic policy as a whole might have been steadier and more consistent. Strong criticism has therefore been directed against Chilean exchange-rate policy in this period. The verdict of two Chilean economists who have served as consultants to the World Bank is damning. In their view, the maintenance of the

> overvalued exchange rate for a long time . . . deepened significantly what should otherwise have been a serious but not devastating crisis generated from adverse foreign shocks . . . . There is little doubt that the manipulation of the exchange rate and ultimate pegging of the peso to the dollar when inflation was still running at a 30 per cent annual rate was an ill-made policy decision.[14]

In the next two years the trade liberalisation was partly retracted. In November 1982 surcharges of up to 30 per cent were imposed on a number of import categories, ostensibly as anti-dumping measures. In March 1983 a general but temporary increase in tariffs to 20 per cent (from the 10 per cent which had been reached in June 1979) was announced. These changes were taken by some observers as signalling official disillusionment with trade liberalisation and the free-market experiment.

The lesson was that, in future liberalisation attempts, exchange-rate policies and anti-inflation programmes should be better designed so that they did not lead to overvalued exchange rates and loss of export competitiveness. More specifically, a floating exchange rate was preferable to a fixed exchange rate (or a fixed rate of currency devaluation). Economists at the World Bank, which in 1980 had published a report fulsome in its praise of the Chilean reforms, took particular note of Chile's troubles with the exchange rate. It became World Bank orthodoxy that trade liberalisation must also be accompanied by a competitive exchange rate.

12.4   Trade liberalisation and fiscal retrenchment in Mexico in the 1980s

Mexico pursued a conscious policy of protection and import substitution in the first thirty-five years after the Second World War, partly in order to demonstrate its economic and political autonomy from the US. While its record of economic growth was very successful in the 1950s and 1960s, the two presidencies of Echeverria (1970–76) and Lopez Portillo (1976–82) saw a marked deterioration in economic policy. The two presidencies saw a sharp rise in government spending and an increase in state control over the economy, which discouraged investment by the private sector. Despite a massive and fortunate boost from rising oil production, the Mexican economy in late 1982 was in turmoil. Its external debts had grown rapidly and unsustainably in the years of the oil boom. On 1 September the Lopez Portillo administration had nationalised the banks and forced people who held dollars in Mexican banks to convert them into pesos at an unfavourable rate. These two acts – which amounted to virtual expropriation – had destroyed the financial confidence of middle-class and wealthy Mexicans.

It was in this difficult economic environment that Mexican policy-makers embarked on a major re-appraisal of trade policy. Pressure for more outward-looking policies came from the World Bank and the International Monetary Fund, on whom they increasingly relied for financial support. An agreement on àn IMF Extended Fund Facility in November 1982 envisaged import liberalisation as part of a larger programme of export promotion. The first measures came with the publication of a *Plan Nacional de Desarrollo* (National Development Plan) in December 1982, to coincide with the inauguration of the new president, Miguel de la Madrid. Initially, between 1983 and 1985, the emphasis was on the replacement of import permits by tariffs. By the middle of 1985 over 60 per cent (by value) of imports were exempt from permits. When permits were clearly well on the way to being phased out, policy switched to the rationalisation and reduction of tariff rates. In addition to cutting tariffs, the government lowered the number of tariff bands and reduced the dispersion between them. Also important was the ending of a system of 'official prices' for imports, whereby tariffs were assessed not on the actual price of imports, but on an artificial price set by the government. By the autumn of 1987 all import permits had been scrapped and the average tariff rate was about 20 per cent. Although liberalisation had come step by step, the contrast with late 1982 represented a massive opening of the economy.

Throughout this period the exchange rate had been devalued frequently, in line with the IMF and World Bank advocacy of a competitive exchange rate. Export growth followed a pattern similar to that in Chile in the late 1970s. Oil exports (like copper exports in the Chilean case) made little progress, hampered by price weakness and official reluctance to raise production because of quota commitments to other oil producers. But non-oil exports boomed. They climbed from $4.8bn in 1982 to $12.0bn in 1987. Exports of manufactures were particularly strong, rising from $3.0bn to $9.9bn. Undoubtedly helpful to this development was the new ease of importing semi-finished products and raw material inputs, which could then be used in the fabrication of exports. Intermediate inputs rose from $8.4bn in 1982 to $8.8bn in 1987, in contrast to imports as a whole which fell from $14.4bn to $12.2bn.[15] Indeed, the sluggishness of imports is striking in view of the scale of the trade liberalisation which had been undertaken. As a result, the balance of payments was kept under reasonable control despite chronic debt anxieties.

Whereas the first five years of the trade liberalisation were gradual, the final stage was sudden and dramatic. The policies of the de la Madrid presidency had been successful in many respects, but they had not brought down inflation. In fact, an inflation rate of almost 150 per cent in the autumn of 1987 was worse than the figure of just under 100 per cent inherited from Lopez Portillo. Policy-makers therefore decided on an abrupt change in direction. After discussions with the trade unions, the government announced a *Pacto de Solidaridad Económica* (Economic Solidarity Pact) which took measures to cut the public-sector deficit (by raising public-sector prices), to limit future wage increases and, after a large initial devaluation, to freeze the peso exchange rate at 2,300 to the dollar. The anti-inflationary thrust of the pact was reinforced by reductions in tariffs to bring the average rate down to 10 per cent. It was made quite clear by government spokesmen that one intention of the tariff cuts was to curb inflationary pressures. The underlying idea, that lower tariffs would intensify competitive pressure on inefficient domestic suppliers, had nothing to do with the traditional resource-allocation arguments for trade liberalisation.

The parallels between the Chilean and Mexican liberalisation programmes are clear. In both countries the early years of liberalisation saw the abolition of import quotas and large cuts in tariff rates accompanied by deliberate pursuit of a competitive exchange rate. Both countries also enjoyed extremely fast growth of non-traditional exports and satisfactory balance-of-payments performance. But the large devaluations required to maintain export competitiveness hindered progress on inflation. Eventually policy-makers decided, through very deliberate and public announcements, to use the exchange rate as the central instrument to dampen inflation expectations. By so doing, they jeopardised the export dynamism which had previously been so critical to the success of trade liberalisation. Indeed, the Mexican authorities appeared to see the final stage of the tariff cuts as an aspect of anti-inflation policy and not as part of a programme to boost exports. In 1988 – as sceptics of fixed exchange rates would have predicted – the growth rate of Mexican exports slowed down and the current account of the balance of payments slid heavily into the red. The shift from a floating to a fixed exchange rate appeared to have been a mistake.

However, it is important to analyse sympathetically the options confronting the Mexican government in late 1987. Basic to understanding the policy-makers' dilemma is that they could do nothing more to combat inflation by following conventional World Bank and IMF prescriptions.

They had gone to great lengths to reduce government spending since 1982, hoping that less spending would result in a lower budget deficit and that a lower budget deficit would remove the main cause of rapid monetary growth and inflation. Central government current spending on goods, services, transfers and subsidies had indeed been cut drastically (from 14.8 per cent of GDP in 1982 to 6.9 per cent in 1987) and capital expenditure had been savaged, but inflation was higher than at the beginning of the whole process.

The reason for this failure was that interest payments had spiralled out of control, rising from 20.9 per cent of central government expenditures (and 5.4 per cent of GDP) in 1982 to 56.5 per cent of such expenditures (and 17.3 per cent of GDP) in 1987.[16] Most of these interest payments were on domestically held debt. The growth of interest payments was partly due to the expansion of the debt, but it also reflected the need to compensate debt-holders for rising inflation, which was seen as being driven by the fall in the peso exchange rate, and to maintain extraordinarily high real interest rates, which were required to protect savers against future falls in the exchange rate. The problem of the explosion in interest payments was seen as closely interrelated with the problem of exchange-rate competitiveness. (Real interest rates in 1987 and 1988 were often above 40 per cent. Wealthy Mexicans were still wary of holding assets in their own country because they remembered the events of 1982.)

In effect, the present period's inflation was caused by the budget deficit, which was caused by high interest payments, which were caused by both the previous period's inflation and the pervasive lack of financial confidence. Expectations of a continuous fall in the peso's external value were largely responsible for the lack of financial confidence. In these circumstances the Mexican government judged that a sharp break in expectations, administered through the *Pacto de Solidaridad Económica*, was necessary. The fixing of the exchange rate was integral to the pact and essential if expectations were to be changed. The possible brake on exports was recognised to be a weakness of the policy, but export growth could be sacrificed temporarily to combat the urgent threat of hyperinflation. Arguably, the whole of the liberalisation programme since 1982 would have been in peril if the government's image had not been rescued by a successful anti-inflation policy.

12.5   Conclusion: The need to respond to circumstances

Economists have been too quick to conclude that trade liberalisation must always be accompanied by devaluation in order to maintain competitiveness. There are good grounds for thinking that the upsurge in inflation in Latin America in the 1980s has been attributable, at least in part, to the effects of devaluation in economies with widespread indexation. Devaluations have no doubt had the good result of stimulating exports. But they have had the bad result of undermining domestic financial confidence. It is easy to show that, when the erosion of confidence has caused a decline in the desired ratio of money balances to GDP, the same amount of domestic credit (as a share of GDP) is associated with a faster inflation rate.[17] The task of inflation control is that much harder. The Mexican case illustrates the point vividly. Extremely harsh fiscal restraint over the six years of the de la Madrid presidency did not prevent inflation being higher as it approached its end than at its beginning. The persistence of inflation was due not to an inadequate policy response, but to an enduring loss of financial confidence. Expectations of never-ending devaluation were at the root of the malaise.

Policy-makers in Mexico in late 1987 – like those in Chile in similar circumstances in early 1978 (and also in Argentina and Uruguay at about the same time) – decided that the best way to end inflation was to break these expectations. The exchange rate – or, less ambitiously, its rate of depreciation – had to be fixed. There was a risk of exchange rate overvaluation and reduced export growth, but that risk was judged to be worth taking. The Chilean decision has been criticised harshly in retrospect. But it is at least arguable that other features of policy-making between 1978 and 1982 – notably a too hurried approach to financial deregulation – were more to blame for the embarrassments suffered by the free-market experiment than the pegging of the exchange rate.[18] At the time of writing (October 1989) it is far from clear that the Mexican government was wrong to shift the emphasis away from export promotion to inflation control in 1987. In the long run real exchange rates cannot be changed by policy, but sound financial management can reduce real interest rates and raise the desired ratio of money balances to GDP. World Bank economists may have sometimes been too glib in their belief in the beneficence of repeated devaluation to ensure the success of trade liberalisation.

Notes

1. Statistics prepared by Inter-American Development Bank (IDB) in Washington and supplied to the author by Mr Hector Luisi, former IDB representative in London.
2. See Inter-American Development Bank (IDB) (1988)
3. See IDB (1988, p. 17).
4. For a discussion of Prebisch's influence, see Balassa *et al.* (1986, pp. 54–61).

It is interesting that Prebisch himself became concerned about the inefficient results of import-substitution policies in the mid-1960s.

5. The paper 'On the import intensity of import substitution' originally appeared in *Kyklos* (1965).
6. The CERTEX arrangements are discussed in Congdon (1982, pp. 133–48).
7. See Ramos (1988). The *maquiladora* programme is described on pp. 262–3.
8. See Skair (1988). The employment numbers are given on p. 292.
9. See Velasco (1988, p. 24). The statistics were originally given in Giersch (1974).
10. The comments on the import-substitution strategy are in Wells (1979, pp. 243–6).
11. See Barham (1988a, b) and Dawnay (1989). See also Banco de Boston (1988).
12. See, particularly, pp. 159–60 and pp. 167–71 of Finch (1979).
13. The export volume figures are given in Ministerio de Hacienda (1982). It should be emphasised that there are particular problems preparing export price indices in this period, partly because of the large change in the structure of exports. However, there is no doubt that export volumes grew very fast.
14. See Edwards and Edwards (1987).
15. See Secretaria de Programación y Presupuesto, *Indicadores del Sector Externo*, various dates.
16. See IDB (1988, pp. 551–61).
17. To give a simple example, let the demand for money be a linear function of money GDP, i.e. $M = aY$. Domestic credit, C, is equal to the change in the money supply, $dM = a\,dY$, and

$$\frac{C}{Y} = a\,\frac{dY}{Y}$$

Assume that the rate of output growth is given. Then, since dY/Y is equal to the rate of inflation plus the rate of output growth, the higher is a (the ratio of money to GDP), the lower is the inflation rate for any particular ratio of domestic credit to GDP. (A cognate argument is developed at more length in Congdon, 1987.)
18. This viewpoint is argued in Congdon (1985).

13

Export promotion in the Caribbean

Karl Bennett

13.1 Introduction

The economies of the Commonwealth Caribbean countries have, historically, been heavily dependent on the performance of their export sectors. This was a natural consequence of the fact that these countries were originally established by the European colonial powers to be suppliers of tropical produce. Since the end of the Second World War, it has been recognised that in order to provide productive employment for the growing labour force, it would be necessary to reduce the level of dependence on traditional primary exports. Economic diversification into the production of manufactured goods was seen as the way of solving the problems of unemployment and low living standards. However, given the small size of their respective economies, a dynamic industrial sector capable of making a significant contribution to the problems of unemployment and low income would have to be based primarily on export production activity.

All countries in the region have, over the years, implemented policies and institutional arrangements, designed to encourage the establishment of export manufacturing enterprises. However, the countries in the region have been only moderately successful in selling manufactured products on international markets.

The analysis of the Caribbean experience with export promotion will concentrate on the experiences of three island economies, Barbados, Jamaica, and Trinidad and Tobago. Firstly, there will be a brief review of the overall trend in exports, as well as exports of manufactured products for the three countries since 1965. This will be followed by an analysis of the original arguments for an export-based industrial sector presented by

Lewis (1950). Many of the features of the original industrialisation strategies were strongly influenced by his arguments. Thirdly, we will analyse the implications for exports of the change in emphasis during the 1960s and 1970s towards a regional approach to export promotion. Finally, there will be an analysis of developments in the 1980s which have given rise to greater emphasis being placed on extra-regional trading.

13.2   Trends in exports: Barbados, Jamaica, Trinidad and Tobago 1965–85

The export performance of Jamaica and Trinidad and Tobago over the period was determined primarily by the market conditions for their principal exports. These were bauxite and alumina for Jamaica and petroleum for Trinidad and Tobago. Peak values were achieved for Trinidad and Tobago in 1980 and Jamaica in 1981. In Trinidad, exports grew at an annual average rate of 16.8 per cent between 1965 and 1980. The period of most rapid growth, 28.7 per cent, occurred between 1973 and 1980, reflecting the petroleum price increases engineered by OPEC. From 1980, the decline in the international petroleum market gave rise to a situation where the value of exports in 1985 amounted to only 51 per cent of the peak value of 1980.

Jamaican exports grew at an annual average rate of 10 per cent between 1965 and 1981. The subsequent collapse in demand for bauxite and alumina led to export values in 1985 amounting to only 58 per cent of the 1981 value. The post-1981 developments then resulted in the country recording a relatively poor export performance for the 1965–85 period of 5 per cent per annum.

The pattern of total export growth for Barbados differed from that of the other two countries in that developments in export markets for one commodity did not determine overall export performance. Between 1965 and 1975 sugar was the major export item, accounting in most years for approximately 50 per cent of the value of exports. Consequently, in that decade the export trend largely mirrored developments in the international sugar market. After 1975, manufactured products were the major items exported and by the end of the period accounted for more than 80 per cent of the value of total exports. The slump in the sugar market after 1980 was more than offset by the growth in exports of manufactured items. As a result, Barbados was able to maintain an impressive annual export growth rate of 11.6 per cent for the period. Moreover, as can be determined from Table 13.1, whereas in 1965, total Barbadian exports amounted to only 13 per cent of the value of Jamaican exports, in 1985, Barbadian exports were 44 per cent of the value of Jamaican exports.

Table 13.1 Total exports and exports of manufactured products: Barbados, Jamaica, Trinidad and Tobago (1965–85) (US$m.).

Year	Barbados			Jamaica		Trinidad and Tobago			
	Total	Mfg. products	Electronic components	Total	Mfg. products	Total	Total excl. petroleum	Mfg. products	Chemicals
1965	27.7	1.1	0.0	214.2	14.6	395.1	66.8	27.7	21.0
1966	29.2	1.3	0.0	227.9	16.5	417.3	78.6	41.3	33.4
1967	30.6	1.6	0.0	196.0	17.5	430.7	90.6	52.6	44.3
1968	29.7	3.1	0.9	219.6	18.2	460.7	92.2	50.6	40.6
1969	28.6	6.3	2.8	289.1	21.5	466.0	100.9	58.1	44.3
1970	31.1	7.9	3.2	341.8	21.7	472.2	100.2	55.2	37.8
1971	27.2	7.4	1.9	344.1	28.1	511.7	100.6	56.6	36.4
1972	32.6	11.5	2.2	375.2	26.6	544.3	113.5	62.6	39.8
1973	42.8	17.5	3.3	390.1	27.7	691.8	115.9	65.1	38.2
1974	61.2	21.8	4.3	604.0	35.9	1916.6	185.5	99.8	67.2
1975	88.3	26.2	4.7	759.3	45.5	1778.6	218.5	102.3	62.7
1976	68.8	32.9	6.9	630.1	48.7	2197.6	183.9	95.6	61.4
1977	75.6	38.3	9.2	723.9	48.9	2166.4	165.3	90.8	62.7
1978	93.3	56.2	19.0	782.1	50.4	2004.2	175.6	112.0	84.3
1979	116.4	74.8	22.6	814.7	61.4	2575.1	174.9	92.7	63.9
1980	168.7	98.4	31.7	962.7	75.1	4056.3	228.0	143.2	108.2
1981	148.5	105.2	38.7	974.0	66.3	3634.2	238.1	161.7	115.6
1982	186.3	139.5	60.9	767.4	95.4	2994.6	285.2	218.1	158.0
1983	255.1	219.5	133.2	685.7	84.0	2263.2	307.8	251.6	186.6
1984	291.9	245.2	168.0	738.7	88.6	2101.8	364.8	309.2	234.1
1985	248.2	205.9	152.1	568.6	106.4	2082.4	371.2	312.9	261.8

Sources: Central Bank of Barbados, *Statistical Digest*, Annual Trinidad and Tobago Central Statistical Office, *Overseas Trade Report*, Statistical Institute of Jamaica, *External Trade of Jamaica*.

In view of the fact that all of the countries had been publicly committed to encourage exports of manufactured products, the developments in that regard are of particular importance. In 1965, Barbadian exports of manufactured products were insignificant. However, as indicated above, by 1976 manufactured products constituted the major share of export products. Over the twenty-year period exports of manufactured products grew at an annual average rate of 30 per cent. Most of this growth can be attributed to one sector, electrical components. Between 1975 and 1984 exports of electrical components expanded at an annual average rate of 53 per cent.

In spite of this rather impressive rate of growth, the high degree of commodity specialisation suggests that the success could likely be only transitory. A change in market conditions could result in an equally dramatic reversal in the growth pattern. This was in fact what occurred after 1984. The assembly of electronic components started in the 1970s. Firms from the United States established subsidiaries to produce components which would be exported in their entirety back to the United States. Transferring the most labour-intensive parts of production activity to low-wage countries has been an increasingly common practice of American firms over the past twenty years. Real cost savings can be realised as under the provisions of Item 807 of the US tariff schedule, firms importing products from overseas affiliates manufactured from components shipped from the United States are charged duty only on the value added in the foreign country. The rapid growth in Barbadian exports of electronic components, starting in the late 1970s, was a direct reflection on the strength of the market for computers in the United States at that time and, consequently, the demand for semiconductors. However, the slump in the US computer market after 1984 had an immediate dramatic impact on the country's sale of these items. By the end of 1986, the value of exports of electronic components had fallen by almost 30 per cent below that of 1984 and there was a further 42 per cent decline in 1987 (Central Bank of Barbados, 1985, 1986, 1987).

The growth of Jamaican exports of manufactured products over the period was substantially lower than that of Barbados, averaging 10.4 per cent. Manufactured products accounted for 7 per cent of total exports in 1965, was 6 per cent in 1975 and had risen to 19 per cent in 1985. The substantial increase in the share of manufactured products in total exports in the later period was more a reflection of the decline in the value of exports of bauxite and alumina than of any major increase in export sales of manufactured products. The annual average rate of growth of sales of manufactured products in that period was less than 9 per cent.

In the case of Trinidad and Tobago exports of manufactured products over the period grew at an annual average rate of 13 per cent. As was the case with Barbados, there was a high degree of commodity specialisation. In this instance the dominant items were chemical products. Since 1977, on average more than two-thirds of total exports of manufactured products has consisted of these items.

In summary, although all countries have made some modest headway in promoting exports of manufactured products, none of them could be said to have established a firm export base in these items. Barbados and more recently Jamaica have experienced some success in exporting to the United States under the provisions of Item 807 of that country's tariff schedule. The rest of this chapter will be directed towards providing an explanation of why this has been the case even though throughout the period there has been a strong commitment to the promotion of exports of manufactured goods.

13.3 Export promotion and industrialisation

A major problem faced by countries in the region in the period following the end of the Second World War was that of providing productive employment for those currently unemployed, as well as those expected to enter the labour force in the coming decades. The solution to this problem was seen to rest on the establishment of manufacturing industries. The first comprehensive argument for industrialisation was set out in an article by Lewis (1950), and his arguments and policy recommendations have had a lasting impact on subsequent industrialisation strategies. Consequently, we will outline in substantial detail the major elements of the Lewis argument.

Lewis based his argument on the following factors. He began by establishing that the relative scarcity of land in the island economies meant that reliance could not be placed on agriculture to absorb the unemployed and provide a reasonable standard of living (Lewis, 1950, p. 7). An alternative to agriculture then had to be found and the logical alternative was to industrialise. He then proceeded to address the issue of what were the major impediments to industrialisation in the islands and how these could be overcome. The major obstacles, as he saw them, were the small size of the island markets, the scarcity of domestic investment capital and limited marketing skills. Recognition of the need to overcome the size constraint led him to stress two important requirements for a successful programme of industrialisation. The first was that if manufacturing industry was to provide the level of employment desired, the islands would have to produce products for export markets. Import-substitution industrialisation would offer very limited scope for addressing the employment issue (p. 16). Secondly, he argued that since there were very few industries in which the islands together could support more than a single factory able to operate at a reasonably economic scale, a customs union among the islands was an essential requirement to take advantage of the limited opportunities for import substitution (p. 30). These two issues, the importance of extra-regional markets and regional economic integration, have continued to be raised over the years whenever development strategies are discussed. Nevertheless, as will be shown later, instead of these issues establishing the basis for a policy consensus, they have tended to highlight the divisiveness among the countries of the region.

Lewis argued that the other major obstacles to industrialisation, capital scarcity and a lack of marketing skills, could be overcome by adopting the strategy which had been used by Puerto Rico. This strategy, which subsequently became known in the Caribbean as 'industrialisation by invitation', was based on attracting foreign firms to establish plants in the region to produce items for extra-regional markets. Given the importance of external economies in a firm's decision as to where to locate a new plant, firms would not normally be attracted to establish new plants in areas without industry like the Caribbean. He argued that special incentives, such as temporary monopoly rights, tariff protection and tax holidays, would have to be provided to industrialists as inducements. His views in this regard are best reflected in the following frequently quoted statement: 'The islands cannot be industrialised to anything like the extent that is necessary without a considerable inflow of foreign capital and capitalists, and a period of wooing and fawning upon such people' (p. 38).

Lewis was adamant in asserting that the industrialisation of a new country could not be left to market forces but would require specific government action. This action would be of two kinds, the provision of special incentives referred to above and the creation of special institutions which would have the responsibility for carrying out the policy (p. 44). With respect to the matter of institutions he called for the creation of a regional Industrial Development Corporation. This agency, even though it would be responsible to government, would have to be granted a substantial degree of autonomy to enable it to function effectively. Not only would the Corporation have the responsibility of bringing to the attention of business firms the incentives available in the form of tax holidays and subsidies, it would have to be provided with funding sufficient to engage in providing additional incentives, such as low-cost factory buildings, capital equipment and serviced industrial estates. It would also be necessary to complement the Industrial Development Corporation with an Industrial Development Bank. The role of the Bank would be to function strictly as a lender of last resort since emphasis ought to be placed on attracting foreign capital into the area (p. 48).

Although emphasis was placed on the importance of providing incentives to attract industries, it was recognised that it might be necessary as well to combine the incentives with the potential penalty of loss of access to markets in the region. Consequently, he argued that tariffs could be used to restrict market access. This, it was recognised, might have the potential negative consequence of encouraging inefficient local production. Nevertheless, foreign firms faced with a potential loss of markets might then be induced to establish branch plants which, after a time, might become involved in export production.

In summary, Lewis's major concern was to challenge what he regarded as conventional thinking concerning appropriate economic policy for the region. At the same time he stated explicitly that if the policy initiatives he recommended were to be effective there would be a need for innovations at the political level and in terms of institutions. This was reflected in his unqualified assertion that industrialisation in the region could not be of any real significance in the absence of a customs union, a political federation and the associated regional institutions.

The industrialisation policy initiatives enacted by countries in the region during the 1950s were, in a limited way, in keeping with the basic thrust of the Lewis argument. Indeed, Jamaica, with the passage of the Pioneer Industries Encouragement Law with its income tax relief and customs duty concessions, had acted to encourage the establishment of manufacturing enterprises prior to the publication of the Lewis article. This law was effectively superseded by the Industrial Incentives Law of 1956 which provided a model for the incentive legislation enacted by Barbados and other countries in the Leeward and Windward Islands (MacFarlane, 1965, p. 23). Trinidad had enacted an Aid to Pioneer Industries Ordinance in 1950 (Carrington, 1967, p. 60). The factors which would determine whether a firm would qualify for the exemptions embodied in the legislation were: the impact on existing industries, the degree of usage of local raw materials or skills available, whether the existing capacity for manufacture of the product was sufficient to meet demand and judgement concerning the likelihood for success of the enterprise (MacFarlane, 1964, p. 23). The income tax benefits were primarily in the form of exemptions from income tax payments on profits earned for a seven-year period. Companies were allowed to wait up to three years following the start of production activity before electing to begin to exercise this incentive. This was designed to avoid the potential redundancy in the tax concession which could arise if countries were restricted to the first seven years of operations, since in the very early stages no profits might be earned on its operations. Apart from the income tax benefit, companies operating under these laws were allowed to import capital equipment duty-free.

In addition to the passage of incentive laws Jamaica and Trinidad and Tobago established Industrial Development Corporations and Barbados a Development Board during the 1950s, which were given the responsibility of promoting industrial development.

In proceeding with the passage of incentive legislation, the countries in the region were responding in a highly superficial way to the Lewis challenge. Specifically, by pursuing what was essentially a national rather than a regional approach to industrialisation they were adopting an approach which was fundamentally inconsistent with the substance of the Lewis argument. Furthermore, in formulating their incentives, insufficient attention was paid to the warning by Lewis that if industrialisation was to make an important contribution towards the employment problems of the islands, the plants which were established would have to be engaged primarily in export production. Consequently, in simply providing a package of incentives, the industrialisation strategy was effectively heavily biased towards import substitution. Furthermore, the fact that industrialisation was not being promoted in the context of a regional market meant that there would be, given the small size of individual country markets, relatively inefficient, high-cost enterprises. This would render more difficult an evolution from pure import substitution to export activity. The Jamaican government at the time of the introduction of the Industrial Incentive Law in 1956 introduced the Export Industry Encouragement Law, which provided a package of incentives for firms engaged exclusively in export production. The major difference in the incentives provided under this law was that firms were allowed to import raw materials in addition to capital equipment duty-free. In passing such a law it meant that export industries were seen as a special feature rather than an integral part of the industrialisation process.

Jamaica and Trinidad and Tobago, as indicated above, were the first to introduce incentive legislation and during the 1950s experienced the most significant growth in manufacturing of the island economies. By the mid-1960s there were 149 firms operating under incentive laws in Jamaica and 139 in Trinidad and Tobago. The contributions these plants made to direct employment in both countries were modest. It was estimated that between 1950 and 1963 the labour force in Trinidad and Tobago increased by nearly 100,000. Over that period the number of jobs created in new manufacturing enterprises was approximately 7,000 (Carrington, 1968, p. 38). In Jamaica, there were just over 9,000 employed in firms operating under incentive laws in 1966 (Jamaica Industrial Development

Corporation, 1967). Heavy out-migration had stabilised the size of the labour force during the 1950s and early part of the 1960s. However, the labour force in the mid-1960s was estimated to be growing by at least 20,000 annually. This then meant that jobs created by firms operating under incentive laws were insufficient to satisfy the additions to the labour force at that time (Jefferson, 1967, p. 4).

Most of the output from these plants was directed to the domestic market of the respective countries. In Jamaica the value of exports amounted to 29 per cent of gross sales of firms operating under incentive laws in 1966. Most of the exports, not surprisingly, were from the eighteen firms operating under the Export Industry Encouragement Law. There was limited commodity diversification. Exports of clothing accounted for more than one-third of total exports of manufactured products at that time (Bennett, 1973, pp. 126–28). In the case of Trinidad and Tobago, exports as a percentage of total manufacturing sales declined over the decade of the 1950s. In 1953 exports represented 17.0 per cent of sales of manufactured products compared with 12.4 per cent in 1962 (Carrington, 1968, p. 40).

The experiences of both countries during the first decade of their industrialisation effort fully vindicated the Lewis argument that only a strategy oriented towards the establishment of export industries could make a significant contribution to employment.

13.4 The regional emphasis and its implications for exports

During the 1960s Caribbean economists challenged with increasing vigour the extent to which orthodox economic theory and its associated policy implications were relevant for Caribbean economies. McIntyre, for example, pointed out the directions in which theoretical thinking on customs unions would have to evolve to provide an appropriate framework for policies to promote regional economic integration (McIntyre, 1965). Demas emphasised the limited applicability of conventional economic analysis given the small size of countries in the region (Demas, 1965). The most radical challenge emanated from a group of economists at the University of the West Indies, who were members of the New World Group.[1] These economists directed their attention towards identifying what they considered were the principal factors contributing to the perpetuation of underdevelopment in the region. The factors which were highlighted were the legacy of the plantation system (Best, 1968; Levitt and Best, 1969; Beckford, 1972) and the role of foreign investment, specifically, the role of transnational corporations in the economy (Girvan, 1967, 1971; Girvan and Jefferson, 1968). Essentially what they argued was that the plantation legacy and the dominant role of the transnational corporations had given rise to societies that had developed a set of characteristics not conducive to promoting development. Evidence of this could be seen in a lack of social cohesion, the absence of significant linkages between various sectors of the economy, as well as the existence of economic and social institutions that were designed to serve narrow sectoral interests as opposed to national needs. The economies were highly open and heavily external dependent. The analysis of these New World economists was very much in line with that of the Latin American Dependency School reflected in the writings of Sunkel, Furtardo and Dos Santos. They saw such strategies as the industrialisation by invitation advocated by Lewis as simply working to reinforce the structural weaknesses contributing to the perpetuation of underdevelopment.

A theme which was pursued through various issues of the *New World Quarterly* was that real development required a complete socioeconomic transformation of countries in the region. The process of economic transformation would not be achieved through reliance on the price mechanism. There would be a need for specific government intervention to curb the activities of the transnational corporations. In addition, governments would have to become actively involved in the formulation of plans to achieve a more effective use of resources.

In 1967 a number of studies[2] were produced which were directed at resolving the following issues:

1. What were the essential requirements for establishing a manufacturing sector which would make substantial use of domestic resources and contribute significantly to domestic value added? (Brewster and Thomas, 1967)
2. What could be done to enhance the contribution of the bauxite industry to income and employment in the region? (Girvan, 1967)
3. The potential for expanding intra-Caribbean trade in agricultural products (Beckford and Guscott, 1967).
4. Improving the competitiveness of the banana industry (Beckford, 1967).

In all the studies, emphasis was placed on the importance of regional economic integration if the desired results were to be realised. The authors believed that the removal of internal trade restrictions and the establishment of a common external tariff would not be sufficient. Brewster and Thomas argued that the purpose of regional economic integration was to allow for the creation of industrial complexes based on a pooling of resources and the creation of economic linkages between the different countries in the region. This would be the means through which the structure of production in the region would be deepened and strengthened. Their basic argument was that an advanced industrial structure was based on the use of a few basic materials. These were iron and steel, natural and synthetic textiles, paper, rubber, plastic, glass, aluminium, leather, wood, cement, the industrial chemicals (mainly the alkalis, chlorine and sulphuric acid) and fuels (Brewster and Thomas, 1967, pp. 129–40). They proceeded to demonstrate that the resource base of the region as whole contained most of these basic materials. They then concluded that through planned sectoral integration, resources could be pooled to establish regional industrial complexes which could operate to deepen and strengthen the structure of production in the region.

In adopting this approach Brewster and Thomas placed considerable emphasis on regional import substitution. They argued that this did not mean that they were trying to disregard the importance of export trade in manufactured products. Rather, it was designed to show that there were existing industrial opportunities which could be exploited while avoiding the difficulties of finding extra-regional export markets, and still maintain a high degree of competitiveness with respect to quality and cost of production (Brewster and Thomas, 1967, p. 61).

The other studies also highlighted the potential benefits that could be realised from regional collaboration. Girvan, for example, on the basis of projections of future market demand for aluminium products, proceeded to demonstrate how by exploiting the hydro-electrical potential of Guyana and Surinam the region could move into the smelting of aluminium and the fabrication of aluminium products.

Beckford and Guscott concluded that many of the food products which were imported from extra-regional sources could be easily produced in the region. They suggested that the obstacles to regional trade in these items could be overcome through the establishment of a Regional Agricultural Trade Commission entrusted with the responsibility to (a) coordinate regional trade activities of government marketing agencies; (b) provide market information; (c) standardise the grading and classification of produce and develop a system of inspection; (d) undertake and commission feasibility studies on regional transportation services; (e) advise on the coordination of guarantee price policies; and (f) study tariff mechanisms for expanding trade (Beckford and Guscott, 1967, p. 28).

In his study of the banana industry, Beckford indicated that through regional collaboration, export substitution, a concept introduced by McIntyre (1965) could be employed to allow the low-cost Windward Island producers to be ceded new markets by the higher-cost Jamaican producers. Jamaica might be convinced to allow this if it could be assured that it would be able to replace the lost banana exports with exports of manufactured products and food-stuff to the Windward Islands (Beckford, 1967, pp. 23, 24).

The degree of collaboration among governments which would be required to carry out the strategies advocated by the New World economists would require an explicit acceptance by all the governments of their diagnosis of the problem, as well as a common view as to the appropriate role of government in economic activity. Most governments in the region at that time were not philosophically inclined to assume the major role in the economy implicit in the strategies proposed by those economists. However, the governments were quite willing to accept in principle the notion of the necessity for greater economic collaboration. In 1968, the initial steps were taken in that direction with the establishment of the Caribbean Free Trade Area Association (CARIFTA). The CARIFTA agreement was a standard free-trade agreement. Accordingly, it was far removed from the type of regional association envisaged by the authors quoted above. There were no provisions for regional industrial programming. There were two instruments for the harmonisation of agricultural production and trade under the Agreement. These were the Agricultural Marketing Protocol and the Oils and Fats Agreement. Both of these instruments were designed to regulate prices for specified products and allocate markets for them among the participating countries on the basis of declared surpluses and deficits. Neither of these measures had the effect of contributing to regional import substitution in food to a significant extent (Chernick, 1978, p. 20).

The CARIFTA agreement did provide a stimulus to the regional export trade, particularly trade in manufactured products from countries like Jamaica and Trinidad and Tobago, which had established a small manufacturing base centred on production of consumer products. There was, however, sustained interest in a further deepening of the regional integration process. This culminated in 1973 when Barbados, Jamaica, Trinidad and Tobago, and Guyana signed a treaty establishing a Caribbean Community and Common Market (CARICOM). In the following year all the remaining CARIFTA members acceded to the Community Agreement.

The concept of the Community covered functional cooperation, foreign-policy coordination and economic integration. The dimensions of economic integration were set out in a special Annex to the Treaty. The principal elements were the following:

1. The creation of an integrated regional market for goods through the adoption of a Common External Tariff and a Common Protective Policy.

2. There was agreement that there should be:
   (a) coordination of national development planning, regional industrial programming and the rationalisation of regional agriculture;
   (b) the joint development of regional natural resources and regional consultation in monetary balance-of-payments and exchange-rate policies;
   (c) the harmonisation of fiscal incentives to industry;
   (d) intra-regional tax harmonisation and double taxation agreements;
   (e) the harmonisation of commercial legislation including company laws;
   (f) the formulation of a process list as a criterion of the establishment of the origin of goods.
   These were all set out to promote coordinated regional development.
3. There was a provision for the negotiation of external trade agreements on a joint basis.
4. The formulation of a regime for the less developed member countries (Chernick, 1978, pp. 35, 36).

The CARICOM agreement was clearly more in keeping with the concept of regional integration advocated by Caribbean economists during the 1960s. In spite of this there did not emerge new manufacturing enterprises based on a pooling of resources from different member countries. Furthermore, there were no major changes in the types of products which dominated intra-regional trade. The hoped-for rationalisation of trade in agricultural and mineral products was also not realised. The wider protected market, for a limited time period, encouraged regional import substitution. In the period up to 1976, as indicated in Table 13.2, Barbados, Jamaica, and Trinidad and Tobago all increased their export sales to regional trading partners significantly. An analysis of the pattern of regional trade during that period concluded that the preferential market was an important contributor to the growth of exports of manufactured products to the region by Jamaica and Trinidad and Tobago (Bennett, 1982b). However, most of the items traded were consumer goods which had been produced in those countries prior to the CARIFTA/CARICOM agreements. These products were heavily dependent on imported inputs and lacking in domestic linkages. An expansion in sales of these items was then not addressing a fundamental structural weakness of the manufacturing sector in those countries.

The post-1976 period was associated with limited growth in intra-regional trade. The failure of the CARICOM agreement to generate the expected expansion in intra-regional trade and more effective use of

Table 13.2 Exports to CARICOM partners: 1969–85 (US$m.).

Year	Barbados	Jamaica	Trinidad and Tobago Total	Total (excluding fuels)
1969	7.1	9.2	36.2	20.6
1970	8.3	10.5	41.6	26.6
1971	8.9	13.8	51.0	32.2
1972	11.7	19.9	58.9	36.5
1973	14.0	24.2	73.4	43.4
1974	19.0	31.3	135.9	57.9
1975	19.8	34.4	155.4	71.5
1976	22.9	51.4	162.2	69.2
1977	23.3	48.5	145.8	51.9
1978	32.1	42.4	142.8	51.1
1979	38.1	61.6	194.1	55.3
1980	63.4	57.0	302.2	163.1
1981	60.6	68.5	296.0	73.0
1982	70.7	78.4	273.7	67.1
1983	69.5	84.6	206.5	58.1
1984	88.0	52.9	196.8	39.4
1985	82.2	40.6	240.8	38.9

Sources: Same as for Table 13.1.

regional resources can be attributed to the following factors. Although, as indicated, the agreement embodied most of the requirements necessary to support close regional collaboration, the governments never really fullfilled their commitments to consult each other on important matters. A graphic example of this can be found in the tentative agreement worked out between Jamaica and Trinidad and Tobago in 1974, which involved the construction of an aluminium smelter in Trinidad to convert Jamaican alumina. The smelter was to be powered by electricity generated from the large quantities of natural gas available in Trinidad. This was an example of the sectoral integration and resource pooling advocated by Caribbean economists, such as Brewster, Thomas and Girvan. The Jamaican government, without consulting the Trinidadian government, subsequently concluded an agreement in 1975 with Mexico, whereby it agreed to supply alumina for a smelter to be constructed in that country. The Trinidadians argued that in light of the expected global demand for aluminium a new Mexican smelter meant that a smelter in Trinidad would no longer be viable.

There was also a general inability on the part of governments to implement projects that were identified as being feasible. Arising from the CARICOM Heads of Government Conference in 1975 a comprehensive regional food plan was prepared. It outlined in substantial detail the items to be produced, production targets and the manner in which production was to be allocated among member countries. This plan was never effectively implemented. Furthermore, the Caribbean Community Secretariat conducted a series of studies which identified several agricultural and manufactured items which could be produced in the region (Caribbean Community Secretariat, 1974, 1975). However, in most instances these projects were not implemented.

The deepening of the regional integration process was also undermined by the severe decline in the economies of Jamaica and Guyana after 1976. Both countries had virtually exhausted their foreign exchange reserves. Their balance-of-payments problems forced them to impose stringent import restrictions. In Table 13.3 is set out the value of exports from Barbados and Trinidad and Tobago to Guyana and Jamaica. Evidence of the restrictions is seen in the stagnation in sales from 1977 through 1979. Since, as indicated above, consumer products tended to be the major items traded in the region, their trade restrictions in response to their balance-of-payments problems tended to fall disproportionably on items imported from their trading partners.

The difficulties created for the operation of CARICOM arising from the balance-of-payments problems of Jamaica and Guyana highlight a major shortcoming of the agreement. The Annex to the Treaty did specify that countries should consult with each other and cooperate on balance-of-payments and exchange-rate policies. The government of Trinidad and Tobago did provide balance-of-payments support to Jamaica. However, what was required was a comprehensive payments arrangement to complement the trading arrangements. In 1978, the member countries established the CARICOM Multilateral Clearance Facility (CMCF). The CMCF was useful in that by allowing intra-regional trade payments to be settled on a multilateral as opposed to bilateral basis it economised on the foreign exchange required to support regional trade. Moreover, since final settlements had to be made on a semi-annual basis and debtors were required only to partially discharge their obligations, the Facility did provide limited balance-of-payments support.

In view of the fact that there was full awareness of the high degree of openness of these economies and, indeed, regional integration was promoted as a mechanism for reducing this openness, more emphasis should have been placed on formally instituting an arrangement providing for balance-of-payments support to countries experiencing global payments problems. Consideration might have been given, for example, to a partial pooling of reserves by member countries, which could have been used to provide balance-of-payments support (Bennett, 1982a, ch. IV).

Table 13.3   Exports from Barbados and Trinidad and Tobago to Guyana and Jamaica: 1976–85 (US$m.).

Year	Barbados Exports to		Trinidad and Tobago Exports to		Exports excl. petroleum to	
	Guyana	Jamaica	Guyana	Jamaica	Guyana	Jamaica
1976	2.6	3.6	67.2	26.8	17.3	16.7
1977	1.8	2.4	60.3	24.7	13.6	9.3
1978	1.2	3.4	53.6	26.7	11.9	9.8
1979	0.9	2.1	71.0	30.8	10.2	10.3
1980	0.6	5.9	90.0	62.4	12.5	28.7
1981	0.9	9.7	106.9	64.8	9.0	25.5
1982	0.3	8.0	109.0	47.0	7.8	24.9
1983	0.7	9.2	64.6	32.0	7.2	14.9
1984	1.1	4.3	70.0	20.7	8.0	6.6
1985	0.9	3.7	64.3	39.1	7.3	5.3

Sources: Central Bank of Barbados, *Statistical Digest*, Annual; Central Statistical Office, Trinidad and Tobago, *Overseas Trade Report*, Annual.

In summary, the expectation that regional integration would lead to a major expansion in trade between the participating countries, and make it possible to establish production on a firm competitive basis for entering extra-regional markets, was not realised. The early stimulus to intra-regional trade based on traditional import substitution was short-lived. By the early 1980s considerable disillusionment had set in with respect to the potential benefits that could be derived from regional integration. There emerged a renewed interest in developing extra-regional market outlets, that is, more traditional export-oriented policies.

13.5   Trade strategies in the 1980s

The emphasis placed on developing extra-regional exports after 1980 can be traced to a number of domestic and external economic and political developments. The balance of payments and growing problem of external indebtedness experienced by Jamaica and Guyana underscored the need for foreign exchange earnings to satisfy debt-service obligations and facilitate import requirements. The Jamaican elections of 1980 brought to power a government which was committed to a radical reversal of the economic policies that had been pursued by the previous government. Specifically, the Seaga government saw the solution to the economic problems faced by Jamaica as resting in allowing the private sector to play the leading role in economic activity. The regional approach with its emphasis on very active state intervention in wide areas of economic activity was thus not in keeping with the thinking of the Seaga government.

The external debt problem also contributed to a limitation in the policy options which would be open to any government, irrespective of its ideological persuasion. The Jamaican payments problems forced the country, starting in 1977, to seek financial assistance from the International Monetary Fund. The Fund, as a condition for providing assistance, usually insisted on a country adopting a set of policy reforms. These well-known reforms in the areas of exchange-rate management, pricing, monetary and fiscal policy are designed to restore the primacy of the market mechanism in the production of goods and services and the allocation of economic resources. Since Mr Seaga became Prime Minister of Jamaica in 1980, that country has operated continuously under a series of Fund-supported programmes. The orthodox policies espoused by the Fund were willingly accepted by the government.

The basic IMF position was that it was necessary for Jamaica to adopt an outward-looking or export-oriented development strategy. However, before such a strategy could be implemented effectively the economy would have to be restored to a competitive footing. The Jamaican government accepted willingly the IMF adjustment programmes which that agency viewed as being essential to establish the necessary competitiveness. Its programme of structural adjustment was aimed at reducing the size of the government role in the economy through divestment of state enterprises and a severely reduced fiscal deficit. In addition, subsidies, price controls and exchange controls were to be de-emphasised in the interest of facilitating the operation of the market mechanism.

Although Jamaica was the first country to try to initiate a radical change in policy direction, elsewhere in the region the generally poor performance of state enterprises also worked to undermine confidence as to the benefits to be derived from very active state intervention in the economy. Moreover, the problems in sustaining regional export positions operated to heighten the interest in extra-regional export strategies.

Another major factor which had an important impact on economic policies in the region was the US election of 1980, which brought to power a president with a conservative agenda and who was concerned to see that developments in the region were consistent with his agenda. In February of 1982 President Reagan announced his Caribbean Basin Initiative (CBI). This trade-and-aid package was expected to generate a private sector-led era of prosperity in the region. The CBI was promoted as an important complement to what was deemed necessary for the area, namely, an outward-looking development strategy. The expectation was that US firms, encouraged by tax and investment credits, would establish production facilities in the region. These would be engaged in the production of items that would be exported to the United States taking advantage of the duty exemptions embodied in the proposal.[3]

The emphasis on more outward-looking policies since 1980 was not reflected in any marked change in export performance up to 1985. Barbados up to 1984 experienced remarkable growth in its exports of electronic components, primarily semiconductors to the United States. However, as mentioned earlier, the slump in the US computer market led to a collapse in export sales of these items. In the case of Jamaica there was modest growth in exports of manufactured products. Since 1986, when a Bilateral Textile Agreement was concluded with the United States, there has been a rapid expansion in exports of garments which more than doubled to slightly in excess of US$100 million in 1987 (Bank of Jamaica, *Report and Statement of Accounts* 1987). In the post-1980 period Trinidad and Tobago expanded its exports of chemical products. This arose from a government decision to invest in the construction of petrochemical production facilities based on its petroleum and natural gas reserves.

The Caribbean Basin Initiative did not live up to the expectations of

Table 13.4 Net private long-term capital flows: Barbados, Jamaica, Trinidad and Tobago (1980–86).

Year	Barbados	Jamaica	Trinidad and Tobago
1980	6.8	−121.5	137.0
1981	28.3	−14.8	203.3
1982	−3.0	19.6	265.6
1983	−6.5	−110.2	115.1
1984	−23.6	119.8	96.4
1985	−17.1	55.0	−41.7
1986	−41.0	32.9	−68.5

Sources: Bank of Jamaica, *Report and Statement of Accounts*, Annual; Central Bank of Barbados, *Statistical Abstract*, 1987; Central Bank of Trinidad and Tobago, *Annual Report*.

either the governments in the Caribbean or that of the Unites States. At the time of its announcement, the US economy was experiencing its worst recession in fifty years. Many traditional industries had been forced to close in the face of strong overseas competition. This gave rise to an upsurge of strong protectionist sentiment in the United States. The recession contributed to a dampened investment climate for both domestic and overseas investment. Moreover, the strength of the protectionist lobby raised serious questions with respect to the potential duration of the tariff concession embodied in the proposal. When the US economy emerged from the recession in 1983 and entered a phase of rapid growth, the range of attractive investment opportunities at home dampened interest in investing in an area like the Caribbean.

The result of all these developments was that there were no significant inflows of long-term private investment capital to countries in the region from the United States. Private long-term capital flows as shown in Table 13.4 were negative in each year after 1982 for Barbados and displayed a steady decline in the case of Trinidad and Tobago. In Jamaica, substantial outflows in 1983 were offset by an inflow of almost equivalent value in 1984. However, the overall pattern since 1982 reveals no discernible trend. The Jamaican situation in this regard is of particular interest. The Reagan administration had made a considerable effort to mobilise investment funds for that country in an effort to make it a regional showpiece for the benefits to be derived from private enterprise. Leading business figures such as banker David Rockefeller were recruited to help mobilise investments for that country. Yet, in spite of these efforts there was no upsurge in the flow of investment capital to that country.

13.6 Conclusions

In this chapter the underlying theme has been that the limited success realised by countries in the region in diversifying and expanding their exports could be attributed to policy deficiencies and, to some extent, policy inconsistencies. In the early years export promotion was treated as basically an extension to industrialisation policies rather than being central to the success of such policies. During the 1960s and 1970s there was wide acceptance of the view that external dependence was at the basis of the problems faced by the countries of the region and that regional integration was the mechanism through which such dependency could be reduced. This resulted in primacy being placed on regional import substitution and less emphasis was placed on extra-regional trade. However, there was never realised the degree of collaboration, as well as development of institutional mechanisms, which those who argued for this approach explicitly recognised as necessary, if regional integration was to reduce external dependency. As a result, what emerged was a traditional free-trade area/customs union arrangement, which was sustained for a time by the potential for import substitution in a protected regional market.

In the period since 1980 a renewed emphasis has been placed on the promotion of extra-regional exports. Barbados for a time was able to develop a growing export trade in semiconductors to the United States. Jamaica has experienced limited success in exporting winter vegetables and clothing, also to the United States. The strategy which has been followed has been a relatively passive one. It has involved the standard promotional packages directed at trying to attract foreign business in general to establish export facilities in the region. It has also involved, especially in the case of Jamaica with its foreign-exchange constraint, the establishment of credit lines and export credit insurance to assist domestic producers to develop export markets. The objective was to develop labour-intensive export activities. However, Caribbean countries, relative to such Pacific countries as the Philippines and Indonesia, are not low-wage countries. The major devaluations of the Jamaican and Guyanese currencies since 1983 have temporarily placed both of those countries on a more competitive footing in terms of labour costs. The success which Jamaica has realised in attracting garment manufacturers in that period is indicative of this development.

Those countries which have been successful in following an export-oriented strategy, have been able to realise their success by being able to adjust their product lines in response to changing market conditions. The relatively passive promotional policies pursued by countries in the region are not likely to lead to an export sector with that element of dynamism.

Instead, what we have witnessed is a highly product-concentrated export sector which goes through periods of rapid expansion and sudden collapse in response to cyclical market trends for the product.

Export promotion in the Caribbean ought properly to be thought of as an important measure in contributing to an over-all improvement in the mobilisation and use of resources. Emphasis ought to be placed on targeting specific sectors and to the potential evolution of markets for those products likely to fall within the feasible set of those which can be produced in the region.

Notes

1. The New World Group was an association of Caribbean intellectuals, many of whom were associated with the University of the West Indies. The Group's main objective was to transform the mode of living and thinking of the Caribbean people by engaging in two complementary forms of activity: the formulation of ideas about the social, political and economic conditions of our societies; and the making of personal contact with the community in the form of discussion meetings and talks with the hope that such interaction would broaden and expand the process of self education both of the Group and community (Editorial, *New World Quarterly*, 4(4), 1968).
2. These studies on Regional Economic Integration were undertaken under the joint initiative of members of staff of the University of the West Indies and the Governments of the English Speaking Caribbean.
3. See Bennett (1987) for an assessment of the potential significance of the duty-exemption provisions.

14

Export promotion in sub-Saharan Africa

David Greenaway

14.1 Introduction

'Sub-Saharan Africa' (SSA) is a vast region encompassing some 33 countries. Most of these countries are low-income countries according to World Bank criteria. In fact, two-thirds of the total set of low-income countries are in SSA. Of those which are not classified as low-income countries all, save one (Gabon), are classified as lower middle-income countries. Moreover, notwithstanding a recent World Bank report which offers some cause for optimism (World Bank, 1989) (but which has been challenged by an ECA report), the medium-term prospects of the SSA countries are such that they can be expected to continue as the largest component of the low-income country group.

Cynics might question the necessity, in a volume of this type, of evaluating export promotion in SSA. After all, there is no great heritage of export promotion in that region. Indeed, the reverse experience is the order of the day – taxation of primary producers, and protection of manufactures. Arguably, however, export promotion in SSA is worthy of analysis for at least three reasons. First, it is certainly true that many SSAs have been highly protectionist. Protection is a relative concept. Import protection inevitably generates an anti-export bias. This is no more than *negative* export promotion. Second, there are a few exceptions to this general rule: some SSA countries have made use of various instruments of *positive* export promotion. Third, a major plank in the World Bank's Structural Adjustment Programme (SAP) in SSA has been the reduction of anti-export bias. To this end a number of instruments of export promotion have been introduced. This programme has become increasingly important in an SSA context. As a result, positive export promotion can be expected to become more, rather than less, important over the next decade. It is these considerations which provide the motivation for this chapter.

The remainder of the chapter is organised as follows. Section 14.2 looks at the details of negative export promotion in SSA. Section 14.3 focuses on positive export promotion in those few countries with such experience. Section 14.4 is directed at structural adjustment loans (SALs) in SSA, with particular reference to positive export promotion. Finally, Section 14.5 offers some concluding comments.

14.2   Protection in sub-Saharan Africa

As noted in the Introduction, promotion and protection are relative concepts. They describe how the structure of relative prices departs from that associated with neutrality, i.e. the free-trade alignment of relative prices. If one introduces an export subsidy, all other things being equal, one promotes the export sector relative to the import-substitute sector by raising the price of exportables *relative* to importables. This is a very obvious point. Nevertheless, it is one which is often forgotten, particularly when its converse holds, i.e. import protection. Thus, if one introduces an import tariff, all other things being equal, one raises the price of importables relative to exportables. This is a crucially important point to make in the context of SSA where, in most countries, negative export promotion via positive import protection was the order of the day.

With a few exceptions, SSA economies are highly protected; just how highly protected can be seen in Tables 14.1 and 14.2. These tables summarise the evidence extant on the characteristics of trade and exchange-rate requirements in SSA for the periods 1965–73 and 1973–84. The information contained in these tables is necessarily qualitative. They report details of effective protection and its range, as well as qualitative information on the use made of direct controls, the presence of export incentives, and the evidence, if any, on exchange-rate misalignment. Effective protection is a widely used indicator of the orientation of trade policy. Some controversy surrounds its use. In the present context it should be noted that the evidence reported has been drawn from a large number of studies which use different measurement techniques and which make their calculations at alternative levels of statistical aggregation. Thus, direct comparisons are problematic. Notwithstanding that, several points are worth making. First, average levels of effective protection are relatively high. Second, the range of effective rates is, in most cases, relatively wide. Both of these refer to comparisons with LDCs in South East Asia and, to a lesser degree, Latin America. Third, for almost all these cases where tentative inter-temporal comparisons can be made, the average rate of effective protection appears to have increased, and the range widened, between the later 1960s/early 1970s, and the late 1970s/early 1980s.

In general, effective protection is measured by reference to the price-distorting effects of tariffs. Many LDCs rely to a greater or lesser degree on direct controls of one form or another. Direct controls take a variety of forms. The most obvious type of intervention is the quantitative restriction (QR). This is deployed pervasively on both competing and non-competing imports. Insofar as QRs apply to intermediate inputs which are used by the export sector, they can constitute an important source of anti-export bias. Little evidence of the price effects of direct controls in the countries of SSA exists. Individual country reports do, however, provide information on the scale of use. Tables 14.1 and 14.2 summarise this in a qualitative sense. As one can see, all the countries listed make some use of direct controls – in many cases extensive use. Clearly such a summary is wholly descriptive and inevitably involves an element of arbitrariness. In the present context, however, all we are concerned with pointing out is that direct controls are widely used in SSA and, other things being equal, will tend to reinforce the anti-export bias associated with relatively high rates of effective protection.

A widely noted concomitant of protectionist trade regimes is exchange-rate overvaluation. Typically this follows from attempts to resist the inflationary consequences of exchange-rate depreciation. As a result, import and export prices are held at artificially low levels. Exchange-rate overvaluation depresses the prices of the output of the tradable sector as a whole. In general, however, it has a greater disincentive effect for exports than for imports for the simple reason that the costs of exporting typically exceed those of producing for the domestic market. There have been some attempts to estimate the degree of exchange-rate misalignment in SSA countries. Tables 14.1 and 14.2 summarise these results in qualitative terms. As with direct controls we are again dealing with a crude qualitative indicator involving a degree of arbitrariness. The point to note, however, is that in all cases, save one, some degree of overvaluation is identified. Again it points to another possible source of anti-export bias.

It does not automatically follow, of course, that positive effective protection, direct controls and some degree of exchange-rate overvaluation must lead to anti-export bias. The disincentive effects of these instruments can, in principle, be counter-balanced by introducing other instruments of positive promotion designed to offset the effects of protection. The example *par excellence* of effective use of this particular strategy is Korea, where a very vigorous programme of export promotion was implemented alongside continued protection of the import-substitute sector. Such export incentives could take a variety of forms. For example, duty drawback schemes may offer a mechanism for exporters to reclaim duty paid on imported inputs; export retention schemes permit exporters to retain some proportion of their export earnings, thereby ameliorating some of the effects of exchange-rate overvaluation; direct export subsidies may be offered on exported output; or institutional support might reduce the transactions cost of market research and appraisal. Tables 14.1 and 14.2 report on the evidence or otherwise of positive export incentives. With a few exceptions which we will discuss in detail in the next section, positive export incentives have not been widely used in SSA. Moreover, where they have been in evidence, they have tended to be neither sufficiently pervasive, nor sufficiently attractive to offset the disincentive effects of import protéction. In the context of Table 14.1, the 'minimal' and 'negligible' incentives which applied in Ivory Coast, Nigeria and Ghana refer to small export subsidies in a narrow range of products. Likewise with Nigeria and Ghana in Table 14.2. The one case where incentives were more substantial is one we shall address in the next section, namely Mauritius.

14.3   Counter-examples

The previous section presents an image of remarkable uniformity across the region with regard to negative export promotion. As we shall see in the next section, policy reforms associated with structural adjustment programmes have resulted in the introduction of a wide range of instruments of export promotion in the second half of the 1980s. Prior to evaluating these reforms, however, it is worth while briefly reviewing a few 'counter-examples'. In the 1960s and 1970s, a handful of the SSA countries made some provisions intended to stimulate some export promotion in some degree, however modest.

14.3.1   *Ivory Coast*

As can be seen from Table 14.1, Ivory Coast had a relatively low level of effective protection in the 1965–73 period, made relatively little use of direct controls, and maintained a realistic exchange rate. By comparison with the other countries of SSA, these were relatively low levels of protection. Indeed, in the 1960s Ivory Coast was widely regarded as having a relatively liberal trade-and-payments regime (see for instance Rimmer, 1984). This regime did include several instruments of export

Table 14.1 Characteristics of trade and exchange-rate regimes in sub-Saharan Africa: 1965–73.

Country	Average EPR (%)	Range of EPRs (%)	Use of direct controls	Export incentives	Exchange-rate alignment
Ivory Coast	41	−25 to 278	Minimal	Minimal	Realistic
Senegal	70 (1971)	n.a.	Modest	n.a.	Low overvalued
Kenya	92 (1967)	−9 to 539	Moderate		Low overvalued
Nigeria	99 (1968)	−27 to 1,063	Extensive	Negligible	Overvalued
Ghana	143 (1968) 105 (1972)	−10 to 1,633	Extensive	Negligible	Significantly overvalued
Tanzania	116 (1966)	−1 to 538	Extensive		

Source: Drawn from Greenaway and Nam (1988).

Table 14.2 Characteristics of trade and exchange-rate regimes in sub-Saharan Africa: 1973–87.

Country	Average EPR (%)	Range of EPRs (%)	Use of direct controls	Export incentives	Exchange-rate alignment
Cameroon	31 (1975)		Moderate		Low overvalued
Ivory Coast	76 (1978)	−8 to 118	Moderate	Limited	Overvalued
Nigeria	82 (1979)	−62 to 119	Extensive	Negligible	Significantly overvalued
Mauritius	128 (1980)	23 to 269	Moderate	EPZ incentives	Moderately overvalued
Ghana	131 (1982)	−82 to 2,632	Extensive	Negligible	Moderately overvalued
Burundi	91 (1984)	−4 to 7,896	Extensive	None.	Moderately overvalued
Zambia	161 (1975)	−22 to 1,251	Extensive		Low overvalued
Madagascar	164 (1982)	−23 to 4,330	Extensive	None	Moderately overvalued
Tanzania	470 (1984)	5 to 5,258	Extensive	None	Significantly overvalued

Source: Drawn from Greenaway and Nam (1988).

promotion. Thus, under the 1959 Investment Code 'priority firms' were entitled to duty exemptions on imports of intermediates. Moreover, new firms were guaranteed fixed tax rates for up to 20 years after establishment. It has been estimated that the implicit nominal subsidy from this regime did not exceed 5 per cent (World Bank, 1987), with the exceptions of food processing, leather products and wood products. Many of these incentives were also available to firms producing for domestic consumption. They nevertheless intermixed with relatively low tariffs and a realistic exchange rate to provide an environment conducive to exporting in some product lines, most notably processed foodstuffs. With the proliferation of import quotas from the mid-1970s and an increase in nominal tariffs, the impact of these modest export incentives weakened, anti-export bias increased, and export performance deteriorated.

14.3.2 *Mauritius*

Export promotion in Mauritius dates back to 1970 and the creation of the Export Processing Zone. This was created as a basis for reducing the economy's dependence on primary-product exports. At that time it was overwhelmingly dependent on exports of sugar. The EPZ offered a variety of incentives to non-traditional exporters setting up in the zone. These included subsidised energy inputs, duty drawback on imported inputs, a ten-year tax holiday on profits, advance factories and simplified export procedures. Although the zone itself was not confined to any specific location, it did operate as a free zone in that products fabricated by EPZ companies could not be sold on the local market. In other words, the minimum export requirement was 100 per cent.

These EPZ provisions did encourage investment for export. For example, the number of EPZ units increased from 10 to 101 between 1970 and 1980, and these units employed over 20,000 workers. Moreover, the output was in non-traditionals, in particular textiles and clothing, but also toys, watches and processed foodstuffs. It is notable, however, that the most impressive growth in EPZ activity has occurred in the 1980s, with a fivefold increase in the number of units, and a fourfold increase in total employment. This is partly a consequence of changes in external circumstances, but more so as a consequence of the fact that during the 1980s the exchange rate has gradually moved towards a market-determined rate, and many of the incentives provided to the import-substitute sector have declined. Notwithstanding this, the fact remains that positive export-promotion policies have been in place in Mauritius for some twenty years. In this regard it is quite unusual in the context of SSA.

14.4 Structural adjustment lending and export promotion

The second oil shock had a dramatic impact on LDCs. To be more precise, the combination of a severe terms-of-trade shock and the drying up of adjustment finance created a major payments problem. One response to this crisis was the initiation of the Structural Adjustments Programme by the World Bank.

Structural Adjustment Loans (SALs) appeared to contrast quite sharply with Stabilisation Loans disbursed by the IMF, in several repects: they were conceived as being medium-term loans; they were conditional upon medium-term economic reforms; conditionality focused upon supply-side reforms. By contrast, IMF Stabilisation Loans, which are also conditional, tend to focus more on short-run demand-side policy changes. As it has turned out, there is more overlap between SALs and the IMF's stabilisation programmes than envisaged, an outcome which has resulted in tension between the two organisations.

The SAL programme is then a stick-and-carrot package. Incentives are offered in the form of concessional lending which is not tied to specific projects. In return a commitment is required in the form of policy reform. Although the detailed package of reforms varies from country to country, as well as from time to time in a particular country, the overall objectives of reform are much the same. In terms of Figure 4.1 (Chapter 4) these are to alter the relative price ratio (P_T) towards the international price ratio (P_W), and to eliminate distortions such that production takes place on the production frontier at a point such as 'e', rather than within it, at 'f'. Reforms are therefore directed at 'making prices work' and mobilising domestic resources.

Table 14.3 lists the percentage of 51 SALs disbursed to some 40 LDCs, with conditions in a range of policy areas. The table also lists the equivalent percentages for 13 SALs to SSA in the sample. If we take first the column pertaining to all countries one can see that trade policies figure more frequently than any other area of policy, in over three-quarters of all cases. The proportion is almost the same for loans to SSA. Note in addition, however, that the other areas of policy reform which pertain most directly to export performance also figure prominently in the SSA list, namely exchange-rate policy, industrial policy and agricultural policy. These are areas of policy which overlap with trade policy. In all cases the percentage of loans with conditions in these areas exceeds the equivalent figure for all countries. Clearly the reform of trade and related policies has figured prominently in the SAL programme thus far.

Table 14.4 breaks down the main components of trade policy reform in 40 countries which were in receipt of SALs prior to 1988. These figures suggest that overall import policy reform was significant in about half of

Table 14.3 Content of policy-conditioned lending operations.

Item	Percentage of total number of loans with conditions in various policy areas	
	SSA countries (13)	All countries* (51)
Exchange rate	30.8	15.7
Trade policies	76.9	78.4
Fiscal policy	61.5	64.7
Budget/public expenditures	69.2	51.0
Public enterprises	61.5	52.9
Financial sector	38.5	39.2
Industrial policy	53.8	25.5
Energy policy	7.7	23.5
Agricultural policy	76.9	49.0
Other	23.1	13.7

*Numbers in parentheses are total numbers of loans.

Source: World Bank (1989).

the cases whilst overall export policy reform was significant in about one-third of all cases. For the SSA countries in this sample, over half were countries where reforms in these areas were regarded as significant. With regard to the reform of import policy, it is important to recall the point made in section 14.2, namely that import protection is negative export promotion. Thus, within the context of SAL-driven reform, import liberalisation has been viewed as a crucial factor in the reduction of anti-export bias.

Table 14.5 gives a flavour of the specific liberalisation components of SALs for 17 SSA countries. Changes in the overall protection level were regarded as negligible in only one instance. Disentangling this into changes in tariff levels and changes in protective QRs, one finds negligible changes in only seven and five cases respectively. The desire to reduce anti-export bias has been a strong driving force in SALs and, in many cases, the intended liberalisation has been significant. Thus in Ghana a target cluster of tariff rates of 20–25 per cent was proposed, together with reduced coverage of QRs; in Nigeria a 30 per cent import levy was discontinued, advance payments of import duties were reduced from 100 per cent to 25 per cent and many import bans eliminated; in Ivory Coast an attempt to cluster effective tariffs around a target of 40 per cent was implemented in 1985, down from an average of over 90 per cent; in Burundi average nominal tariffs were reduced and rationalised around

Table 14.4 Main components of trade policy in 40 SAL countries.

Area of reform	Number of countries where reforms were:						
	Significant	Less significant	Negligible	Total	Present	Not present	Total
Overall import policy[a]	19	10	11	40	–	–	–
QRs on non-competitive imports	12	16	12	40	–	–	–
Protective QRs	12	17	11	40	–	–	–
Tariff level	7	20	13	40	–	–	–
Tariff dispersion	8	22	10	40	–	–	–
Protection level	13	26	1	40	–	–	–
Schedule of future reduction	6	29	5	40	–	–	–
Protection studies	–	–	–	–	28	12	40
Overall export policy[a]	15	14	11	40	–	–	–
Exchange rate[b]	–	–	–	–	38	2	40
Export promotion[c]	–	–	–	–	33	7	40
Imports for exports	17	15	8	40	–	–	–

Note: The assessments refer to proposals supported by the Bank. They do not necessarily refer to policy implementation.
[a] Judgement on the significance of the overall reform proposals.
[b] Often these were not explicit conditions, but constituted understandings, frequently made under the programme.
[c] Includes such schemes as export credits, insurance, guarantees, and institutional development.

Source: CECTP, World Bank (1989).

Table 14.5 Trade liberalisation components of adjustment lending: intensity of reduction of restrictions.

Country	Overall imports	Exports	Import for	QRs on non-competing imports	Protective QRs	Tariff level	Overall protection level	Tariff dispersion	Schedule of future reduction	Forms of export promotion	Studying forms of protection
Burundi	LS	S	LS	IN	LS	LS	LS	LS	S	OTH	N
CAR	S	LS	LS	S	S	LS	S	LS	LS	OTH	Y
Ghana	LS	S	LS	LS	LS	LS	LS	LS	S	OTH	Y
Ivory Coast	S	LS	LS	LS	S	S	S	S	S	OTH	Y
Kenya	S	S	LS	LS	LS	S	S	LS	LS	ER	Y
Madagascar	S	S	S	LS	LS	LS	LS	S	LS	OTH	Y
Malawi	IN	IN	IN	IN	IN	IN	IN	IN	LS	OTH	N
Mauritania	IN	LS	LS	LS	LS	LS	LS	LS	LS	OTH	N
Mauritius	S	S	IN	S	S	LS	LS	LS	LS	OTH	N
Niger	IN	IN	IN	IN	LS	IN	LS	LS	LS	OTH	N
Nigeria	S	S	S	S	LS	IN	LS	LS	LS	ER	Y
Senegal	S	LS	LS	S	LS	LS	LS	LS	LS	OTH	Y
Tanzania	IN	LS	S	IN	IN	IN	LS	IN	IN	OTH	N
Togo	IN	LS	IN	IN	IN	IN	LS	IN	IN	N	Y
Zaire	LS	S	IN	IN	S	LS	S	S	S	OTH	Y
Zambia	S	LS	LS	S	S	IN	LS	IN	IN	OTH	Y
Zimbabwe	S	LS	S	IN	IN	S	LS	S	IN	ER	Y

Note: S = significant; LS = less significant; IN = insignificant or negligible; OTH = other; ER = exchange rate; N = no; Y = yes.

CAR = Central African Republic

Source: Halevi (1988).

Table 14.6 Summary of trade policy reform measures: Kenya (SALs agreed: 1980, 1982).

Policy instruments	Initial reforms	Subsequent reforms
Import duties	Tariffs on some items, including capital and intermediate goods, increased (maximum rate of 100%) Temporary 10% tariff surcharge imposed on all durable items	Intention to produce more moderate and uniform tariff rates, including some use of tariff-equivalents for removed QRs
Quantitative import restrictions	Removal of import bans	Progressive reduction of QRs on most imports planned
Export taxes/subsidies	Rate of export compensation raised from 10% to 20% and list of eligible exports expanded No change to export taxes	
Exchange-rate policy	Depreciation in February 1981 of 5% and of 15% in September 1981	Further depreciations

a relatively small number of target rates; in Madagascar QRs were liberalised and tariff rates reduced.

Tables 14.6, 14.7 and 14.8 provide a yet more detailed breakdown of the trade policy components of three SAL programmes in Kenya, Mauritius and Ivory Coast. In these three countries the full range of measures directed at reducing anti-export bias has been introduced, although the combination of instruments used, and their phasing, differs from one case to another. In Mauritius tariff and quota changes have been implemented with a view to reducing relative protection of the import-substitute sector (as well as reducing relative protection within that sector). In addition, however, a key instrument has been the reduction in exemptions applicable to firms operating in this sector. There is evidence to suggest that duty exemptions available to import-substituting firms operated as a clear disincentive to invest in the export sector (Greenaway and Milner, 1989a). In Kenya liberalisation of import bans and quantitative restrictions was seen as a key element in reducing anti-export bias. Note initially, however, that in this case some tariffs actually *increased*, and some tariff surcharges were *introduced*. Although these changes were not explicitly calibrated as tariff equivalents of the QRs, they went some way to fulfilling that function, thereby replacing quota rents with tariff revenue. In turn this was intended to make the

Table 14.7   Summary of trade policy reform measures: Mauritius (SALs agreed: 1981, 1983).

Policy instruments	Initial reforms	Subsequent reforms
Import duties	Consolidation of some duties Lowering of average tariff levels Reduced exemptions to duty Import surcharge in 1984–85	Intention to reduce spread of tariffs Intention to consolidate fiscal, customs and stamp duty into one tax
Quantitative import restriction	QRs lifted in Jan. 1985	Intention to introduce tariff equivalents
Export taxes/subsidies	Increased exemptions to export tax Extension of duty drawback to exporting firms	
Exchange-rate policy	Depreciation of 45% against dollar between 1981 and 1985	
Institutional and other reforms	Creation of MEDIA Creation of ICU Introduction of ECGI scheme Negotiation of double taxation agreements	

Table 14.8   Summary of trade policy reform measures: Ivory Coast (SALs agreed: 1981, 1983, 1986).

Policy instruments	Initial reforms	Subsequent reforms
Import duties	Reduction in nominal tariffs to achieve uniform effective tariffs Reduction in some exemptions	
Quantitative import restriction		Planned abolition of QRs and replacement with temporary surcharges
Export taxes/subsidies	Provision of export subsidies Increase in producer prices in agricultural sector	
Institutional and other reforms	New Investment Code	Planned privatisation

introduction of positive export incentives easier than otherwise. The details of the Ivorian reforms are different again. Nominal tariffs were reduced with the intention of generating a uniform effective tariff across all activities (of 40 per cent). Moreover, export subsidies were provided in an attempt to supply exporting activities with an equivalent degree of effective protection. Thus in this case the tariff reforms were designed, not just to reduce anti-export bias, but to eliminate it completely.

These examples are cited for illustrative purposes only. They are intended to give an indication of the type of programme introduced with a view to reducing anti-export bias, a theme which pervades most SALs. It is important to note, however, that intentions and outcomes may differ. One cannot take sustainability for granted in SSA. The structure of property rights to the rents from protection are well established in many countries, resulting in widespread resistance to reform. Moreover, changes in external constraints often challenge commitment to reform at an early stage. In some countries, 'sustainability limits' have already been broached and the programmes have either collapsed, or been significantly diluted: Zambia is an example of the former, Ivory Coast of the latter. In addition, governments have shown themselves to be adept in the art of instrument substitution – replacing one form of intervention with another. Thus, for example, although the tariff structure was rationalised in Nigeria and average tariffs reduced, a variety of criteria for surcharging was introduced. Specifically, surcharges could be obtained on luxury imports, industries which required safeguard protection and industries facing competition from 'dumped' imports. The definition of each turned out to be somewhat elastic. As a result, by the end of 1986, a remarkably high proportion of imports fell under one of these headings. One therefore needs to acknowledge the fact that whilst a given *intention* may be expressed in SALs, actual outcomes may differ. Where, however, outcomes are consistent with intentions there is no doubt that anti-export bias should be reduced, providing an opportunity for improved export performance. It is as yet premature to evaluate fully this aspect of SAL programmes. Two recent studies have however strongly emphasised the beneficial aspects of such changes. Whalley (1990) argues that 'adopting import liberalizing . . . measures are widely seen in policy circles in these countries . . . (Kenya, Tanzania and Nigeria) . . . as central to any new effort to reverse the decline of their economies' (p. 3). World Bank (1989) goes even further in arguing that these policy changes have already had a measurable impact on performance. This last assessment has to be treated with some caution, particularly where SSA countries are concerned. Reform progress here has been slower than in other parts of the world and the issue of any actual improvement in performance is a matter of debate. We will return to this point later.

. As one can see from Tables 14.4, 14.6, 14.7 and 14.8, conditionality has been directed not only at anti-export bias, but also at pro-export bias, in other words at explicit export promotion. As these tables show, this has taken the form of exchange-rate policy reform, or other export-promoting measures. As we saw earlier, exchange-rate overvaluation is a common feature of an inward-oriented trade regime. That it provides a disincentive to export is not in doubt. Consequently a variety of instruments has been assigned to reducing exchange-rate overvaluation. *Inter alia* these have included some kind of auction system for foreign exchange (e.g. Ghana, Uganda); two-tier exchange rates with convergence (e.g. Nigeria, Ghana); foreign-exchange retention schemes (e.g. Tanzania and Kenya); depreciation/devaluation followed by a floating exchange rate (e.g. Mauritius). In many cases the extent of depreciation has been dramatic. For example, the Ghanaian cedi moved from $1 = 2.75 cedi to $1 = 30 cedi between April and October 1983 and had reached 90 cedis by the end of 1985; in Tanzania the exchange rate moved from $1 = 15 TSch to $1 = 95 TSch between late 1984 and early 1987. This kind of experience is not untypical and is crucial to any sustained stimulus to export growth.

Another common pro-export reform has been changes in producer prices. Many SSA economies are heavily dependent on exports of primary products. The taxation of these commodities has traditionally been an important source of government revenue (see Greenaway, 1984). Such taxation has, however, served to depress domestic prices of the commodities concerned, often with fundamental effects on incentive structures (see for example Bevan *et al.*, 1987, on Tanzania and Kenya). To some extent this too has shown signs of change. Export taxes have been reduced and/or exemption rules changed and/or producer prices set by marketing boards raised in a number of countries, for example Mauritius, Tanzania, Kenya, Ivory Coast, Ghana, Senegal, Madagascar and Burundi.

Producer price changes of this type pertain of course to traditional exportables. The great challenge facing most SSAs is export diversification away from traditional, and towards non-traditional exportables. Some modest steps have been taken in this direction in a few SSA countries. For example, in Mauritius, duty drawback provisions were improved for non-traditional exporters. There some companies benefited from corporate tax concessions. In addition a variety of infrastructural/ systemic reforms were introduced including the creation of an Industrial Coordination Unit to assist potential investors; an export credit guarantee scheme; a Mauritius export-development agency and the simplification of export-related procedures. Mauritius has moved more quickly and further, with regard to non-traditional exportables, than any other SSA.

However, some innovations have taken place elsewhere. Duty drawback or duty exemption provisions have, for instance, been introduced in Nigeria, Tanzania and Kenya; export procedures have been simplified in Madagascar, Burundi and Ivory Coast; infrastructural support provided in Tanzania, Ivory Coast and Cameroon; and export subsidies provided in Kenya and Ivory Coast. In addition, more liberal arrangements on export retention and import licensing are aimed at encouraging greater activity in non-traditional exportables in Tanzania and Kenya.

14.5 Evaluation

It is clear that, until recently, the SSA countries as a whole can be fairly described as inward oriented. Some of the most highly protected economies in the world are in the region and their protective structures are often regimes of bewildering complexity. One very important by-product of this inward orientation has been strong anti-export bias. The last decade has seen some modest changes in outlook and in actual policy. As Whalley (1990) contends, this is partly due to a changed intellectual climate and more favourable conditions in the OECD countries. Arguably, however, the principal driving force has been policy-lending conditionality from the IMF, and even more so the World Bank. Some change is therefore underway.

Whether this modest reorientation will be sustained and reinforced is an open question. On the one hand, the resistance to change should not be underestimated – many influential interest groups have long-established claims on the rents from protection. On the other hand, the wider benefits of liberalisation have been felt in some economies. Mauritius is an obvious example. However, they have not gone unrecorded in some of the newer reformers (e.g. Tanzania, Madagascar and Burundi). The steps which have been taken are tentative steps on a somewhat difficult path. The prospects for sustainability are to some extent in the hands of the policy-makers in the countries concerned. They will also, however, be fashioned by changes in the external environment, most notably in the openness of OECD markets, and by the terms of trade and perceptions regarding the effects of policy reform thus far. This is an extremely difficult issue. It is early days to pass final judgement on the SAL programme. The most favourable analysis thus far has been provided by World Bank (1989). This study compared the performance of SSA countries subject to SALs with that of a group of comparable countries. The results were mixed. Less than half showed an improvement over the control group on GDP growth, investment growth and budgetary balance. On the other hand, more than a half showed an improvement over the control on export growth, the real exchange rate and the current account. Overall, 51 per cent of the countries showed some improvement. This was a lower proportion than that recorded for manufacturing exporters, low-income countries and high-income countries; but a higher share than the highly indebted countries. Since these countries received a significant share of total adjustment lending, this may appear to be a somewhat disappointing outcome. One could argue, however, that the share showing improvement would have been much less in the absence of SALs, and point out that for those SSA countries which were subject to 'intensive' adjustment lending, the share showing improvement was higher (albeit still only at 58 per cent).

This issue is likely to continue to be a subject for debate for some time to come. Although the exact detail of improvements in economic performance may not yet be clear, it does seem as though improvements in export performance have occurred in a substantial number of SSAs, and that this is related to the reform programmes which have been implemented. It is also clear, however, that there is a long way to go.

15

Export promotion in the Mediterranean Basin

Richard Pomfret

15.1 Introduction

The Mediterranean region offers a rich variety of case studies for the relationship between public policy and export performance. For over a decade exports from the region have enjoyed duty-free access to their main market, the European Community (EC), but the various countries have shown great variations in their response to this export opportunity. Economic policy differences are not the only reason for the varied response – invasion, revolution and civil war have disrupted exports from Cyprus, Portugal and the Lebanon – but policy has played a clear role in many cases.

The next two sections of this chapter contain a summary of the economic performance and export-promotion policies of the countries in the Mediterranean region. The aim of these sections is to draw some conclusions about the effectiveness of export-promotion policies from comparative analysis. The drawback of this approach is that, within the space constraints of a single chapter, there is little room for detail. The following three sections provide case studies of Israel as an example of the semi-industrialised countries which shifted to more outward-oriented development strategies during the 1960s (section 15.4), Turkey as a country attempting similar trade liberalisation during the 1980s (section 15.5), and Malta as a successful exporter currently offering a well-designed package of export incentives (section 15.6).

I am grateful to Philo Scerri for helpful advice on section 15.6 and to Marian Gibbon for assistance in preparing the tables.

285

15.2   The historical record

Mediterranean trade patterns during the 1950s consisted overwhelmingly of bilateral trade between the poorer countries and western Europe; indeed some areas were still colonies or departments of Britain or France, and others had only recently ceased to be protectorates of these two powers. Formation of the EC and in particular the EC's Common Agricultural Policy forced the Mediterranean non-member countries to reassess their trade policies, as they faced long-run loss of market for their traditional agricultural exports. Several Mediterranean countries were able to sign preferential trade agreements with the EC, and acceleration of this process after 1967 encouraged the EC to standardise the arrangements in 1972 by adopting a global Mediterranean policy (GMP), of which a core component was duty-free access to EC markets for the Mediterranean countries' manufactured exports by 1977. All Mediterranean countries except Albania and Libya have signed agreements within the GMP framework and, although Greece, Portugal and Spain have moved on to full EC membership during the 1980s, the situation of duty-free access for manufactured exports from non-member Mediterranean countries remains.[1] In sum, facing a favourable external market situation, these countries have been among the developing countries best placed to adopt a development strategy based upon manufactured export expansion.

Tables 15.1 and 15.2 summarise the main economic characteristics and export record of the Mediterranean countries.[2] The variety of income levels and population size is immediately apparent. Israel, Spain and Greece are usually characterised as newly industrialising countries, with living standards and economic structures approaching those of the industrialised countries. The island economies of Cyprus and Malta also have relatively high income levels, but they have less developed economic structures, constrained in part by small size. Algeria, Syria and, to a lesser extent, Egypt and Tunisia all benefited from the oil-price increases of the 1970s and Morocco from the phosphate boom of the mid-1970s, but of these countries only Tunisia has had much success in export diversification. Among the poorer countries in the region there was a rather clear division in economic growth rates during the 1960s and 1970s between the success stories of Malta and Tunisia and the laggards, Morocco and Turkey; the cumulative effect of differential growth rates can be seen from the fact that Morocco and Tunisia started their independent careers in the late 1950s with similar income levels, but by 1985 Tunisian per capita income was double that of Morocco.

The relationship between export performance and economic growth has been analysed in Part 1 of this book, and will not be taken up here beyond stating that the Mediterranean countries' experience confirms a positive relationship. In this chapter the focus will be on explaining export performance, and in particular relating it to export-promotion policies. In some cases export performance is explained by favourable natural-resource endowment; Algeria's reliance on oil and natural gas exports is obvious from the tables; less clear is the dependence of Egypt's accelerated growth on oil prices since Egypt benefited indirectly from labour migration to the Arab Gulf countries and from Suez Canal fees, as well as from the oilfields regained after the Camp David agreement. In some cases adverse political conditions hurt export growth, e.g. Portugal and Cyprus in the 1970s, although recovery of exports was remarkably rapid in both of these cases. Other cases are less readily explained by exogenous factors.

Some comparisons of export performance are striking. Greece and Turkey both signed agreements with the EC in the early 1960s, but while Greek manufactured exports grew rapidly, Turkey's were stagnant until 1980. Morocco and Tunisia both signed agreements with the EC in 1969, but in the 1970s Tunisian exports increased twelvefold while Morocco's increased less than fivefold – raw materials were critical for both countries, but an important difference was Tunisia's success in developing new export industries such as electronics and clothing. Spain and Israel took advantage of easy access to EC markets to increase their manufactured exports, but so did the less developed island economy of Malta; level of economic development is not a sufficient explanation of export success, although the poorer eastern Mediterranean Arab countries on the whole fared less well. Finally, the export environment generally deteriorated for these countries during the first half of the 1980s, but a few countries avoided the trend, of which the most spectacular exception was Turkey.

Why were some countries more successful exporters than others? Why did some countries manage to diversify their exports from dependence on agricultural and other primary products while others did not? Why did some of the 'success stories' falter during the 1980s? To a large extent, the answers to these questions lie in economic policies. This is not a new finding; it was perceived by the countries in the region and led to major policy reforms by Tunisia in 1971–72, by Egypt after 1973 and Morocco in the 1980s (both to some degree trying to imitate the Tunisian model), and by Turkey after 1980. A final question, then, is why did some policy reforms (by Tunisia and Turkey) succeed better than others (by Egypt and Morocco) in promoting exports?

Table 15.1 Basic data for some Mediterranean countries.

	Population mid-1985 (million)	GNP per capita (US$)		Average annual growth rates (percentages)			Export/GDP ratio (percentages)			
		1985	mid-1950s	GNP per capita 1965–80	Exports 1965–80	Exports 1980–85	1965	1970	1977	1985
Greece	9.9	3,550	(239)	3.6	12.0	2.5	9	10	16	21
Portugal	10.2	1,970	(201)	3.3	3.4	10.0	26	23	18	39
Spain	38.6	4,290	(254)	2.6	5.5	2.6	10	13	15	23
Algeria	21.9	2,550	(176)	3.6	1.6	0.9	20	22	33	22
Cyprus	0.7	3,790	(374)	*	*	*	32	38	45	*
Egypt	48.5	610	(133)	3.1	2.0	3.9	18	14	18	14
Israel	4.2	4,990	(540)	2.5	8.9	5.0	19	25	38	33
Malta	0.4	3,310	*	8.1	*	*	54	50	87	*
Morocco	21.9	560	(159)	2.2	3.6	3.5	18	18	18	18
Tunisia	7.1	1,190	(131)	4.0	8.5	−1.8	19	22	26	24
Turkey	50.2	1,080	(276)	2.6	5.5	25.3	6	6	4	17

Note: * Data not available in these sources.

Sources: World Bank data from *World Development Report 1987* and *World Tables*, except for col. 3 from Bhagwati (1966).

Table 15.2 Export data for some Mediterranean countries.

	Exports (US$m.)			Composition of exports (percentages)						Share of total exports going to EC (Nine) (%)	
				Fuels		Other primary products		Manufs.			
	1970	1980	1984	1970	1980	1970	1980	1970	1980	1966	1984
Greece	643	5142	4864	1	16	83	51	16	34	41	54
Portugal	949	4629	5208	2	6	43	31	54	62	41	57
Spain	2387	20827	23283	5	4	48	42	46	55	45	48
Algeria	1009	15624	11861	70	98	26	1	4	1	90	64
Cyprus	109	533	575	0	5	85	42	14	52	66[c]	25
Egypt	762	3046	3120	5	64	71	26	24	10	15	42
Israel	776	5540	5803	0	0	40	34	60	66	42	31
Lebanon	198	394[a]	n/a	0	0[a]	51	37[a]	49	63[a]	13	6[a]
Malta	29	432	358	0	0	23	8	77	92	58[c]	71
Morocco	488	2403	2172	0	5	92	82	7	13	68[c]	50
Syria	203	2108	1854	17	72[b]	73	21[b]	10	7[b]	17	34
Tunisia	183	2234	1796	27	52	68	25	5	22	56[c]	58
Turkey	589	2910	7134	1	1	93	75	6	23	42[c]	37

Notes: [a] 1977, [b] 1979, [c] 1967; the export composition groups are SITC 3 (fuels), SITC 0 + 1 + 2 + 4 + 5 + 67 + 68 (other primary products), and SITC 6 − 67 − 68 + 7 + 8 (manufactures).

Sources: UNCTAD *Handbook of International Trade and Development Statistics* (cols 1–9); UN *International Trade Statistics Yearbook* (cols 10–11).

15.3   Export-promotion policies in the region: An overview

The principal determinant of export success or failure has been the outward or inward orientation of each country's development strategy. All of the independent countries were pursuing import-substituting industrialisation strategies during the 1950s, and manufactured export growth was slow throughout the region. By the 1960s Greece, Israel, Portugal and Spain had shifted towards greater balance between the incentive to produce for the domestic and for foreign markets, and their manufactured exports grew at a reasonable pace through this and the next two decades. In contrast, Turkey, the other semi-industrialised nation in the region, continued to pursue an inward-oriented development strategy with far greater incentives for import substitutes than for exports throughout the 1960s and 1970s. Malta and Cyprus had domestic markets too small to permit meaningful import-substitution policies, and exports were not seriously discriminated against; Malta enjoyed one of the highest export growth rates in the world during the 1970s, and Cypriot manufactured export performance was not bad in view of the disruption following the partition of the island in the mid-1970s. All of the North African countries adopted import-substitution industrialisation policies during the 1960s, characterised by rather bureaucratic state controls. Tunisia opened her doors to export-oriented direct foreign investment in 1972 and, perhaps more importantly, removed much of the red tape tying up private enterprise; the result was spectacular export growth during the 1970s, almost on a par with the Maltese performance, and as in Malta substantially driven by foreign investment in labour-intensive manufacturing activities producing for duty-free export to the EC.

Outward orientation does not preclude an active government policy. *Laissez-faire* is one way to equalise incentives to produce for home and foreign markets, but this can also be achieved by government intervention offering substantial but balanced incentives for each type of activity. All of the Mediterranean countries are characterised by more or less active economic policy-making. In the successful exporters, policy has rarely involved 'picking winners', but rather encouraging (or not discouraging) market-selected winners. Government intervention has been harmful when it involves too many rules and regulations which obscure market signals and/or increase the cost of doing international business; for example, excessive red tape underlies the failure of shifts towards more outward-oriented policies in Egypt and Morocco. In sum, although outward orientation can be achieved by mutually offsetting barriers to imports and subsidies to exports, the greater these trade policy interventions, the greater the probability of their not promoting exports in practice.[3] The Turkish experience since 1980 illustrates one country's experience, with temporarily offsetting policies being replaced by greater reliance on the exchange rate.

Exchange-rate and macroeconomic policies are at least as important as trade policies in creating an environment in which exports are promoted. In countries such as Turkey and Egypt during the 1960s and 1970s exports were discouraged by overvalued exchange rates as well as by high barriers to imports. Even a successful exporter like Malta lost her way in the 1980s when the government pursued a strong currency policy. When exports are involved, correct investment decisions must be based upon a viable long-run exchange rate, and investors cannot be confident about what this rate is if the government pursues unsustainable or erratic exchange-rate policies. Similarly, hyperinflation makes rational economic decision making difficult and is likely to hinder export growth even if the real exchange rate does not become overvalued. In Israel inflation reached several hundred per cent per year during the early 1980s and, although adverse income distribution effects were reduced by widespread indexing, the negative microeconomic consequences were finally recognised by the 1984 national unity government which made price stabilisation its number one priority.

Finally, the relationship between export promotion and policies towards direct foreign investment is complex. Export promotion does not necessarily require a liberal policy towards foreign investment, and in the region's newly industrialising countries indigenous firms have been the main force behind export growth.[4] In less developed economies direct foreign investment can, however, provide crucial inputs and market-access information lacking to domestic entrepreneurs. In both Tunisia and Malta export-oriented direct foreign investment played a major facilitating role in the manufactured export booms of the 1970s. The 1972 policy reform in Tunisia referred to earlier was in fact primarily concerned with promoting foreign investment and the current Maltese incentives described in section 15.5 are aimed at investment decisions. In both countries foreign investors are attracted by a range of considerations (e.g. political stability, proximity and duty-free access to EC markets) to locate labour-intensive activities, which primarily consist of making up clothing and assembly of electronic equipment, but also a range of light industries from spectacle frames to automotive parts.[5] Since these activities typically involve imported inputs, foreign firms are put off by import restrictions or cumbersome bureaucratic procedures to obtain exemption from such restrictions. Thus attracting export-oriented direct foreign investment requires more than simply a package of export or investment incentives, as Egypt and Morocco have discovered.

15.4   The transition from inward-oriented to outward-oriented development in Israel

Israel's development strategy underwent a dramatic transformation during the first 25 years of the state's existence. In the early 1950s an inward-looking strategy of import-substituting industrialisation was adopted, but the emphasis gradually shifted between the late 1950s and the late 1960s to a more even-handed treatment of import substitutes and exports. Over the whole period from the mid-1950s to 1973 exports grew rapidly (at a rate exceeded only by South Korea, Libya, Iran and a few micro-states), but the growth rate was especially high in the sub-periods 1958–63 and 1968–73. Perhaps the best summary indicator of the shift from inward- to outward-oriented economic development is the share of commodity exports in GNP, which increased from 6 per cent in 1954 to 34 per cent in 1972.

The instruments of export-promotion policy have not changed much, and they can be divided into three groups: direct financial incentives in the form of export premiums or subsidies, indirect assistance to exporters, and allocation of investment funds. What did change over time was the emphasis given to export promotion *vis-à-vis* the promotion of import substitutes.

During the 1950s financial incentives increased the Israeli pound return per dollar of exports substantially above the official exchange rate. Table 15.3 provides estimates for the late 1950s showing an increasing level of direct financial incentives for exports. The third row of Table 15.3, however, reveals that the Israeli pound return for a dollar of imports saved by producers of import substitutes was substantially higher. Thus, the net effect of direct trade policies was biased in favour of production for the home market and against exports.

During the 1950s the Israeli government also tried to reduce non-price obstacles to exporting by establishing institutions aimed at providing information about foreign market conditions and standards requirements. Institutions to provide risk insurance, to organise trade fairs and exhibitions, and to give help with design and packaging were also set up. These indirect assistance measures doubtless helped Israeli exporters, but the resources devoted to them were small before the mid-1960s.

The most important policy instrument, given the large proportion of available capital controlled by the Israeli government, was the allocation of investment funds. During the 1950s export potential was one of the criteria governing this allocation, but it tended to be subordinated to import-substituting potential. Thus, ten industrial sectors with export/sales ratios below 10 per cent received 62 per cent of new investment in the two years 1958–59 while the remaining eight, more export-oriented, sectors received 38 per cent. An indication of the 1962 policy shift towards more outward-oriented trade policies is that these shares were 43 per cent and 57 per cent respectively in 1962–63 (Michaely, 1975, p. 173).

The centrepiece of the 1962 policy package was devaluation of the Israeli pound from 1.8 to 3.0 to the US dollar. Initially, it was thought that this would be sufficient to encourage exports, and direct subsidies for most exports were eliminated. The belief was misplaced because even at a less overvalued exchange rate import-substitute production was still favoured over exports due to the continued existence of tariffs and import quotas. After 1965 export premiums were revived and indirect assistance was increased; direct and indirect assistance to exports increased from IL17 and IL3 million in 1965 to IL195 and IL67 million in 1969 (Pomfret, 1976, p. 49). Meanwhile, by 1968 the removal of quantitative restrictions on imports had been completed and reduction of the effective rates of protection for import-competing industries was under way, so that net discrimination against exports was substantially reduced.

The Israeli experience illustrates the possibility of successfully shifting from an inward-oriented to an outward-oriented development strategy even in the context of a continuing high degree of government intervention. In this context reliance on the price mechanism alone, as intended by the 1962 package, is likely to be inadequate. Existing intervention will typically favour import substitution, and the bias against exports will remain. Active export-promotion policies can offset the resource pull from import-substitution policies. In Israel, the key feature was not the nature of the export-promotion policies, which changed little, but the extent to which export incentives counterbalanced the incentives to produce for the home market. Such a balance had been roughly achieved by the late 1960s and contributed to a doubling of exports per capita between 1967 and 1973.

Table 15.3 Official and estimated actual exchange rates (ER), Israel (1956–60).

	1956	1957	1958	1959	1960
Official ER (IL per $)	1.80	1.80	1.80	1.80	1.80
Average ER on exports (IL per $ earned)	2.05	2.21	2.37	2.49	2.58
Average ER on import substitutes (IL per $ saved)	3.26	2.91	2.63	3.16	3.47

Note: For definitions and methods see the source; the import measure is probably biased downwards because it omits rents on quantitative restrictions on imports and because of the averaging procedure.

Source: Michaely (1975, p. 97).

During the 1970s and 1980s Israel maintained export growth momentum by shifting to less interventionist trade policies which make the balance between export and import-substitution incentives easier to maintain. By signing free-trade agreements with the EC in 1975 and the United States in 1985, Israel, uniquely, has free access to these markets for her manufactured exports while permitting practically free access to imports. From a purely trade policy perspective this is ideal, although exports were harmed in the 1980s by macroeconomic policies leading to hyperinflation.

15.5 Trade liberalisation in Turkey after 1980

Turkish experience offers a more recent and dramatic example of a country successfully shifting from an inward-oriented to an outward-oriented development strategy. Industrialisation in modern Turkey had been oriented towards the domestic market and made inflexible by the dominant position of state enterprises whose products were uncompetitive on world markets. By the end of the 1970s foreign-exchange scarcity had led to ever-tighter import restrictions, such that less than one-sixth of total imports were exempt from the complicated system of quantitative restrictions. Moreover, importers were required to pay an interest-free advanced deposit in order to obtain an import licence (by 1979 the deposit was 20 per cent for imports for industrial use and 40 per cent for imports for commercial purposes) and imports were subject to a variety of taxes (i.e. tariffs, stamp duty, wharf charges), all of which raised the rate of return in import-substitute industries. The bias against exports was exacerbated by an overvalued exchange rate, and only partially and unevenly offset by tax rebates, credits and other export incentives. Most primary goods and some industrial exports were also subject to export price controls and licensing.

The 1980 liberalisation package had four component parts: a large nominal devaluation, simplification of import licensing procedures, reduced levels of protection, and credit subsidies for exports. In January 1980 the lira was devalued from TL47 to TL70 per dollar and after several subsequent adjustments a crawling peg replaced the fixed exchange rate in May 1981, and by 1983 free purchase and sale of foreign exchange were permitted; the real effective exchange rate fell by 23 per cent in 1980 and then by an average of 3 per cent per annum over the next five years (Kopits, 1987, p. 19). Advanced deposits were reduced and quantitative restrictions replaced by licensing requirements. The major change in import policies, however, occurred with the announcement in December 1983 of the 1984 Import Regime, under which all goods still subject to restrictions of licensing were specifically listed (rather than listing only those imports permitted without licences). This was accompanied by a downward revision of tariff rates, and the total effect was a much less protective import regime than the pre-1980 one.[6] Subsidised export credits increased rapidly between 1980 and 1984, but were then replaced by a direct subsidy of up to 4 per cent of the export value. Other export incentives, especially preferential foreign-exchange allocation and retention schemes, were also important in the early 1980s, but were then cut back in late 1983, although income tax benefits for exporters remained in place.

The Turkish liberalisation episode thus moved very quickly through two stages. First, substantial incentives to import-substitute producers were balanced by substantial direct export incentives in 1980–84. In the second stage, greater reliance was placed on the exchange rate as the major trade policy instrument with some, but more modest, tariff and subsidy elements remaining. In this process Turkey avoided the unrealistic hope that devaluation alone could reverse the bias against exports (as Israel had hoped in 1962), but experienced the problems of trying to balance incentives in a complex system. Thus, while import-substitute producers inevitably complained about reduced protection, people took advantage of increased export subsidies to make fictitious exports (Akder, 1987, p. 553). Enforcement and equity issues provided a strong incentive to liberalise imports as fast as possible in order to prevent a complex export-subsidy system from becoming too set in place, although pressure on the government budget provided the immediate incentive for reducing direct export subsidies.

The Turkish experience must be rated a success. Merchandise export volume more than tripled between 1980 and 1985, and exports were diversified as industrial goods' share increased from about one-third to three-quarters. Thus Turkey experienced an export-led economic recovery at a time of substantial deterioration in her terms of trade and generally weak demand conditions in the major world markets. Turkey was helped by favourable demand trends in Middle East markets (i.e. Iran, Iraq and the Arabian oil-producers), but demand in these markets was for different goods than those which Turkey sold to the EC.[7] The clearest measure of successful export promotion is that, alone among the Mediterranean non-member countries, Turkey substantially increased her manufactured exports to the EC during the 1980s.

15.6   Export-promotion measures in Malta

During the export boom of the 1970s Malta had rather limited export-promotion measures, contained within various investment incentive schemes. In 1980 a Trade Documentation Unit was established within the Central Bank to provide information to exporters about market access, regulation, etc., and in 1986 an Export Stabilisation Scheme was introduced to provide exporters with partial insurance against exchange-rate risk. After the 1987 election these activities were consolidated under the Malta Development Corporation's (MDC) direction and on the whole expanded.

The current investment incentive package, effective June 1987 and applying to all limited-liability companies registered in Malta and involved in manufacturing industries, is summarised in Table 15.4. The bias in favour of exporters is apparent both indirectly, in the need for MDC approval for which export orientation is one criterion, and directly, in the limitation of some items solely to export-oriented companies. To qualify for the ten-year tax holiday a company must export at least 95 per cent of its output. The more limited tax concessions under the export-incentive scheme are tied to achievement of specified rates of export growth. Export-oriented companies also receive more favourable soft-loans provisions. Finally, there are a standard relief from customs duty on imported inputs and a new Export Promotion Allowance which apply only to exporting companies. In sum, the package described in Table 15.4 is an investment package but because of its strong bias in favour of export-oriented activities it is simultaneously a package to promote exports.

Export-promotion measures more narrowly defined consist of incentives for firms to seek out markets plus direct activity by the MDC. The Export Promotion Allowance provides a tax incentive to foster export marketing efforts, and is granted whether or not these are successful in leading to actual sales. In 1987–88 an Export Promotion Division of the MDC was reorganised, incorporating the Trade Documentation Unit (now referred to as a trade information service and run by the MDC research section) and administering the Export Stabilisation Scheme. Once reorganisation is completed the MDC's Export Promotion Division will also cover market development, trade fairs and publicity with desk officers specialising by geographical area (EC/EFTA, the Americas, North Africa/Middle East, Far East, Rest of World). A research section will oversee publication of directories, a newsletter, etc., as well as providing information to exporters on market access and regulations, and other support services will be provided by specialists in export credit, pricing, packaging and quality control.

The whole programme of investment/export incentives plus export-promotion measures contains elements common to other countries' schemes, although the Maltese measures are among the most generous and best organised in the region; the last feature is important for a small economy where the absolute number of skilled personnel who can be devoted to these activities is limited.

15.7 Conclusions

Economic developments in the Mediterranean region since the 1950s provide a fascinating picture. Economic growth in the area has been rapid, despite its reputation for political instability. Overall, the key to success has lain in transforming economies from a high degree of dependence on agricultural exports to export-led industrialisation; a process stimulated by the EC's adoption of a restrictive agricultural policy, in compensation for which the Mediterranean non-member countries were offered preferential access to EC markets for their manufactured exports. Countries seeking to maintain their traditional agrarian structure (e.g. Morocco) or to pursue an import-substituting industrialisation strategy (e.g. Turkey) have fallen behind those countries which adopted development strategies based on manufactured export expansion in the 1960s (e.g. Greece and Israel) or 1970s (e.g. Tunisia).

The cumulative impact of policy differences became clear over the past three decades. Estimates of GNP per capita for the 1950s are in most cases rough estimates (hence the parentheses in Table 15.1), but they do provide a guide to relative starting-points. Turkey's GNP per capita was higher than that of Spain or Greece in the mid-1950s, but had fallen well behind these relatively advanced economies by the 1980s and even behind countries such as Portugal and Tunisia which were much poorer than Turkey in the 1950s. Among the North African countries in Table 15.1, Tunisia had the lowest per capita income in the 1950s but was second to oil-rich Algeria by the 1980s and had a per capita income roughly double that of Morocco or Egypt. There are well-known drawbacks to relying solely on GNP estimates to draw welfare implications, but relative changes of this magnitude give clear guides to the success of different governments in meeting their people's material wants which in the countries listed here are supported by casual evidence visible to any eyewitness. The average Tunisian is better off than the average Moroccan or Egyptian and the average Turk is worse off than the average Spaniard or Greek, and in large part this situation has been brought about by government policies.

The crucial element in the successful national policies has been not to favour production for the domestic market over production for export. Since all countries had import barriers, this policy requirement in effect involved offering export incentives comparable with the incentives given

Table 15.4 Incentives for industrial development in Malta.

FISCAL	ELIGIBILITY	THE SCHEME
1. Tax holidays	New export-oriented companies (minimum 95% export)	10-year tax holiday

2. Export incentive scheme	(a) New companies (that do not qualify for tax holiday)
	(b) Existing companies which either
	  i. Take up exports
	  ii. Increase exports by a certain amount over a base
		Additional profits resulting from increased export sales will be exempt from income tax
		
		A company can qualify for a 10-year period
		The scheme is operational up to the year 2000

3. Investment allowance and accelerated depreciation allowance	(a) An MDC-approved project (b) If Maltese controlled (a) An MDC-approved project (b) If Maltese controlled	(a) Plant and machinery: +30%; indust. Bldgs. and structures: +15% (b) Plant and machinery: +33%; indust. Bldgs and structures: +16.5% (a) Plant and machinery: 4 yrs; indust. Bldgs and structures: 25 yrs (b) Plant and machinery: 3 yrs; indust. Bldgs. and structures: 20 yrs.
4. Reduced rates of company tax	Companies that plough back profits for MDC-approved projects	15% Tax on ploughed back profits
5. Export promotion allowance	Export promotion costs directly incurred by a local company	Export promotion costs can be increased by an additional 20% for tax purposes Maximum allowance: Lm 20,000 or 5% of export sales (whichever is higher)
6. Research and development allowance	Any local company which undertakes approved Research and Development Schemes	R&D costs can be increased by an additional 20% for tax purposes Maximum allowance: not higher than 5% of the company's turnover
7. Training costs allowance	Industries organising in-house or outside training courses to increase skills of their employees	Industrial training costs can be increased by an additional 20% for tax purposes Maximum amount to be claimed in any one year is not to exceed 5% of payroll

GRANTS

1. Training grants	Companies offering training programmes to their newly recruited full-time employees	50% of the minimum wage for up to twelve months
2. Management service grant	Maltese-controlled companies with an annual turnover not exceeding Lm350,000	An annual grant (for three years) equivalent to 25% of additional management costs incurred. Maximum grant: Lm5,000 p.a.

SOFT LOANS

		(a) Lm100,000	(b) Lm100,000
(a) Export-oriented and intermediary companies	Min. cap. inv. new projects		
(b) Other projects	Min. cap. inv. existing projects	Lm 75,000	Lm 75,000
Finance for capital investment in plant, machinery and other fixed assets excluding land and bldgs	Max. amount	Up to 33%	Up to 33%
	Int. rate sub.:	4% p.a.	2% p.a.
	Repayment period:	6–10 yrs	6–10 yrs
	Moratorium period:	2 yrs	2 yrs
	%Cap. non-MDC financed allowed to rank prior to MDC's hypothecary rights:	Up to 17‰	Up to 17‰

OTHER

1. Relief from customs duty	MDC-approved projects	Duty-free importation of plant, machinery and other equipment as well as materials, components and accessories used for the production of exported goods
2. Factory buildings	Any MDC-approved projects	The rates charged for factory bldgs shall be as follows: First 3 yrs Lm175 per sq mt. Following 13 yrs up to Lm400 per sq mt.
3. Work permits	MDC-approved projects	Expatriate personnel: 3-yr basis Major shareholders (or nominee): Indefinite
4. Gozo	MDC-approved projects setting up or operating in Gozo	The neutralising of cost differential between Malta and Gozo

Source: Malta Development Corporation.

for import substitution. Highly complex trade regimes do, however, lead to inefficiencies and often fail to make exporting as attractive as producing for the home market. Thus, the most successful export-promotion packages have involved liberalisation of imports and of the exchange rate, so that the positive incentives for exports need not be too extensive.

Notes

1. Some non-tariff barriers have been introduced since 1977, most notably quantitative restrictions on 'sensitive' textile and clothing items, but these have been less stringent than EC restrictions on similar imports from non-preferred developing countries. The most restrictive NTBs have been on T-shirt exports by Turkey during the 1980s, and these have been insufficient to distract Turkey from shifting successfully to an export-promotion strategy.
2. The EC included Portugal and Jordan in the GMP despite their lack of Mediterranean coastline. The tables and discussion make little if any reference to Jordan, the Lebanon and Syria because despite participation in the GMP they have made little effort to promote manufactured exports to the EC or any other market. A more complete description and analysis of the EC's Mediterranean policy is contained in Pomfret (1986).
3. Bhagwati (1987) argues that a more interventionist policy balancing incentives for export and import-substituting activities is likely to be inferior in practice to a less interventionist policy because the former provides greater incentives for evasion and bribery, upsetting the balance, as well as for economically wasteful rent-seeking activity (e.g. lobbying for export subsidies and import barriers).
4. In Spain, however, direct foreign investment (by Ford and General Motors) was crucial in establishing automobiles as the leading export product after the mid-1970s. In Greece there is evidence of export-oriented direct foreign investment having increased after the 1961 agreement with the EC. Nevertheless, in both of these countries and even more so in Israel, indigenous firms were dynamic exporters.
5. Pomfret (1986) provides more details. For a small country reliance on foreign firms may introduce some potential instability, e.g. a quarter of Maltese exports during the late 1970s and early 1980s were supplied by a single US-owned jeans manufacturer and reduction in that firm's activity during the mid-1980s contributed to Malta's poor export performance. Even in this extreme case the outcome was arguably due to changing Maltese conditions (a policy-induced currency appreciation and growing political instability) rather than to capricious (or more sinister) decisions taken by foreigners.
6. According to World Bank estimates the number of goods subject to licensing fell from 821 in 1983 to 373 in 1984 while tariffs on some 800 products were lowered from an average of 19 per cent to 12 per cent (Riedel, 1987, p. 82). Further wide-ranging tariff cuts were made in 1986, although the net impact was offset by increased use of dollar-denominated levies on specific import items (the number of items subject to such levies had increased from the original 73 in December 1983 to 347 by Spring 1986). Proliferation of the

levies illustrates the fatal temptation offered by flexible sources of immediate government revenue, even when their impact will contradict long-run policy goals.
7. The post-1980 export boom was also facilitated by the excess capacity left over from negative economic growth in 1978 and 1979. Some of the measured export growth may be illusory because exports were under-invoiced in the 1970s (to avoid declaring all foreign-currency earnings) and overstated in the early 1980s (to obtain export subsidies), but if appropriate revisions were possible they would be unlikely to change the general picture.

Bibliography

Adams, C. and D. Gros (1986), 'The consequences of real exchange rate rules for inflation: some illustrative examples', *IMF Staff Papers*, September, 439–76.

Adelman, I. (1984), 'Beyond export-led growth', *World Development*, **12**(9), 937–49.

Agarwala, R. (1983), 'Price distortions and growth in developing countries', *World Bank Staff Working Paper*, 575 (Washington, DC: The World Bank).

Aghazadeh, E. and H. D. Evans (1988), 'Price distortions, efficiency and growth', mimeo (Brighton: IDS, University of Sussex).

Ahmad, E. (1987), *Trade Regime and Export Strategies with Reference to South Asia*, London School of Economics, Development Research Programme, DP 4.

Akder, H. (1987), 'Turkey's export expansion in the Middle East, 1980–1985', *The Middle East Journal*, **41**, 553–67.

Ariff, M. and H. Hill (1985), *Export-oriented Industrialization: The ASEAN Experience* (Sydney: Allen and Unwin).

Arndt, H. W. and R. M. Sundrum (1984), 'Devaluation and inflation: the 1978 experience, *Bulletin of Indonesian Economic Studies*, **20**, 83–97.

Bagchi, A. (1981), 'Export incentives in India: a review', in A. K. Bagchi and N. Banerjei (eds), *Change and Choice in Indian Industry* (Calcutta: K. P. Bagchi & Co., for the Centre of Studies in Social Sciences).

Balassa, B. (1971), *The Structure of Protection in Developing Countries* (Baltimore, Md.: Johns Hopkins University Press).

Balassa, B. (1978), 'Exports and economic growth: further evidence', *Journal of Development Economics*, **5**, 181–89.

Balassa, B. (1982), *Development Strategies in Semi Industrialised Countries* (Washington, DC: The World Bank).

Balassa, B. (1983), 'External shocks and adjustment policies in twelve less-developed countries: 1974–76 and 1979–81', paper presented to the annual meeting of the American Economic Association, San Francisco, December.

Balassa, B. (1984), 'Adjustment to external shocks in developing economies', *World Bank Staff Working Paper*, 472 (Washington, DC: The World Bank).

Balassa, B. and C. Balassa (1984), 'Industrial protection in the developed countries', *The World Economy*, **7**, 179–96.

303

Balassa, B., G. Bueno, P. Kuczynski and M. E. Simonsen (1986), *Towards Renewed Economic Growth in Latin America* (Washington, DC: Institute for International Economics).

Balasubramanyam, V. N. (1984), 'Incentives and disincentives for foreign direct investment in less-developed countries', *Weltwirtschaftliches Archiv*, **120**, 720–35.

Balasubramanyam, V. N. (1988), 'Export processing zones in developing countries: theory and empirical evidence', in D. Greenaway (ed.), *Economic Development and International Trade* (London: Macmillan).

Baldwin, R. (1982), *The Inefficacy of Trade Policy*, Princeton University Department of Economics, Frank D. Graham Memorial Lecture, Essays in International Finance, 150.

Baldwin, R. (1985), 'Ineffectiveness of protection in promoting social goals', *The World Economy*, June, 109–18.

Banco de Boston (1988), 'Industrial policy: modernization efforts in the forefront', *Newsletter Brazil*, 13 June 1988.

Bank of Jamaica, *Report and Statement of Accounts*, annual.

Bank of Jamaica, *Statistical Digest*, monthly.

Bardhan, P. K. (1984), *The Political Economy of Development in India* (Oxford: Basil Blackwell).

Barham, J. (1988a), 'Brazil gives details of industrial policy', *Financial Times*, 28 September 1988.

Barham, J. (1988b), 'Brazil lifts ban on 1,250 items', *Financial Times*, 23 November 1988.

Beals, R. E. (1987), 'Trade patterns and trends of Indonesia', in C. I. Bradford Jun. and W. H. Branson (eds), *Trade and Structural Change in Pacific Asia* (Chicago: University of Chicago Press, for the National Bureau of Economic Research), 515–45.

Beckford, G. L. (1967), *The West Indian Banana Industry* (Mona, Jamaica: Institute of Social and Economic Research).

Beckford, G. L. (1972), *Persistent Poverty* (New York: Oxford University Press).

Beckford, G. L. and M. H. Guscott (1967), *Intra Caribbean Agricultural Trade* (Mona, Jamaica: Institute of Social and Economic Research).

Beenstock, M. (1984), *The World Economy in Transition* (London: Allen and Unwin).

Behrman, J. (1984), 'Rethinking global negotiations: trade', in J. N. Bhagwati and J. Russie (eds), *Power, Passions and Purpose* (Cambridge, Mass.: MIT Press).

Bennett, K. M. (1973), 'Industrialisation by invitation: an examination of the Jamaican and Puerto Rican experience', unpublished PhD thesis, McGill University.

Bennett, K. M. (1982a), *Trade and Payments in the Caribbean Common Market* (Mona, Jamaica: Institute of Social and Economic Research).

Bennett, K. M. (1982b), 'An evaluation of the contribution of CARICOM to intra regional Caribbean trade', *Social and Economic Studies*, **31**, 74–89.

Bennett, K. M. (1987), 'The Caribbean Basin Initiative and its implications for CARICOM exports', *Social and Economic Studies*, **36**(2), 21–40.

Best, L. (1968), 'A model of pure plantation economy', *Social and Economic Studies*, **17**, 283–326.

Bevan, D., A. Bigsten, P. Collier and J. Gunning (1987), *Lessons of East African Liberalisation*, Thames Essay (London: Trade Policy Research Centre).

Bhagwati, J. N. (1966), *The Economics of Under-developed Countries* (New York: McGraw-Hill).

Bhagwati, J. N. (1968), *The Theory and Practice of Commercial Policy*, Princeton University Department of Economics, Frank D. Graham Memorial Lecture, Essay in International Finance, 8.
Bhagwati, J. N. (1971), 'The generalized theory of distortions and welfare', in J. N. Bhagwati *et al.* (eds), *Trade, Balance of Payments and Growth*, Essays in honour of C. P. Kindleberger (Amsterdam: North-Holland).
Bhagwati, J. N. (1973), 'The theory of immiserizing growth: further applications' in M. Connolly and A. Swoboda (eds), *International Trade and Money* (Toronto: University of Toronto Press).
Bhagwati, J. N. (1978), *Foreign Trade Regimes and Economic Development: Anatomy and Consequences of Exchange Control Regimes* (Cambridge, Mass.: Ballinger, for the NBER).
Bhagwati, J. N. (1980), 'Lobbying and welfare', *Journal of Public Economics*, **14**, 355–63.
Bhagwati, J. N. (1982a), 'Shifting comparative advantage, protectionist demands, and policy response', in J. N. Bhagwati (ed.), *Import Competition and Response* (Chicago: Chicago University Press).
Bhagwati, J. N. (1982b), 'Directly-unproductive, profit-seeking (DUP) activities', *Journal of Political Economy*, **90**, 988–1002.
Bhagwati, J. N. (1985a), in G. Grossman (ed.), *Wealth and Poverty: Essays in Development Economics*, 1 (Cambridge, Mass.: MIT Press).
Bhagwati, J. N. (1985b), in G. Grossman (ed.), *Dependence and Interdependence: Essays in Development Economics*, 2 (Cambridge, Mass.: MIT Press).
Bhagwati, J. N. (1985c), 'Protectionism: old wine in new bottles', *Journal of Policy Modelling*, **7**, 23–33.
Bhagwati, J. N. (1985d), *Growth and Poverty*, Michigan State University Center for Advanced Study of International Development, Occasional Paper 5.
Bhagwati, J. N. (1985e), 'Export promotion as a development strategy', in Toshio Shishido and Ryuzo Sata (eds), *Essays in Honor of Saburo Okita* (Boston: Auburn House).
Bhagwati, J. N. (1986a), *Export Promoting Trade Strategy: Issues and Evidence*, Development Policy Issues Series, Discussion Paper, Report VPERS 7 (Washington, DC: The World Bank).
Bhagwati, J. N. (1986b), *Investing abroad*, Esmee Fairbairn Lecture, University of Lancaster, England.
Bhagwati, J. N. (1986c), 'VERs, trade and foreign investment', paper presented to the Western Economic Association Conference, San Francisco, July.
Bhagwati, J. N. (1986d), 'Rethinking trade strategy', in J. Lewis and V. Kallab (eds), *Development Strategies Reconsidered* (Washington, DC: Overseas Development Council).
Bhagwati, J. N. (1987), 'Outward orientation: trade issues', in V. Corbo, M. Goldstein and M. Khan (eds), *Growth-Oriented Adjustment Programs* (Washington, DC: IMF/World Bank) pp. 257–90.
Bhagwati, J. N. (1988), 'Export promoting trade strategy: issues and evidence', *The World Bank Research Observer*, **3**, 27–58.
Bhagwati, J. N., R. Brecher, E. Dinopoulos and T. N. Srinivasan (1987), '*Quid pro quo* investment and policy intervention: a political-economy theoretic analysis', *Journal of Development Economics*, **27**, 127–38.
Bhagwati, J. N., R. Brecher and T. N. Srinivasan (1984), 'DUP activities and economic theory', *European Economic Review*, **28**, 291–307.
Bhagwati, J. N. and S. Chakravarthy (1969), 'Contribution to Indian economic analysis: a survey', *American Economic Review*, **59** (supplement), 1–73.

Bhagwati, J. N. and P. Desai (1970), *India: Planning for Industrialisation* (London: Oxford University Press).

Bhagwati, J. N. and E. Dinopoulos (1986), '*Quid pro quo* investment and market structure', paper presented to the Western Economic Association Conference, San Francisco, July.

Bhagwati, J. N. and V. K. Ramswami (1963), 'Domestic distortions, tariffs and the theory of optimum subsidy', *Journal of Political Economy*, **6**, 44–50.

Bhagwati, J. N. and T. N. Srinivasan (1975), *Foreign Trade Regimes and Economic Development* (New York: Columbia University Press, for the National Bureau of Economic Research).

Bhagwati, J. N. and T. N. Srinivasan (1979), 'Trade policy and development', in R. Dornbusch and J. Frenkel (eds), *International Economic Policy: Theory and Evidence* (Baltimore, Md.: Johns Hopkins University Press).

Bhagwati, J. N. and T. N. Srinivasan (1982), 'The welfare consequences of directly-unproductive profit-seeking (DUP) activities', *Journal of International Economics*, **13**, 33–44.

Bhagwati, J. N. and T. N. Srinivasan (1983), *Lectures on International Trade* (Cambridge, Mass.: MIT Press).

Bliss, C. J. (1988), 'Taxation, cost-benefit analysis and effective protection', in D. Newbery and N. Stern (eds), *The Theory of Taxation for Developing Countries* (New York: Oxford University Press, for the World Bank), pp. 141–62.

Bliss, C. J. (1989), 'Trade and development theoretical issues and policy implications', ch. 24 in H. Chenery and T. N. Srinivasan (eds), *Handbook of Development Economics* (Amsterdam: North-Holland).

Booth, A. and P. McCawley (eds) (1981), *The Indonesian Economy During the Soeharto Era* (Kuala Lumpur: Oxford University Press).

Bowles, S. (1985), 'The production process in a competitive economy: Walrasean, neo-Hobbesian and Marxian models', *American Economic Review*, **75**, 16–36.

Brecher, R. and C. Diaz-Alejandro (1977), 'Tariffs, foreign capital and immiserizing growth', *Journal of International Economics*, **14**, 317–22.

Brewster, H. and C. Y. Thomas (1967), *The Dynamics of West Indian Economic Integration* (Mona, Jamaica: Institute of Social and Economic Research).

Bruno, M. and S. Fischer (1986), 'The inflationary process in Israel: shocks and accommodation', in Y. Ben-Porath (ed.), *The Israeli Economy* (Cambridge, Mass.: Harvard University Press), pp. 347–71.

Buiter, W. (1986), 'Fiscal prerequisites for a viable managed exchange regime: a non-technical eclectic introduction', *NBER Working Paper 2041*, October.

Calvo, G. (1986), 'Incredible reforms', mimeo.

Cairncross, A. (1962), *Factors in Economic Development* (London: Allen and Unwin).

Caribbean Community Secretariat (1974), *Co-ordinated Emergency Action Programme for Industrial Development*, mimeo.

Caribbean Community Secretariat (1975), *Towards an Action Plan for Joint Agricultural and Industrial Development*, mimeo.

Carrington, E. (1967), 'Trinidad post-war economy', *New World Quarterly*, **4**, 45–67.

Carrington, E. (1968), 'Industrialisation by invitation in Trinidad and Tobago since 1950', *New World Quarterly*, **4**, 37–43.

Castro, J. S. (1982), 'The Bataan export processing zone', Asian Employment Programme Working Papers, ILO-ARTEP, Bangkok, mimeo.

Caves, R. E. and R. W. Jones (1985), *World Trade and Payments: An Introduction*, 4th edn. (Boston: Little, Brown).

Central Bank of Barbados (1985, 1986, 1987), *Annual Report*.

Central Bank of Barbados, *Statistical Digest*, annual.

Central Bank of Trinidad and Tobago, *Annual Report*.

Central Statistical Office, Trinidad and Tobago, *Overseas Trade Report*, annual.

Chenery, H. B., S. Shishido and T. Watanabe (1962), 'The pattern of Japanese growth, 1914–1954', *Econometrica*, **30**, 98–139.

Chenery, H. B. and M. Syrquin (1975), *Patterns of Development 1950–70*, (Oxford: Oxford University Press, for the World Bank).

Chenery, H. B. and M. Syrquin (1986), 'Patterns of development: 1950 to 1983', draft, June.

Chernick, S. (1978), *The Commonwealth Caribbean: The Integration Experience* (Baltimore and London: Johns Hopkins University Press).

Clements, K. W and L. A. Sjaastad (1985), 'How protection taxes exporters', *Thames Essay*, 40, (London: Trade Policy Research Centre).

Cline, W. (1982), 'Can the East Asian model of development be generalized?', *World Development*, February, 81–90.

Cline, W. (1985), 'Reply', *World Development*, April.

Colclough, C. and J. Manor (eds) (1990), *Imperfect Markets or Imperfect States? Neo-Liberalism and the Development Policy Debate* (Oxford: Oxford University Press).

Congdon, T. G. (1982), '*Apertura* policies in the cone of Latin America', *The World Economy* (London: Trade Policy Research Centre).

Congdon, T. G. (1985), *Economic Liberalism in the Cone of Latin America* (London: Trade Policy Research Centre).

Congdon, T. G. (1987) 'The link between budget deficits and inflation: some contrasts between developed and developing countries' in M. J. Boskin, J. S. Fleming and S. Gorini (eds), *Private Saving and Public Debt* (Oxford and New York: Basil Blackwell).

Corbo, V. and J. de Melo (1987), 'Lessons from the southern cone policy reforms', *World Bank Economic Review*, **2**, 111–42.

Corden, W. M. (1974a), *Trade Policy and Economic Welfare* (Oxford: Clarendon Press).

Corden, W. M. (1974b), 'The theory of international trade', in J. H. Dunning (ed.), *Economic Analysis and the Multinational Enterprise* (London: Allen and Unwin).

Corden, W. M. (1985), *Protection Growth and Trade: Essays in International Economics* (Oxford: Basil Blackwell).

Cornia, A. C., R. Jolly and F. Stewart (eds) (1987), *Adjustment with a Human Face: Protecting the Vulnerable and Promoting Growth* (Oxford: Oxford University Press).

Datta-Chaudhuri, M. (1980), 'The role of free trade zones in the creation of employment and industrial growth in Malaysia', ILO-ARTEP Working Papers, Bangkok, mimeo.

Dawnay, I. (1989), 'Brazil to ease import ban', *Financial Times*, 2 June 1989.

Demas, W. G. (1965), *The Economics of Development of Small Countries* (Montreal: McGill University Press).

Demas, W. G. (1972), *From CARIFTA to Caribbean Community* (Georgetown, Guyana: Commonwealth Caribbean Regional Community Secretariat).

Demas, W. G. (1976), *Essays on Caribbean Integration and Development* (Mona, Jamaica: Institute of Social and Economic Research).

De Melo, J. (1988), 'Computable general equilibrium models for trade policy analysis in developing countries: a survey', Trade Policy Division, Country Economics Department, The World Bank, mimeo.

Dervis, K., J. de Melo and S. Robinson (1981), 'A general equilibrium analysis of foreign exchange shortages in a developing economy', *Economic Journal*, December, 891–906.

Desai, P. (1979), 'Alternative measures of import substitution', *Oxford Economic Papers*, **31**, 312–24.

Diaz-Alejandro, C. F. (1970), 'Direct foreign development in Latin America', in C. P. Kindleberger (ed.), *The Multinational Corporation* (Cambridge, Mass.: MIT Press).

Dixit, A. (1985), 'Tax policy in open economics', in A. J. Auerbach and M. Feldstein (eds), *Handbook of Public Economics*, 1 (Amsterdam: North-Holland).

Donges, J. B. (1976), 'A comparative survey of industrialisation in fifteen semi-industrialised countries', *Weltwirtschaftliches Archiv*, **112**, 626–59.

Dornbusch, R. (1986), 'Impacts on debtor countries of world economic conditions', paper presented to a seminar on external debt, saving and growth in Latin America, 13–16 October, mimeo.

Edgren, G. (1982), 'Spearheads of industrialization or sweatshops in the sun?: a critical appraisal of labour conditions in Asian export processing zones', Asian Employment Programme Working Papers, ILO-ARTEP, Bangkok, mimeo.

Edwards, S. (1984), 'The order of liberalization of the external sector in developing countries', *Essays in International Finance*, 156 (Princeton: Princeton University Press).

Edwards, S. (1985), 'Trend in real exchange rate behaviour in selected developing countries', *CPD Discussion Paper* **16**, The World Bank, April.

Edwards, S. (1987), 'Economic liberalization and the equilibrium real exchange rate in developing countries', *NBER Working Paper 2179*, March.

Edwards, S. and A. C. Edwards (1987), *Monetarism and Liberalization: The Chilean Experiment* (Cambridge, Mass.: Ballinger).

Edwards, S. and P. Montiel (1988), 'Devaluation crises and the macroeconomic consequences of postponed adjustment in developing countries', mimeo.

Emery, R. (1967), 'The relation of exports and economic growth', *Kyklos*, **20**, 470–86.

Evans, H. D. (1989a), 'Alternative perspectives on trade and development', ch. 24 in H. Chenery and T. N. Srinivasan (eds), *Handbook of Development Economics*, II (Amsterdam: North-Holland).

Evans, H. D. (1989b), *Comparative Advantage and Growth: Trade and Development in Theory and Practice* (Hemel Hempstead: Harvester Wheatsheaf).

Evans, H. D. (1990), 'Visible and invisible hands in trade policy reform', in C. Colclough and J. Manor (eds), *Imperfect Markets and Imperfect States? Neo-Liberalism and the Development Policy Debate* (Oxford: Oxford University Press).

Fajana, O. (1979), 'Trade and growth: the Nigerian experience', *World Development*, **7**, 73–8.

Fane, G. and C. Phillips (1987), 'Effective protection in Indonesia', report submitted to the Department of Industry, Jakarta.

Feder, G. (1983), 'On exports and economic growth', *Journal of Development Economics*, **12**, 59–73.

Feenstra, R. and J. N. Bhagwati (1982), in J. N. Bhagwati (ed.), *Import Competition and Response* (Chicago: Chicago University Press).

Fields, G. (1984), 'Employment, income distribution and economic growth in seven small open economies', *Economic Journal*, **94**, 74–83.

Finch, M. H. J. (1979), 'Stabilisation policy in Uruguay since the 1950s', in R. Thorp and L. Whitehead (eds), *Inflation and Stabilisation* (London and Basingstoke: Macmillan, in association with St Anthony's College, Oxford).

Findlay, R. (1984a), 'Trade and development: theory and Asian experience', *Asian Development Review*, 23–42.

Findlay, R. (1984b), 'Growth and development in trade models' in R. W. Jones and P. B. Kenen (eds), *Handbook of International Economics*, 1 (Amsterdam: North-Holland).

Finger, J. M. (1982), 'Incorporating the gains from trade into policy', *The World Economy*, **5**, 367–77.

Fischer, S. (1987), 'Economic growth and economic policy', in V. Corbo, M. Goldstein and M. S. Khan (eds), *Growth-oriented Adjustment Programs* (Washington, DC: International Monetary Fund and the World Bank), 151–78.

Fitzgerald, B. D. (1987), 'Export bans for industrial development: the costs of Indonesian plywood', unpublished paper, Country Policy Department, World Bank, Washington, DC.

Giersch, H. (ed.) (1974), *The International Division of Labour* (Tübingen: J. C. B. Mohr Paul Siebeck).

Gillis, M. (1985), 'Micro and macroeconomics of tax reform: Indonesia', *Journal of Development Economics*, **19**, 221–54.

Girvan, N. (1967), *The Caribbean Bauxite Industry* (Mona, Jamaica: Institute of Social and Economic Research).

Girvan, N. (1971), *Foreign Capital and Economic Underdevelopment in Jamaica* (Mona, Jamaica: Institute of Social and Economic Research).

Girvan, N. and O. Jefferson (1968), 'Corporate vs Caribbean integration', *New World Quarterly*, **4**, 45–56

Goldstein, M. and M. S. Khan (1982), 'Effects of slowdown in industrial countries on growth in non-oil developing countries', Occasional Paper 12, International Monetary Fund, Washington, DC, August.

Grais, W., J. de Melo and S. Urata (1986), 'A general equilibrium estimate of the effects of reductions in tariffs and quantitative restrictions in Turkey in 1978', in T. N. Srinivasan and J. Whalley (eds), *General Equilibrium Trade Policy Modelling* (Cambridge, Mass.: MIT Press).

Granger, C. W. J. (1969), 'Investigating causal relationships by econometric models and cross spectral methods', *Econometrica*, **37**, 424–38.

Gray, C. (1979), 'Civil service compensation in Indonesia', *Bulletin of Indonesian Economic Studies*, **15**, 85–113.

Greenaway, D. (1984), 'A statistical analysis of fiscal dependence on trade taxes and economic development', *Public Finance*, **39**, 79–89.

Greenaway, D. (1986), 'Characteristics of industrialisation and economic performance under alternative development strategies', mimeo, background paper for ch. 5, *World Development Report 1987* (Washington, DC: The World Bank).

Greenaway, D. and C. R. Milner (1986), *The Economics of Intra Industry Trade* (Oxford: Basil Blackwell).

Greenaway, D. and C. R. Milner (1987), ' "True protection" concepts and their role in evaluating trade policies in LDCs', *Journal of Development Studies*, **23**, 200–19.

Greenaway, D. and C. R. Milner (1988), 'Intra-industry trade and the shifting of protection across sectors', *European Economic Review*, **32**, 927–45.

Greenaway, D. and C. R. Milner (1989a), 'Did Mauritius really provide a "case study" in Malthusian economics?', mimeo.

Greenaway, D. and C. R. Milner (1989b), 'Industrial incentives, domestic resource costs and resource allocation in Madagascar', CREDIT Research Paper, No. 89/1, University of Nottingham.

Greenaway, D. and C. R. Milner (1990a), 'South–south trade, theory, evidence and policy implications', *World Bank Research Observer*.

Greenaway, D. and C. R. Milner (1990b), 'The fiscal implications of trade policy reform: theory and evidence', Report to Trade Policy Division, World Bank.

Greenaway, D. and C.-H. Nam (1988), 'Industrialisation and macroeconomic performance in developing countries under alternative liberalisation scenarios', *Kyklos*, **41**, 419–35.

Grubel, H. G. (1982), 'Towards a theory of free economic zones', *Weltwirtschaftliches Archiv*, **118**, 38–61.

Halevi, N. (1988), 'Trade liberalization in adjustment lending', mimeo, World Bank.

Hamada, K. (1974), 'An economic analysis of the duty-free zone', *Journal of International Economics*, **4**, 225–41.

Hamilton, C. and L. E. O. Svensson (1982), 'On the welfare economics of a duty-free zone', *Journal of International Economics*, **13**, 45–64.

Hamilton, C. and L. E. O. Svensson (1983), 'On the choice between capital import and labor export', *European Economic Review*, **20**, 167–92.

Harris, R. (1986), 'Market structure and trade liberalization: a general equilibrium assessment', in T. N. Srinivasan and J. Whalley (eds), *General Equilibrium Trade Policy Modelling* (Cambridge, Mass.: MIT Press).

Harrod, R. (1951), *The Life of John Maynard Keynes* (New York: Harcourt Brace).

Havrylyshyn, O. and Alikhani, I. (1989), 'Changing comparative advantage and trade among developing countries' in J. Black and A. MacBean (eds), *Causes of Changes in the Structure of International Trade* (London: Macmillan).

Helleiner, G. K. (1977), 'Transnational enterprises and the new political economy of Unites States trade policy', *Oxford Economic Papers*, **29**, 102–16.

Hill, H. (1986), 'LDC manufactured exports: do definitions matter? Some examples from ASEAN', *ASEAN Economic Bulletin*, 3(2), 269–74.

Hill, H. (1987), 'Survey of recent developments', *Bulletin of Indonesian Economic Studies*, **23**, 1–33.

Hill, H. (1988), *Foreign Investment and Industrialization in Indonesia* (Singapore: Oxford University Press).

Hong, W. T. (1979), *Trade, Distortions and Employment Growth in Korea* (Seoul: KDI Press).

Hufbauer, G. and J. Schott (1985), *Trading for Growth: The Next Round of Trade Negotiations* (Washington, DC: Institute for International Economics).

Hughes, G. A. (1983), 'Shadow prices and economic policy in Indonesia' unpublished manuscript, Faculty of Economics and Politics, University of Cambridge.

Hughes, H. and A. O. Krueger (1984), 'Effects of protection in developed countries on developing countries', in R. Baldwin and A. Krueger (eds), *The*

Structure and Evolution of Recent US Trade Policy (Chicago: Chicago University Press, for NBER).

Inter-American Development Bank (1985), *Economic and Social Progress in Latin America: 1985 Report* (Washington).

Inter-American Development Bank (1988), *Economic and Social Progress in Latin America: 1988 Report* (Washington).

International Monetary Fund (1988), *IMF Survey*, Washington, DC, 29 August, p. 287.

Jamaica Industrial Development Corporation (1967), *Statistical Report of Manufacturing Firms Operating Under Incentive Laws*.

Jayasuriya, S. and C. Manning (1988), 'Survey of recent developments', *Bulletin of Indonesian Economic Studies*, **24**, 3–41.

Jefferson, O. (1967) 'Some aspects of the post-war economic development of Jamaica', *New World Quarterly*, **III**, 1–11.

Jones, R. W. (1980), 'Comparative and absolute advantage', *Swiss Journal of Economics and Statistics*, **3**, 235–60.

Jung, W. S. and G. Lee (1986), 'The effectiveness of export promotion policies: the case of Korea', *Weltwirtschaftliches Archiv*, **122**, 340–57.

Jung, W. S. and P. J. Marshall (1985), 'Exports, growth and causality in developing countries', *Journal of Development Economics*, **18**, 1–13.

Kaldor, N. (1966), *Causes of the Slow Economic Growth of the United Kingdom* (Cambridge: Cambridge University Press).

Kavoussi, R. M. (1984), 'Export expansion and economic growth', *Journal of Development Economics*, **14**, 241–50.

Kavoussi, R. M. (1985), 'International trade and economic development: the recent experience of developing countries', *Journal of Developing Areas*, **19**, 379–92.

Keesing, D. B. (1979), 'Trade policy for developing countries', *World Bank Staff Working Paper*, 353.

Khan, M. S. (1986), 'Developing country exchange rate policy responses to exogenous shocks', *American Economic Review*, **76**, 84–87.

Khan, M. S. and P. Montiel (1987), 'Real exchange rate dynamics for a small, primary-exporting country', *IMF Staff Papers*, December, 681–710.

Khan, M. S. and R. Zahler (1985), 'Trade and financial liberalization given external shocks and inconsistent domestic policies', *IMF Staff Papers*, **32**, March, 22–55.

Koo Bohn-Young (1981), 'A preliminary estimate of shadow price parameters in Korea' (in Korean), *Hankuk Kaebal Yongu*, 3.

Kopits, G. (1987), 'Structural reform, stabilization and growth in Turkey', *IMF Occasional Paper*, 52.

Krause, L. B. (1982), *US Economic Policy Towards the Association of Southeast Asian Nations: Meeting the Japanese Challenge* (Washington, DC: The Brookings Institution).

Kravis, I. (1970), 'Trade as a handmaiden of growth: similarities between the nineteenth and twentieth centuries', *Economic Journal*, December, 850–72.

Krueger, A. O. (1961), 'Export prospects and economic growth: India: a comment', *Economic Journal*, **71**, 436–42.

Krueger, A. O. (1974), 'The political economy of the rent-seeking society', *American Economic Review*, **64**, 291–303.

Krueger, A. O. (1978), *Foreign Trade Regimes and Economic Development: Liberalization Attempts and Consequences* (Cambridge, Mass.: Ballinger, for NBER).

312   *Bibliography*

Krueger, A. O. (1980), 'Trade policy as an input to development', *American Economic Review*, **70**, 288–92.

Krueger, A. O. (1981a), 'Interactions between inflation and trade regime objectives in stabilization programs', in W. Cline and S. Weintraub (eds), *Economic Stabilization in Developing Countries* (Washington, DC: The Brookings Institution), pp. 83–118.

Krueger, A. O. (1981b), *Trade and Employment in Developing Countries* (Chicago: University of Chicago Press).

Krueger, A. O. (1982), *Trade and Employment in Developing Countries: Synthesis and Conclusions* (Chicago: University of Chicago Press).

Krueger, A. O. and B. Tuncer (1980), 'Estimating total factor productivity growth in a developing country', *World Bank Staff Working Paper*, 422, (Washington, DC)

Krugman, P. (ed.) (1986), *Strategic Trade Policy and the New International Economics* (Cambridge, Mass.: MIT Press).

Lal, D. (1979), 'Indian export incentives', *Journal of Development Economics*, **6**, 103–17.

Lal, D. and S. Rajapatirana (1986), 'Trade regimes and economic growth in developing countries', paper prepared for the Kiel Conference on Free Trade, June.

Lavergne, R. and G. K. Helleiner (1985), 'United States transnational corporations and the structure of United States trade barriers: an empirical investigation', mimeo.

Leudde-Neurath, R. (1986), *Import Controls and Export Oriented Development: A Re-assessment of the South Korean Case* (Boulder and London: Westview Press).

Levitt, K. and L. Best (1969), *Externally Propelled Growth and Industrialisation in the Caribbean*, 1 (Montreal: McGill Centre for Developing Area Studies), mimeo.

Lewis, W. A. (1950), 'The industrialisation of the British West Indies', *Caribbean Economic Review*, **2**, 1–61.

Lewis, W. A. (1980), 'The slowing down of the engine of growth', *American Economic Review*, **70**, 555–64.

Lin, C.-Y. (1987), 'Policy reforms, international competitiveness, and export performance: Chile and Argentina versus the Republic of Korea and Taiwan, Province of China', *IMF WP/87/49*, July.

Lindsay, H. (forthcoming), 'The Indonesian log export ban: an estimation of forgone export earnings', *Bulletin of Indonesian Economic Studies*.

Lipton, M. and J. K. Firn (1975), *The Erosion of a Relationship: India and Britain Since 1960* (London: Oxford University Press).

Little, I., T. Scitovsky and M. Scott (1970), *Industry and Trade in Some Developing Countries* (London: Oxford University Press).

Lloyd, P. J. (1974), 'A more general theory of price distortions in open economies', *Journal of International Economics*, **4**, 365–86.

Low, P. (1982), 'The definition of "export subsidies" in GATT', *Journal of World Trade Law*, **16**, 375–90.

Lucas, R. E. B. (1988), 'Liberalisation of Indian trade and industrial licensing: a disaggregated econometric model with simulations', *Journal of Development Economics*, **29**, 63–75.

MacBean, A. (1988), 'Uruguay and the developing countries', draft paper presented to the Annual Conference of the International Economics Study Group, Isle of Thorns, mimeo (Lancaster: University of Lancaster).

McCawley, P. (1981), 'The growth of the industrial sector', in A. Booth and P. McCawley (eds), *The Indonesian Economy During the Soeharto Era* (Kuala Lumpur: Oxford University Press), pp. 62–101.

McCawley, P. (1983), 'Industrial licensing in Indonesia', unpublished paper, Australian National University, Canberra.

McDonald, D. (1985), 'Trade data discrepancies and the incentive to smuggle: an empirical analysis', *IMF Staff Papers*, **32**, 668–92.

MacFarlane, D. (1964), 'A comparative study of incentive legislation in the Leeward Islands, Windward Islands, Barbados and Jamaica', *Social and Economic Studies*, Supplement to vol. 13.

McIntyre, A. (1965), 'Decolonization and trade policy in the West Indies', in F. Andic and T. Matthews (eds), *The Caribbean in Transition* (Rio Piedras: Institute of Caribbean Studies, University of Puerto Rico).

Mackie, J. (1989), 'Indonesian political developments, 1987–88', in H. Hill and J. Mackie (eds), *Indonesia Assessment 1988*, Political and Social Change Monograph 8, Research School of Pacific Studies, Australian National University, pp. 13–38.

Maddison, A. (1982), *Phases of Capitalist Development* (Oxford: Oxford University Press).

Manalaysay, C. P. (1979), 'Estimating the shadow price of capital', in R. M. Bautista, J. H. Power and Associates, *Industrial Promotion Policies in the Philippines* (Manila: Philippine Institute for Development Studies).

Mayer, W. (1984a), 'Endogenous tariff formation', *American Economic Review*, **74**, 970–85.

Mayer, W. (1984b), 'The infant-export industry argument', *Canadian Journal of Economics*, **17**, 249–69.

Meade, J. (1951), *Trade and Welfare, The Theory of International Economic Policy*, 2, (London: Oxford University Press).

Medalla, E. A. and J. H. Power (1984), 'Estimating the shadow exchange rate, the shadow wage rate and the social rate of discount for the Philippines', Staff Paper Series 84-03, Philippine Institute for Development Studies, Manila.

Michaely, M. (1975), *Foreign Trade Regimes and Economic Development: Israel* (New York: National Bureau of Economic Research).

Michaely, M. (1977a), 'Exports and growth: an empirical investigation', *Journal of Development Economics*, **4**, 49–53.

Michaely, M. (1977b), *Theory of Commercial Policy: Trade and Protection* (Oxford: Philip Allan).

Michaely, M. (1986), 'The timing and sequencing of trade policy reform', in A. M. Choksi and D. Papageorgiou (eds), *Economic Liberalization in Developing Countries* (Oxford: Basil Blackwell).

Michalopoulos, C. and K. Jay (1973), 'Growth of exports and income in the developing world: a neoclassical view', *AID Discussion Paper*, 28, Washington, DC.

Miller, M. (1985), 'Big US semiconductor makers expected to sue over "dumping" of Japanese chips', *Wall Street Journal*, 1 October.

Milner, C. R. (1988), 'On tariff uniformity, optimal effective protection and tariff reform in developing countries', mimeo.

Milner, C. R. (1989), 'True protection in "capital-rich" and "capital-poor" developing countries: some policy implications', *Journal of Economic Studies*, **16**, 5–22.

Milner, C. R. (1990), 'Trade policy reform in Burundi' in J. Bates and V. N. Balasubramanyam (eds), *Case Studies in Development Economics*, vol. 1 (London: Macmillan).

Ministerio de Hacienda (1982), *Exposición sobre el Estado de la Hacienda Pública 1982* (Santiago).

Moschos, D. (1989), 'Export expansion, growth and the level of economic development', *Journal of Development Economics*, **16**, 99–102.

Munasinghe, M. (1980), 'Energy pricing policy: the case of electricity' (Washington, DC: The World Bank).

Murray, R. *et al.* (1987), 'Cyprus industrial strategy: report of the UNDP/ UNIDO mission' (Brighton: IDS, University of Sussex).

Mussa, M. (1986), 'The effects of commercial, fiscal, monetary, and exchange rate policies on the real exchange rate', in S. Edwards and L. Ahamed (eds), *Economic Adjustment and Exchange Rates in Developing Countries* (Chicago: The University of Chicago Press), pp. 43–88.

Nam, C.-H. (1981a), 'Trade and industrial policies, and the structure of protection in Korea', in W. Hong and L. B. Krause (eds), *Trade and Growth of the Advanced Developing Countries in the Pacific Basin* (Seoul: Korea Development Institute).

Nam, C.-H. (1981b), 'The industrial incentives and structure of protection in Korea' (in Korean), Korea Development Institute, Seoul, mimeo.

Nam, C.-H. (1986), 'Trade policy and economic development in Korea', World Bank, mimeo, April.

Nam, C.-H. (1987), 'Export-promoting subsidies, countervailing threats, and the general agreement on tariffs and trade', *The World Bank Economic Review*, **1**, 727–44.

Narsey, W. (1987), 'A re-interpretation of the history and theory of colonial monetary systems', unpublished DPhil thesis, University of Sussex.

Neary, J. P. (1988), 'Export subsidies and national welfare', *Austrian Economic Papers*, *Empirica*, **2**, 243–61.

Nishimizu, M. and S. Robinson (1984), 'Trade policies and productivity change in semi-industrialized countries', *Journal of Development Economics*, October, 177–206.

Nurkse, R. (1953), *Problems of Capital Formation in Underdeveloped Countries* (Oxford: Basil Blackwell).

Nurkse, R. (1959), *Patterns of Trade and Development*, Wicksell Lectures (Stockholm: Almquist and Wicksell).

Olson, M. (1971), *The Logic of Collective Action: Public Goods and the Theory of Groups* (Cambridge, Mass.: Harvard University Press).

Pack, H. L. and L. E. Westphal (1986), 'Industrial strategy and technological change: theory versus reality', *Journal of Development Economics*, **22**, 87–128.

Pangestu, M. (1987), 'Survey of recent developments', *Bulletin of Indonesian Economic Studies*, **23**, 1–39.

Pangestu, M. (1989), 'East Kalimantan: beyond the timber and oil boom', in H. Hill (ed.), *Unity and Diversity: Regional Economic Development in Indonesia Since 1970* (Kuala Lumpur: Oxford University Press).

Pangestu, M. and P. Boediono (1986), 'Indonesia: the structure and causes of manufacturing sector protection', in C. Findlay and R. Garnaut (eds), *The Political Economy of Manufacturing Protection: Experiences of ASEAN and Australia* (Sydney: Allen and Unwin), pp. 1–47.

Park, C. K. (1981), *Human Resources and Social Development in Korea* (Seoul: KDI Press).

Parker, S. (1985), 'A study of Indonesian trade policy between 1980 and 1984', unpublished paper, Washington.

Parsan, E. (1988), 'An investigation into the potential for south–south trade: a case study of Trinidad and Tobago – Brazil trade in petrochemicals', unpublished DPhil. thesis, University of Sussex.

Pitt, M. M. (1981), 'Alternative trade strategies and employment in Indonesia' in A. O. Krueger, H. B. Lary, T. Monson, N. Akransanee (eds), *Trade and Employment in Developing Countries. 1: Individual Studies* (Chicago: University of Chicago Press).

Pomfret, R. (1976), *Trade Policies and Industrialization in a Small Country: The Case of Israel* (Tubingen: JCB Mohr).

Pomfret, R. (1986), *Mediterranean Policy of the European Community* (London: Macmillan).

Poot, H. *et al.* (forthcoming), *Industrialization and Trade in Indonesia* (Yogyakarta: Gadjah Mada University Press).

Prebisch, R. (1952), 'Problemas teóricos y prácticos del crecimiento económico', United Nations, Economic Commission for Latin America.

Prebisch, R. (1959), 'The role of commercial policies in underdeveloped countries', *American Economic Review* (Papers and Proceedings), **49**, 251–6.

Prebisch, R. (1984), 'Five stages in my thinking about development', in P. Bauer, G. Meier and D. Seers (eds), *Pioneers in Development* (New York: Oxford University Press).

Ramos, M. H. (1988), 'Policies of the Mexican government towards the northern frontier region of Mexico', in G. Philip (ed.), *The Mexican Economy* (London and New York: Routledge).

Ranis, G. (1985), 'Can the East Asian model of development be generalized?', *World Development*, **13**, 543–45.

Rhee, Y. W. (1985), 'Instruments of export policy and administration', *Staff Working Paper*, 725 (Washington, DC: The World Bank).

Riedel, J. (1984), 'Trade as the engine of growth in developing countries, revisited', *Economic Journal*, **84**, 56–73.

Riedel, J. (1987), 'Macroeconomic crises and long-run growth in developing countries: a case study of Turkey', unpublished ms, World Bank.

Rimmer, D. (1984), *The Economies of West Africa* (London: Weidenfeld and Nicolson).

Robison, R. (1986), *Indonesia: The Rise of Capital* (Sydney: Allen and Unwin).

Rodriguez, C. A. (1976), 'A note on the economics of the duty-free zone', *Journal of International Economics*, **6**, 385–8.

Roemer, J. E. (1977), 'The effect of sphere of influence and economic distance on composition of trade in manufactures', *Review of Economics and Statistics*, **59**, 318–27.

Roepstorff, T. M. (1985), 'Industrial development in Indonesia: performance and prospects', *Bulletin of Indonesian Economic Studies*, **21**, 32–61.

Rudra, A. (1973), *Indian Plan Models* (New Delhi: Allied Publishers).

Ruggie, J. (ed.) (1983), *The Antimonies of Interdependence: National Welfare and the International Division of Labor* (New York: Columbia University Press, New York).

Ruzicka, I. (1979), 'Rent appropriation in Indonesian logging: East Kalimantan 1972/3–1976/7', *Bulletin of Indonesian Economic Studies*, **15**, 45–74.

Sachs, J. (1985), 'External debt and macroeconomic performance in Latin America and East Asia', *Brookings Papers on Economic Activity*, **2**, 523–75.

Sachs, J. (1987), 'Trade and exchange-rate policies in growth-oriented adjustment programs', in V. Corbo, M. Goldstein and M. Khan (eds), *Growth-oriented Adjustment Programs* (Washington, DC: International Monetary Fund and World Bank), pp. 291–325.

Salvatore, D. (1989), 'Exports and economic growth with alternative trade strategies', paper presented to the International Economics Study Group Conference, University of Sussex, September.

Sargent, T. and N. Wallace (1981), 'Some unpleasant monetarist arithmetic', *Federal Reserve Bank of Minneapolis Quarterly Review*, Fall, 159–90.

Sarkar, P. and H. W. Singer (1989), 'Debt pressure and the transfer burden of the third world countries', IDS, University of Sussex, mimeo.

Scott, M. F. G., (1979), 'Foreign trade', in W. Galenson (ed.), *Economic Growth and Structural Change in Taiwan* (Ithaca: Cornell University Press), pp. 308–83.

Seabury, P. (1983), 'Industrial policy and national defense', *Journal of Contemporary Studies*, **3**, 5–15.

Shome, P. (ed.) (1986), *Fiscal Issues in South-East Asia: Comparative Studies of Selected Economies* (Singapore: Oxford University Press).

Singer, H. W. (1950), 'The distribution of gains between investing and borrowing countries, *American Economic Review* Papers and Proceedings), **40**, 473–5.

Singer, H. W. (1988), 'The World Development Report 1987 on the blessings of outward orientation: a necessary correction', *Journal of Development Studies*, **24**, 232–6.

Singer, H. W. (1989), 'Industrialisation and world trade: ten years after the Brandt Report', paper prepared for the International Symposium 'The crisis of the global system: the world ten years after the Brandt Report, crisis management for the nineties'.

Singer, H. W. and P. Gray (1988), 'Trade policy and growth of developing countries: some new data', *World Development*, **16**, 395–404.

Singh, M. (1964), *India's Export Trends* (Oxford: Clarendon Press).

Sjaastad, L. A. (1980), 'Commercial policy, true tariffs and relative prices', in J. Black and B. V. Hindley (eds), *Current Issues in Commercial Policy and Diplomacy* (London: Macmillan).

Sjaastad, L. A. and K. W. Clements (1981), 'The incidence of protection: theory and measurement', in L. A. Sjaastad (ed.), *The Free Trade Movement in Latin America* (London: Macmillan).

Skair, L. (1988), 'Mexico's *maquiladora* programme: a critical evaluation', in G. Philip (ed.), *The Mexican Economy* (London and New York: Routledge).

Smith, A. (1986), 'The infant industry argument and the reform of trade policy', background study for the *World Development Report*, World Bank, 1987, mimeo, University of Sussex.

Soehoed, A. R. (1988), 'Reflections on industrialisation and industrial policy in Indonesia', *Bulletin of Indonesian Economic Studies*, **24**, 43–57.

Spinanger, D. (1984), 'Objectives and impact of economic activity zones – some evidence from Asia', *Weltwirtschaftliches Archiv*, **120**, 64–89.

Srinivasan, T. N. (1986a), 'Development strategy: is the success of outward orientation at an end?', in S. Guhan and Manu Shroff (eds), *Essays on Economic Progress and Welfare* (New Delhi: Oxford University Press).

Srinivasan, T. N. (1986b), 'International trade for developing countries in the nineteen eighties: problems and prospects', in J. Dunning and M. Usui (eds), *Economic Independence* (London: Macmillan).

Srinivasan, T. N. (1987), 'Distortions' in J. Eatwell, M. Milgate and P. Newman (eds), *The New Palgrave: A Dictionary of Economics* (London: Macmillan).

Srinivasan, T. N. (1989), 'International aspects: introduction to Part 5', in H. Chenery and T. N. Srinivasan (eds), *Handbook of Development Economics* (Amsterdam: North-Holland).

Stern, N. (1988), 'Aspects of the general theory of tax reform', in D. Newbery and N. Stern (eds), *The Theory of Taxation for Developing Countries* (New York: Oxford University Press, for the World Bank), 60–91.

Stern, N. (1989), 'The economics of development: a survey', *The Economic Journal*, **99**, 629–30.

Stewart, F. (1987), 'Back to Keynesianism', *World Policy Journal*, Summer, 467–83.

Streeten, P. (1982), 'A cool look at "outward-looking" strategies for development', *The World Economy* (September), 159–69.

Sundrum, R. M. (1986), 'Indonesia's rapid economic growth: 1968–81', *Bulletin of Indonesian Economic Studies*, **22**, 40–69.

Sundrum, R. M. (1988), 'Indonesia's slow economic growth', *Bulletin of Indonesian Economic Studies*, **24**, 37–72.

Syrquin, M. and H. B. Chenery (1989), 'Patterns of development: 1950 to 1983', *World Bank Discussion Paper*, 41.

Taylor, L. (1986), 'Trade and growth', *The Review of Black Political Economy*, **14**, 17–36.

Thee, K. W. (1988), *Industrialisasi Indonesia: Analisis dan Catatan Kritis* (Industrialisation in Indonesia: Analysis and Critical Notes), Pustaka Sinar Harpan, Indonesia.

Thee, K. W. and K. Yoshihara (1987), 'Foreign and domestic capital in Indonesian industrialization', *Southeast Asian Studies*, **24**, 327–49.

Tyler, W. (1981), 'Growth and export expansion in developing countries: some empirical evidence', *Journal of Development Economics*, **3**, 337–49.

United Nations (1985), *An Evaluation of Export Processing Zones in Selected Asian Countries*, ESCAP/UNCTC Publication Series B, 8 (ST/ESCAP/395), Bangkok.

Uzawa, H. (1969), 'Shihon jiyuka to kokumin keizai' (Liberalisation of foreign investments and the national economy), *Economisuto*, 106–22 (in Japanese).

van Wijnbergen, S (1981), 'Short-run macroeconomic adjustment policies in South Korea: a quantitative analysis', *Staff Working Paper*, 510 (Washington, DC: The World Bank).

Veitch, M. (1977, 1979, 1984), 'National parameters for project evaluation in Malaysia', UNDP/World Bank State and Rural Development Project, Kuala Lumpur.

Velasco, A. (ed.) (1988) *Trade, Development and the World Economy: Selected Essays of Carlos Diaz-Alejandro* (Oxford: Basil Blackwell).

Verghese, S. K. (1978), 'Export assistance policy and export performance in the seventies', *Economic and Political Weekly* (Annual Number, February), 245–76.

Vernon, R. (1966), 'International investment and international trade in the product cycle', *Quarterly Journal of Economics*, **80**, 190–207.

Wade, R. (1989), *Governing the Market: Economic Theory and Role of Government in East Asian Industrialization* (Princeton: Princeton University Press).

Wall, D. (1976), 'Export processing zones', *Journal of World Trade Law*, **10**, 478–89.

Warr, P. G. (1983), 'The Jakarta export processing zone: benefits and costs', *Bulletin of Indonesian Economics Studies*, **20**, 53–89.

Warr, P. G. (1984a), 'Korea's Masan free export zone: benefits and costs', *The Developing Economies*, **22**, 167–84.

Warr, P. G. (1984b), 'Exchange rate protection in Indonesia', *Bulletin of Indonesian Economic Studies*, **20**, 53–89.

Warr, P. G. (1985), 'Export processing zones in the Philippines', *ASEAN – Australia Economics Papers*, 20, Australian National University, Canberra.

Warr, P. G. (1986), 'Indonesia's other Dutch disease: economic effects of the petroleum boom', in J. P. Neary and S. van Wijnbergen (eds), *Natural Resources and the Macroeconomy* (Oxford: Basil Blackwell).

Warr, P. G. (1987a), 'Export promotion via industrial enclaves: the Philippines Bataan export processing zone', *Journal of Development Studies*, **23**, 220–42.

Warr, P. G. (1987b), 'Malaysia's industrial enclaves: benefits and costs', *The Developing Economies*, **25**, 30–55.

Warr, P. G. (1989), 'Export processing zones: the economics of enclave manufacturing', *World Bank Research Observer*, **4**, 65–88.

Wells, J. R. (1979), 'Brazil and the post-1973 crisis in the international economy', in R. Thorp and L. Whitehead (eds), *Inflation and Stabilisation in Latin America* (London and Basingstoke: Macmillan, in association with St Anthony's College, Oxford).

Whalley, J. (1990), 'Recent trade liberalization in developing countries', in D. Greenaway, R. C. Hine, A. O'Brien and R. Thornton (eds), *Global Protectionism* (London: Macmillan).

White, G. (1984), 'Development states and socialist industrialisation in the third world', *Journal of Development Studies*, **21**, 97–120.

White, G. and R. Wade (eds) (1988), *Developmental States and Markets in East Asia* (London: Macmillan).

Williamson, R. (1978), 'The role of exports and foreign capital in Latin American economic growth', *Southern Economic Journal*, **45**, 410–20.

Wolf, M. (1982), *India's Exports* (New York: Oxford University Press, for the World Bank).

Wood, A. and T. King (1989), 'North–south trade and the demand for labour', discussion draft of Report to ODA, IDS, University of Sussex.

World Bank (1983), *World Development Report* (New York: Oxford University Press, for International Bank for Reconstruction and Development).

World Bank (1987), *World Development Report 1987* (New York: Oxford University Press).

World Bank (1989), *Adjustment Lending: An Evaluation of Ten Years of Experience* (Washington, DC: The World Bank).

Yoffie, D. (1983), *Power and Protectionism* (New York: Columbia University Press).

Yusuf, S. and K. Peters (1985), 'Capital accumulation and economic growth: the Korean paradigm', *Staff Working Paper*, 712 (Washington, DC: The World Bank).

Index